C000319103

BRITISH RAILWAYS
LOCOMOTIVES &
COACHING STOCK
2003

The Complete Guide to all
Locomotives & Coaching Stock which
operate on Network Rail & Eurotunnel

Peter Fox, Robert Pritchard & Peter Hall

ISBN 1 902336 31 3

© 2003. Platform 5 Publishing Ltd., 3 Wyvern House, Sark Road, Sheffield,
S2 4HG, England.

CONTENTS

SECTION 5 – LOCO-HAULED NON-PASSENGER COACHING STOCK

SECTION 6 – CODES

UPDATES

An update to this book is published every month in the Platform 5 magazine, **entrain**, which contains news and rolling stock information on the railways of Britain. For further details of **entrain**, please see the advertisement on page 4 of this book.

COVER PHOTOGRAPHS

Front Cover: Fragonset liveried 31452 "MINOTAUR" and 31602 "CHIMAERA" pass Church Fenton with a Green Express charter to Edinburgh on 4 May 2002. **Jason Rogers**

Rear Cover: Old WAGN liveried outer suburban Class 317 unit No. 317 652 passes Bethnal Green with the 09.19 London Liverpool Street–Cambridge on 13 December 2002. **Robert Pritchard**

PROVISION OF INFORMATION

This book has been compiled with care to be as accurate as possible, but in some cases official information is not available and the publisher cannot be held responsible for any errors or omissions. We would like to thank the companies and individuals which have been co-operative in supplying information to us. The authors of this book will be pleased to receive notification of any inaccuracies readers may find in the series, and also any additional information to supplement our records and thus enhance future editions. Please send comments to:

Locomotives, DMUs & EMUs: Robert Pritchard, Platform 5 Publishing Ltd., Wyvern House, Sark Road, Sheffield, S2 4HG, England.
Tel: 0114 255 2625 Fax: 0114 255 2471
e-mail: platfive@platfive.freeserve.co.uk

Coaching Stock: Peter Hall, 4 Ladies Spring Court, Ladies Spring Grove, Dore, Sheffield, S17 3LR. (Tel: 0114 262 0693; e-mail: peter@hall59.freeserve.co.uk)

Both the author and the staff of Platform 5 regret they are unable to answer specific queries regarding locomotives and rolling stock.

This book is updated to 1 January 2003.

ACKNOWLEDGEMENTS

The author would like to thank the following companies for their help and co-operation with the compilation of this book:

Angel Trains Ltd.
Anglia Railways
c2c Rail
Cotswold Rail
Direct Rail Services
Freightliner Ltd.
GB Railfreight Ltd.
Heathrow Express
HSBC Rail (UK) Ltd.
Midland Mainline
Porterbrook Leasing Company Ltd.
Rolling Stock Library
ScotRail
South West Trains
Valley Lines
Virgin Trains

Thanks are also due to the following individuals for their reports of changes observed during 2002 and for corrections given to the "pocket book" series:

Brian Loughlin, Mark Beal, Donald J. Bishop, Alan Costello, David Haydock, Tony Russell, Roger Templeman, Keith Foster, J. Wolton, Nick Bartlett, DJ Day and many others – keep the observations coming!

BRITAIN'S RAILWAY SYSTEM

INFRASTRUCTURE & OPERATION

Britain's national railway infrastructure is now owned by a "not for dividend" company, Network Rail, following the demise of Railtrack. Many stations and maintenance depots are leased to and operated by Train Operating Companies (TOCs), but some larger stations remain under Network Rail control. The only exception is the infrastructure on the Isle of Wight, which is nationally owned and is leased to the Island Line franchisee.

Trains are operated by TOCs over Network Rail, regulated by access agreements between the parties involved. In general, TOCs are responsible for the provision and maintenance of the locomotives, rolling stock and staff necessary for the direct operation of services, whilst Network Rail is responsible for the provision and maintenance of the infrastructure and also for staff needed to regulate the operation of services.

DOMESTIC PASSENGER TRAIN OPERATORS

The large majority of passenger trains are operated by the TOCs on fixed term franchises. Franchise expiry dates are shown in parentheses in the list of franchisees below:

Franchise	Franchisee	Trading Name
Anglia Railways	GB Railways plc. (until 4 April 2004)	Anglia Railways
Central Trains	National Express Group plc (until 1 April 2004)	Central Trains
Chiltern Railways	M40 Trains Ltd. (until December 2021)	Chiltern Railways
Cross-Country	Virgin Rail Group Ltd.* (until March 2012)	Virgin Trains
Gatwick Express	National Express Group plc (until 27 April 2011)	Gatwick Express
Great Eastern Railway	First Group plc (until 4 April 2004)	First Great Eastern
Great Western Trains	First Group plc (until 3 February 2006)	First Great Western
InterCity East Coast	GNER Holdings Ltd. (until 4 April 2005)	Great North Eastern Railway
InterCity West Coast	Virgin Rail Group Ltd.* (until 8 March 2012)	Virgin Trains
Island Line	Stagecoach Holdings plc (until February 2007)	Island Line
LTS Rail	National Express Group plc (until 25 May 2011)	c2c
Merseyrail Electrics	Arriva Trains Ltd. (until 20 July 2003)	Arriva Trains Merseyside

Midland Main Line	National Express Group plc (until 27 April 2008)	Midland Mainline
North London Railways	National Express Group plc (until 1 September 2004)	Silverlink Train Services
North West Regional Railways	First Group plc (until 1 April 2004)	First North Western
Regional Railways North East	Arriva Trains Ltd (until 3 January 2004)	Arriva Trains Northern
ScotRail	National Express Group plc (until 30 March 2004)	ScotRail
South Central	GoVia Ltd. (Go-Ahead/Keolis). (until May 2010)	South Central
South Eastern	Connex Transport UK Ltd. (until 12 October 2011)	Connex
South West	Stagecoach Holdings plc (until 3 February 2007)	South West Trains
Thames	Go-Ahead Group (until 12 April 2004)	Thames Trains
Thameslink	GoVia Ltd. (until 1 April 2004)	Thameslink Rail
Wales & Borders§	National Express Group plc (until 30 April 2004)	Wales & Borders Trains
Wessex Trains§	National Express Group plc (until 30 April 2004)	Wessex Trains
West Anglia Great Northern	National Express Group plc (until 4 April 2004)	WAGN

Notes: * Franchise to be renegotiated by April 2004.

§ For the present, Wales & West PassengerTrains is the legal trading name of Wessex Trains and the Cardiff Railway Company is the legal name for Wales & Borders.

A major reorganisation of franchises is under way. See **entrain** for developments.

The following operators run non-franchised services only:

Operator	Trading Name	Route
British Airports Authority	Heathrow Express	London Paddington–Heathrow Airport
Hull Trains	Hull Trains	London King's Cross–Hull
West Coast Railway Co.	West Coast Railway	Fort William–Mallaig* York–Scarborough*

* Special summer-dated services only.

INTERNATIONAL PASSENGER OPERATIONS

Eurostar (UK) operates international passenger-only services between the United Kingdom and continental Europe, jointly with French National Railways (SNCF) and Belgian National Railways (SNCB/NMBS). Eurostar (UK) is a subsidiary of London & Continental Railways, which is jointly owned by National Express Group PLC and British Airways.

In addition, a service for the conveyance of accompanied road vehicles through the Channel Tunnel is provided by the tunnel operating company, Eurotunnel.

FREIGHT TRAIN OPERATIONS

The following operators operate freight train services under 'Open Access' arrangements:

English Welsh & Scottish Railway Ltd. (EWS)
Freightliner Ltd.
GB Railfreight Ltd.
Direct Rail Services Ltd.
Mendip Rail Ltd.

1. LOCOMOTIVES

SCOPE

This section contains details of all locomotives which can run on Britain's national railway network, plus those of Eurotunnel. Locomotives which are owned by EWS and Freightliner which have been withdrawn from service and awaiting disposal are now listed in the main list, as are those owned by companies such as Fragonset, Harry Needle and DRS which are awaiting possible restoration to service. Only preserved locomotives which are currently used or are likely to be used on the national network in the foreseeable future are included. Others, which may be Network Rail registered but not at present certified for use, are not included, but will be found in the Platform 5 book, "Preserved locomotives and Multiple Units".

LOCO CLASSES

Loco classes are listed in numerical order of class. Principal details and dimensions are quoted for each class in metric and/or imperial units as considered appropriate bearing in mind common UK usage. Abbreviations used are shown in Section 4.5.

All dimensions and weights are quoted for locomotives in an 'as new' condition with all necessary supplies (e.g. oil, water and sand) on board. Dimensions are quoted in the order length x width. Lengths quoted are over buffers or couplers as appropriate. All widths quoted are maxima. Where two different wheel diameter dimensions are shown, the first refers to powered wheels and the second refers to non-powered wheels.

NUMERICAL LISTINGS

Locomotives are listed in numerical order. Where numbers actually carried are different from those officially allocated, these are noted in class headings where appropriate. Where locomotives have been recently renumbered, the most immediate previous number is shown in parentheses. Each locomotive entry is laid out as in one of the following examples:

RSL No.	Detail	Livery	Owner	Pool	Allocn.	Name
37411	r	**E**	E	WKBM	ML	The Scottish Railway Preservation Society

In some cases where few members of a class are named, names are appended as a separate list at the end of the class listings to save space.

Detail Differences. Only detail differences which currently affect the areas and types of train which locomotives may work are shown. All other detail differences are specifically excluded. Where such differences occur within a class or part class, they are shown in the 'Detail' column alongside the individual locomotive number.
Standard abbreviations used are:

a	Train air brake equipment only.
b	Drophead buckeye couplers.

c	Scharfenberg couplers.
k	Swinghead automatic combination or "buckeye" couplers.
p	Train air, vacuum and electro-pneumatic brakes.
r	RETB signalling equipment fitted.
s	Slow Speed Control equipment.
v	Train vacuum brake only.
x	Train air and vacuum brakes ('Dual brakes').
+	Additional fuel tank capacity.
§	Sandite laying equipment.

In all cases use of the above abbreviations indicates the equipment indicated is normally operable. Meaning of non-standard abbreviations and symbols is detailed in individual class headings.

Note: Where a locomotive pool code indicates a detail difference, e.g. as in WBBM which is a special pool for RETB fitted locos, then the fitting is not shown separately.

Codes. Codes are used to denote the livery, owner, pool and depot of each locomotive. Details of these will be found in section 6 of this book. Where a unit or spare car is off-lease, the operation column will be left blank.

Names. Only names carried with official sanction are listed. As far as possible names are shown in UPPER/lower case characters as actually shown on the name carried on the vehicle(s).

GENERAL INFORMATION

CLASSIFICATION AND NUMBERING

All locomotives are classified and allocated numbers by the Rolling Stock Library under the TOPS numbering system, introduced in 1972. This comprises a two-digit class number followed by a three-digit serial number. Where the actual number carried by a locomotive differs from the allocated number, or where an additional number is carried to the allocated number, this is shown by a note in the class heading.

For diesel locomotives, class numbers offer an indication of engine horsepower as shown in the table below.

Class No. Range	Engine h.p.
01–14	0–799
15–20	800–1000
21–31	1001–1499
32–39	1500–1999
40–54, 57	2000–2999
55–56, 58–69	3000+

For electric locomotives class numbers are allocated in ascending numerical order under the following scheme:

Class 70–80	direct current and DC/diesel dual system locomotives.
Class 81 onwards	alternating current and AC/DC dual system locos.

Numbers in the 89xxx series (except 89001) are allocated by the Rolling Stock Library to locomotives which have been de-registered but subsequently re-registered for use on the Network Rail network and whose original number has already been re-used. 89xxx numbers are normally only carried inside locomotive cabs and are not carried externally in normal circumstances.

WHEEL ARRANGEMENT

For main line locomotives the number of driven axles on a bogie or frame is denoted by a letter (A = 1, B = 2, C = 3 etc.) and the number of non-powered axles is denoted by a number. The use of the letter 'o' after a letter indicates each axle is individually powered, whilst the '+' symbol indicates bogies are inter-coupled.

For shunting locomotives, the Whyte notation is used. In this notation the number of leading wheels are given, followed by the number of driving wheels and then the trailing wheels.

HAULAGE CAPABILITY OF DIESEL LOCOMOTIVES

The haulage capability of a diesel locomotive depends upon three basic factors:

1. Adhesive weight. The greater the weight on the driving wheels, the greater the adhesion and more tractive power can be applied before wheelslip occurs.

2. The characteristics of its transmission. To start a train the locomotive has to exert a pull at standstill. A direct drive diesel engine cannot do this, hence the need for transmission. This may be mechanical, hydraulic or electric. The present British Standard for locomotives is electric transmission. Here the diesel engine drives a generator or alternator and the current produced is fed to the traction motors. The force produced by each driven wheel depends on the current in its traction motor. In other words, the larger the current, the harder it pulls. As the locomotive speed increases, the current in the traction motor falls, hence the *Maximum Tractive Effort* is the maximum force at its wheels the locomotive can exert at a standstill. The electrical equipment cannot take such high currents for long without overheating. Hence the *Continuous Tractive Effort* is quoted which represents the current which the equipment can take continuously.

3. The power of its engine. Not all power reaches the rail, as electrical machines are approximately 90% efficient. As the electrical energy passes through two such machines (the generator or alternator and the traction motors), the *Power at Rail* is approximately 81% (90% of 90%) of the engine power, less a further amount used for auxiliary equipment such as radiator fans, traction motor blowers, air compressors, battery charging, cab heating, Electric Train Supply (ETS) etc. The power of the locomotive is proportional to the tractive effort times the speed. Hence when on full power there is a speed corresponding to the continuous tractive effort.

HAULAGE CAPABILITY OF ELECTRIC LOCOMOTIVES

Unlike a diesel locomotive, an electric locomotive does not develop its power on board and its performance is determined only by two factors, namely its weight and the characteristics of its electrical equipment. Whereas a diesel locomotive tends to be a constant power machine, the power of an electric locomotive varies considerably. Up to a certain speed it can produce virtually a constant tractive effort. Hence power rises with speed according to the formula given in section three above, until a maximum speed is reached at which tractive effort falls, such that the power also falls. Hence the power at the speed corresponding to the maximum tractive effort is lower than the maximum speed.

BRAKE FORCE

The brake force is a measure of the braking power of a locomotive. This is shown on the locomotive data panels so operating staff can ensure sufficient brake power is available on freight trains.

ELECTRIC TRAIN SUPPLY (ETS)

A number of locomotives are equipped to provide a supply of electricity to the train being hauled to power auxiliaries such as heating, cooling fans, air conditioning and kitchen equipment. ETS is provided from the locomotive by means of a separate alternator (except Class 33 locos, which have a DC generator). The ETS index of a locomotive is a measure of the electrical power available for train supply.

Similarly, most loco-hauled coaches also have an ETS index, which in this case is a measure of the power required to operate equipment mounted in the coach. The sum of the ETS indices of all the hauled vehicles in a train must not exceed the ETS index of the locomotive.

ETS is commonly (but incorrectly) known as ETH (Electric Train Heating), which is a throwback to the days before loco-hauled coaches were equipped with electrically powered auxiliary equipment other than for train heating.

ROUTE AVAILABILITY (RA)

This is a measure of a railway vehicle's axle load. The higher the axle load of a vehicle, the higher the RA number on a scale from 1 to 10. Each Network Rail route has a RA number and in general no vehicle with a higher RA number may travel on that route without special clearance. A map showing route availability on all routes is published on the Network Rail internet web site.

MULTIPLE & PUSH-PULL WORKING

Multiple working between vehicles (i.e. two or more powered vehicles being driven from one cab) is facilitated by jumper cables connecting the vehicles. However, not all types are compatible with each other, and a number of different systems are in use, each system being incompatible with any other.

Association of American Railroads (AAR) System: Classes 59, 66, and 67.
Blue Star Coupling Code: Classes 20, 25, 31, 33, & 37.
Green Circle Coupling Code: Class 47 (not all equipped).
Orange Square Coupling Code: Class 50.
Red Diamond Coupling Code: Classes 56 and 58.
SR System: Classes 33/1, 73 and various electric multiple units.
Within Own Class only: Classes 43 and 60.

Many locomotives use a time-division multiplex (TDM) system for push-pull and multiple working which utilises the existing RCH jumper cables fitted to coaching stock vehicles. Previously these cables had only been used to control train lighting and public address systems.

Class 47 locos 47701–47717 were equipped with a older non-standard TDM system.

1.1. DIESEL LOCOMOTIVES

Note: The 01/5 series has been allocated for shunting locomotives of various types which may operate on the Network Rail system. Only those actually registered on TOPS, or ex-BR locos are included here.

SERIES 01/5   H-B/CATERPILLAR   0-6-0

Built: 1971 by The Hunslet Engine Company at Leeds (Works No. 7018), for the National Coal Board, Western Area (No. 8D). Subsequently sold to Hunslet-Barclay, Kilmarnock and rebuilt prior to sale to The Felixstowe Dock and Railway Company in 1999. Registered for use on the Railtrack network in 1999. Normally used at Felixstowe South Container Terminal.
Engine: Caterpillar 3412C DITA of 475 kW (640 h.p.) at ? r.p.m.
Transmission: Hydraulic. Twin Disc 13800 series torque converter coupled to a Hunslet final drive.
Maximum Tractive Effort: 180 kN (40365 lbf).
Train Brakes: Air.
Brake Force: 48 t.   **Dimensions:** 3.95 x 2.51 m.
Weight: 64.3 t.   **Wheel Diameter:** 1143 mm.
Design Speed: 15 m.p.h.   **Maximum Speed:** 15 m.p.h.
Fuel Capacity: 930 litres.   **RA:** 7.
Train Supply: Not equipped.   **Multiple Working:** Not equipped.
Non standard numbering: Also carries number H4323.

| 01531 | **FX** | FX | MBDL | FX | COLONEL TOMLINE |

SERIES 01/5   ENGLISH ELECTRIC/RR   0-4-0

Built: 1966 by English Electric at Vulcan Foundry, Newton le Willows (Works No. D1122), for the Central Electricity Generating Board at Croydon 'B' Power Station (No. 2). Subsequently acquired by RFS(E), Doncaster (now Wabtec). Registered for use on the Railtrack network in 2000, and hired to Aggregate Industries UK for use at Croft Quarry, Leicestershire.
Engine: ? of 235 kW (315 h.p.) at ? r.p.m.
Transmission: Hydraulic.
Maximum Tractive Effort:
Train Brakes: Air.
Brake Force: 10 t.   **Dimensions:** 7.32 x ? m.
Weight: 24.0 t.   **Wheel Diameter:**
Design Speed: 10 m.p.h.   **Maximum Speed:** 10 m.p.h.
Fuel Capacity: 1365 litres.   **RA:** 0.
Train Supply: Not equipped.   **Multiple Working:** Not equipped.
Non standard livery: RFS(E) livery of blue, lined out in silver.

| 01551 | **0** | WA | MBDL | ZB | |

SERIES 01/5   HNRC/ROLLS-ROYCE   0-6-0

Built: 1966 by Thomas Hill at Vanguard Works, Kilnhurst (Works No. 167V), for ICI

Billingham (No. D3). Subsequently sold to Harry Needle Railroad Company in 1995 and rebuilt 2000. Registered for use on the Railtrack network in 2000, and hired to Creative Logistics, for use at Salford International Railfreight Terminal.
Engine: Rolls Royce 8-cylinder of 275 kW (370 h.p.) at ? r.p.m.
Transmission: Hydraulic. Twin Disc 11800 torque converter coupled to a RF final drive unit.
Maximum Tractive Effort:
Train Brakes: Air.

Brake Force: 19 t.	**Dimensions:** 9.14 x ? m.
Weight: 49.0 t.	**Wheel Diameter:**
Design Speed: 10 m.p.h.	**Maximum Speed:** 10 m.p.h.
Fuel Capacity: 1360 litres.	**RA:** 5.
Train Supply: Not equipped.	**Multiple Working:** Not equipped.

Non standard livery: Creative Logistics livery of blue and green.

01552	**0**	HN	MBDL	BH	

SERIES 01/5   BR/ENGLISH   ELECTRIC   0-6-0

Built: 1950 by BR at Derby Locomotive Works to LMS design as BR 12082. Withdrawn from service in 1971 and sold to Shellstar (UK), Ince (later UK Fertilisers) in 1972. Purchased by Harry Needle in 19??, and registered for use on the Railtrack network in 2000. Part of the Harry Needle Railroad Company hire fleet. **Engine:** English Electric 6KT of 260 kW (350 h.p.) at 600 r.p.m.
Main Generator: English Electric 801.
Traction Motors: Two English Electric 506.
Maximum Tractive Effort: 156 kN (35000 lbf).
Continuous Tractive Effort: ? at 8.5 m.p.h.

Power at Rail:	**Train Brakes:** Air.
Brake Force: 19 t.	**Dimensions:** 8.88 x 2.59 m.
Weight: 48.60 t.	**Wheel Diameter:** 1232 mm.
Design Speed: 20 m.p.h.	**Maximum Speed:** 20 m.p.h.
Fuel Capacity: 3000 litres.	**RA:** 5.
Train Supply: Not equipped.	**Multiple Working:** Not equipped.

Non-standard numbering: Also carries original number 12082.

01553 (12082)	**HN**	HN HNRL	ZB	

CLASS 03   BR/GARDNER   0–6–0

Built: 1962 by BR at Swindon Works. Used at Hornsey T&RSMD.
Engine: Gardner 8L3 of 152 kW (204 h.p.) at 1200 r.p.m.
Transmission: Mechanical. Fluidrive type 23 hydraulic coupling to Wilson-Drewry CA5R7 gearbox with SCG type RF11 final drive.
Maximum Tractive Effort: 68 kN (15300 lbf).
Continuous Tractive Effort: 68 kN (15300 lbf) at 3.75 m.p.h.
Train Brakes: Air & vacuum.

Brake Force: 13 t.	**Dimensions:** 7.93 x 2.59 m.
Weight: 31.3 t.	**Wheel Diameter:** 1092 mm.
Design Speed: 28.5 m.p.h.	**Maximum Speed:** 28.5 m.p.h.
Fuel Capacity: 1364 litres.	**RA:** 1.
Train Supply: Not equipped.	**Multiple Working:** Not equipped.

Originally numbered D 2179.

| 03179 | **WN** WN HQXX | HE | CLIVE |

CLASS 07 RUSTON & HORNSBY/PAXMAN 0-6-0

Built: 1962 by Ruston & Hornsby, Lincoln, as BR D2985 for shunting duties in Southampton Docks. Withdrawn from service in 1977 and sold to Tilsley & Lovatt, Stoke-on-Trent in 1978. Resold to Staveley Lime Company (later Peakstone Ltd.), Peak Dale, in 1978. Purchased by Harry Needle in 1989 and registered for use on the Railtrack network in 2000. Part of the Harry Needle Railroad Company hire fleet.
Engine: Paxman 6RPHL Mk. 3 of 204 kW (275 h.p.) at 1360 r.p.m.
Main Generator: AEI RTB 6652.
Traction Motors: AEI RTA 6652.
Maximum Tractive Effort: 126 kN (28240 lbf).
Continuous Tractive Effort: ? at 4.4 m.p.h.

Power at Rail:	**Train Brakes:** Air.
Brake Force: 21 t.	**Dimensions:** 8.13 x 2.57 m.
Weight: 42.25 t.	**Wheel Diameter:** 1067 mm.
Design Speed: 20 m.p.h.	**Maximum Speed:** 20 m.p.h.
Fuel Capacity:	**RA:** 6.
Train Supply: Not equipped.	**Multiple Working:** Not equipped.

Originally numbered D 2985.

| 07001 | **HN** HN HNRL | BH |

CLASS 08   BR/ENGLISH ELECTRIC   0-6-0

Built: 1955–1962 by BR at Crewe, Darlington, Derby Locomotive, Doncaster or Horwich Works.
Engine: English Electric 6KT of 298 kW (400 h.p.) at 680 r.p.m.
Main Generator: English Electric 801.
Traction Motors: Two English Electric 506.
Maximum Tractive Effort: 156 kN (35000 lbf).
Continuous Tractive Effort: 49 kN (11100 lbf) at 8.8 m.p.h.

Power At Rail: 194 kW (260 h.p.)	**Train Brakes:** Air & vacuum.
Brake Force: 19 t.	**Dimensions:** 8.92 x 2.59 m.
Weight: 49.6–50.4 t.	**Wheel Diameter:** 1372 mm.
Design Speed: 20 m.p.h.	**Maximum Speed:** 15 m.p.h.
Fuel Capacity: 3037 litres.	**RA:** 5.
Train Supply: Not equipped.	**Multiple Working:** Not equipped.

Notes: † – Equipped with remote control (Hima Sella system) for working at Allied Steel & Wire, Cardiff.
z – Equipped with remote control (Cattron system) for evaluation purposes.

Non-standard liveries/numbering:

08414 is as **DG**, but with BR & Railfreight Distribution logos and large bodyside numbers. Carries number D3529.
08460 is light grey with black underframe, cab doors, window surrounds and roof. Carries number D3575.

08500 is red, lined out in black & white. Carries bodyside name "THOMAS 1".
08527 is light grey with a black roof, blue bodyside stripe and "Ilford Level 5" branding.
08573 is light grey.
08601 is London Midland & Scottish Railway style black.
08616 carries number 3783.
08629 is red with italic numbers.
08642 is London & South Western Railway style black. Carries number D3809.
08649 is grey with blue, white and red stripes and WTL logo. Carries number D3816.
08678 is Glaxochem grey and blue.
08682 is dark blue with a grey roof.
08715 is "Day-glo" orange.
08721 is as **B**, but with a black roof and "Express parcels" branding with red and yellow stripe.
08782 is in Corus silver livery.
08785 is silver grey.
08801 carries number 801.
08805 is London Midland & Scottish Railway style maroon. Carries number 3973.
08809 is plain light grey.
08834 is in RFS(E) livery of blue with silver lining.
08879 is green and black with Railfreight Distribution logos.
08883 is Caledonian Railway style blue.
08928 is as **F0** with large bodyside numbers and light blue solebar.

Originally numbered in series D 3000–4192.

Class 08/0. Standard Design.

08077	**FL**	P	DFLS	FD		08481	**B**	E	WSXX	CF
08308 a	**CS**	RT	MOLO	IS		08482 a	**E**	E	WSAS	OC
08331	**GN**	WA	RFSH	ZB		08483 a	**GL**	FG	HJXX	PM
08375 a	**RT**	RT	MOLO	ZB		08484 a	**DG**	AM	KWSW	ZN
08389 a	**E**	EF	WSNE	IM		08485 a	**B**	EF	WSNW	AN
08393 a	**FE**	EF	WSNE	IM		08489 a	**E**	E	WSSC	ML
08397 a	**E**	E	WSNW	AN		08492 a	**B**	E	WSYX	ML
08401 a	**DG**	E	WSNE	IM		08493 a	**B**	E	WNZX	CF
08402 a	**E**	E	WSSC	ML		08495	**E**	E	WSNE	IM
08405 a	**E**	E	WSMD	TO		08499 a	**B**	E	WSGW	CF
08410 a	**GL**	FG	HJXX	LA		08500	**0**	E	WSGW	CF
08411 a	**B**	E	WSSC	ML		08506 a	**B**	E	WSAS	OC
08414 a	**0**	E	WSWX	OC		08507 a	**HN**	HN	HNRL	CZ
08417 a	**B**	SO	CDJD	ZA		08509 a	**F**	E	WSWX	IM
08418 a	**E**	E	WSMD	TO		08510 a	**B**	E	WSNE	IM
08428 a	**B**	E	WSNE	IM		08511 a	**E**	E	WSSC	ML
08441 a	**E**	E	WSSC	ML		08512 a	**F**	E	WSNE	IM
08442 a	**F**	E	WSNE	IM		08514 a	**E**	E	WSNE	IM
08451	**GB**	VW	ATLO	WN		08516 a	**DG**	E	WSMD	TO
08454	**VP**	VW	ATLO	WN		08523	**ML**	E	WSXX	CD
08460 a	**0**	E	WSNW	AN		08525	**F**	MA	HISL	NL
08466 a†| **E**	E	WSAW	CF		08526	**E**	E	WSAS	OC
08472 a	**BR**	WA	RFSH	BN		08527	**0**	BT	KCSI	ZI
08480 a	**G**	E	WSMD	TO		08528	**DG**	E	WSMD	TO

08529		B	E	WSWX	DR	08648	DG	RT	HJSL	ZB (S)
08530		FL	P	DFLS	FD	08649	O	AM	KESE	ZG
08531	a	DG	P	DFLS	FD	08651	a	DG	E	WSGW	CF
08534		DG	E	WSWX	ML	08653	FE	EF	WSWX	FB
08535		DG	EF	WSXX	CD	08655	F	EF	WSNE	IM
08536		B	MA	HISE	DY (S)	08661	a	FE	EF	WNZX	SP
08538		DG	E	WSMD	TO	08662	E	E	WSGW	CF
08540		DG	E	WSMD	TO	08663	a	GL	FG	HJSL	LA
08541		DG	E	WSXX	OC	08664	E	E	WSAS	OC
08542		F	E	WSXX	BS	08665	B	E	WSNE	IM
08543		DG	E	WSMD	TO	08666	B	E	WSYX	SP
08561		B	E	WSNW	AN	08669	a	WA	WA	RFSH	PM
08567		B	E	WSMD	TO	08670	a	E	E	WSSC	ML
08568	a	B	AM	KGSS	ZH (S)	08673	IM	E	WNZX	SP
08569		B	E	WSMD	TO	08675	F	E	WSXX	ML
08571	a	B	WA	HBSH	PC	08676	B	E	WSWX	FB
08573		O	RT	KCSI	ZB	08678	O	WC	MBDL	DY
08575		FL	P	DFLS	FD	08682	O	BT	KDSD	ZF
08576		B	E	WNZX	CF	08683	E	E	WSMD	TO
08577		E	E	WSMD	TO	08685	B	E	WSGW	CF
08578		E	E	WSNE	IM	08689	a	E	E	WSNE	IM
08580		B	E	WSMD	TO	08690	MA	MA	HISE	DY (S)
08582	a	DG	E	WSNE	IM	08691	G	WA	DFLS	FD
08585		FL	P	DFLS	FD	08694	a	E	EF	WSAS	OC
08587		B	E	WSNE	IM	08695	a	E	E	WSSC	ML
08588		BR	MA	HISL	NL (S)	08696	a	V	VW	ATLO	LO
08593		E	E	WSSC	ML	08697	B	MA	HISE	DY (S)
08596	a†	WA	WA	RFSH	ZB	08698	a	E	E	WSMD	TO
08597		E	E	WSNE	IM	08701	a	RX	E	WSNW	AN
08599		E	E	WSNE	IM	08702	B	E	WSXX	ZB
08601		O	E	WSXX	AN	08703	a	E	EF	WSMD	TO
08605		B	E	WSNE	IM	08706	E	E	WSNW	AN
08611		V	VW	ATLO	LL	08709	E	E	WSMD	TO
08613		K	RT		ZI	08711	RX	E	WSGW	CF
08616		GW	MA	HGSS	TS	08714	E	E	WSMD	TO
08617		VP	VW	ATLO	WN	08715	v	O	E	WSWX	FB
08623		E	E	WSNE	IM	08720	a	E	E	WSXX	ML
08624		B	P	DFLS	FD	08721	O	VW	ATLO	LO
08628		B	E	WSXX	SY	08724	WA	WA	HBSH	NL
08629		O	AM	KWSW	ZN	08730	K	AM	KGSS	ZH
08630		E	E	WSGW	CF	08735	E	E	WSNE	IM
08631		N	FG	SDFR	DF	08737	a	FE	EF	WSNW	AN
08632		E	E	WSNW	AN	08738	E	E	WSNW	AN
08633		E	E	WSNE	IM	08739	B	EF	WSXX	AN
08635		E	E	WSAS	OC	08740	F	E	WSXX	FB
08641		FP	FG	HJSL	LA	08742	RX	E	WSMD	TO
08642		O	P	DFLS	SZ (S)	08743	EN	EN	MBDL	BG
08643		GL	FG	HJXX	PM (S)	08745	FE	P	DFLS	SZ (S)
08644		GL	FG	HJSL	LA	08746	DG	HN	HNRS	DR
08645		FP	FG	HJSL	LA	08750	a	K	RT	MOLO	BF
08646		F	E	WSAS	OC	08751	FE	EF	WSYX	ZB

08752	†	**E**	E	WSAW	CF
08754		**FL**	RT	MOLO	ZB
08756		**DG**	E	WNZX	CF
08757		**RG**	E	WSMD	TO
08758		**B**	E	WSXX	FB
08762		**B**	RT	MOLO	ZB
08765		**DG**	E	WSMD	TO
08768		**B**	E	WSSC	ML
08770	a	**DG**	E	WSGW	CF
08775		**E**	E	WSAS	OC
08776	a	**DG**	E	WSAS	OC
08782	a	**0**	E	WSNW	AN
08783		**E**	E	WSAS	OC
08784		**B**	EF	WSWX	FB
08785	a	**0**	P	DFLS	FD
08786	a	**DG**	E	WSAS	OC
08788		**RT**	RT	MOLO	IS
08790		**B**	VW	ATLO	LO
08792		**F**	E	WSGW	CF
08795		**FP**	FG	HJSE	LE
08798		**B**	E	WSGW	CF
08799	a	**E**	EF	WSAS	OC
08801		**B**	E	WNZX	CF
08802		**RX**	E	WSNW	AN
08804		**E**	E	WSAS	OC
08805		**0**	MA	HGSS	TS
08806	a	**F**	E	WSXX	TE
08807		**BR**	E	WSSC	ML
08809		**0**	CD	CREL	NC
08810	a	**AR**	CD	CREL	NC
08813	a	**DG**	E	WSYX	TE
08815		**B**	E	WSYX	SP
08817		**BR**	E	WSXX	AN
08818		**HN**	HN	DFLS	FD
08819		**DG**	E	WNZX	CF
08822		**GL**	FG	HJSE	ZB
08823	a	**B**	BT	KDSD	ZF
08824	ak	**F**	E	WSNE	IM
08825	a	**B**	EF	WSWX	OC
08827	a	**B**	E	WSYX	ML
08828	a	**E**	E	WSMD	TO
08830		**LW**	WB	HLSV	CP
08834		**0**	WA	HBSH	BN
08836		**GL**	FG	HJXX	OO
08837		**DG**	EF	WSXX	AN
08842		**E**	EF	WSNW	AN
08844		**B**	EF	WSNE	IM
08847		**B**	CD	CREL	DR
08853	a	**B**	WA	RFSH	ZB
08854	†	**E**	E	WSAS	OC
08856		**B**	EF	WSAW	CF
08865		**B**	E	WSAS	OC
08866		**B**	E	WSNW	AN
08867		**K**	E	WSWX	FB
08868		**B**	HN	HNRL	BH
08869		**G**	CD	CROL	LB
08870		**RL**	RL	MBDL	NC
08871		**CD**	CD	CREL	ZB
08872		**E**	EF	WSAS	OC
08873		**RX**	RT	MOLO	CP
08874		**SL**	RT	MOLO	CP
08877		**DG**	E	WSWX	SP
08879		**0**	EF	WSNE	IM
08880		**B**	E	WSXX	AN
08881		**DG**	E	WSSC	ML
08883		**0**	E	WSSC	ML
08884		**B**	E	WSMD	TO
08886	z	**E**	E	WSNE	IM
08887	a	**VP**	VW	ATLO	LO
08888		**E**	E	WSNE	IM
08890		**DG**	E	WSAS	OC
08891		**B**	P	DFLS	FD
08892		**GN**	WA	RFSH	BN
08893		**DG**	E	WSYX	FB
08894		**B**	E	WSXX	AN
08896		**E**	E	WSGW	CF
08897		**E**	E	WSNW	AN
08899		**MM**	MA	HISE	DY
08900		**DG**	E	WSAS	OC
08901		**B**	E	WSYX	FB
08902		**B**	EF	WSXX	AN
08903		**EN**	EN	MBDL	BG
08904		**B**	E	WSGW	CF
08905		**E**	EF	WSMD	TO
08906		**B**	E	WSXX	ML
08907		**LW**	EF	WSWX	FB
08908		**MM**	MA	HISL	NL
08909		**ML**	E	WSNW	AN
08910		**B**	E	WSXX	FB
08911		**DG**	E	WSNE	IM
08912		**B**	E	WSWX	FB
08913		**DG**	EF	WSGW	CF
08914		**B**	E	WSXX	FB
08915		**F**	E	WSNW	AN
08918		**DG**	E	WSAS	OC
08919		**RX**	E	WSAS	OC
08920		**F**	E	WSMD	TO
08921	†	**E**	E	WSAS	OC
08922		**DG**	E	WSNW	AN
08924		**E**	E	WSSC	ML
08925		**B**	E	WSWX	DR
08926		**B**	EF	WSXX	AN

08927		**B**	E	WSSC	ML	08946	**FE**	EF	WSWX	AN
08928		**O**	CD	CROL	LB (S)	08947	**B**	E	WSAS	OC
08931		**B**	E	WSYX	FB	08948	c	**EP**	EU	GPSS	OC
08932		**B**	E	WSXX	CD	08950		**IM**	MA	HISL	NL (S)
08933		**E**	E	WSSC	ML	08951	†	**DG**	EF	WSAW	CF
08934	a	**VP**	VW	ATLO	WN	08953	a	**DG**	E	WSNE	IM
08936		**B**	HN	HNRL	DY	08954		**F**	E	WSNW	AN
08939		**B**	EF	WSMD	TO	08955		**F**	E	WSXX	CF
08940		**B**	E	WNZX	SP	08956		**B**	SO	CDJD	ZA
08941		**B**	E	WSGW	CF	08957		**E**	E	WNZX	CF
08942		**B**	E	WSXX	FB						

Names:

08389	NOEL KIRTON OBE
08483	DUSTY Driver David Miller
08649	G.H. Stratton
08664	DON GATES 1952–2000
08682	Lionheart
08694	PAT BARR
08701	The Sorter
08714	Cambridge
08743	Brian Turner
08782	CASTLETON WORKS
08790	M.A. SMITH

08804	RICHARD J.WENHAM EASTLEIGH DEPOT DECEMBER 1989–JULY 1999
08818	MOLLY
08872	TONY LONG Stratford Depot 1971–2002
08874	Catherine
08896	STEPHEN DENT
08903	John W Antill
08905	Danny Daniels
08919	Steep Holm
08950	Neville Hill 1st

Class 08/9. Reduced height cab. Converted 1985–87 by BR at Landore T&RSMD.

08993		**E**	E	WSGW	CF	ASHBURNHAM
08994	a	**E**	E	WSGW	CF	GWENDRAETH
08995	a	**E**	E	WSGW	CF	KIDWELLY

CLASS 09   BR/ENGLISH ELECTRIC   0-6-0

Built: 1959–1962 by BR at Darlington or Horwich Works.
Engine: English Electric 6KT of 298 kW (400 h.p.) at 680 r.p.m.
Main Generator: English Electric 801.
Traction Motors: English Electric 506.
Maximum Tractive Effort: 111 kN (25000 lbf).
Continuous Tractive Effort: 39 kN (8800 lbf) at 11.6 m.p.h.
Power At Rail: 201 kW (269 h.p.).
Brake Force: 19 t.
Weight: 50 t.
Design Speed: 27 m.p.h.
Fuel Capacity: 3037 litres.
Train Supply: Not equipped.
Train Brakes: Air & vacuum.
Dimensions: 8.92 x 2.59 m.
Wheel Diameter: 1372 mm.
Maximum Speed: 27 m.p.h.
RA: 5.
Multiple Working: Not equipped.

Class 09/0 were originally numbered D 3665–71, 3719–21, 4099–4114.

Class 09/0. Built as Class 09.

09001	**E**	E	WSGW	CF
09003	**E**	E	WSGW	CF
09005	**E**	E	WSNE	IM

09006	**ML**	E	WSAS	OC	
09007	**ML**	E	WSNE	IM	
09008	**E**	E	WSGW	CF	
09009	**E**	E	WSAS	OC	Three Bridges C.E.D.
09010	**DG**	E	WSAS	OC	
09011	**DG**	EF	WSGW	CF	
09012	**DG**	E	WSAS	OC	Dick Hardy
09013	**DG**	E	WSGW	CF	
09014	**DG**	E	WSNE	IM	
09015	**E**	E	WSGW	CF	
09016	**E**	E	WSGW	CF	
09017	**E**	E	WSGW	CF	
09018	**E**	E	WSAS	OC	
09019	**ML**	E	WSAS	OC	
09020	**E**	E	WSNW	AN	
09021	**E**	EF	WSNW	AN	
09022 a	**E**	EF	WSNW	AN	
09023 a	**E**	E	WSNE	IM	
09024	**ML**	E	WSAS	OC	
09025	**CX**	SC	HWSU	SU	
09026	**G**	SC	HWSU	BI	William Pearson

Class 09/1. Converted from Class 08/0. 110 V electrical equipment.

Converted: 1992–1993 by RFS Industries, Kilnhurst.

09101 (08833)	**DG**	E	WSGW	CF
09102 (08832)	**DG**	E	WSGW	CF
09103 (08766)	**DG**	E	WSSC	ML
09104 (08749)	**DG**	E	WSXX	AN
09105 (08835)	**DG**	E	WSGW	CF
09106 (08759)	**DG**	E	WSNE	IM
09107 (08845)	**DG**	E	WSNE	IM

Class 09/2. Converted from Class 08. 90 V electrical equipment.

Converted: 1992 by RFS Industries, Kilnhurst.

09201 (08421)	ak	**DG**	E	WSNE	IM
09202 (08732)		**DG**	E	WSNE	IM
09203 (08781)		**DG**	E	WSGW	CF
09204 (08717)		**DG**	E	WSNE	IM
09205 (08620)		**DG**	E	WSSC	ML

CLASS 20   ENGLISH ELECTRIC   Bo-Bo

Built: 1957–1968 by English Electric Company at Vulcan Foundry, Newton le Willows or by Robert Stephenson & Hawthorn at Darlington.
Engine: English Electric 8SVT Mk. II of 746 kW (1000 h.p.) at 850 r.p.m.
Main Generator: English Electric 819/3C.
Traction Motors: English Electric 526/5D or 526/8D.
Maximum Tractive Effort: 187 kN (42000 lbf).
Continuous Tractive Effort: 111 kN (25000 lbf) at 11 m.p.h.
Power At Rail: 574 kW (770 h.p.).   **Train Brakes:** Air & vacuum.

Brake Force: 35 t.	**Dimensions:** 14.25 x 2.67 m.
Weight: 73.4–73.5 t.	**Wheel Diameter:** 1092 mm.
Design Speed: 75 m.p.h.	**Maximum Speed:** 75 m.p.h.
Fuel Capacity: 1727 litres.	**RA:** 5.
Train Supply: Not equipped.	**Multiple Working:** Blue Star.

Non-standard liveries:

20088, 20105, 20108, 20113, 20145, 20159 and 20175 are in RFS grey.
20092 is in Central Services grey & red livery.
20132, 20138 and 20215 are as **FO** but with a red solebar stripe.
20905 is in Hunslet-Barclay two-tone grey with a red solebar.

Originally numbered in series D 8007–8190, 8315–8325.

Class 20/0. Standard Design.

20016	B	DR	XHSS	LT
20032	B	DR	XHSS	LT
20057	B	DR	XHSS	LT
20066	B	DR	XHSS	LT
20072	B	DR	XHSS	LT
20073	B	DR	XHSS	LT
20081	B	DR	XHSS	LT
20088	0	DR	XHSS	LT
20092	0	DR	XHSS	LT
20094	B	DR	XHSS	ZH
20105	0	DR	XHSS	LT
20108	0	DR	XHSS	LT
20113	0	DR	XHSS	KM
20121	B	DR	XHSS	LT
20132	0	DR	XHSS	LT
20135	B	DR	XHSS	ZH
20138	0	DR	XHSS	LT
20145	0	DR	XHSS	LT
20159	0	DR	XHSS	LT
20175	0	DR	XHSS	KM
20215	0	DR	XHSS	LT

Class 20/3. Direct Rail Services refurbished locos.

Details as Class 20/0 except:

Refurbished: 1995–1996 by Brush Traction at Loughborough (20301–305) or 1997–98 by RFS(E) at Doncaster (20306–315). Disc indicators or headcode panels removed.
Train Brakes: Air. **Fuel Capacity:** 2900 (+ 4909) litres.
Brake Force: 31 t.
Multiple Working: Blue Star (20301–305 at nose end only).

20301	(20047)	+	**DR**	DR XHSD	KM	Max Joule 1958–1999
20302	(20084)		**DR**	DR XHSD	KM	
20303	(20127)	+	**DR**	DR XHSD	KM	
20304	(20120)		**DR**	DR XHSD	KM	
20305	(20095)		**DR**	DR XHSD	KM	
20306	(20131)	+	**DR**	DR XHSD	KM	

20307	(20128)	+ **DR**	DR XHSD	KM	
20308	(20187)	+ **DR**	DR XHSD	KM	
20309	(20075)	+ **DR**	DR XHSD	KM	
20310	(20190)	+ **DR**	DR XHSD	KM	
20311	(20102)	+ **DR**	DR XHSD	KM	
20312	(20042)	+ **DR**	DR XHSD	KM	
20313	(20194)	+ **DR**	DR XHSD	KM	
20314	(20117)	+ **DR**	DR XHSD	KM	
20315	(20104)	+ **DR**	DR XHSD	KM	

Class 20/9. Direct Rail Services (former Hunslet-Barclay) refurbished locos.

Details as Class 20/0 except:

Refurbished: 1989 by Hunslet-Barclay at Kilmarnock.
Train Brakes: Air.   **Fuel Capacity:** 1727 (+ 4727) litres.

20901	(20041)	**DR**	DR XHSD	KM	
20902	(20060)	+ **DR**	DR XHSD	KM	
20903	(20083)	+ **DR**	DR XHSD	KM	
20904	(20101)	**DR**	DR XHSD	KM	
20905	(20225)	+ **0**	DR XHSS	ZB	
20906	(20219)	**DR**	DR XHSD	KM	

CLASS 31 BRUSH/ENGLISH ELECTRIC A1A-A1A

Built: 1958–1962 by Brush Traction at Loughborough.
Engine: English Electric 12SVT of 1100 kW (1470 h.p.) at 850 r.p.m.
Main Generator: Brush TG160-48.   **Traction Motors:** Brush TM73-68.
Maximum Tractive Effort: 160 kN (35900 lbf).
Continuous Tractive Effort: 83 kN (18700 lbf) at 23.5 m.p.h.
Power At Rail: 872 kW (1170 h.p.).   **Train Brakes:** Air & vacuum.
Brake Force: 49 t.   **Dimensions:** 17.30 x 2.67 m.
Weight: 106.7–111 t.   **Wheel Diameter:** 1092/1003 mm.
Design Speed: 90 m.p.h.   **Maximum Speed:** 90 m.p.h.
Fuel Capacity: 2409 litres.   **RA:** 5 or 6.
Train Supply: Not equipped.   **Multiple Working:** Blue Star.

Originally numbered D 5520–5699, 5800–5862 (not in order).

Non-standard livery/numbering:

31110 carries number D5528.
31301 is as **F0** but with a red solebar stripe.

Class 31/1. Standard Design. RA: 5.

31102	**CE**	E	WNZX	CD	
31105	**F**	NR	QADD	BH	
31106	**FR**	HJ	SDFR	DF	SPALDING TOWN
31107	**CE**	NR	QADD	DF	
31110 a	**G**	E	WMOC	BH	TRACTION magazine
31113	**CE**	E	WNXX	OC	
31128	**FR**	FR	SDFR	DF	CHARYBDIS

31154	**CE**	FR	SDXL	DF	
31190	**RK**	PO	SDFR	DF	GRYPHON
31200	**F**	HN	HNRS	CS	
31206	**CE**	CD	CROL	LB	
31207	**CE**	E	WNXX	OC	
31233	**CE**	NR	QADD	DF	
31275	**F**	E	WNZX	CS	
31285	**CE**	NR	QADD	DF	
31296	**F**	E	WNZX	CP	
31301	**0**	FR	SDXL	DF	
31306	**CE**	E	WNXX	OC	
31308	**CE**	E	WNXX	OC	
31319	**F**	HN	HNRS	CS	

Class 31/4. Electric Train Supply equipment. RA: 6.
Class 31/5. Train Heating Equipment isolated. RA: 6.

31407	**ML**	FR	SDXL	BH	
31410	**RR**	E	WNZX	CS	
31411	**DG**	FR	SDXL	BH	
31412	**CE**	FR	SDXL	BH	
31514	**CE**	E	WNXX	OC	
31415	**B**	FR	SDXL	DF	
31417	**DG**	FR	SDXL	BH	
31420	**IM**	E	WNXX	OC	
31421	**RR**	HN	HNRS	CS	
31422	**IM**	FR	SDXL	TM	
31423	**IM**	FR	SDXL	DF	
31424	**CE**	FR	SDXL	BH	
31426	**CE**	FR	SDXL	DF	
31427	**B**	E	WNXX	OC	
31433	**CE**	FR	SDXL	BH	
31437	**CE**	FR	SDXL	DF	
31439	**RR**	FR	SDXL	DF	
31449	**CE**	FR	SDXL	TM	
31452	**FR**	FR	SDFR	DF	MINOTAUR
31454	**CE**	FR	SDXL	DF	
31458	**CE**	FR	SDXL	TM	
31459	**FR**	FR	SDFR	DF	CERBERUS
31460	**B**	FR	SDXL	BH	
31461	**DG**	FR	SDXL	DF	
31462	**DG**	FR	SDXL	TM	
31465	**RR**	E	WNXX	OC	
31466 a	**E**	E	WNXX	OC	
31468	**FR**	FR	SDFR	DF	HYDRA

Class 31/6. ETS through wiring and controls. RA: 5.

| 31601 | (31186) | **RK** | FR | SDFR | DF | BLETCHLEY PARK 'STATION X' |
| 31602 | (31191) | **FR** | FR | SDFR | DF | CHIMAERA |

CLASS 33   BRCW/SULZER   Bo-Bo

Built: 1960–1962 by the Birmingham Railway Carriage & Wagon Company at Smethwick.
Engine: Sulzer 8LDA28 of 1160 kW (1550 h.p.) at 750 r.p.m.
Main Generator: Crompton Parkinson CG391B1.
Traction Motors: Crompton Parkinson C171C2.
Maximum Tractive Effort: 200 kN (45000 lbf).
Continuous Tractive Effort: 116 kN (26000 lbf) at 17.5 m.p.h.
Power At Rail: 906 kW (1215 h.p.).   **Train Brakes:** Air & vacuum.
Brake Force: 35 t.   **Dimensions:** 15.47 x 2.82 (2.64 m. 33/2).
Weight: 77.7 t.   **Wheel Diameter:** 1092 mm.
Design Speed: 85 m.p.h.   **Maximum Speed:** 85 m.p.h.
Fuel Capacity: 3410 litres.   **RA:** 6.
Train Supply: Electric, index 48 (750 V DC only).
Multiple Working: Blue Star.

Originally numbered in series D 6500–97 but not in order.

Notes:

Fragonset operated 33021, 33103, 33108 and 33202 are currently on hire to South West Trains.

Non-standard numbering:

33051 also carries number 6569.
33109 also carries number D6525.
33116 also carries number D6535.
33208 also carries number D6593.

Class 33/0. Standard Design.

33002	**CE**	DR	XHSS	LT	
33008	**G**	DR	XHSS	LT	
33021	**FR**	WF	SDFR	DF	Eastleigh
33023	**B**	DR	XHSS	ZH	
33025	**DR**	DR	XHSD	KM	
33026	**CE**	HN	HNRS	EH	
33029	**B**	DR	XHSS	DF	
33030	**DR**	DR	XHSD	KM	
33046	**CE**	FR	SDXL	EH	
33051	**B**	HN	HNRS	EH	Shakespeare Cliff
33053	**F**	DR	XHSS	LT	
33057	**CE**	DR	XHSS	LT	

Class 33/1. Fitted with buckeye couplings & SR multiple working equipment for use with SR EMUs, TC stock & Class 73. Also fitted with flashing light adaptor for use on Weymouth Quay line.

33103	b	**FR**	CM	SDFR	DF	SWORDFISH
33108	b	**FR**	11	SDFR	DF	VAMPIRE
33109	b	**B**	71	MBDL	RL	Captain Bill Smith RNR
33116	b	**B**	E	WNZX	OC	

Class 33/2. Built to former loading gauge of Tonbridge–Battle Line.
All equipped with slow speed control.

33202	**FR**	FR	SDFR	DF	METEOR
33203	**F**	DR	XHSS	LT	
33205	**F**	DR	XHSS	OC	
33207	**DR**	DR	XHSD	KM	
33208	**G**	71	MBDL	RL	

CLASS 37   ENGLISH ELECTRIC   Co-Co

Built: 1960–1965 by English Electric Company at Vulcan Foundry, Newton le Willows or by Robert Stephenson & Hawthorn at Darlington.
Engine: English Electric 12CSVT of 1300 kW (1750 h.p.) at 850 r.p.m.
Main Generator: English Electric 822/10G.
Traction Motors: English Electric 538/A.
Maximum Tractive Effort: 245 kN (55500 lbf).
Continuous Tractive Effort: 156 kN (35000 lbf) at 13.6 m.p.h.

Power At Rail: 932 kW (1250 h.p.).	**Train Brakes:** Air & vacuum.
Brake Force: 50 t.	**Dimensions:** 18.75 x 2.74 m.
Weight: 102.8–108.4 t.	**Wheel Diameter:** 1092 mm.
Design Speed: 90 m.p.h.	**Maximum Speed:** 80 m.p.h.
Fuel Capacity: 4046 (+ 7678) litres.	**RA:** 5 (§ 6).
Train Supply: Not equipped.	**Multiple Working:** Blue Star.

Originally numbered D 6600–8, 6700–6999 (not in order).

Non-standard liveries/numbering:

37131 also carries number 6831.
37351 carries number 37002 on one side only.
37403 carries number D6607.
37906 is as **FO** but with a red solebar stripe.

Class 37/0. Standard Design. Details as above.

37010 a	**CE**	E	WNYX	SP	
37012	**CE**	DR	XHSS	LB	
37013	**ML**	DR	XHSS	LB	
37019	**F**	DR	XHSS	LB	
37023	**ML**	E	WNXX	OC	Stratford TMD
37029 §	**DR**	DR	XHSD	KM	
37037 a	**F**	E	WNYX	SP	
37038	**CE**	IR	MBDL	BQ	
37040	**E**	E	WNYX	SP	
37042 r+	**E**	E	WKAD	CD	
37043	**CE**	DR	XHSS	LB	
37045	**F**	X		TT	
37046 a	**CE**	E	WNXX	TY	
37047 +	**ML**	E	WKAC	OC	
37048	**F**	X		TT	
37051	**E**	E	WKAC	OC	
37054	**CE**	E	WNYX	ML	

37055	+	**ML**	E	WNXX	TE	
37057	+	**E**	E	WKAC	OC	Viking
37058	a+	**CE**	E	WNXX	TY	
37059	a+	**DR**	DR	XHSS	LB	
37065	+	**ML**	E	WKAD	CD	
37068		**F**	DR	XHSS	LB	
37069	a+	**CE**	DR	XHSS	LB	
37071	a+	**CE**	E	WNYX	SP	
37072		**DG**	HN	HNRS	BH	
37073	a+	**F**	E	WNZX	SP	
37074	a+	**ML**	E	WNYX	SP	
37077	a	**ML**	E	WNXX	TY	
37078		**F**	HN	HNRS	SP	
37079		**F**	HN	HNRS	BH	
37087		**CE**	HN	HNRS	BH	
37095		**CE**	HN	HNRS	BH	
37097		**CE**	E	WNYX	MH	
37100	a	**F**	E	WNXX	TY	
37109		**E**	E	WKAC	OC	
37111		**F**	DR	XHSS	DP	
37114	r+	**E**	E	WKAD	CD	City of Worcester
37116	+	**B**	E	WNYX	EH	Sister Dora
37131	+	**F**	E	WNYX	SP	
37133	a	**CE**	E	WNYX	SP	
37137		**?**	X		TT	
37139		**F**	E	WNZX	TE	
37141		**CE**	HN	HNRS	CS	
37142		**CE**	HN	HNRS	BH	
37144		**F**	DR	XHSS	LB	
37146	a	**CE**	E	WNXX	TY	
37152		**I**	E	WNYX	ML	
37153		**CE**	HN	HNRS	BH	
37162	+	**DG**	E	WNYX	SP	
37165	a+	**CE**	HN	HNRS	CS	
37170	a	**CE**	E	WNYX	SP	
37174	a	**E**	E	WKAC	OC	
37175	a	**CE**	E	WMOC	OC	
37178	+	**F**	E	WNYX	EH	
37185	+	**CE**	E	WNYX	SP	
37188		**CE**	HN	HNRS	CS	
37194		**HN**	HN	HNRL	BH	
37196	a	**CE**	E	WNXX	TY	
37197		**IR**	IR	MBDL	BQ	
37198	+	**ML**	E	WNXX	TO	
37201		**CE**	HN	HNRS	BH	
37203		**ML**	E	WKAC	OC	
37211		**CE**	DR	XHSS	LB	
37212	+	**F**	E	WNYX	EH	
37213		**F**	X		TT	
37214		**F**	HN	HNRS	SP	
37216	+	**ML**	E	WKAC	OC	

37217	+	**B**	E	WNZX	AY	
37218		**DR**	DR	XHSD	KM	
37219		**ML**	E	WNXX	EH	
37220	+	**E**	E	WNXX	TO	
37221	a	**F**	E	WNXX	TY	
37222		**F**	HN	HNRS	CS	
37223		**F**	DR	XHSS	LB	
37225	+	**F**	E	WNYX	SP	
37227		**F**	HN	HNRS	BH	
37229	§	**DR**	DR	XHSD	KM	
37230	+	**CE**	E	WNYX	TO	
37235		**F**	IR	MBDL	BQ	
37238	a+	**F**	E	WNXX	TY	
37242		**ML**	HN	HNRS	BH	
37248	+	**ML**	E	WKAC	OC	Midland Railway Centre
37250	a+	**F**	E	WNXX	TY	
37254		**CE**	HN	HNRS	BH	
37255		**CE**	FR	SDXL	SP	
37259		**DR**	DR	XHSD	KM	
37261	a+	**F**	IR	MBDL	BQ	
37262	+	**DG**	DR	XHSS	LB	Dounreay
37263		**CE**	E	WNYX	EH	
37264		**CE**	E	WNZX	TM	
37275	+	**B**	E	WNYX	TO	
37278		**F**	X		TT	
37293	a+	**ML**	E	WNXX	TY	
37294	a+	**CE**	E	WKAD	CD	
37298	a+	**E**	E	WNYX	SP	
37308	+	**B**	E	WKAC	OC	

Class 37/3. Re-geared (CP7) bogies.

Details as Class 37/0 except:

Maximum Tractive Effort: 250 kN (56180 lbf).
Continuous Tractive Effort: 184 kN (41250 lbf) at 11.4 m.p.h.
Design Speed: 80 m.p.h.

37331		**F**	HN	HNRS	BH	
37334		**F**	DR	XHSS	LB	
37340		**F**	DR	XHSS	LB	
37341		**F**	HN	HNRS	BH	
37343		**CE**	X		TT	
37344		**F**	DR	XHSS	LB	
37345		**F**	HN	HNRS	IM	
37351	+	**CE**	E	WNXX	CD	
37358	+	**F**	E	WNZX	IM	
37359		**F**	HN	HNRS	CS	
37370	a	**E**	E	WNYX	SP	
37372		**ML**	E	WKAC	OC	
37375	a+	**ML**	E	WKAC	OC	
37376	a+	**F**	E	WNYX	SP	
37377	+	**CE**	E	WNXX	EH	

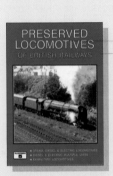

37379 a	**ML**	E	WNXX	EH		Ipswich WRD Quality Approved
37383 +	**ML**	DR	XHSS	CP	
37384	**CE**	DR	XHSS	LB	

Class 37/4. Refurbished with electric train supply equipment.
Main generator replaced by alternator. Re-geared (CP7) bogies. Details as Class
37/0 except:

Main Alternator: Brush BA1005A.   **Power At Rail:** 935 kW (1254 h.p.).
Maximum Tractive Effort: 256 kN (57440 lbf).
Continuous Tractive Effort: 184 kN (41250 lbf) at 11.4 m.p.h.
Weight: 107 t.   **Design Speed:** 80 m.p.h.
Fuel Capacity: 7678 litres.   **Train Supply:** Electric, index 38.

37401	**GS**	E	WKBM	ML	The Royal Scotsman
37402	**F**	E	WKCK	CF	Bont Y Bermo
37403 ar	**G**	E	WNYX	MG	Ben Cruachan
37405 r	**E**	E	WKBM	ML	
37406	**F**	E	WNSS	CF	The Saltire Society
37407	**F**	E	WNXX	CD	
37408 r	**E**	E	WKCK	CF	Loch Rannoch
37409	**F**	E	WKAM	ML	
37410 r	**F**	E	WKAM	ML	Aluminium 100
37411 r	**E**	E	WKBM	ML	The Scottish Railway Preservation Society
37412	**F**	E	WNSS	CF	Driver John Elliott
37413 r	**E**	E	WNXX	CF	
37414	**RR**	E	WNYX	SP	
37415 r	**E**	E	WKBM	ML	
37416 r	**E**	E	WKBM	ML	Sir Robert McAlpine/Concrete Bob
37417 a	**E**	E	WNSS	CF	
37418	**E**	E	WKCK	CF	East Lancashire Railway
37419	**E**	E	WKCK	CF	
37420	**RR**	E	WNXX	CD	The Scottish Hosteller
37421 r	**E**	E	WKBM	ML	
37422	**RR**	E	WNSS	CF	
37423	**F**	E	WNXX	ML	Sir Murray Morrison 1873–1948
					Pioneer of the British Aluminium Industry
37424	**F**	E	WNXX	ML	
37425	**E**	E	WKCK	CF	
37426 r	**E**	E	WKBM	ML	
37427 r	**E**	E	WKBM	ML	
37428 r	**GS**	E	WKBM	ML	Loch Long/Loch Awe
37429	**RR**	E	WNXX	TO	
37430 a	**F**	E	WNXX	ML	Cwmbrân

**Class 37/5. Refurbished without train supply equipment. Main generator
replaced by alternator. Re-geared (CP7) bogies.**

Details as Class 37/4 except:
Maximum Tractive Effort: 248 kN (55590 lbf).
Weight: 106.1–110.0) t.

37503 r§	**E**	E	WKAD	CD	
37505 a§	**F**	E	WNXX	AY	British Steel Workington

37509 a§ F	E	WNXX	CF	
37510 a I	E	WNXX	TE	
37513 as§ LH	E	WNXX	OC	
37515 as F	E	WNXX	TE	
37516 s§ LH	E	WNSS	BS	
37517 as§ LH	E	WKAD	CD	
37518 a§ F	E	WNXX	AY	
37519 F	E	WNYX	EH	
37520 r§ E	E	WNXX	CD	
37521 r§ E	E	WKAD	CD	English China Clays

Class 37/6. Originally refurbished for Nightstar services. Main generator replaced by alternator, re-geared bogies and UIC jumpers. Details as Class 37/5 except:

Maximum Speed: 90 m.p.h.   **Train Brake:** Air.
Train Supply: Not equipped, but electric through wired.
Multiple Working: TDM († plus Blue Star).

37601	EP	EU	GPSV	OC	
37602 †	DR	DR	XHSD	KM	
37603	EP	EU	GPSV	OC	
37604	EP	EU	GPSV	OC	
37605 †	DR	DR	XHSD	KM	
37606 †	DR	DR	XHSD	KM	
37607 †	DR	DR	XHSD	KM	
37608 †	DR	DR	XHSD	KM	
37609 †	DR	DR	XHSD	KM	
37610 †	DR	DR	XHSD	KM	The MALCOLM Group
37611 †	DR	DR	XHSD	KM	
37612 †	DR	DR	XHSD	KM	

Class 37/5 continued.

37667 rs§ E	E	WKAM	ML	Meldon Quarry Centenary
37668 s§ E	E	WNSS	DR	
37669 r§ E	E	WKAD	CD	
37670 r§ E	E	WKAD	CD	St. Blazey T&RS Depot
37671 a F	E	WNXX	TY	
37672 as F	E	WNXX	TE	
37673 § F	E	WNXX	TE	
37674 § F	E	WKAD	CD	Saint Blaise Church 1445-1995
37675 as§ F	E	WNSS	CA	Margam TMD
37676 as§ F	E	WNSS	CA	
37677 a§ F	E	WNSS	DR	
37678 a§ F	E	WNXX	BS	
37679 a§ F	E	WNXX	AY	
37680 a§ F	E	WNXX	TE	
37682 r§ E	E	WKAD	CD	Hartlepool Pipe Mill
37683 a F	E	WNXX	TE	
37684 ar§ E	E	WKAD	CD	Peak National Park
37685 a§ I	E	WNSS	PB	
37686 a F	E	WNYX	SP	
37688 § E	E	WNXX	IM	

37689 a§	F	E	WKAD	CD	
37692 s§	F	E	WNSS	CA	Didcot Depot
37693 as	F	E	WNXX	TY	
37694 §	E	E	WKAC	OC	
37695 s§	E	E	WKAD	CD	
37696 as	F	E	WNXX	TY	
37697 §	E	E	WNXX	TT	
37698 a§	LH	E	WKAD	CD	

Class 37/7. Refurbished locos. Main generator replaced by alternator. Re-geared (CP7) bogies. Ballast weights added. Details as Class 37/5 except:
Main Alternator: GEC G564AZ (37796–803) Brush BA1005A (others).
Maximum Tractive Effort: 276 kN (62000 lbf).
Weight: 120 t.   **RA:** 7.

37701 as	F	E	WNXX	OC	
37702 s	GIF	E	WKGS	ES	
37703	GIF	E	WKGS	ES	
37704 s	E	E	WNSS	WA	
37705	F	E	WNXX	ML	
37706	E	E	WNSS	EH	
37707	E	E	WKAD	CD	
37708 a	F	E	WNXX	DR	
37709	F	E	WNXX	IM	
37710	LH	E	WNSS	TE	
37711	F	E	WNYX	TT	
37712 a	E	E	WKAD	CD	
37713	LH	E	WNXX	CD	
37714 a	GIF	E	WKGS	ES	
37715	F	E	WNYX	SP	
37716	GIF	E	WKGS	ES	
37717	E	E	WKAD	CD	Berwick Middle School
					Railsafe Trophy Winners 1998
37718	GIF	E	WKGS	ES	
37719 a	F	E	WNXX	OC	
37796 as	F	E	WNXX	TY	
37797 s	E	E	WKAD	CD	
37798	ML	E	WNSS	CD	
37799 as	GIF	E	WKGS	ES	
37800 a	GIF	E	WKGS	ES	
37801 a	GIF	E	WKGS	ES	
37802 s	GIF	E	WKGS	ES	
37803 a	ML	E	WNXX	TY	
37883	GIF	E	WKGS	ES	
37884	GIF	E	WKGS	ES	
37885	GIF	E	WNXX	ES	
37886	E	E	WKAC	OC	Sir Dyfed/County of Dyfed
37887 s	F	E	WNXX	IM	
37888	GIF	E	WKGS	ES	
37889	F	E	WNYX	CD	
37890 a	F	E	WNSS	CD	
37891 a	F	E	WNXX	TY	

37892	F	E	WNXX	OC	Ripple Lane
37893	E	E	WKGR	IT	
37894 as	F	E	WNXX	TY	
37895 s	E	E	WKGR	IT	
37896 s	F	E	WNSS	CD	
37897 s	F	E	WNXX	BS	
37898 s	F	E	WNYX	MG	
37899 s	GIF	E	WNXX	ES	

Class 37/9. Refurbished locos. New power unit. Main generator replaced by alternator.
Ballast weights added. Details as Class 37/4 except:
Engine: Mirrlees MB275T of 1340 kW (1800 h.p.) at 1000 r.p.m. (§ Ruston RK270T of 1340 kW (1800 h.p.) at 900 r.p.m.).
Train supply: Not equipped.
Main Alternator: Brush BA1005A (§ GEC G564AZ).
Maximum Tractive Effort: 279 kN (62680 lbf).
Continuous Tractive Effort: 184 kN (41250 lbf) at 11.4 m.p.h.
Weight: 120 t.   **RA:** 7.

37902	F	DR	XHSS	KM
37903	F	HN	HNRS	CD
37904	F	HN	HNRS	CS
37905 §s	F	E	WNYX	IM
37906 §s	FO	E	WMOC	KR

CLASS 40   ENGLISH ELECTRIC   1Co-Co1

Built: 1958–1962 by the English Electric Co. at Vulcan Foundry, Newton le Willows.
Engine: English Electric 16SVT Mk2 of 1490 kW (2000 h.p.) at 850 r.p.m.
Main Generator: English Electric 822.
Traction Motors: English Electric 526/5D.
Maximum Tractive Effort: 231 kN (52000 lbf).
Continuous Tractive Effort: 137 kN (30900 lbf) at 18.8 m.p.h.
Power At Rail: 1160 kW (1550 h.p.).   **Train Brakes:** Air & vacuum.
Brake Force: 51 t.   **Dimensions:** 21.18 x 2.78 m.
Weight: 132 t.   **Wheel Diameter:** 914/1143 mm.
Design Speed: 90 m.p.h.   **Maximum Speed:** 90 m.p.h.
Fuel Capacity: 3250 litres.   **RA:** 6.
Train Supply: Steam.   **Multiple Working:** Not equipped.

Also carries original number D 345.

| 40145 | G | PO | MBDL | BQ |

CLASS 43   BREL/PAXMAN   Bo-Bo

Built: 1976–1982 by BREL at Crewe Works.
Engine: Paxman Valenta 12RP200L of 1680 kW (2250 h.p.) at 1500 r.p.m.
(* Paxman 12VP185 of 1680 kW (2250 h.p.) at 1500 r.p.m.).
Main Alternator: Brush BA1001B.
Traction Motors: Brush TMH68–46 or GEC G417AZ, frame mounted.
Maximum Tractive Effort: 80 kN (17980 lbf).
Continuous Tractive Effort: 46 kN (10340 lbf) at 64.5 m.p.h.
Power At Rail: 1320 kW (1770 h.p.).   **Train Brakes:** Air.
Brake Force: 35 t.   **Dimensions:** 17.79 x 2.71 m.
Weight: 70.25 t.   **Wheel Diameter:** 1020 mm.
Design Speed: 125 m.p.h.   **Maximum Speed:** 125 m.p.h.
Fuel Capacity: 4500 litres.   **RA:** 5.
Train Supply: Three-phase electric.
Multiple Working: Within class, jumpers at non-driving end only.

Notes: † = Buffer fitted.
43196 carries its name on one side only.

43002	FG	A	IWRP	PM	TECHNIQUEST
43003	FG	A	IWRP	PM	
43004	FP	A	IWRP	PM	Borough of Swindon
43005	FP	A	IWRP	PM	
43006	V	A	IECP	EC	
43007	V	A	IMLP	NL	
43008	V	A	IECP	EC	
43009	FP	A	IWRP	PM	
43010	FP	A	IWRP	PM	
43012	FP	A	IWRP	PM	
43013 †	Y	P		NL	
43014 †	Y	P		NL	
43015	FP	A	IWRP	PM	
43016	FG	A	IWRP	PM	Peninsula Medical School
43017	FG	A	IWRP	LA	
43018	FP	A	IWRP	LA	The Red Cross
43019	FG	A	IWRP	LA	City of Swansea/Dinas Abertawe
43020	FG	A	IWRP	LA	John Grooms
43021	FG	A	IWRP	LA	
43022	FG	A	IWRP	LA	
43023	FG	A	IWRP	LA	County of Cornwall
43024	FG	A	IWRP	LA	
43025	FG	A	IWRP	LA	Exeter
43026	FG	A	IWRP	LA	City of Westminster
43027	FG	A	IWRP	LA	Glorious Devon
43028	FP	A	IWRP	LA	
43029	FG	A	IWRP	LA	
43030	FP	A	IWRP	PM	Christian Lewis Trust
43031	FP	A	IWRP	PM	
43032	FG	A	IWRP	PM	The Royal Regiment of Wales
43033	FP	A	IWRP	PM	

43034	FP	A	IWRP	PM	The Black Horse
43035	FP	A	IWRP	PM	
43036	FP	A	IWRP	PM	
43037	FP	A	IWRP	PM	
43038	GN	A	IECP	EC	
43039	GN	A	IECP	EC	The Royal Dragoon Guards
43040	FG	A	IWRP	PM	
43041	FG	A	IWRP	LA	City of Discovery
43042	FP	A	IWRP	LA	
43043	MM	P	IMLP	NL	LEICESTERSHIRE COUNTY CRICKET CLUB
43044	MM	P	IMLP	NL	Borough of Kettering
43045	MM	P	IMLP	NL	
43046	MM	P	IMLP	NL	Royal Philharmonic
43047 *	MM	P	IMLP	NL	
43048 *	MM	P	IMLP	NL	
43049 *	MM	P	IMLP	NL	Neville Hill
43050	MM	P	IMLP	NL	
43051	MM	P	IMLP	NL	
43052 *	MM	P	IMLP	NL	
43053	MM	P	IMLP	NL	Leeds United
43054	MM	P	IMLP	NL	
43055 *	MM	P	IMLP	NL	Sheffield Star
43056	MM	P	IMLP	NL	
43057	MM	P	IMLP	NL	
43058	MM	P	IMLP	NL	MIDLAND PRIDE
43059 *	MM	P	IMLP	NL	
43060	MM	P	IMLP	NL	COUNTY OF LEICESTERSHIRE
43061	MM	P	IMLP	NL	
43062	Y	P		NL	
43063	V	P	ICCM	MA	Maiden Voyager
43064	MM	P	IMLP	NL	
43065 †	V	P	ICCP	LA	
43066	MM	P	IMLP	NL	Nottingham Playhouse
43067 †	V	P	ICCP	LA	
43068 †	V	P	ICCP	LA	The Red Arrows
43069	V	P	ICCM	MA	
43070	V	P	ICCM	MA	
43071	V	P	ICCM	MA	Forward Birmingham
43072 *	MM	P	IMLP	NL	Derby Etches Park
43073	MM	P	IMLP	NL	
43074 *	MM	P	IMLP	NL	BBC EAST MIDLANDS TODAY
43075 *	MM	P	IMLP	NL	
43076	MM	P	IMLP	NL	THE MASTER CUTLER 1947–1997
43077	MM	P	IMLP	NL	
43078	V	P	ICCM	MA	Golowan Festival Penzance
43079	V	P	ICCM	MA	
43080 †	V	P	ICCP	LA	
43081	MM	P	IMLP	NL	
43082	MM	P	IMLP	NL	DERBYSHIRE FIRST
43083	MM	P	IMLP	NL	

Number						Name
43084	†	V	P	ICCP	LA	County of Derbyshire
43085		MM	P	IMLP	NL	
43086		V	P	ICCM	MA	
43087		V	P	ICCM	MA	
43088		V	P	ICCM	MA	
43089		V	P	ICCM	MA	
43090		V	P	ICCP	LA	
43091		V	P	ICCP	LA	
43092		V	P	ICCP	LA	Institution of Mechanical Engineers 150th Anniversary 1847–1997
43093		V	P	ICCP	LA	Lady in Red
43094		V	P	ICCP	LA	
43095		GN	A	IECP	EC	
43096		GN	A	IECP	EC	Stirling Castle
43097		V	P	ICCP	LA	railwaychildren
43098		V	P	ICCP	LA	
43099		V	P	ICCP	LA	
43100		V	P	ICCP	LA	
43101		V	P	ICCP	LA	HST Silver Jubilee
43102		V	P	ICCP	LA	Helston Furry Dance
43103		V	P	ICCP	LA	
43104		V	A	IMLP	NL	City of Inverness
43105		GN	A	IECP	EC	
43106		GN	A	IECP	EC	
43107		GN	A	IECP	EC	Old Course St. Andrews
43108		GN	A	IECP	EC	
43109		GN	A	IECP	EC	
43110		GN	A	IECP	EC	Scone Palace
43111		GN	A	IECP	EC	Doncaster
43112		GN	A	IECP	EC	
43113		GN	A	IECP	EC	
43114		GN	A	IECP	EC	
43115		GN	A	IECP	EC	
43116		GN	A	IECP	EC	Bonnie Prince Charlie
43117		GN	A	IECP	EC	City of Kingston upon Hull
43118		GN	A	IECP	EC	
43119		GN	A	IECP	EC	
43120		GN	A	IECP	EC	
43121		V	P	ICCP	LA	South Yorkshire Metropolitan County
43122		V	P	ICCP	LA	
43123	†	V	P	ICCP	LA	
43124		FP	A	IWRP	LE	Merchant Venturer
43125		FP	A	IWRP	LE	City of Bristol
43126		FP	A	IWRP	LE	
43127		FG	A	IWRP	LE	
43128		FP	A	IWRP	LE	
43129		FP	A	IWRP	LE	Sulis Minerva
43130		FG	A	IWRP	LE	Sir Felix Pole
43131		FP	A	IWRP	LE	
43132		FP	A	IWRP	LE	
43133		FP	A	IWRP	LE	

43134	FP	A	IWRP	LE	County of Somerset
43135	FP	A	IWRP	LE	
43136	FP	A	IWRP	LE	
43137	FG	A	IWRP	LE	Newton Abbot 150
43138	FG	A	IWRP	LE	
43139	FP	A	IWRP	LE	
43140	FG	A	IWRP	LE	
43141	FG	A	IWRP	LE	
43142	FG	A	IWRP	LE	
43143	FP	A	IWRP	LE	
43144	FP	A	IWRP	LE	
43145	FP	A	IWRP	LE	
43146	FP	A	IWRP	LE	
43147	FP	A	IWRP	LE	
43148	FP	A	IWRP	LE	
43149	FP	A	IWRP	LE	B.B.C. Wales Today
43150	FP	A	IWRP	LE	Bristol Evening Post
43151	FP	A	IWRP	LE	
43152	FP	A	IWRP	LE	
43153	V	P	ICCP	LA	THE ENGLISH RIVIERA TORQUAY PAIGNTON BRIXHAM INTERCITY
43154	V	P	ICCP	LA	
43155	V	P	ICCM	MA	City of Aberdeen
43156	V	P	ICCM	MA	
43157	V	P	ICCP	LA	
43158	V	P	ICCP	LA	Dartmoor The Pony Express
43159	V	P	ICCM	MA	
43160	V	P	ICCP	LA	
43161	V	P	ICCM	MA	
43162	V	P	ICCM	MA	
43163	FP	A	IWRP	LA	
43164	FP	A	IWRP	LA	
43165 *	FG	A	IWRP	LA	
43166	V	A	IMLP	NL	
43167	GN	A	IECP	EC	
43168 *	FP	A	IWRP	LA	
43169 *	FP	A	IWRP	LA	The National Trust
43170 *	FP	A	IWRP	LA	Edward Paxman
43171	FP	A	IWRP	LA	
43172	FP	A	IWRP	LA	
43174	FP	A	IWRP	LA	Bristol–Bordeaux
43175 *	FP	A	IWRP	LA	
43176	FP	A	IWRP	LA	
43177 *	FP	A	IWRP	LA	University of Exeter
43178	V	A	IMLP	NL	
43179 *	FP	A	IWRP	LA	Pride of Laira
43180	V	P	ICCM	MA	City of Newcastle upon Tyne
43181	FP	A	IWRP	LA	Devonport Royal Dockyard 1693–1993
43182	FP	A	IWRP	LA	
43183	FP	A	IWRP	LA	

43184	V	A	IMLP	NL	
43185	FP	A	IWRP	LA	Great Western
43186	FP	A	IWRP	LA	Sir Francis Drake
43187	FP	A	IWRP	LA	
43188	FP	A	IWRP	LA	City of Plymouth
43189	FP	A	IWRP	LA	RAILWAY HERITAGE TRUST
43190	FP	A	IWRP	LA	
43191 *	FP	A	IWRP	LA	Seahawk
43192	FG	A	IWRP	LA	City of Truro
43193	V	P	ICCM	MA	Plymouth SPIRIT OF DISCOVERY
43194	V	P	ICCM	MA	
43195	V	P	ICCM	MA	British Red Cross 125th Birthday 1995
43196	V	P	ICCM	MA	The Newspaper Society Founded 1836
43197	V	P	ICCM	MA	The RAILWAY MAGAZINE
43198	V	P	ICCM	MA	HMS Penzance

CLASS 45   BR/SULZER   1Co-Co1

Built: 1963 by BR at Derby Locomotive Works.
Engine: Sulzer 12LDA28B of 1860 kW (2500 h.p.) at 750 r.p.m.
Main Generator: Crompton-Parkinson CG426 A1.
Traction Motors: Crompton-Parkinson C172 A1.
Maximum Tractive Effort: 245 kN (55000 lbf).
Continuous Tractive Effort: 134 kN (31600 lbf) at 22.3 m.p.h.
Power At Rail: 1490 kW (2000 h.p.).   **Train Brakes:** Air & vacuum.
Brake Force: 63 t.   **Dimensions:** 20.70 x 2.78 m.
Weight: 140 t.   **Wheel Diameter:** 914/1143 mm.
Design Speed: 90 m.p.h.   **Maximum Speed:** 90 m.p.h.
Fuel Capacity: 3591 litres.   **RA:** 7.
Train Supply: Electric, index 66.   **Multiple Working:** Not equipped.

Originally numbered D 61.

45112	B	FR	SDMS	DF	THE ROYAL ARMY ORDNANCE CORPS

CLASS 46   BR/SULZER   1Co-Co1

Built: 1963 by BR at Derby Locomotive Works.
Engine: Sulzer 12LDA28B of 1860 kW (2500 h.p.) at 750 r.p.m.
Main Generator: Brush TG160-60.   **Traction Motors:** Brush TM73-68 Mk3.
Maximum Tractive Effort: 245 kN (55000 lbf).
Continuous Tractive Effort: 141 kN (31600 lbf) at 22.3 m.p.h.
Power At Rail: 1460 kW (1960 h.p.).   **Train Brakes:** Air & vacuum.
Brake Force: 63 t.   **Dimensions:** 20.70 x 2.78 m.
Weight: 140 t.   **Wheel Diameter:** 914/1143 mm.
Design Speed: 90 m.p.h.   **Maximum Speed:** 75 m.p.h.
Fuel Capacity: 3591 litres.   **RA:** 7.
Train Supply: Not equipped.   **Multiple Working:** Not equipped.

46035	B	CN	MBDL	CQ	

CLASS 47   BR/BRUSH/SULZER   Co-Co

Built: 1963–1967 by Brush Traction, at Loughborough or by BR at Crewe Works.
Engine: Sulzer 12LDA28C of 1920 kW (2580 h.p.) at 750 r.p.m.
Main Generator: Brush TG160-60 Mk4 or TM172-50 Mk1.
Traction Motors: Brush TM64-68 Mk1 or Mk1A.
Maximum Tractive Effort: 267 kN (60000 lbf).
Continuous Tractive Effort: 133 kN (30000 lbf) at 26 m.p.h.
Power At Rail: 1550 kW (2080 h.p.).   **Train Brakes:** Air.
Brake Force: 61 t.   **Dimensions:** 19.38 x 2.79 m.
Weight: 111.5–120.6 t.   **Wheel Diameter:** 1143 mm.
Design Speed: 95 m.p.h.   **Maximum Speed:** 95 m.p.h. (* 75 m.p.h.).
Fuel Capacity: 3273 (+ 5550).
Train Supply: Not equipped.
Multiple Working: Green Circle (n – not equipped).

Originally numbered in series D 1100–11, 1500–1999 not in order.

Note: The DFFT loco has "Dock Mode" slow speed traction control system for
working trains from Felixstowe North Container Terminal.

Non-standard liveries/numbering:
47004 also carries number D1524.
47114 is as **GG**, but with Freightliner logos.
47145 is dark blue with Railfreight Distribution logos.
47515 is livery **IM** on one side and all-over white on the other side.
47519 also carries number D1102.
47803 is yellow and white with a red stripe.
47829 is in a special "Police" livery of white with a broad red band outlined in yellow.
47853 is in "XP64 blue" with red cabside panels.
47972 is in BR Central Services livery of red and grey.

Class 47/0 (Dual braked locos) or Class 47/2 (Air braked locos). Standard Design.
Details as above.

47004 xn	**GG**	E	WMOC	OC
47033	**FE**	CD	CROL	ZB
47052	**FF**	P	DHLT	BA
47053 +	**FE**	FR	SDXL	BH
47095 +	**FE**	EF	WNYX	SP
47114 +	**O**	FL	DHLT	CD
47145 +	**O**	FR	SDXL	CD
47146 +	**FE**	EF	WNYX	SP
47150 *+	**FL**	FL	DFLH	FD
47152 +	**FF**	FL	DHLT	SZ
47156	**F**	HN	HNRS	ZH
47157 +	**FF**	P	DHLT	BA
47186 +	**FE**	FR	SDXL	KT
47188 +	**FE**	CD	CROL	CD
47193 n	**FL**	P	DHLT	BA
47194	**F**	FR	SDXL	CS
47197 n*	**FF**	P	DFLH	FD

Johnson Stevens Agencies

47200	+	**CD**	CD	IANA	NC	The Fosse Way
47201	+	**FE**	FR	SDXL	KT	
47205	+	**FF**	FL	DHLT	SZ	
47206	n	**FF**	P	SBXL	LB	The Morris Dancer
47207	+	**FF**	P	DHLT	SZ	
47209	+	**FF**	P	SBXL	LB	
47211	+	**F**	FR	SDXL	EH	
47212	xn*	**FL**	P	DFLH	FD	
47213	+	**F**	CD	CROL	CD	
47217	+	**FE**	EF	WNYX	SP	
47219	+	**FE**	FR	SDXL	KT	
47223		**F**	HN	HNRS	ZH	
47224	xn*	**F**	P	DFLH	FD	
47226	+	**F**	FR	SDXL	KT	
47228	+	**FE**	FR	SDXL	KT	
47229	+	**F**	FR	SDXL	BH	
47234	+	**FF**	P	DHLT	BA	
47236	+	**FE**	FR	SDXL	CS	
47237	+	**FE**	DR	XHSS	ZH	
47241	+	**FE**	EF	WNYX	SP	
47245	+	**FE**	HN	HNRS	DR	
47258	+	**FL**	FL	DHLT	CD	
47270	*n	**FL**	P	DFLH	FD	Cory Brothers 1842–1992
47279	*+	**FL**	P	DFLH	FD	
47280	+	**F**	FR	SDXL	KT	
47283	n	**FF**	FL	DHLT	SZ	
47285	+	**FE**	FR	SDXL	DF	
47287	+	**F**	FL	DHLT	CP	
47289	*+	**FF**	P	DFLM	FD	
47290	+	**FF**	FL	DHLT	BA	
47292	*+	**FL**	P	DFLH	FD	
47293	+	**FE**	FR	SDXL	KT	
47295	an	**F**	FL	DHLT	IP	
47296	xn	**FF**	P	DHLT	SZ	
47298	+	**F**	DR	XHSS	ZH	

Class 47/3 (Dual braked locos) or Class 47/2 (Air braked locos).
Details as Class 47/0 except:
Weight: 113.7 t.

47301	+	**FF**	P	DHLT	BA	Freightliner Birmingham
47302	+	**FF**	FL	DHLT	BA	
47303	*+	**FF**	P	DFLM	FD	Freightliner Cleveland
47305	n	**FF**	P	DHLT	BA	
47306	+	**FE**	EF	WMOC	OC	The Sapper
47307	+	**FE**	FR	SDXL	KT	
47308	+	**FF**	FL	DHLT	BA	
47309	*+	**FF**	FL	DFFT	FD	European Rail Operator of The Year
47310	+	**FE**	EF	WNYX	SP	
47312	+	**FE**	EF	WNZX	SP	
47313	+	**F**	FR	SDXL	KT	
47314	+	**F**	FR	SDXL	KT	

47316 +	FE	CD	CROL	ZB	
47323 +	FF	P	DHLT	CD	
47326 +	FE	CD	CROL	CD	
47328 +	F	EF	WNYX	SP	
47330 +	FF	P	SBXL	LB	
47331 xns	CE	E	WNZX	SP	
47334 n	FF	P	DHLT	SZ	
47335 +	F	FR	SDXL	KT	
47337 +	FF	P	SBXL	LB	
47338 +	FE	CD	CROL	CD	
47339 n	FF	P	DHLT	BA	
47345 n	FF	P	DHLT	BA	
47348 +	FE	FR	SDXL	DF	St. Christopher's Railway Home
47349 xn	FF	P	SBXL	LB	
47353 n	FF	FL	DHLT	BA	
47354	FF	FL	DHLT	BA	
47355	FB	FR	SDFR	DF	AVOCET
47358 *+	FF	P	DFLM	FD	
47360 +	FE	FR	SDXL	KT	
47361 +	FF	P	DHLT	SZ	
47363	F	FR	SDXL	CS	
47365 +	FE	EF	WNYX	MG	
47368 xn	F	FR	SDXL	CS	
47370 *+	FF	P	DFLM	FD	Andrew A Hodgkinson
47371 n	FF	P	SBXL	LB	
47372 n	FF	P	SBXL	LB	
47375 +	FE	FR	SDXL	BH	
47377 n	FF	P	DHLT	BA	

Class 47/4. Electric Train Supply equipment.
Details as Class 47/0 except:
Weight: 120.4–125.1 t.   **Fuel Capacity:** 3273 (+ 5887) litres.
Train Supply: Electric. ETH 66.   **RA:** 7.
Multiple Working: Not equipped (m – Green Circle).

47462 x	RG	E	WNZX	TT	
47471 x	IM	E	WNZX	CW	
47474 x	RG	E	WNYX	SP	
47475 x	RX	E	WNZX	HM	
47476 x	RG	E	WNYX	TT	
47478 x	B	E	WNZX	SP	
47481 x	BL	P	SBXL	LB	
47484 x	GW	DR	XHSS	ZH	
47488 x	GG	FR	SDFR	DF	
47489 x	RG	FR	SDXL	CS	
47492 x	RX	E	WNZX	OC	
47501 x	RG	DR	XHSS	ZH	
47513 x	BL	E	WNYX	SP	
47515 x	O	E	WNZX	CW	
47519 x+	GG	E	WNYX	CD	
47524 x	RX	E	WNZX	CW	
47525 x	FE	FR	SDXL	CS	

47526	x	BL	FR	SDXL	CS	
47528	x	IM	E	WNZX	HM	
47535	x	RX	E	WNZX	OC	
47536	x	RX	E	WNYX	SP	
47540	xm	CE	E	WNZX	CW	The Institution of Civil Engineers
47547		N	E	WNZX	CD	
47550	x	IM	FR	SDXL	IR	
47565	x	RX	E	WNZX	SP	
47566	x	RX	E	WNYX	SP	
47574	x	RG	E	WNZX	CD	
47575	x	RG	E	WMOC	ML	City of Hereford
47576	x	RX	E	WNYX	SP	
47596	x	RX	E	WNZX	CD	
47624	x	RX	E	WNYX	SP	
47628	x	RX	FR	SDXL	BH	
47634	x	RG	E	WNXX	SY	Holbeck
47635	x	RG	E	WHDD	CD	
47640		RG	E	WNYX	CD	University of Strathclyde

Class 47/7. Fitted with an older form of TDM.
Details as Class 47/4 except:
Weight: 118.7 t.　　　　　　　　　　　**Fuel Capacity:** 5887 litres.

47701	x	FR	WF	SDFR	DF	Waverley
47702	x	V	E	WNYX	TO	County of Suffolk
47703	x	FR	FR	SDFR	DF	HERMES
47704	x	RX	FR	SDXL	BA	
47707	x	RX	FR	SDXL	BH	Holyrood
47709	x	FR	FR	SDFR	DF	DIONYSOS
47710	x	FR	FR	SDFR	DF	
47711	x	V	E	WNYX	TO	County of Hertfordshire
47712	x	FR	FR	SDFR	DF	ARTEMIS
47714	x	RX	CD	IANA	NC	
47715		N	FR	SDXL	DF	
47716	x	RX	FR	SDXL	CW	
47717	x	RG	FR	SDXL	DF	

Class 47/7. Former Railnet dedicated locos.
All have twin fuel tanks and are fitted with RCH jumper cables for operating with propelling control vehicles (PCVs).

47721		RX	E	WNXX	TO	Saint Bede
47722		V	E	WNXX	TO	
47725		RX	E	WHCD	CD	Bristol Barton Hill
47726		RX	E	WNXX	TO	Manchester Airport Progress
47727		E	E	WHCD	CD	Castell Caerffili/Caerphilly Castle
47732	x	RX	E	WHDD	CD	Restormel
47733		RX	E	WHTN	TO	Eastern Star
47734		RX	E	WHTN	TO	Crewe Diesel Depot
47736		RX	E	WHTN	TO	Cambridge Traction & Rolling Stock Depot
47737		RX	E	WHCD	CD	Resurgent
47738		RX	E	WNZX	SP	
47739		RX	E	WHCD	CD	Resourceful

47741	V	E	WHTN	TO	Resilient
47742	RX	E	WNXX	TO	The Enterprising Scot
47744	E	E	WHCD	CD	Royal Mail Cheltenham
47745 x	RX	E	WNYX	TO	Royal London Society for the Blind
47746	RX	E	WHCD	CD	The Bobby
47747	E	E	WHCD	CD	Florence Nightingale
47749	RX	E	WHCD	CD	Atlantic College
47750	V	E	WHCD	CD	
47756	RX	E	WHDD	CD	Royal Mail Tyneside
47757	RX	E	WHCD	CD	Restitution
47758	E	E	WHDD	CD	
47759	RX	E	WHCD	CD	
47760	E	E	WHCD	CD	Ribblehead Viaduct
47761	RX	E	WHCD	CD	
47762	RX	E	WNXX	CD	
47763	RX	E	WNXX	ML	
47764	RX	E	WNYX	SP	Resounding
47765 x	RX	E	WNXX	PY	
47766 x	RX	E	WNXX	TT	Resolute
47767	RX	E	WHCD	CD	Saint Columba
47768 x	RX	E	WNXX	CD	
47769	V	E	WNXX	TT	Resolve
47770	RX	E	WHDD	CD	Reserved
47771	RX	E	WNXX	TO	Heaton Traincare Depot
47772 x	RX	E	WHDD	CD	
47773	E	E	WHCD	CD	The Queen Mother
47774 x	RX	E	WNXX	CD	Poste Restante
47775 x	RX	E	WNXX	CD	Respite
47776 x	RX	E	WHDD	CD	Respected
47777 x	RX	E	WNXX	TO	
47778	E	E	WHTN	TO	Duke of Edinburgh's Award
47779	RX	E	WNXX	CD	
47780	RX	E	WHCD	CD	
47781	RX	E	WHCD	CD	Isle of Iona
47782	RX	E	WHCD	CD	
47783	RX	E	WNXX	CD	
47784	RX	E	WHCD	CD	Saint Peter
47785	E	E	WHCD	CD	Condover Hall
47786	E	E	WHCD	CD	Fiona Castle
47787	E	E	WHCD	CD	Roy Castle OBE
47789	RX	E	WHCD	CD	Windsor Castle
47790	E	E	WHCD	CD	Lindisfarne
47791	RX	E	WHTN	TO	
47792	RX	E	WHTN	TO	Saint Cuthbert
47793	RX	E	WHCD	CD	Saint Augustine

Class 47/4 continued. RA6.

47798	RP	E	WHRD	CD	Prince William
47799	RP	E	WHRD	CD	Prince Henry
47802 +	DR	DR	XHSS	ZH	
47803	O	FR	SDXL	PR	

47805 +	V	P	ATLO	WN	Pride of Toton
47810 +	V	P	ATLO	WN	PORTERBROOK
47811 +	GL	P	IWLA	LE	
47812 +	V	P	ATLO	WN	Pride of Eastleigh
47813 +	GL	P	IWLA	LE	S.S. Great Britain
47815 +	GL	P	IWLA	LE	Abertawe Landore
47816 +	GL	P	SBXL	CD	
47818 +	V	P	ATLO	WN	Strathclyde
47826 +	I	P	ATLO	WN	Springburn
47828 +	V	P	ATLO	WN	Severn Valley Railway
					Kidderminster Bewdley Bridgnorth
47829 +	O	P	ATLO	WN	
47830 +	GL	P	SBXL	CD	
47832 +	GL	P	IWLA	LE	Tamar
47839 +	RV	RV	RTLO	CP	
47840 +	B	P	ATLO	WN	NORTH STAR
47841 +	V	P	ATLO	WN	Spirit of Chester
47843 +	V	P	ATLO	WN	VULCAN
47844	V	P	SBXL	ZC	
47847 +	BL	P	ATLO	WN	Railway World Magazine/Brian Morrison
47848 +	V	P	ATLO	WN	Newton Abbot Festival of Transport
47851 +	GG	P	ATLO	WN	Traction Magazine
47853 +	O	RV	RTLO	CP	RAIL EXPRESS
47854 +	V	P	ATLO	WN	Women's Royal Voluntary Service
47972 +	O	FR	SDXL	BA	

CLASS 50   ENGLISH ELECTRIC   Co-Co

Built: 1967–1968 by English Electric at Vulcan Foundry, Newton-le-Willows.
Engine: English Electric 16CVST of 2010 kW (2700 h.p.) at 850 r.p.m.
Main Generator: English Electric 840/4B.
Traction Motors: English Electric 538/5A.
Maximum Tractive Effort: 216 kN (48500 lbf).
Continuous Tractive Effort: 147 kN (33000 lbf) at 23.5 m.p.h.
Power At Rail: 1540 kW (2070 h.p.).   **Train Brakes:** Air & vacuum.
Brake Force: 59 t.   **Dimensions:** 20.88 x 2.78 m.
Weight: 116.9 t.   **Wheel Diameter:** 1092 mm.
Design Speed: 105 m.p.h.   **Maximum Speed:** 90 (* 100) m.p.h.
Fuel Capacity: 4796 litres.   **RA:** 6.
Train Supply: Electric, index 66.   **Multiple Working:** Orange Square.

Originally numbered D 416–49, 400.

Non-standard livery/numbering:

50017 is "LMS Coronation Scot" style maroon with four gold bands.
50044 carries number D444.

50017 *	O	JK	MBDL	TM	
50031	B	50	MBDL	OC	Hood
50044	GG	50	MBDL	OC	
50049	B	PD	MBDL	OC	Defiance
50050	BL	HS	DNLL	TS	Fearless

CLASS 52   WESTERN   C-C

Built: 1961–1964.
Engine: Two Maybach MD655 of 1007 kW (1350 h.p) at 1500 r.p.m.
Transmission: Hydraulic. Voith L630rV.
Maximum Tractive Effort: 297 kN (66700 lbf).
Continuous Tractive Effort: 201 kN (45200 lbf) at 14.5 m.p.h.
Power At Rail: 1490 kW (2000 h.p.).   **Train Brakes:** Air & vacuum.
Brake Force: 65 t.   **Dimensions:** 20.7 x 2.78 m.
Weight: 111 t.   **Wheel Diameter:** 1092 mm.
Design Speed: 90 m.p.h.   **Maximum Speed:** 90 m.p.h.
Fuel Capacity: 3900 litres.   **RA:** 7.
Train Supply: Steam.   **Multiple Working:** Not equipped.

Non-standard livery: Golden ochre.

Never allocated a TOPS number.

D1015	0	DT	MBDL	OC	WESTERN CHAMPION

CLASS 55   ENGLISH ELECTRIC   Co-Co

Built: 1961 by English Electric at Vulcan Foundry, Newton-le-Willows.
Engine: Two Napier-Deltic D18-25 of 1230 kW (1650 h.p.) each at 1500 r.p.m.
Main Generators: Two English Electric 829.
Traction Motors: English Electric 538/A.
Maximum Tractive Effort: 222 kN (50000 lbf).
Continuous Tractive Effort: 136 kN (30500 lbf) at 32.5 m.p.h.
Power At Rail: 1969 kW (2640 h.p.).   **Train Brakes:** Air & vacuum.
Brake Force: 51 t.   **Dimensions:** 21.18 x 2.68 m.
Weight: 104.7 t.   **Wheel Diameter:** 1092 mm.
Design Speed: 105 m.p.h.   **Maximum Speed:** 100 m.p.h.
Fuel Capacity: 3755 litres.   **RA:** 5.
Train Supply: Electric, index 66.   **Multiple Working:** Not equipped.

Originally numbered D 9009–19, 9000.

Non-standard numbering:

55009 carries number D9009.
55016 carries number 9016.
55022 carries number D9000.

55009	GG	DP	MBDL	BH	ALYCIDON
55016	P	90	DNLL	CP	GORDON HIGHLANDER
55019	B	DP	MBDL	BH	ROYAL HIGHLAND FUSILIER
55022	GG	90	MBDL	TM	ROYAL SCOTS GREY

CLASS 56   BRUSH/BR/PAXMAN   Co-Co

Built: 1976–1984 by Electroputere at Craiova, Romania (as sub contractors for Brush) or BREL at Doncaster or Crewe Works.
Engine: Ruston Paxman 16RK3CT of 2460 kW (3250 h.p.) at 900 r.p.m.

Main Alternator: Brush BA1101A.
Traction Motors: Brush TM73-62.
Maximum Tractive Effort: 275 kN (61800 lbf).
Continuous Tractive Effort: 240 kN (53950 lbf) at 16.8 m.p.h.
Power At Rail: 1790 kW (2400 h.p.).   **Train Brakes:** Air.
Brake Force: 60 t.   **Dimensions:** 19.36 x 2.79 m.
Weight: 125.2 t.   **Wheel Diameter:** 1143 mm.
Design Speed: 80 m.p.h.   **Maximum Speed:** 80 m.p.h.
Fuel Capacity: 5228 litres.   **RA:** 7.
Train Supply: Not equipped.   **Multiple Working:** Red Diamond.

Notes: All equipped with Slow Speed Control.
56110 carries its name on one side only.

Non-standard liveries:

56019 is as **F0** but with a red solebar stripe.
56063 is as **F**, but with the light grey replaced by a darker grey.
56027 and 56109 are **LH** but with the Loadhaul branding on one side only.

56003	LH	E	WNXX	TO
56004	B	E	WNYX	SP
56006	B	E	WGAI	IM
56007	F	E	WGAI	IM
56010	F	E	WNYX	DR
56011	E	E	WNXX	IM
56018	E	E	WGAI	IM
56019	0	E	WNYX	IM
56021	LH	E	WNXX	IM
56022	F	E	WNXX	IM
56025	F	E	WNXX	IM
56027	LH	E	WGAT	TE
56029	F	E	WNYX	SP
56031	CE	E	WNXX	IM
56032	E	E	WGAI	IM
56033	F	E	WGAI	IM	Shotton Paper Mill
56034	LH	E	WNYX	SP	Castell Ogwr/Ogmore Castle
56036	CE	E	WNYX	SP
56037	E	E	WGAT	TE
56038	E	E	WGAT	TE
56039	LH	E	WNYX	TE
56040	F	E	WNXX	IM
56041	E	E	WGAT	TE
56043	F	E	WNXX	IM
56044	F	E	WNYX	IM
56045	LH	E	WNYX	IM	British Steel Shelton
56046	CE	E	WNTR	IM
56047	CE	E	WNYX	IM
56048	CE	E	WNXX	IM
56049	CE	E	WGAT	TE
56050	LH	E	WNYX	TO	British Steel Teesside
56051	E	E	WGAT	TE
56052	F	E	WNXX	IM

56053	F	E	WNXX	DR	
56054	F	E	WGAI	IM	British Steel Llanwern
56055	LH	E	WGAI	IM	
56056	F	E	WGAT	TE	
56057	E	E	WNYX	IM	British Fuels
56058	E	E	WGAT	TE	
56059	E	E	WGAT	TE	
56060	E	E	WGAT	TE	
56061	F	E	WNYX	TT	
56062	E	E	WGAI	IM	
56063	O	E	WNXX	IM	
56064	F	E	WNXX	IM	
56065	E	E	WGAT	TE	
56066	F	E	WNYX	SP	
56067	E	E	WGAT	TE	
56068	E	E	WGAT	TE	
56069	E	E	WGAI	IM	Wolverhampton Steel Terminal
56070	F	E	WGAI	IM	
56071	E	E	WGAT	TE	
56072	F	E	WGAI	IM	
56073	F	E	WNXX	IM	Tremorfa Steelworks
56074	LH	E	WGAI	IM	
56075	F	E	WNYX	TT	
56076	F	E	WNXX	IM	
56077	LH	E	WNSS	CD	
56078	F	E	WGAI	IM	
56079	F	E	WNXX	IM	
56081	E	E	WGAI	IM	
56082	F	E	WNXX	IM	
56083	LH	E	WGAT	TE	
56084	LH	E	WNXX	IM	
56085	LH	E	WNXX	TE	
56086	F	E	WNXX	IM	The Magistrates' Association
56087	E	E	WGAI	IM	ABP Port of Hull
56088	E	E	WGAI	IM	
56089	E	E	WNXX	IM	
56090	LH	E	WGAI	IM	
56091	E	E	WGAI	IM	Stanton
56093	F	E	WNXX	DR	
56094	E	E	WGAT	TE	Eggborough Power Station
56095	E	E	WGAT	TE	
56096	E	E	WGAI	IM	
56098	F	E	WGAT	TE	
56099	F	E	WGAI	IM	
56100	LH	E	WGAT	TE	
56101	F	E	WNXX	IM	Mutual Improvement
56102	LH	E	WGAI	IM	
56103	E	E	WGAI	IM	STORA
56104	F	E	WGAI	IM	
56105	E	E	WGAT	TE	
56106	LH	E	WGAT	TE	

56107	LH	E	WGAI	IM	
56108	F	E	WNXX	TE	
56109	LH	E	WGAT	TE	
56110	LH	E	WNSS	IM	Croft
56111	LH	E	WGAI	IM	
56112	LH	E	WGAI	IM	Stainless Pioneer
56113	E	E	WGAI	IM	
56114	E	E	WGAT	TE	
56115	E	E	WGAI	IM	Barry Needham
56116	LH	E	WGAI	IM	
56117	E	E	WGAT	TE	
56118	LH	E	WGAI	IM	
56119	E	E	WGAT	TE	
56120	E	E	WGAI	IM	
56121	F	E	WNYX	CU	
56123	F	E	WNYX	IM	Drax Power Station
56124	F	E	WNYX	KY	
56125	F	E	WNXX	IM	
56127	F	E	WNXX	TE	
56128	F	E	WNXX	IM	
56129	F	E	WGAI	IM	
56130	LH	E	WNXX	TT	
56131	F	E	WNXX	IM	Ellington Colliery
56132	F	E	WNYX	SP	
56133	F	E	WGAT	TE	
56134	F	E	WNXX	IM	Blyth Power
56135	F	E	WNYX	IM	

CLASS 57   BRUSH/GM   Co-Co

Built: 1964–1965 by Brush Traction at Loughborough or BR at Crewe Works as Class 47. Rebuilt 1997–2003 by Brush Traction at Loughborough. 57301–57312 are undergoing conversion for Virgin Trains use.
Engine: General Motors 645-12E3 of 1860 kW (2500 h.p.) at 900 r.p.m.
Main Alternator: Brush BA1101A.
Traction Motors: Brush TM68-46.
Maximum Tractive Effort: 244.5 kN (55000 lbf).
Continuous Tractive Effort: 140 kN (31500 lbf) at ?? m.p.h.
Power at Rail: 1507 kW (2025 h.p.).
Brake Force: 80 t.
Weight: 120.6 t.
Design Speed: 75 m.p.h.
Fuel Capacity: 5550 litres.
Train Supply: Not equipped.
Train Brakes: Air.
Dimensions: 19.38 x 2.79 m.
Wheel Diameter: 1143 mm.
Maximum Speed: 75 m.p.h.
RA: 6
Multiple Working: Not equipped.

Class 57/0. No Train Supply Equipment.

57001	(47356)	FL	P	DFTZ	FD	Freightliner Pioneer
57002	(47322)	FL	P	DFTZ	FD	Freightliner Phoenix
57003	(47317)	FL	P	DFTZ	FD	Freightliner Evolution
57004	(47347)	FL	P	DFTZ	FD	Freightliner Quality
57005	(47350)	FL	P	DFTZ	FD	Freightliner Excellence

57006	(47187)	**FL**	P	DFTZ	FD	Freightliner Reliance
57007	(47332)	**FL**	P	DFTZ	FD	Freightliner Bond
57008	(47060)	**FL**	P	DFTZ	FD	Freightliner Explorer
57009	(47079)	**FL**	P	DFTZ	FD	Freightliner Venturer
57010	(47231)	**FL**	P	DFTZ	FD	Freightliner Crusader
57011	(47329)	**FL**	P	DFTZ	FD	Freightliner Challenger
57012	(47204)	**FL**	P	DFTZ	FD	Freightliner Envoy

Class 57/3. Electric Train Supply Equipment. Details as Class 57/0 except.

Engine: General Motors 645-F3B-12 Cylinder of 2050 kW (2750 h.p.).
Fuel Capacity: 5887 litres.   **Train Supply:** Electric, index 100.
Design Speed: 95 m.p.h.   **Maximum Speed:** 95 m.p.h.
Brake Force: 60 t.   **Weight:** 117 t.

57301	(47845)	**VT**	P	ATLO	WN	SCOTT TRACY
57302	(47827)	**VT**	P	ATLO	WN	VIRGIL TRACY
57303	(47705)	**VT**	P	ATLO	WN	ALAN TRACY
57304	(47807)	**VT**	P	ATLO	WN	GORDON TRACY
57305	(47822)	**VT**	P	ATLO	WN	JOHN TRACY
57306	(47814)	**VT**	P			
57307	(47225)	**VT**	P			
57308	(47846)	**VT**	P			
57309	(47806)	**VT**	P			
57310	(47831)	**VT**	P			
57311	(47817)	**VT**	P			
57312	(47)	**VT**	P			

Class 57/6. Electric Train Supply Equipment. Prototype loco. Details as Class 57/0 except:

Fuel Capacity: 5887 litres.   **Train Supply:** Electric, index 95.
Design Speed: 95 m.p.h.   **Maximum Speed:** 95 m.p.h.

| 57601 | (47825) | **P** | P | IWLA | LE | |

Class 57/6. Electric Train Supply Equipment. On order. Details as Class 57/3.

57602	(47)		P			
57603	(47)		P			
57604	(47)		P			

CLASS 58   BREL/PAXMAN   Co-Co

Built: 1983–1987 by BREL at Doncaster Works.
Engine: Ruston Paxman 12RK3ACT of 2460 kW (3300 h.p.) at 1000 r.p.m.
Main Alternator: Brush BA1101B.   **Traction Motors:** Brush TM73-62.
Maximum Tractive Effort: 275 kN (61800 lbf).
Continuous Tractive Effort: 240 kN (53950 lbf) at 17.4 m.p.h.
Power At Rail: 1780 kW (2387 h.p.).   **Train Brakes:** Air.
Brake Force: 62 t.   **Dimensions:** 19.13 x 2.72 m.
Weight: 130 t.   **Wheel Diameter:** 1120 mm.
Design Speed: 80 m.p.h.   **Maximum Speed:** 80 m.p.h.
Fuel Capacity: 4214 litres.   **RA:** 7.
Train Supply: Not equipped.   **Multiple Working:** Red Diamond.

Notes: All equipped with Slow Speed Control.
Locos in the WFGA pool are due to move to the Netherlands for hire to ACTS in 2003.

58001	F	E	WNXX	EH	
58002	ML	E	WNXX	EH	Daw Mill Colliery
58003	F	E	WNXX	TO	Markham Colliery
58004	F	E	WNXX	DD	
58005	ML	E	WNXX	LR	
58006	F	E	WNXX	HM	
58007	F	E	WNXX	HM	
58008	ML	E	WNXX	TT	
58009	F	E	WNXX	EH	
58010	F	E	WNXX	HM	
58011	F	E	WNXX	HM	
58012	F	E	WNXX	DD	
58013	ML	E	WNXX	EH	
58014	ML	E	WNXX	TO	
58015	F	E	WNXX	DR	
58016	E	E	WNXX	EH	
58017	F	E	WNXX	DR	
58018	F	E	WNXX	HM	High Marnham Power Station
58019	F	E	WNXX	TO	Shirebrook Colliery
58020	F	E	WNXX	OC	Doncaster Works
58021	ML	E	WNXX	EH	Hither Green Depot
58022	F	E	WNXX	CD	
58023	ML	E	WNXX	TO	
58024	E	E	WNXX	OC	
58025	F	E	WNXX	EH	
58026	F	E	WNXX	EH	
58027	F	E	WNXX	DD	
58028	F	E	WNXX	TO	
58029	F	E	WNXX	EH	
58030	E	E	WNXX	EH	
58031	F	E	WNXX	EH	
58032	ML	E	WNXX	HM	Thoresby Colliery
58033	E	E	WNXX	OC	
58034	F	E	WNXX	DR	
58035	F	E	WNXX	DD	
58036	ML	E	WFGA	TO	
58037	E	E	WNXX	EH	
58038	ML	E	WFGA	TO	
58039	E	E	WFGA	DR	
58040	F	E	WNXX	HM	Cottam Power Station
58041	F	E	WNXX	EH	Ratcliffe Power Station
58042	ML	E	WNXX	EH	
58043	F	E	WNXX	EH	
58044	F	E	WFGA	TO	
58045	F	E	WNXX	OC	
58046	ML	E	WFGA	TO	
58047	E	E	WNXX	OC	
58048	E	E	WNXX	TO	

| 58049 | E | E | WNXX | EH | Littleton Colliery |
| 58050 | E | E | WNXX | EH | Toton Traction Depot |

CLASS 59   GENERAL MOTORS   Co-Co

Built: 1985 (59001/002/004) or 1989 (59005) by General Motors, La Grange, Illinois, USA or 1990 (59101–4), 1994 (59201) and 1995 (59202–6) by General Motors, London, Ontario, Canada.
Engine: General Motors 645E3C two stroke of 2460 kW (3300 h.p.) at 900 r.p.m.
Main Alternator: General Motors AR11 MLD-D14A.
Traction Motors: General Motors D77B.
Maximum Tractive Effort: 506 kN (113 550 lbf).
Continuous Tractive Effort: 291 kN (65 300 lbf) at 14.3 m.p.h.
Power At Rail: 1889 kW (2533 h.p.).   **Train Brakes:** Air.
Brake Force: 69 t.   **Dimensions:** 21.35 x 2.65 m.
Weight: 121 t.   **Wheel Diameter:** 1067 mm.
Design Speed: 60 (* 75) m.p.h.   **Maximum Speed:** 60 (* 75) m.p.h.
Fuel Capacity: 4546 litres.
Train Supply: Not equipped.   **Multiple Working:** AAR System.

Class 59/0. Owned by Foster-Yeoman.

59001	**FY**	FY	XYPO	MD	YEOMAN ENDEAVOUR
59002	**MR**	FY	XYPO	MD	ALAN J DAY
59004	**YO**	FY	XYPO	MD	PAUL A HAMMOND
59005	**FY**	FY	XYPO	MD	KENNETH J PAINTER

Class 59/1. Owned by Hanson Quarry Products.

59101	**HA**	HA	XYPA	MD	Village of Whatley
59102	**HA**	HA	XYPA	MD	Village of Chantry
59103	**HA**	HA	XYPA	MD	Village of Mells
59104	**HA**	HA	XYPA	MD	Village of Great Elm

Class 59/2. Owned by EWS.

59201	*	**E**	E	WDAG	HG	Vale of York
59202	*	**E**	E	WDAG	HG	Vale of White Horse
59203	*	**E**	E	WDAG	HG	Vale of Pickering
59204	*	**E**	E	WDAG	HG	Vale of Glamorgan
59205	b*	**E**	E	WDAG	HG	L. Keith McNair
59206	b*	**E**	E	WDAG	HG	Pride of Ferrybridge

CLASS 60   BRUSH/MIRRLEES   Co-Co

Built: 1989–1993 by Brush Traction at Loughborough.
Engine: Mirrlees 8MB275T of 2310 kW (3100 h.p.) at 1000 r.p.m.
Main Alternator: Brush BA1000.   **Traction Motors:** Brush TM216.
Maximum Tractive Effort: 500 kN (106500 lbf).
Continuous Tractive Effort: 336 kN (71570 lbf) at 17.4 m.p.h.
Power At Rail: 1800 kW (2415 h.p.)   **Train Brakes:** Air.
Brake Force: 74 (+ 62) t.   **Dimensions:** 21.34 x 2.64 m.
Weight: 129 (+ 131) t.   **Wheel Diameter:** 1118 mm.
Design Speed: 62 m.p.h.   **Maximum Speed:** 60 m.p.h.

Fuel Capacity: 4546 (+ 5225) litres.   **RA:** 7.
Train Supply: Not equipped.   **Multiple Working:** Within class.

Notes: All equipped with Slow Speed Control.
60021, 60034, 60046, 60064, 60065, 60072, 60073, 60077, 60082, 60084, and
60088 carry their names on one side only.

Non-standard livery:

60006/033 are in "Corus" livery of silver with red logos.

60001	**E**	E	WCAT	TE	The Railway Observer
60002 +	**E**	E	WCAT	TE	High Peak
60003 +	**E**	E	WCAK	CF	FREIGHT TRANSPORT ASSOCIATION
60004 +	**E**	E	WCAK	CF	
60005 +	**E**	E	WCAK	CF	BP Gas Avonmouth
60006	**0**	E	WCAT	TE	Scunthorpe Ironmaster
60007 +	**LH**	E	WCAI	IM	
60008	**LH**	E	WCAT	TE	GYPSUM QUEEN II
60009 +	**E**	E	WCAI	IM	
60010 +	**E**	E	WCAK	CF	
60011	**ML**	E	WCAT	TE	
60012 +	**E**	E	WCAI	IM	
60013	**F**	E	WCAT	TE	Robert Boyle
60014	**F**	E	WCAT	TE	Alexander Fleming
60015 +	**F**	E	WCAK	CF	Bow Fell
60016	**E**	E	WCAN	TO	RAIL Magazine
60017 +	**E**	E	WCAT	TE	Shotton Works Centenary Year 1996
60018	**E**	E	WCAT	TE	
60019	**E**	E	WCAN	TO	
60020 +	**E**	E	WCAI	IM	
60021 +	**F**	E	WCAI	IM	Pen-y-Ghent
60022 +	**E**	E	WCAI	IM	
60023 +	**E**	E	WCAI	IM	
60024 +	**E**	E	WCAN	TO	
60025 +	**E**	E	WCAI	IM	Caledonian Paper
60026 +	**E**	E	WCAK	CF	
60027 +	**E**	E	WCAI	IM	
60028 +	**F**	E	WCAI	IM	John Flamsteed
60029	**E**	E	WCAN	TO	Clitheroe Castle
60030 +	**E**	E	WCAK	CF	
60031	**E**	E	WCAN	TO	ABP Connect
60032	**F**	E	WCAN	TO	William Booth
60033 +	**0**	E	WCAT	TE	Tees Steel Express
60034	**F**	E	WCAN	TO	Carnedd Llewelyn
60035	**E**	E	WCAT	TE	
60036	**E**	E	WCAN	TO	GEFCO
60037 +	**E**	E	WCAK	CF	Aberthaw/Aberddawan
60038 +	**E**	E	WCAI	IM	AvestaPolarit
60039	**E**	E	WCAT	TE	
60040	**E**	E	WCAT	TE	
60041 +	**E**	E	WCAK	CF	
60042 +	**E**	E	WCAT	TE	The Hundred of Hoo

60043	E	E	WCAT	TE	
60044	ML	E	WCAT	TE	
60045	E	E	WCAT	TE	The Permanent Way Institution
60046 +	F	E	WCAN	TO	William Wilberforce
60047 +	E	E	WCAN	TO	
60048	E	E	WCAT	TE	EASTERN
60049 +	E	E	WCAT	TE	
60050 +	E	E	WCAT	TE	
60051 +	E	E	WCAK	CF	
60052 +	E	E	WCAK	CF	Glofa Twr – The last deep mine in Wales – Tower Colliery
60053 +	E	E	WCAT	TE	NORDIC TERMINAL
60054 +	F	E	WCAN	TO	Charles Babbage
60055 +	F	E	WCAI	IM	Thomas Barnardo
60056 +	F	E	WCAK	CF	William Beveridge
60057	F	E	WCAN	TO	Adam Smith
60058 +	F	E	WCAI	IM	John Howard
60059 +	LH	E	WCAK	CF	Swinden Dalesman
60060	F	E	WCAT	TE	James Watt
60061	F	E	WCAT	TE	Alexander Graham Bell
60062	F	E	WCAT	TE	Samuel Johnson
60063	F	E	WCAT	TE	James Murray
60064 +	F	E	WCAK	CF	Back Tor
60065	F	E	WCAT	TE	Kinder Low
60066	F	E	WCAN	TO	John Logie Baird
60067 +	F	E	WCAN	TO	James Clerk-Maxwell
60068	F	E	WCAN	TO	Charles Darwin
60069	F	E	WCAN	TO	Humphry Davy
60070 +	F	E	WCAK	CF	John Loudon McAdam
60071 +	E	E	WCAN	TO	
60072	F	E	WCAN	TO	Cairn Toul
60073	F	E	WCAT	TE	Cairn Gorm
60074	F	E	WCAT	TE	
60075	E	E	WCAN	TO	
60076	F	E	WCAN	TO	
60077 +	F	E	WCAK	CF	Canisp
60078	ML	E	WCAT	TE	
60079	F	E	WCAT	TE	Foinaven
60080 +	E	E	WCAI	IM	Little Eaton Primary School Little Eaton Railsafe Trophy Winners 2002
60081 +	GW	E	WCAK	CF	ISAMBARD KINGDOM BRUNEL
60082	F	E	WCAT	TE	Mam Tor
60083	E	E	WCAT	TE	Mountsorrel
60084	F	E	WCAN	TO	Cross Fell
60085	E	E	WCAT	TE	MINI Pride of Oxford
60086	F	E	WCAT	TE	Schiehallion
60087	F	E	WCAN	TO	Slioch
60088	F	E	WCAT	TE	Buachaille Etive Mor
60089 +	E	E	WCAK	CF	THE RAILWAY HORSE
60090 +	F	E	WCAI	IM	Quinag
60091 +	F	E	WCAK	CF	An Teallach

60092	F	E	WCAT	TE	Reginald Munns
60093	F	E	WCAT	TE	Jack Stirk
60094	F	E	WCAN	TO	Tryfan
60095	F	E	WCAN	TO	
60096 +	E	E	WCAK	CF	
60097 +	E	E	WCAI	IM	ABP Port of Grimsby & Immingham
60098 +	E	E	WCAK	CF	Charles Francis Brush
60099	F	E	WCAT	TE	Ben More Assynt
60100	F	E	WCAN	TO	Boar of Badenoch

CLASS 66   GENERAL MOTORS   Co-Co

Built: 1998–2001 by General Motors, London, Ontario, Canada (Model JT42CWR).
Engine: General Motors 12N-710G3B-EC two stroke of 2385 kW (3200 h.p.) at 900 r.p.m.
Main Alternator: General Motors AR8/C86.
Traction Motors: General Motors D43TR.
Maximum Tractive Effort: 409 kN (92000 lbf).
Continuous Tractive Effort: 260 kN (58390 lbf) at 15.9 m.p.h.
Power At Rail: 1850 kW (2480 h.p.).   **Train Brakes:** Air.
Brake Force: 68 t.   **Dimensions:** 21.35 x 2.64 m.
Weight: 126 t.   **Wheel Diameter:** 1120 mm.
Design Speed: 87.5 m.p.h.   **Maximum Speed:** 75 m.p.h.
Fuel Capacity: 6550 litres.   **RA:** 7.
Train Supply: Not equipped.   **Multiple Working:** AAR System.

Notes: All equipped with Slow Speed Control.
Locos in pool WBBM are fitted with RETB.
66002 carries its name on one side only.

Class 66/0. EWS operated locomotives.

66001		E	A	WBAT	TE	66021	k	E	A	WBAK	CF
66002		E	A	WBAN	TO	66022	k	E	A	WBAN	TO
66003	k	E	A	WBAT	TE	66023	k	E	A	WBAI	IM
66004	k	E	A	WBAN	TO	66024	k	E	A	WBAN	TO
66005	k	E	A	WBAI	IM	66025	k	E	A	WBAN	TO
66006	k	E	A	WBAT	TE	66026	k	E	A	WBAI	IM
66007	k	E	A	WBAI	IM	66027	k	E	A	WBAI	IM
66008	k	E	A	WBAK	CF	66028	k	E	A	WBAM	ML
66009	k	E	A	WBAH	EH	66029	k	E	A	WBAK	CF
66010	k	E	A	WBAI	IM	66030	k	E	A	WBAT	TE
66011	k	E	A	WBAI	IM	66031	k	E	A	WBAK	CF
66012	k	E	A	WBAI	IM	66032	k	E	A	WBAK	CF
66013	k	E	A	WBAH	EH	66033	k	E	A	WBAH	EH
66014	k	E	A	WBAI	IM	66034		E	A	WBAH	EH
66015	k	E	A	WBAH	EH	66035		E	A	WBAM	ML
66016	k	E	A	WBAH	EH	66036	k	E	A	WBAI	IM
66017	k	E	A	WBAN	TO	66037	k	E	A	WBAN	TO
66018	k	E	A	WBAI	IM	66038	k	E	A	WBAN	TO
66019	k	E	A	WBAK	CF	66039	k	E	A	WBAI	IM
66020	k	E	A	WBAT	TE	66040	k	E	A	WBAN	TO

66041	k	E	A	WBAT	TE	66092		E	A	WBAK	CF

66041	k	E	A	WBAT	TE	66092		E	A	WBAK	CF
66042	k	E	A	WBAN	TO	66093	k	E	A	WBAT	TE
66043	k	E	A	WBAK	CF	66094	k	E	A	WBAI	IM
66044	k	E	A	WBAT	TE	66095	k	E	A	WBBM	ML
66045	k	E	A	WBAI	IM	66096		E	A	WBBM	ML
66046	k	E	A	WBAI	IM	66097		E	A	WBBM	ML
66047	k	E	A	WBAT	TE	66098	k	E	A	WBBM	ML
66048	k	E	A	WBAI	IM	66099		E	A	WBBM	ML
66049	k	E	A	WBAM	ML	66100		E	A	WBBM	ML
66050	k	E	A	WBAI	IM	66101		E	A	WBBM	ML
66051	k	E	A	WBAT	TE	66102		E	A	WBBM	ML
66052	k	E	A	WBAI	IM	66103		E	A	WBBM	ML
66053		E	A	WBAI	IM	66104		E	A	WBBM	ML
66054	k	E	A	WBAK	CF	66105		E	A	WBBM	ML
66055	k	E	A	WBAK	CF	66106		E	A	WBBM	ML
66056	k	E	A	WBAK	CF	66107		E	A	WBBM	ML
66057	k	E	A	WBAK	CF	66108	k	E	A	WBBM	ML
66058	k	E	A	WBAK	CF	66109	k	E	A	WBBM	ML
66059	k	E	A	WBAN	TO	66110	k	E	A	WBBM	ML
66060	k	E	A	WBAI	IM	66111		E	A	WBBM	ML
66061	k	E	A	WBAH	EH	66112		E	A	WBBM	ML
66062	k	E	A	WBAN	TO	66113		E	A	WBBM	ML
66063	k	E	A	WBAI	IM	66114	k	E	A	WBBM	ML
66064		E	A	WBAH	EH	66115		E	A	WBAK	CF
66065	k	E	A	WBAM	ML	66116	k	E	A	WBAM	ML
66066	k	E	A	WBAM	ML	66117	k	E	A	WBAN	TO
66067	k	E	A	WBAN	TO	66118	k	E	A	WBAT	TE
66068	k	E	A	WBAI	IM	66119		E	A	WBAN	TO
66069	k	E	A	WBAI	IM	66120	k	E	A	WBAI	IM
66070	k	E	A	WBAT	TE	66121	k	E	A	WBAI	IM
66071	k	E	A	WBAI	IM	66122	k	E	A	WBAH	EH
66072	k	E	A	WBAI	IM	66123	k	E	A	WBAI	IM
66073		E	A	WBAI	IM	66124	k	E	A	WBAI	IM
66074		E	A	WBAN	TO	66125	k	E	A	WBAT	TE
66075		E	A	WBAN	TO	66126		E	A	WBAN	TO
66076	k	E	A	WBAK	CF	66127		E	A	WBAK	CF
66077	k	E	A	WBAI	IM	66128	k	E	A	WBAI	IM
66078	k	E	A	WBAT	TE	66129		E	A	WBAN	TO
66079	k	E	A	WBAK	CF	66130	k	E	A	WBAI	IM
66080	k	E	A	WBAK	CF	66131	k	E	A	WBAI	IM
66081	k	E	A	WBAI	IM	66132	k	E	A	WBAH	EH
66082		E	A	WBAH	EH	66133		E	A	WBAM	ML
66083	k	E	A	WBAT	TE	66134	k	E	A	WBAI	IM
66084	k	E	A	WBAI	IM	66135		E	A	WBAK	CF
66085	k	E	A	WBAI	IM	66136	k	E	A	WBAM	ML
66086	k	E	A	WBAN	TO	66137	k	E	A	WBAI	IM
66087		E	A	WBAN	TO	66138	k	E	A	WBAT	TE
66088	k	E	A	WBAK	CF	66139	k	E	A	WBAI	IM
66089	k	E	A	WBAT	TE	66140	k	E	A	WBAT	TE
66090		E	A	WBAK	CF	66141	k	E	A	WBAI	IM
66091	k	E	A	WBAI	IM	66142		E	A	WBAN	TO

66143		E	A	WBAK	CF	66194		E	A	WBAN	TO
66144		E	A	WBAK	CF	66195	k	E	A	WBAN	TO
66145		E	A	WBAK	CF	66196	k	E	A	WBAN	TO
66146	k	E	A	WBAH	EH	66197	k	E	A	WBAI	IM
66147	k	E	A	WBAI	IM	66198	k	E	A	WBAT	TE
66148		E	A	WBAN	TO	66199		E	A	WBAK	CF
66149	k	E	A	WBAT	TE	66200	k	E	A	WBAM	ML
66150		E	A	WBAN	TO	66201	k	E	A	WBAI	IM
66151	k	E	A	WBAK	CF	66202	k	E	A	WBAK	CF
66152	k	E	A	WBAM	ML	66203	k	E	A	WBAT	TE
66153	k	E	A	WBAI	IM	66204	k	E	A	WBAI	IM
66154	k	E	A	WBAI	IM	66205	k	E	A	WBAI	IM
66155	k	E	A	WBAI	IM	66206	k	E	A	WBAK	CF
66156	k	E	A	WBAT	TE	66207	k	E	A	WBAI	IM
66157		E	A	WBAK	CF	66208	k	E	A	WBAN	TO
66158	k	E	A	WBAI	IM	66209	k	E	A	WBAI	IM
66159	k	E	A	WBAN	TO	66210	k	E	A	WBAN	TO
66160	k	E	A	WBAI	IM	66211	k	E	A	WBAT	TE
66161	k	E	A	WBAT	TE	66212	k	E	A	WBAK	CF
66162	k	E	A	WBAH	EH	66213	k	E	A	WBAI	IM
66163	k	E	A	WBAN	TO	66214	k	E	A	WBAK	CF
66164	k	E	A	WBAK	CF	66215	k	E	A	WBAK	CF
66165	k	E	A	WBAK	CF	66216	k	E	A	WBAH	EH
66166	k	E	A	WBAI	IM	66217	k	E	A	WBAH	EH
66167	k	E	A	WBAI	IM	66218	k	E	A	WBAN	TO
66168		E	A	WBAK	CF	66219	k	E	A	WBAN	TO
66169		E	A	WBAH	EH	66220	k	E	A	WBAI	IM
66170	k	E	A	WBAT	TE	66221	k	E	A	WBAI	IM
66171	k	E	A	WBAN	TO	66222	k	E	A	WBAK	CF
66172	k	E	A	WBAI	IM	66223	k	E	A	WBAT	TE
66173	k	E	A	WBAH	EH	66224	k	E	A	WBAT	TE
66174	k	E	A	WBAN	TO	66225	k	E	A	WBAN	TO
66175	k	E	A	WBAN	TO	66226	k	E	A	WBAI	IM
66176		E	A	WBAK	CF	66227	k	E	A	WBAT	TE
66177	k	E	A	WBAI	IM	66228	k	E	A	WBAI	IM
66178	k	E	A	WBAN	TO	66229	k	E	A	WBAK	CF
66179		E	A	WBAK	CF	66230	k	E	A	WBAI	IM
66180	k	E	A	WBAM	ML	66231	k	E	A	WBAN	TO
66181	k	E	A	WBAK	CF	66232	k	E	A	WBAN	TO
66182	k	E	A	WBAN	TO	66233	k	E	A	WBAT	TE
66183	k	E	A	WBAI	IM	66234	k	E	A	WBAI	IM
66184	k	E	A	WBAT	TE	66235	k	E	A	WBAK	CF
66185	k	E	A	WBAI	IM	66236	k	E	A	WBAK	CF
66186	k	E	A	WBAM	ML	66237	k	E	A	WBAI	IM
66187		E	A	WBAK	CF	66238	k	E	A	WBAH	EH
66188	k	E	A	WBAN	TO	66239	k	E	A	WBAK	CF
66189		E	A	WBAH	EH	66240	k	E	A	WBAI	IM
66190	k	E	A	WBAT	TE	66241	k	E	A	WBAK	CF
66191		E	A	WBAK	CF	66242	k	E	A	WBAI	IM
66192	k	E	A	WBAT	TE	66243	k	E	A	WBAN	TO
66193		E	A	WBAM	ML	66244	k	E	A	WBAT	TE

66245 k **E**	A	WBAI	IM	66248 k **E**	A	WBAM	ML
66246 k **E**	A	WBAN	TO	66249 k **E**	A	WBAH	EH
66247 k **E**	A	WBAN	TO	66250 k **E**	A	WBAK	CF

Name:

66002 Lafarge Buddon Wood.

Class 66/4. Direct Rail Services operated locomotives. On order.

Details as Class 66/0.

66401	P
66402	P
66403	P
66404	P
66405	P
66406	P
66407	P
66408	P
66409	P
66410	P

Class 66/5. Freightliner operated locomotives.

Details as Class 66/0.

66501	**FL**	P	DFGM	FD	Japan 2001
66502	**FL**	P	DFGM	FD	Basford Hall Centenary 2001
66503	**FL**	P	DFGM	FD	
66504	**FL**	P	DFGM	FD	
66505	**FL**	P	DFGM	FD	
66506	**FL**	H	DFRT	FD	Crewe Regeneration
66507	**FL**	H	DFRT	FD	
66508	**FL**	H	DFRT	FD	
66509	**FL**	H	DFRT	FD	
66510	**FL**	H	DFRT	FD	
66511	**FL**	H	DFRT	FD	
66512	**FL**	H	DFRT	FD	
66513	**FL**	H	DFRT	FD	
66514	**FL**	H	DFRT	FD	
66515	**FL**	H	DFRT	FD	
66516	**FL**	H	DFRT	FD	
66517	**FL**	H	DFRT	FD	
66518	**FL**	H	DFRT	FD	
66519	**FL**	H	DFRT	FD	
66520	**FL**	H	DFRT	FD	
66521	**FL**	H	DHLT	ZF	
66522	**FL**	H	DFHH	FD	
66523	**FL**	H	DFHH	FD	
66524	**FL**	H	DFHH	FD	
66525	**FL**	H	DFHH	FD	
66526	**FL**	P	DFHH	FD	Driver Steve Dunn (George)
66527	**FL**	P	DFHH	FD	Don Raider
66528	**FL**	P	DFHH	FD	

66529	**FL**	P	DFHH	FD	
66530	**FL**	P	DFHH	FD	
66531	**FL**	P	DFHH	FD	
66532	**FL**	P	DFGM	FD	P&O Nedlloyd Atlas
66533	**FL**	P	DFGM	FD	
66534	**FL**	P	DFGM	FD	OOCL Express
66535	**FL**	P	DFGM	FD	
66536	**FL**	P	DFGM	FD	
66537	**FL**	P	DFGM	FD	
66538	**FL**	H	DFGM	FD	
66539	**FL**	H	DFGM	FD	
66540	**FL**	H	DFGM	FD	
66541	**FL**	H	DFGM	FD	
66542	**FL**	H	DFGM	FD	
66543	**FL**	H	DFGM	FD	
66544	**FL**	P	DFHH	FD	
66545	**FL**	P	DFHH	FD	
66546	**FL**	P	DFHH	FD	
66547	**FL**	P	DFHH	FD	
66548	**FL**	P	DFHH	FD	
66549	**FL**	P	DFHH	FD	
66550	**FL**	P	DFHH	FD	
66551	**FL**	P	DFHH	FD	
66552	**FL**	P	DFHH	FD	
66553	**FL**	P	DFHH	FD	
66554	**FL**	H	DFHH	FD	
66555	**FL**	H	DFHH	FD	
66556	**FL**	H	DFHH	FD	
66557	**FL**	H	DFHH	FD	
66558	**FL**	H	DFHH	FD	
66559	**FL**	H	DFHH	FD	
66560	**FL**	H	DFHH	FD	
66561	**FL**	H	DFHH	FD	
66562	**FL**	H	DFHH	FD	
66563	**FL**	H	DFHH	FD	
66564	**FL**	H	DFHH	FD	
66565	**FL**	H	DFHH	FD	
66566	**FL**	H	DFHH	FD	

Class 66/6. Freightliner operated locomotives with modified gear ratios.

Details as Class 66/0 except:

Maximum Tractive Effort: 467 kN (105080 lbf).
Continuous Tractive Effort: 296 kN (66630 lbf) at 14.0 m.p.h.
Design Speed: 87.5 m.p.h.   **Maximum Speed:** 65 m.p.h.

66601	FL	P	DFHH	FD	The Hope Valley
66602	FL	P	DFRT	FD	
66603	FL	P	DFRT	FD	
66604	FL	P	DFRT	FD	
66605	FL	P	DFRT	FD	
66606	FL	P	DFRT	FD	
66607	FL	P	DFHH	FD	
66608	FL	P	DFHH	FD	
66609	FL	P	DFHH	FD	
66610	FL	P	DFHH	FD	
66611	FL	P	DFHH	FD	
66612	FL	P	DFHH	FD	

Class 66/7. GB Railfreight operated locomotives.

Details as Class 66/0.

Notes: 66710–66712 are currently on hire to DRS.
66713–66717 are on order.

Non Standard/Advertising Liveries:

66705 is in **GB** livery but with "Union Jack" bodyside vinyls.
66709 is Black and Orange with MEDITE branding.

66701	GB	H	GBRT	WN	Railtrack National Logistics
66702	GB	H	GBRT	WN	Blue Lightning
66703	GB	H	GBRT	WN	Doncaster PSB 1981–2002
66704	GB	H	GBRT	WN	
66705	0	H	GBRT	WN	Golden Jubilee
66706	GB	H	GBRT	WN	
66707	GB	H	GBRT	WN	
66708	GB	H	GBCM	WN	
66709	AL	H	GBCM	WN	Joseph Arnold Davies
66710	GB	H	GBCM	WN	
66711	GB	H	GBCM	WN	
66712	GB	H	GBCM	WN	
66713		H			
66714		H			
66715		H			
66716		H			
66717		H			

CLASS 67   GENERAL MOTORS   Bo-Bo

Built: 1999–2000 by Alstom at Valencia, Spain, as sub-contractors for General Motors (General Motors model JT42 HW-HS).
Engine: General Motors 12N-710G3B-EC two stroke of 2385 kW (3200 h.p.) at 900 r.p.m.
Main Alternator: General Motors AR9/HE3/CA6B.
Traction Motors: General Motors D43FM.
Maximum Tractive Effort: 141 kN (31750 lbf).
Continuous Tractive Effort: 90 kN (20200 lbf) at ?? m.p.h.
Power At Rail: 1860 kW.   **Train Brakes:** Air.
Brake Force: 78 t.   **Dimensions:** 19.74 x 2.72 m.
Weight: 90 t.   **Wheel Diameter:** 965 mm.
Design Speed: 125 m.p.h.   **Maximum Speed:** 110 (* 125) m.p.h.
Fuel Capacity: 4927 litres.   **RA:** 8.
Train Supply: Electric, index 66.   **Multiple Working:** AAR System.

Note: All equipped with slow speed control and swing-head automatic "buckeye" combination couplers.

67001	*	E	A	WAAK	CF	Night Mail
67002	*	E	A	WAAK	CF	Special Delivery
67003		E	A	WAAK	CF	
67004	*	E	A	WAAK	CF	Post Haste
67005	*	E	A	WAAK	CF	Queen's Messenger
67006	*	E	A	WAAK	CF	
67007	*	E	A	WAAK	CF	
67008		E	A	WAAK	CF	
67009	*	E	A	WAAK	CF	
67010	*	E	A	WAAK	CF	Unicorn
67011	*	E	A	WAAK	CF	
67012		E	A	WAAK	CF	
67013	*	E	A	WAAK	CF	
67014		E	A	WAAK	CF	
67015		E	A	WAAK	CF	
67016	*	E	A	WAAK	CF	
67017	*	E	A	WAAK	CF	Arrow
67018	*	E	A	WAAK	CF	Rapid
67019	*	E	A	WAAK	CF	
67020	*	E	A	WAAK	CF	
67021	*	E	A	WAAK	CF	
67022	*	E	A	WAAK	CF	
67023	*	E	A	WAAK	CF	
67024		E	A	WAAK	CF	
67025	*	E	A	WAAK	CF	Western Star
67026		E	A	WAAK	CF	
67027		E	A	WAAK	CF	Rising Star
67028	*	E	A	WAAK	CF	
67029	*	E	A	WAAK	CF	
67030		E	A	WAAK	CF	

▲ EWS liveried 08597 is seen passing Doncaster station with a Wabtec–Belmont Yard trip on 24/05/02. **Simon Wright**

▼ BR green liveried 09026 is seen at Brighton on 28/07/00. This loco is owned by South Central. **Hugh Ballantyne**

▲ DRS liveried 20310 and 20315 leaves Dungeness on 11/06/02 with a return nuclear flask train to Willesden. **Anthony Kay**

▼ Fragonset's 31468 "HYDRA" passes Chester on 29/03/02 with an ex-Class 501 Sandite unit being moved from Birkenhead North to Derby. **Doug Birmingham**

▲ DRS liveried 33025 with "Minimodal" branding passes Normanton-on-Soar on the MML on 09/10/02 whilst en-route from Loughborough to Carlisle. **Bob Sweet**

▼ EWS 37047, still in Mainline Blue livery, passes Carlisle on 30/09/02 with a short engineers train for Tyne Yard. **Robert Pritchard**

A Midland Mainline liveried HST set with power cars 43060 and 43058 passes Hasland, south of Chesterfield with the 13.27 Sheffield–St. Pancras on 12/05/01.

Ian Lyall

A new First Group (Great Western) liveried HST led by power car 43165 passes Horse Cove whilst forming the 11.33 Paddington–Penzance on 01/06/02. **John Chalcraft**

▲ BR Blue liveried 46035 is the only Class 46 that is Railtrack registered. On 01/06/02 it passes Mold Junction with the 05.22 Yeovil–Holyhead charter.
Doug Birmingham

▼ Fragonset's 47703 "HERMES" is seen near Attenborough on 31/05/02 with an e.c.s. from Derby to Nottingham before forming the short-lived 09.30 Nottingham–St. Pancras loco-hauled MML service.
John Rudd

▲ BR Blue liveried 50031 "Hood" and 50049 "Defiance" pass Burton Lane crossing
with an e.c.s. from York on 23/09/02.   **Simon Wright**

▼ Loadhaul liveried 56100 is seen shunting in Workington Docks on 14/09/02.
                                                                   Robert Pritchard

▲ 57301 "SCOTT TRACY" in the new Virgin silver livery passes Kilsby on the WCML with a Euston–Rugby e.c.s. on 24/09/02.　　**Bob Sweet**

▼ Hanson liveried 59101 "Village of Whatley" passes Great Cheverell on the Berks and Hants line with the 12.49 Acton–Merehead empty stone train on 22/09/00.　　**John Chalcraft**

▲ EWS liveried 60089 "THE RAILWAY HORSE" is seen on a Stoke–St. Blazey China Clay service as it heads west along the sea wall at Dawlish on 16/07/02.
John Chalcraft

▼ EWS liveried 66236 passes Charing Heath with a Hothfield–Hither Green empty stone train on 22/08/02.
Rodney Lissenden

Freightliner's 66531 is seen with 4Z42, the 12.15 Gascoigne Wood-Hunterston empty Heavy Haul coal train passing Cummertrees near Annan on 20/06/02.
Dave McAlone

67019 passes Defford, Gloucestershire with the 1E43 15.09 Plymouth–Low Fell mail train on 27/06/02.   **Doug Birmingham**

Two of only three EWS Class 73s still in service as this book went to press are seen here at St. Denys with Pathfinders "Soton Vinegar" railtour from Derby to Southampton on 14/09/02. Mainline Blue liveried 73136 "Kent Youth Music" and 73133 "The Bluebell Railway" were the two locos in charge.

Anthony Kay

▲ 86218 "NHS 50" waits for departure from Norwich on 12/09/02 with the
13.40 Anglia service to Liverpool Street.   **Robert Pritchard**

▼ Class 86s are still in use with Virgin West Coast. On 03/09/02 86247 "Abraham
Darby" passes Canley with the 14.15 Birmingham New Street–Euston.
                                                             Andy Flowers

87029 "Earl Marischal" passes Rugby on 20/08/01 with a Euston–Manchester working formed of Mark 2s.   John Rudd

▲ EWS liveried 90031 speeds through Winwick near Warrington with a northbound TPO on 18/06/01. **Paul Senior**

▼ Pairs of Class 92s on freights are rare, however on 15/08/02 92013 "Puccini" and 92005 "Mozart" power the 09.47 Wembley–Dollands Moor intermodal past Otford Junction. **Anthony Kay**

91110 "David Livingstone" with 91128 "Peterborough Cathedral" dead in train on a Kings Cross–Glasgow train at Peterborough on 24/07/02.   **John Rudd**

1.2. ELECTRO-DIESEL & ELECTRIC LOCOMOTIVES

CLASS 73/1   BR/ENGLISH ELECTRIC   Bo-Bo

Electro-diesel locomotives which can operate either from a DC supply or using power from a diesel engine.

Built: 1965–1967 by English Electric Co. at Vulcan Foundry, Newton le Willows.
Main Generator: English Electric 824/5D.
Traction Motors: English Electric 546/1B.
Maximum Tractive Effort (Electric): 179 kN (40000 lbf).
Maximum Tractive Effort (Diesel): 160 kN (36000 lbf).
Continuous Rating (Electric): 1060 kW (1420 h.p.) giving a tractive effort of 35 kN (7800 lbf) at 68 m.p.h.
Continuous Tractive Effort (Diesel): 60 kN (13600 lbf) at 11.5 m.p.h.
Maximum Rail Power (Electric): 2350 kW (3150 h.p.) at 42 m.p.h.
Train Brakes: Air, vacuum & electro-pneumatic († Air & electro-pneumatic).
Brake Force: 31 t.   **Dimensions:** 16.36 x 2.64 m.
Weight: 77 t.   **Wheel Diameter:** 1016 mm.
Design Speed: 90 m.p.h.   **Maximum Speed:** 90 m.p.h.
Fuel Capacity: 1409 litres.
Train Supply: Electric, index 66 (on electric power only).
Multiple Working: SR System.

Formerly numbered E 6001–20/22–26/28–49 (not in order).

Notes: Locomotives numbered in the 732xx series are classed as 73/2 and were originally dedicated to Gatwick Express services. 73201 and 73202 are to be retained by Gatwick Express as standby locos. These two locos, along with 73208 and 73235 were available for use on service trains as this book closed for press.

73101	**PC**	E	WNXX	HG	The Royal Alex'
73103	**IM**	E	WNZX	EH	
73104	**IM**	FR	SDXL	EH	
73105	**CE**	FR	SDXL	OC	
73106	**DG**	E	WNXX	HG	
73107	**CE**	E	WNZX	OC	Redhill 1844–1994
73108	**CE**	E	WNXX	TO	
73109	**ST**	SW	HYSB	BM	Battle of Britain 50th Anniversary
73110	**CE**	E	WNXX	OC	
73114	**ML**	FR	SDXL	OC	
73117	**IM**	E	WNZX	EH	University of Surrey
73118 †tc	**EP**	EU	GPSN	OC	
73119	**CE**	E	WNZX	OC	Kentish Mercury
73128	**E**	E	WNXX	HG	
73129	**N**	E	WNXX	HG	City of Winchester
73130 †tc	**EP**	EU	GPSN	OC	
73131	**E**	E	WPAG	HG	

73132	**IM**	E	WNYX	SP	
73133	**ML**	E	WPAG	HG	The Bluebell Railway
73134	**IM**	E	WNZX	EH	Woking Homes 1885–1985
73136	**ML**	E	WPAG	HG	Kent Youth Music
73138	**CE**	E	WNZX	OC	
73139	**IM**	FR	SDXL	EH	
73201 †	**GX**	P	IVGA	SL	
73202 †	**GX**	P	IVGA	SL	
73203 †	**GX**	GB	GBZZ	PY (S)	
73204 †	**GX**	GB	GBZZ	PY (S)	
73205 †	**GX**	GB	GBZZ	PY (S)	
73206 †	**GX**	GB	GBZZ	PY (S)	
73207 †	**GX**	GB	GBZZ	PY (S)	
73208 †	**GX**	P	IVGA	SL	
73209 †	**GX**	GB	GBZZ	PY (S)	
73210 †	**GX**	P	IVGA	ZG (S)	
73211 †	**GX**	P	IVGA	SL (S)	
73212 †	**RK**	NR	QAED	DF	
73213 †	**RK**	NR	QAED	DF	
73235 †	**GX**	P	IVGA	SL	

CLASS 86   BR/ENGLISH   ELECTRIC   Bo-Bo

Built: 1965–1966 by English Electric Co. at Vulcan Foundry, Newton le Willows or by BR at Doncaster Works.
Electric Supply System: 25 kV AC 50 Hz overhead.
Train Brakes: Air.   **Brake Force:** 40 t.
Dimensions: 17.83 x 2.65 m.   **Weight:** 83–86.8 t.
RA: 6.   **Multiple Working:** TDM system.
Train Supply: Electric, index 74.

Formerly numbered E 3101–3200 (not in order).
Non standard Liveries:
86227 is as **AR** but with "Union Jack" bodyside vinyls.
86233 is in BR "Electric Blue" livery.

Class 86/1. Class 87-type bogies & motors.

Maximum Tractive Effort: 258 kN (58000 lbf).
Traction Motors: GEC 412AZ frame mounted.
Continuous Rating: 3730 kW (5000 h.p.) giving a tractive effort of 95 kN (21300 lbf) at 87 m.p.h.
Maximum Rail Power: 5860 kW (7860 h.p.) at 50.8 m.p.h.
Weight: 86.8 t.   **Wheel Diameter:** 1150 mm.
Design Speed: 110 m.p.h.   **Maximum Speed:** 110 m.p.h.

| 86101 | **I** | H | SAXL | LT | |
| 86102 | **I** | H | SAXL | LT | Robert A Riddles |

Class 86/2. Standard Design rebuilt with resilient wheels and Flexicoil suspension.

Traction Motors: AEI 282BZ axle hung.
Maximum Tractive Effort: 207 kN (46500 lbf).
Continuous Rating: 3010 kW (4040 h.p.) giving a tractive effort of 85 kN (19200 lbf) at 77.5 m.p.h.
Maximum Rail Power: 4550 kW (6100 h.p.) at 49.5 m.p.h.
Wheel Diameter: 1156 mm.   **Weight:** 85–86.2 t.
Design Speed: 125 m.p.h.   **Maximum Speed:** 100 m.p.h.

86205	V	H	IWPA	WN	City of Lancaster
86206	V	H	SAXL	IR	City of Stoke on Trent
86207	I	H	SAXL	LT	City of Lichfield
86208	I	E	WNZX	CE	City of Chester
86209	I	H	IANA	NC	City of Coventry
86210 x	RX	E	WNXX	CE	C.I.T. 75th Anniversary
86212	V	H	IWPA	WN	Preston Guild 1328–1992
86213	I	H	SAXL	BH	Lancashire Witch
86214	I	H	SAXL	LT	Sans Pareil
86215	AR	H	IANA	NC	
86216	I	H	SAXL	ZH	
86217	AR	H	IANA	NC	City University
86218	AR	H	IANA	NC	NHS 50
86220	AR	H	SAXL	LT	
86221	AR	H	IANA	NC	B.B.C. Look East
86222	V	H	SAXL	LT	Clothes Show Live
86223	AR	H	IANA	NC	Norwich Union
86224	I	H	SAXL	LT	
86225	V	H	SAXL	LT	Hardwicke
86226	V	H	SAXL	IR	CHARLES RENNIE MACKINTOSH
86227	0	H	IANA	NC	Golden Jubilee
86228	I	H	IWPA	WN	Vulcan Heritage
86229	V	H	IWPA	WN	Lions Clubs International
86230	AR	H	IANA	NC	
86231	V	H	SAXL	IR	Starlight Express
86232	AR	H	IANA	NC	Norfolk and Norwich Festival
86233	0	H	IWPA	WN	ALSTOM Heritage
86234	AR	H	IANA	NC	Suffolk Relax.Refresh.Return
86235	AR	H	IANA	NC	Crown Point
86236	V	H	SAXL	LT	Josiah Wedgwood
86237	AR	H	IANA	NC	University of East Anglia
86238	AR	H	IANA	NC	European Community
86240	V	H	SAXL	IR	Bishop Eric Treacy
86241	RX	E	WNZX	CE	Glenfiddich
86242	AR	H	IANA	NC	Colchester Castle
86243 x	RX	E	WNXX	CE	
86244	V	H	SAXL	LT	The Royal British Legion
86245	V	H	IWPA	WN	Caledonian
86246	AR	H	IANA	NC	Royal Anglian Regiment
86247	V	H	IWPA	WN	Abraham Darby
86248	V	H	SAXL	ZH	Sir Clwyd/County of Clwyd

86249	**I**	H	SAXL	ZH	County of Merseyside
86250	**AR**	H	IANA	NC	
86251	**V**	H	SAXL	IR	The Birmingham Post
86253	**I**	H	SAXL	ZH	The Manchester Guardian
86254 x	**RX**	E	WNXX	CE	
86256	**V**	H	SAXL	LT	Pebble Mill
86257	**AR**	H	SAXL	LT	
86258	**V**	H	SAXL	IR	Talyllyn 50 Years of Railway Preservation 1951–2001
86259	**V**	H	IWPA	WN	Les Ross
86260	**V**	H	IWPA	WN	Driver Wallace Oakes G.C.
86261 x	**E**	E	WNXX	CE	THE RAIL CHARTER PARTNERSHIP

Class 86/4. EWS owned locomotives.

Traction Motors: AEI 282AZ axle hung.
Maximum Tractive Effort: 258 kN (58000 lbf).
Continuous Rating: 2680 kW (3600 h.p.) giving a tractive effort of 89 kN (20000 lbf) at 67 m.p.h.
Maximum Rail Power: 4400 kW (5900 h.p.) at 38 m.p.h.
Wheel Diameter: 1156 mm.   **Weight:** 83–83.9 t.
Design Speed: 100 m.p.h.   **Maximum Speed:** 100 m.p.h.

Note: 86426 and 86430 are on long term hire from EWS to Freightliner.

86401	**E**	E	WNXX	CE	Hertfordshire Rail Tours
86416 x	**RX**	E	WNXX	TE	
86417 x	**RX**	E	WNXX	CE	
86419 x	**RX**	E	WNZX	CE	
86424	**RX**	E	WNXX	CE	
86425	**RX**	E	WNXX	CE	Saint Mungo
86426 x	**FL**	E	DFNC	FE	
86430 x	**FL**	E	DFNC	FE	

Class 86/5. Regeared locomotive operated by Freightliner.

Details as Class 86/4 except:
Continuous Rating: 2680 kW (3600 h.p.) giving a tractive effort of 117 kN (26300 lbf) at 67 m.p.h.
Maximum Speed: 75 m.p.h.   **Train Supply:** Electric, isolated.

| 86501 (86608) | **FL** | FL | DFGC | FE |

Class 86/6. Freightliner operated locomotives. Details as Class 86/4 except:
Maximum Speed: 75 m.p.h.   **Train Supply:** Electric, isolated.

86602	**FL**	FL	DFNC	FE	
86603	**FE**	FL	DHLT	SP	
86604	**FF**	FL	DFNC	FE	
86605	**FF**	FL	DFNC	FE	
86606	**FF**	FL	DFNC	FE	
86607	**FL**	FL	DFNC	FE	
86609	**FL**	FL	DFNC	FE	
86610	**FL**	FL	DFNC	FE	
86611	**FF**	FL	DFNC	FE	Airey Neave

86612	FF	P	DFNC	FE	Elizabeth Garrett Anderson
86613	FL	P	DFNC	FE	
86614	FF	P	DFNC	FE	
86615	FL	P	DFNC	FE	Rotary International
86618	FF	P	DHLT	CE	
86620	FL	P	DFNC	FE	Philip G Walton
86621	FF	P	DFNC	FE	London School of Economics
86622	FF	P	DFNC	FE	
86623	FF	P	DFNC	FE	
86627	FL	P	DFNC	FE	
86628	FF	P	DFNC	FE	Aldaniti
86631	FL	P	DFNC	FE	
86632	FL	P	DFNC	FE	
86633	FF	P	DFNC	FE	Wulfruna
86634	FL	P	DHLT	CE	
86635	FL	P	DFNC	FE	
86636	FL	P	DHLT	CE	
86637	FF	P	DFNC	FE	
86638	FF	P	DFNC	FE	
86639	FF	P	DFNC	FE	

CLASS 87   BREL/GEC   Bo-Bo

Built: 1973–1975 by BREL at Crewe Works.
Electric Supply System: 25 kV AC 50 Hz overhead.
Traction Motors: GEC G412AZ frame mounted.
Maximum Tractive Effort: 258 kN (58000 lbf).
Continuous Rating: 3730 kW (5000 h.p.) giving a tractive effort of 95 kN (21300 lbf) at 87 m.p.h.
Maximum Rail Power: 5860 kW (7860 h.p.) at 50.8 m.p.h.

Train Brakes: Air.	**Brake Force:** 40 t.
Dimensions: 17.83 x 2.65 m.	**Weight:** 83.3 t.
Wheel Diameter: 1150 mm.	**Design Speed:** 110 m.p.h.
Maximum Speed: 110 m.p.h.	**Train Supply:** Electric, index 95.
RA: 6.	**Multiple Working:** TDM system.

87001	V	P	IWCA	WN	Royal Scot
87002	V	P	IWCA	WN	Royal Sovereign
87003	V	P	IWCA	WN	Patriot
87004	V	P	IWCA	WN	Britannia
87005	V	P	IWCA	WN	City of London
87006	V	P	IWCA	WN	George Reynolds
87007	V	P	IWCA	WN	City of Manchester
87008	V	P	IWCA	WN	City of Liverpool
87009	V	P	IWCA	WN	City of Birmingham
87010	V	P	IWCA	WN	King Arthur
87011	V	P	IWCA	WN	City of Wolverhampton
87012	V	P	IWCA	WN	Coeur de Lion
87013	V	P	IWCA	WN	John O'Gaunt
87014	V	P	IWCA	WN	Knight of the Thistle
87015	V	P	IWCA	WN	Howard of Effingham

87016	V	P	IWCA	WN	Willesden Intercity Depot
87017	V	P	IWCA	WN	Iron Duke
87018	V	P	IWCA	WN	Lord Nelson
87019	V	P	IWCA	WN	Sir Winston Churchill
87020	V	P	IWCA	WN	North Briton
87021	V	P	IWCA	WN	Robert The Bruce
87022	V	P	IWCA	WN	Lew Adams The Black Prince
87023	V	P	IWCA	WN	Polmadie
87024	V	P	IWCA	WN	Lord of the Isles
87025	V	P	IWCA	WN	County of Cheshire
87026	V	P	IWCA	WN	Sir Richard Arkwright
87027	V	P	IWCA	WN	Wolf of Badenoch
87028	V	P	IWCA	WN	Lord President
87029	V	P	IWCA	WN	Earl Marischal
87030	V	P	IWCA	WN	Black Douglas
87031	V	P	IWCA	WN	Hal o' the Wynd
87032	V	P	IWCA	WN	Kenilworth
87033	V	P	IWCA	WN	Thane of Fife
87034	V	P	IWCA	WN	William Shakespeare
87035	V	P	IWCA	WN	Robert Burns

CLASS 89   BRUSH   Co-Co

Built: 1986 by BREL at Crewe Works (as sub-contractors for Brush).
Electric Supply System: 25 kV AC 50 Hz overhead.
Traction Motors: Brush. Frame mounted.
Maximum Tractive Effort: 205 kN (46000 lbf).
Continuous Rating: 4350 kW (5850 h.p.) giving a tractive effort of 105 kN (23600 lbf) at 92 m.p.h.

Maximum Rail Power:	**Train Brakes:** Air.
Brake Force: 50 t.	**Dimensions:** 19.80 x 2.74 m.
Weight: 104 t.	**Wheel Diameter:** 1150 mm.
Design Speed: 125 m.p.h.	**Maximum Speed:** 125 m.p.h.
Train Supply: Electric, index 95.	**RA:** 6.
Multiple Working: TDM system.	

89001   **GN**   SA   IECB   ZB (S)

CLASS 90   GEC   Bo-Bo

Built: 1987–1990 by BREL at Crewe Works (as sub contractors for GEC).
Electric Supply System: 25 kV AC 50 Hz overhead.
Traction Motors: GEC G412CY frame mounted.
Maximum Tractive Effort: 258 kN (58000 lbf).
Continuous Rating: 3730 kW (5000 h.p.) giving a tractive effort of 95 kN (21300 lbf) at 87 m.p.h.
Maximum Rail Power: 5860 kW (7860 h.p.) at 68.3 m.p.h.
Train Brakes: Air.

Brake Force: 40 t.	**Dimensions:** 18.80 x 2.74 m.
Weight: 84.5 t.	**Wheel Diameter:** 1156 mm.

Design Speed: 110 m.p.h.   **Maximum Speed:** 110 m.p.h.
Train Supply: Electric, index 95.   **RA:** 7.
Multiple Working: TDM system.

Non-standard liveries:

90028 is in Belgian Railways style blue and yellow.
90029 is in German Federal Railways style raspberry red and white.
90036 is as **FE**, but has a yellow roof.

Notes:

One (unspecified) locomotive is hired from EWS (Pool WEFE) to Great North Eastern Railway (Pool IECA) on a regular basis. This locomotive is normally used between London King's Cross and Leeds/Bradford Forster Square only.

Locomotives from Pool WEFE are also loaned on a day-to-day basis to West Coast Traincare for operation by Virgin West Coast in pool IWPA.

Two or three Freightliner Class 90s (Pool DFLC) are curently hired to Anglia Railways (pool IANA) for use on London Liverpool Street–Norwich services. More locos are expected to be hired to this pool during 2003.

90001	b	**V**	P	IWCA	WN	BBC Midlands Today
90002	b	**V**	P	IWCA	WN	Mission: Impossible
90003	b	**V**	P	IWCA	WN	THE HERALD
90004	b	**V**	P	IWCA	WN	City of Glasgow
90005	b	**V**	P	IWCA	WN	Financial Times
90006	b	**V**	P	IWCA	WN	Modern Railways Magazine/ Roger Ford
90007	b	**V**	P	IWCA	WN	Keith Harper
90008	b	**V**	P	IWCA	WN	The Birmingham Royal Ballet
90009	b	**V**	P	IWCA	WN	The Economist
90010	b	**V**	P	IWCA	WN	275 Railway Squadron (Volunteers)
90011	b	**V**	P	IWCA	WN	West Coast Rail 250
90012	b	**V**	P	IWCA	WN	British Transport Police
90013	b	**V**	P	IWCA	WN	The Law Society
90014	b	**V**	P	IWCA	WN	Driver Tom Clark O.B.E
90015	b	**V**	P	IWCA	WN	The International Brigades SPAIN 1936–1939
90016	b	**RX**	E	WEFE	CE	
90017	b	**E**	E	WEFE	CE	
90018	b	**E**	E	WEFE	CE	
90019	b	**RX**	E	WEFE	CE	Penny Black
90020	b	**E**	E	WEFE	CE	Sir Michael Heron
90021		**FE**	EF	WEFE	CE	
90022		**FE**	EF	WEFE	CE	Freightconnection
90023		**FE**	EF	WEFE	CE	
90024		**GN**	EF	WEFE	CE	
90025		**F**	EF	WEFE	CE	
90026		**E**	EF	WEFE	CE	
90027		**FE**	EF	WEFE	CE	Allerton T&RS Depot
90028		**O**	EF	WEFE	CE	Vrachtverbinding
90029		**O**	EF	WEFE	CE	Frachtverbindungen

90030	E	EF	WEFE	CE	Crewe Locomotive Works
90031	E	EF	WEFE	CE	The Railway Children Partnership
					Working For Street Children Worldwide
90032	E	EF	WEFE	CE	
90033	FE	EF	WEFE	CE	
90034	E	EF	WEFE	CE	
90035	E	EF	WEFE	CE	
90036	0	EF	WEFE	CE	
90037	E	EF	WEFE	CE	Spirit of Dagenham
90038	FE	EF	WEFE	CE	
90039	F	EF	WEFE	CE	
90040	E	EF	WEFE	CE	The Railway Mission
90041	FF	P	DFLC	FE	
90042	FF	P	DFLC	FE	
90043	FF	P	DFLC	FE	Freightliner Coatbridge
90044	FF	P	DFLC	FE	
90045	FF	P	DFLC	FE	
90046	FF	P	DFLC	FE	
90047	FF	P	DFLC	FE	
90048	FF	P	DFLC	FE	
90049	FF	P	DFLC	FE	
90050	FF	P	DFLC	FE	

CLASS 91   GEC   Bo-Bo

Built: 1988–1991 by BREL at Crewe Works (as sub contractors for GEC).
Electric Supply System: 25 kV AC 50 Hz overhead.
Traction Motors: GEC G426AZ.   **Maximum Tractive Effort:**
Continuous Rating: 4540 kW (6090 h.p.) giving a tractive effort of ?? kN at ?? m.p.h.
Maximum Rail Power: 4700 kW (6300 h.p.) at ?? m.p.h.
Train Brakes: Air.
Brake Force: 45 t.   **Dimensions:** 19.41 x 2.74 m.
Weight: 84 t.   **Wheel Diameter:** 1000 mm.
Design Speed: 140 m.p.h.   **Maximum Speed:** 125 m.p.h.
Train Supply: Electric, index 95.   **RA:** 7.
Multiple Working: TDM system.

Note: This class is near to the completion of a refurbishment programme at Bombardier, Doncaster. Refurbished locomotives are reclassified Class 91/1 and have been renumbered by the addition of 100 to their original number, except 91023 which was renumbered 91132.

91101	GN	H	IECA	BN	City of London
91102	GN	H	IECA	BN	Durham Cathedral
91103	GN	H	IECA	BN	County of Lincolnshire
91104	GN	H	IECA	BN	Grantham
91105	GN	H	IECA	BN	County Durham
91106	GN	H	IECA	BN	East Lothian
91107	GN	H	IECA	BN	Newark on Trent
91108	GN	H	IECA	BN	City of Leeds

91109	GN	H	IECA	BN	The Samaritans
91110	GN	H	IECA	BN	David Livingstone
91111	GN	H	IECA	BN	Terence Cuneo
91112	GN	H	IECA	BN	County of Cambridgeshire
91113	GN	H	IECA	BN	County of North Yorkshire
91014	GN	H	IECA	BN	St. Mungo Cathedral
91115	GN	H	IECA	BN	Holyrood
91116	GN	H	IECA	BN	Strathclyde
91117	GN	H	IECA	BN	Cancer Research UK
91118	GN	H	IECA	BN	Bradford Film Festival
91119	GN	H	IECA	BN	County of Tyne & Wear
91120	GN	H	IECA	BN	Royal Armouries
91021	GN	H	IECA	BN	Archbishop Thomas Cranmer
91122	GN	H	IECA	BN	Double Trigger
91024	GN	H	IECA	BN	Reverend W Awdry
91125	GN	H	IECA	BN	
91126	GN	H	IECA	BN	York Minster
91127	GN	H	IECA	BN	Edinburgh Castle
91128	GN	H	IECA	BN	Peterborough Cathedral
91129	GN	H	IECA	BN	Queen Elizabeth II
91130	GN	H	IECA	BN	City of Newcastle
91131	GN	H	IECA	BN	County of Northumberland
91132	GN	H	IECA	BN	City of Durham

CLASS 92   BRUSH   Co-Co

Built: 1993–1996 by Brush Traction at Loughborough.
Electric Supply System: 25 kV AC 50 HZ overhead or 750 V DC third rail.
Traction Motors: Brush.
Maximum Tractive Effort: 400 kN (90 000 lbf).
Continuous Rating: 5040 kW (6760 h.p.) on AC, 4000 kW (5360 h.p.) on DC.
Maximum Rail Power: **Train Brakes:** Air.
Brake Force: 63 t.   **Dimensions:** 21.34 x 2.67 m.
Weight: 126 t.   **Wheel Diameter:** 1160 mm.
Design Speed: 140 km/h (87 m.p.h.).   **Maximum Speed:** 140 km/h (87 m.p.h.).
Train Supply: Electric, index 108 (AC), 70 (DC).
RA: 7.

Note: Locomotives in pool WTWE are also authorised to operate on the
Eurotunnel network. These locomotives have temporarily had their DC shoegear
removed and may only operate under power between Dollands Moor and
Fréthun.

92001	E	E	WTWE	CE	Victor Hugo
92002	EP	E	WTAE	CE	H.G. Wells
92003	EP	E	WTAE	CE	Beethoven
92004	EP	E	WTAE	CE	Jane Austen
92005	EP	E	WTAE	CE	Mozart
92006	EP	SF	WTWE	CE	Louis Armand
92007	EP	E	WTAE	CE	Schubert
92008	EP	E	WTAE	CE	Jules Verne

92009	EP	E	WTAE	CE	Elgar
92010	EP	SF	WTWE	CE	Molière
92011	EP	E	WTAE	CE	Handel
92012	EP	E	WTWE	CE	Thomas Hardy
92013	EP	E	WTAE	CE	Puccini
92014	EP	SF	WTWE	CE	Emile Zola
92015	EP	E	WTAE	CE	D.H. Lawrence
92016	EP	E	WTAE	CE	Brahms
92017	EP	E	WTAE	CE	Shakespeare
92018	EP	SF	WTWE	CE	Stendhal
92019	EP	E	WTAE	CE	Wagner
92020	EP	EU	WNWX	CE	Milton
92021	EP	EU	WNWX	CE	Purcell
92022	EP	E	WTAE	CE	Charles Dickens
92023	EP	SF	WTWE	CE	Ravel
92024	EP	E	WTAE	CE	J.S. Bach
92025	EP	E	WTAE	CE	Oscar Wilde
92026	EP	E	WTAE	CE	Britten
92027	EP	E	WTWE	CE	George Eliot
92028	EP	SF	WTWE	CE	Saint Saëns
92029	EP	E	WTWE	CE	Dante
92030	EP	E	WTAE	CE	Ashford
92031	E	E	WTAE	CE	The Institute of Logistics and Transport
92032	EP	EU	WNWX	CE	César Franck
92033	EP	SF	WTWE	CE	Berlioz
92034	EP	E	WTAE	CE	Kipling
92035	EP	E	WTAE	CE	Mendelssohn
92036	EP	E	WTAE	CE	Bertolt Brecht
92037	EP	E	WTWE	CE	Sullivan
92038	EP	SF	WTWE	CE	Voltaire
92039	EP	E	WTAE	CE	Johann Strauss
92040	EP	EU	WNWX	CE	Goethe
92041	EP	E	WTAE	CE	Vaughan Williams
92042	EP	E	WTAE	CE	Honegger
92043	EP	SF	WTWE	CE	Debussy
92044	EP	EU	WNWX	CE	Couperin
92045	EP	EU	WNWX	CE	Chaucer
92046	EP	EU	WNWX	CE	Sweelinck

1.3. EUROTUNNEL LOCOMOTIVES

1.3.1. DIESEL LOCOMOTIVES

0001–0005   MaK   Bo-Bo

Built: 1992–93 by MaK at Kiel, Germany (Model DE1004).
Engine: MTU 12V 396 Tc of 1180 kW (1580 h.p.) at 1800 rpm.
Main Alternator: BBC.   **Traction Motors:** BBC.
Maximum Tractive Effort: 305 kN (68600 lbf).
Continuous Tractive Effort: 140 kN (31500 lbf) at 20 mph.
Power At Rail: 750 kW (1012 h.p.).
Brake Force: 120 kN.   **Dimensions:** 16.50 x ?? x ?? m.
Weight: 84 t.   **Wheel Diameter:** 1000 mm.
Design Speed: 120 km/h.   **Maximum Speed:** 120 km/h.
Fuel Capacity: **Train Brakes:** Air.
Train Supply: Not equipped.   **Multiple Working:** Within class.

0001	**GY**	ET	CO
0002	**GY**	ET	CO
0003	**GY**	ET	CO
0004	**GY**	ET	CO
0005	**GY**	ET	CO

0032–0042   HUNSLET/SCHÖMA   0–4–0

Built: 1989–90 by Hunslet Engine Company at Leeds as 900 mm. gauge.
Rebuilt: 1993-94 by Schöma in Germany to 1435 mm. gauge.
Engine: Deutz of 270 kW (200 h.p.) at ???? rpm.
Transmission: Mechanical.   **Maximum Tractive Effort:**
Cont. Tractive Effort: **Power At Rail:**
Brake Force: **Dimensions:**
Weight: **Wheel Diameter:**
Design Speed: 50 km/h.   **Maximum Speed:** 50 km/h.
Fuel Capacity: **Train Brakes:** Air.
Train Supply: Not equipped.   **Multiple Working:** Not equipped.

0031	**Y**	ET	CO	FRANCES
0032	**Y**	ET	CO	ELISABETH
0033	**Y**	ET	CO	SILKE
0034	**Y**	ET	CO	AMANDA
0035	**Y**	ET	CO	MARY
0036	**Y**	ET	CO	LAWRENCE
0037	**Y**	ET	CO	LYDIE
0038	**Y**	ET	CO	JENNY
0039	**Y**	ET	CO	PACITA
0040	**Y**	ET	CO	JILL
0041	**Y**	ET	CO	KIM
0042	**Y**	ET	CO	NICOLE

1.3.2. ELECTRIC LOCOMOTIVES

9001–9113   BRUSH/ABB   Bo-Bo-Bo

Built: 1993–2001 by Brush Traction at Loughborough.
Supply System: 25 kV AC 50 Hz overhead.
Traction Motors: ABB 6PH.   **Maximum Tractive Effort:** 400 kN (90 000 lbf).
Continuous Rating: 5760 kW (7725 h.p.) giving a TE of 310 kN at 65 km/h.
Maximum Rail Power: **Multiple Working:** TDM system.
Brake Force: 50 t.   **Dimensions:** 22.01 x 2.97 x 4.20 m.
Weight: 132 t.   **Wheel Diameter:** 1090 mm.
Design Speed: 175 km/h.   **Maximum Speed:** 160 km/h.
Train Supply: Electric.   **Train Brakes:** Air.

CLASS 9/0. Mixed traffic locomotives.

9001	**ET**	ET	CO	LESLEY GARRETT
9002	**ET**	ET	CO	STUART BURROWS
9003	**ET**	ET	CO	BENJAMIN LUXON
9004	**ET**	ET	CO	VICTORIA DE LOS ANGELES
9005	**ET**	ET	CO	JESSYE NORMAN
9006	**ET**	ET	CO	REGINE CRESPIN
9007	**ET**	ET	CO	DAME JOAN SUTHERLAND
9008	**ET**	ET	CO	ELISABETH SODERSTROM
9009	**ET**	ET	CO	FRANÇOIS POLLET
9010	**ET**	ET	CO	JEAN-PHILIPPE COURTIS
9011	**ET**	ET	CO	JOSÉ VAN DAM
9012	**ET**	ET	CO	LUCIANO PAVAROTTI
9013	**ET**	ET	CO	MARIA CALLAS
9014	**ET**	ET	CO	LUCIA POPP
9015	**ET**	ET	CO	LÖTSCHBERG 1913
9016	**ET**	ET	CO	WILLARD WHITE
9017	**EB**	ET	CO	JOSÉ CARRERAS
9018	**ET**	ET	CO	WILHELMENA FERNANDEZ
9019	**ET**	ET	CO	MARIA EWING
9020	**ET**	ET	CO	Nicolai Ghiaurov
9021	**ET**	ET	CO	TERESA BERGANZA
9022	**ET**	ET	CO	DAME JANET BAKER
9023	**ET**	ET	CO	DAME ELISABETH LEGGE-SCHWARZKOPF
9024	**ET**	ET	CO	GOTTHARD 1882
9025	**ET**	ET	CO	JUNGFRAUJOCH 1912
9026	**ET**	ET	CO	FURKATUNNEL 1982
9027	**ET**	ET	CO	BARBARA HENDRICKS
9028	**ET**	ET	CO	DAME KIRI TE KANAWA
9029	**ET**	ET	CO	THOMAS ALLEN
9031	**ET**	ET	CO	
9032	**ET**	ET	CO	RENATA TEBALDI
9033	**ET**	ET	CO	MONTSERRAT CABALLE
9034	**ET**	ET	CO	MIRELLA FRENI
9035	**ET**	ET	CO	Nicolai Gedda

9036	**ET**	ET	CO	ALAIN FONDARY
9037	**ET**	ET	CO	GABRIEL BACQUIER
9038	**ET**	ET	CO	HILDEGARD BEHRENS
9040	**EB**	ET	CO	

CLASS 9/1. Freight Shuttle dedicated locomotives.

9101	**EB**	ET	CO
9102	**EB**	ET	CO
9103	**EB**	ET	CO
9104	**EB**	ET	CO
9105	**EB**	ET	CO
9106	**EB**	ET	CO
9108	**EB**	ET	CO
9109	**EB**	ET	CO
9110	**EB**	ET	CO
9111	**EB**	ET	CO
9112	**EB**	ET	CO
9113	**EB**	ET	CO

9701–9707   BRUSH/BOMBARDIER   Bo-Bo-Bo

Built: 2001–2002 by Brush Traction at Loughborough.
Supply System: 25 kV AC 50 Hz overhead.

Traction Motors:	**Maximum Tractive Effort:**
Continuous Rating: 7000 kW.	
Maximum Rail Power:	**Multiple Working:**
Brake Force:	**Dimensions:**
Weight:	**Wheel Diameter:**
Design Speed:	**Maximum Speed:**
Train Supply:	**Train Brakes:**

9701	**EB**	ET	CO
9702	**EB**	ET	CO
9703	**EB**	ET	CO
9704	**EB**	ET	CO
9705	**EB**	ET	CO
9706	**EB**	ET	CO
9707	**EB**	ET	CO

2. LOCO-HAULED PASSENGER COACHING STOCK

INTRODUCTION

LAYOUT OF INFORMATION

Coaches are listed in numerical order of painted number in batches according to type.

Each coach entry is laid out as in the following example (former number column may be omitted where not applicable):

No.	Prev. No.	Notes	Livery	Owner	Operation	Depot/Location
3522	(3236)		**FP**	H	*GW*	OO

DETAILED INFORMATION & CODES

Under each type heading, the following details are shown:

- Diagram Code. This consists of the first three characters of the TOPS type code followed by two numbers which relate to the particular design of vehicle.
- 'Mark' of coach (see below).
- Descriptive text.
- Number of first class seats, standard class seats, lavatory compartments and wheelchair spaces shown as F/S nT nW respectively.
- Bogie type (see below).
- Additional features.
- ETH Index.

TOPS TYPE CODES

TOPS type codes are allocated to all coaching stock. For vehicles numbered in the passenger stock number series the code consists of:

(1) Two letters denoting the layout of the vehicle as follows:

AA   Gangwayed Corridor
AB   Gangwayed Corridor Brake
AC   Gangwayed Open (2+2 seating)
AD   Gangwayed Open (2+1 seating)
AE   Gangwayed Open Brake
AF   Gangwayed Driving Open Brake
AG   Micro-Buffet
AH   Brake Micro-Buffet

AI	As 'AC' but with drop-head buckeye and gangway at one end only
AJ	Restaurant Buffet with Kitchen
AK	Kitchen Car
AL	As 'AC' but with disabled person's toilet (Mark 4 only)
AN	Miniature Buffet
AP	Pullman First with Kitchen
AQ	Pullman Parlour First
AR	Pullman Brake First
AS	Sleeping Car
AT	Royal Train Coach
AU	Sleeping Car with Pantry
AX	Generator Van (1000 V DC)
AZ	Special Saloon
GF	DMU/EMU/Mark 4 Barrier Vehicle
AX	Generator Van (415 V AC three-phase)
NM	Sandite Coach

(2) A digit denoting the class of passenger accommodation:

1	First	4	Unclassified
2	Standard (formerly second)	5	None
3	Composite (first & standard)		

(3) A suffix relating to the build of coach.

1	Mark 1	C	Mark 2C	G	Mark 3 or 3A
Z	Mark 2	D	Mark 2D	H	Mark 3B
A	Mark 2A	E	Mark 2E	J	Mark 4
B	Mark 2B	F	Mark 2F		

OPERATING CODES

Operating codes used by train company operating staff (and others) to denote vehicle types in general. These are shown in parentheses adjacent to TOPS type codes. Letters used are:

B	Brake	K	Side corridor with lavatory
C	Composite	O	Open
F	First Class	S	Standard Class (formerly second)

Various other letters are in use and the meaning of these can be ascertained by referring to the titles at the head of each type.

Readers should note the distinction between an SO (Open Standard) and a TSO (Tourist Open Standard) The former has 2+1 seating layout, whilst the latter has 2+2.

BOGIE TYPES

BR Mark 1 (BR1). Double bolster leaf spring bogie. Generally 90 m.p.h., but BR1 bogies may be permitted to run at 100 m.p.h. with special maintenance. Weight: 6.1 t.

BR Mark 2 (BR2). Single bolster leaf-spring bogie used on certain types of non-passenger stock and suburban stock (all now withdrawn). Weight: 5.3 t.

COMMONWEALTH (C). Heavy, cast steel coil spring bogie. 100 m.p.h. Weight: 6.75 t.

B4. Coil spring fabricated bogie. Generally 100 m.p.h., but B4 bogies may be permitted to run at 110 m.p.h. with special maintenance. Weight: 5.2 t.

B5. Heavy duty version of B4. 100 m.p.h. Weight: 5.3 t.

B5 (SR). A bogie originally used on Southern Region EMUs, similar in design to B5. Now also used on locomotive hauled coaches. 100 m.p.h.

BT10. A fabricated bogie designed for 125 m.p.h. Air suspension.

T4. A 125 m.p.h. bogie designed by BREL (now Bombardier Transportation).

BT41. Fitted to Mark 4 vehicles, designed by SIG in Switzerland. At present limited to 125 m.p.h., but designed for 140 m.p.h.

BRAKES

Air braking is now standard on British main line trains. Vehicles with other equipment are denoted:
v   Vacuum braked.
x   Dual braked (air and vacuum).

HEATING & VENTILATION

Electric heating and ventilation is now standard on British main-line trains. Certain coaches for use on charter services may also have steam heating facilities, or be steam heated only.

PUBLIC ADDRESS

It is assumed all coaches are now fitted with public address equipment, although certain stored vehicles may not have this feature. In addition, it is assumed all vehicles with a conductor's compartment have public address transmission facilities, as have catering vehicles.

COOKING EQUIPMENT

It is assumed that Mark 1 catering vehicles have gas powered cooking equipment, whilst Mark 2, 3 and 4 catering vehicles have electric powered cooking equipment unless stated otherwise.

ADDITIONAL FEATURE CODES

d   Secondary door locking.
dg   Driver–Guard communication equipment.
f   Facelifted or fluorescent lighting.
k   Composition brake blocks (instead of cast iron).
n   Day/night lighting.
p   Public telephone.
pg   Public address transmission and driver-guard communication.
pt   Public address transmission facility.

q   Catering staff to shore telephone.
w   Wheelchair space.
z   Disabled persons' toilet.

Standard class coaches with wheelchair space also have one tip-up seat per space.

NOTES ON ETH INDICES

The sum of ETH indices in a train must be not more than the ETS index of the locomotive. The normal voltage on British trains is 1000 V. Suffix 'X' denotes 600 amp wiring instead of 400 amp. Trains whose ETH index is higher than 66 must be formed completely of 600 amp wired stock. Class 33 and 73 locomotives cannot provide a suitable electric train supply for Mark 2D, Mark 2E, Mark 2F, Mark 3, Mark 3A, Mark 3B or Mark 4 coaches. Class 55 locomotives provide an e.t.s. directly from one of their traction generators into the train line. Consequently voltage fluctuations can result in motor-alternator flashover. Thus these locomotives are not suitable for use with Mark 2D, Mark 2E, Mark 2F, Mark 3, Mark 3A, Mark 3B or Mark 4 coaches unless modified motor-alternators are fitted. Such motor alternators were fitted to Mark 2D and 2F coaches used on the East Coast main line, but few remain fitted.

BUILD DETAILS

Lot Numbers
Vehicles ordered under the auspices of BR were allocated a lot (batch) number when ordered and these are quoted in class headings and sub-headings.

Builders
These are shown in class headings. Abbreviations used are found in section 6.8.

Information on sub-contracting works which built parts of vehicles e.g. the underframes etc. is not shown.

In addition to the above, certain vintage Pullman cars were built or rebuilt at the following works:

Metropolitan Carriage & Wagon Company, Birmingham (Now Alstom)
Midland Carriage & Wagon Company, Birmingham
Pullman Car Company, Preston Park, Brighton

Conversions have also been carried out at the Railway Technical Centre, Derby, BR Salisbury Depot and Blakes Fabrications, Edinburgh.

Vehicle Numbers
Where a coach has been renumbered, the former number is shown in parentheses. If a coach has been renumbered more than once, the original number is shown first in parentheses, followed by the most recent previous number. Where the former number of a coach due to be converted or renumbered is known and the conversion and/or renumbering has not yet taken place, the coach is listed under both current number (with depot allocation) and under new number (without allocation).

Numbering Systems
Seven different numbering systems were in use on BR. These were the BR series, the four pre-nationalisation companies' series', the Pullman Car

Company's series and the UIC (International Union of Railways) series. BR number series coaches and former Pullman Car Company series are listed separately. There is also a separate listing of 'Saloon' type vehicles which are registered to run on Network Rail. Please note the Mark 2 Pullman vehicles were ordered after the Pullman Car Company had been nationalised and are therefore numbered in the BR series.

THE DEVELOPMENT OF BR STANDARD COACHES

The standard BR coach built from 1951 to 1963 was the Mark 1. This type features a separate underframe and body. The underframe is normally 64 ft. 6 in. long, but certain vehicles were built on shorter (57 ft.) frames. Tungsten lighting was standard and until 1961, BR Mark 1 bogies were generally provided. In 1959 Lot No. 30525 (TSO) appeared with fluorescent lighting and melamine interior panels, and from 1961 onwards Commonwealth bogies were fitted in an attempt to improve the quality of ride which became very poor when the tyre profiles on the wheels of the BR1 bogies became worn. Later batches of TSO and BSO retained the features of Lot No. 30525, but compartment vehicles – whilst utilising melamine panelling in standard class – still retained tungsten lighting. Wooden interior finish was retained in first class vehicles where the only change was to fluorescent lighting in open vehicles (except Lot No. 30648, which had tungsten lighting). In later years many Mark 1 coaches had BR 1 bogies replaced by B4.

In 1964, a new prototype train was introduced. Known as 'XP64', it featured new seat designs, pressure heating & ventilation, aluminium compartment doors and corridor partitions, foot pedal operated toilets and B4 bogies. The vehicles were built on standard Mark 1 underframes. Folding exterior doors were fitted, but these proved troublesome and were later replaced with hinged doors. All XP64 coaches have been withdrawn, but some have been preserved.

The prototype Mark 2 vehicle (W 13252) was produced in 1963. This was an FK of semi-integral construction and had pressure heating & ventilation, tungsten lighting, and was mounted on B4 bogies. This vehicle has been preserved by the National Railway Museum and is currently stored at MoD Kineton DM. The production build was similar, but wider windows were used. The TSO and SO vehicles used a new seat design similar to that in the XP64 and fluorescent lighting was provided. Interior finish reverted to wood. Mark 2 vehicles were built from 1964–66.

The Mark 2A design, built 1967–68, incorporated the remainder of the features first used in the XP64 coaches, i.e. foot pedal operated toilets (except BSO), new first class seat design, aluminium compartment doors and partitions together with fluorescent lighting in first class compartments. Folding gangway doors (lime green coloured) were used instead of the traditional one-piece variety.

The following list summarises the changes made in the later Mark 2 variants:

Mark 2B: Wide wrap around doors at vehicle ends, no centre doors, slightly longer body. In standard class, one toilet at each end instead of two at one end as previously. Red folding gangway doors.

Mark 2C: Lowered ceiling with twin strips of fluorescent lighting and ducting for air conditioning, but air conditioning not fitted.

Mark 2D: Air conditioning. No opening top-lights in windows.

Mark 2E: Smaller toilets with luggage racks opposite. Fawn folding gangway doors.

Mark 2F: Plastic interior panels. Inter-City 70 type seats. Modified air conditioning system.

The Mark 3 design has BT10 bogies, is 75 ft. (23 m.) long and is of fully integral construction with Inter-City 70 type seats. Gangway doors were yellow (red in RFB) when new, although these are being changed on refurbishment. Loco-hauled coaches are classified Mark 3A, Mark 3 being reserved for HST trailers. A new batch of FO and BFO, classified Mark 3B, was built in 1985 with Advanced Passenger Train-style seating and revised lighting. The last vehicles in the Mark 3 series were the driving brake vans built for West Coast Main Line services.

The Mark 4 design was built by Metro-Cammell for use on the East Coast Main Line after electrification and features a body profile suitable for tilting trains, although tilt is not fitted, and is not intended to be. This design is suitable for 140 m.p.h. running, although is restricted to 125 m.p.h. because the signalling system on the route is not suitable for the higher speed. The bogies for these coaches were built by SIG in Switzerland and are designated BT41. Power operated sliding plug exterior doors are standard.

2.1. BR NUMBER SERIES STOCK
PASSENGER STOCK

AJ11 (RF)   RESTAURANT FIRST

Dia. AJ106. Mark 1. 325 spent most of its life as a Royal Train vehicle and was numbered 2907 for a time. Built with Commonwealth bogies, but B5 bogies substituted. 24/–. ETH 2.

Lot No. 30633 Swindon 1961. 41 t.

325   **PC** VS *SS*   SL

AP1Z (PFK)   PULLMAN FIRST WITH KITCHEN

Dia. AP101. Mark 2. Pressure Ventilated. 18/– 2T. B5 bogies. ETH 6.

Lot No. 30755 Derby 1966. 40 t.

504	**PC** WC *SS*	CS	ULLSWATER
506	**PC** WC *SS*	CS	WINDERMERE

AQ1Z (PFP)   PULLMAN PARLOUR FIRST

Dia. AQ101. Mark 2. Pressure Ventilated. 36/– 2T. B4 bogies. ETH 5.

Lot No. 30754 Derby 1966. 35 t.

546	**PC** WC *SS*	CS	CONISTON WATER
548	**PC** WC *SS*	CS	GRASMERE
549	**PC** WC *SS*	CS	BASSENTHWAITE LAKE
550	**PC** WC *SS*	CS	RYDAL WATER
551	**PC** WC *SS*	CS	BUTTERMERE
552	**PC** WC *SS*	CS	ENNERDALE WATER
553	**PC** WC *SS*	CS	CRUMMOCK WATER

AR1Z (PFB)   PULLMAN BRAKE FIRST

Dia. AR101. Mark 2. Pressure Ventilated. 30/– 2T. B4 bogies. ETH 4.

Lot No. 30753 Derby 1966. 35 t.

586   **PC** WC *SS*   CS   DERWENTWATER

AJ21 (RG)   GRIDDLE CAR

Dia. AJ210. Mark 1. Rebuilt from RF. –/30. B5 bogies. ETH 2.

This vehicle was numbered DB975878 for a time when in departmental service for British Railways

Lot No. 30013 Doncaster 1952. Rebuilt Wolverton 1965. 40 t.

1105   (302)   v   **G**   MH   *SS*   RL

AJ1F (RFB)   BUFFET OPEN FIRST

Dia. AJ104. Mark 2F. Air conditioned. Converted 1988–9/91 at BREL, Derby from
Mark 2F FOs. 1200/1/3/6/11/14–17/20/21/50/2/5/6/9 have Stones equipment,
others have Temperature Ltd. 25/– 1T 1W (except 1217 and 1253 which are 26/
– 1T). B4 bogies. p. q. d. ETH 6X.

1200/3/6/11/14/16/20/52/5/6. Lot No. 30845 Derby 1973. 33 t.
1201/4/5/7/8/10/12/13/15/17–9/21/50/1/4/8/60. Lot No. 30859 Derby 1973–
74. 33 t.
1202/9/53/9. Lot No. 30873 Derby 1974–75. 33 t.

† Fitted with new m.a. sets.
b In use as a Pendolino barrier vehicle.

Note: 1200/03/60 are leased to Riviera Trains.

1200	(3287, 6459)	†	**RV**	H	*SS*	OM
1201	(3361, 6445)	†	**V**	H		TM
1202	(3436, 6456)	†	**V**	H		KT
1203	(3291)	†		H	*SS*	OM
1204	(3401)	†	**V**	H		KT
1205	(3329, 6438)	†	**V**	H		KT
1206	(3319)	†	**V**	H		PY
1207	(3328, 6422)	†	**V**	H		KT
1208	(3393)		**V**	H		KT
1209	(3437, 6457)	†	**V**	H		KT
1210	(3405, 6462)	†	**V**	H		KT
1211	(3305)			H		DY
1212	(3427, 6453)	†	**V**	H		KT
1213	(3419)	†	**V**	H		KT
1214	(3317, 6433)		**AR**	H	*AR*	NC
1215	(3377)		**AR**	H	*AR*	NC
1216	(3302)	†	**V**	H		KT
1217	(3357, 6444)		**CS**	H	*SR*	IS
1218	(3332)		**AR**	H	*AR*	NC
1219	(3418)		**AR**	H	*AR*	NC
1220	(3315, 6432)	†	**V**	H		DY
1221	(3371)			H		DY
1250	(3372)	†	**V**	H		KT
1251	(3383)	†	**V**	H		KT
1252	(3280)	†	**V**	H		KT
1253	(3432)	†	**V**	H		KT
1254	(3391)	†	**V**	H		KT
1255	(3284)	†	**V**	H		KT
1256	(3296)	†		H		DY
1258	(3322)	†b	**V**	H	*FL*	CP
1259	(3439)	†	**V**	H		KT
1260	(3378)	†	**V**	H	*SS*	CP

AK51 (RKB)   KITCHEN BUFFET

Dia. AK502. Mark 1. No seats. B5 bogies. ETH 1.

Lot No. 30624 Cravens 1960–61. 41 t.

1566   **VN** VS   *SS*   CP

AJ41 (RBR)   RESTAURANT BUFFET

Dia. AJ403. Mark 1. Built with 23 loose chairs (Dia. AJ402). All remaining vehicles refurbished with 23 fixed polypropylene chairs and fluorescent lighting. ETH 2 (2X*).

r Further refurbished with 21 chairs, payphone, wheelchair space and carpets (Dia. AJ416).
s Modified for use as servery vehicle with 14 chairs (1680) or 8 chairs (1698).

1651–1699. Lot No. 30628 Pressed Steel 1960–61. Commonwealth bogies. 39 t.
1730. Lot No. 30512 BRCW 1960–61. B5 bogies. 37 t.

Non-standard Liveries:
1651, 1683 and 1699 are Oxford blue.

1651		**O**	RV		CP	1683	r	**O**	RV	*SS*	OM
1658		**BG**	RS	*SS*	BN	1692	xr	**CH**	RV	*SS*	CP
1659	x	**PC**	WT	*SS*	OM	1696		**G**	RS	*SS*	BN
1671	x*	**M**	RS	*SS*	BN	1698	s	**GC**	RS	*SS*	BN
1674			RS	*SS*	BN	1699	r	**O**	RV	*SS*	OM
1679		**G**	RS	*SS*	BN	1730	x	**M**	BK	*SS*	BT
1680	x*s	**GC**	RS	*SS*	BN						

AN2F (RSS)   SELF-SERVICE BUFFET CAR

Dia. AN205. Mark 2F. Air conditioned. Temperature Ltd. equipment. Inter-City 70 seats. Converted 1974 from a Mark 2F TSO as a prototype self-service buffet for APT-P. Sold to Northern Ireland Railways 1983 and regauged to 5'3". Since withdrawn, repatriated to Great Britain and converted back to standard gauge. –/24. B5 bogies. ETH 12X.

Lot No. 30860 Derby 1973–74. 33 t.

1800   (5970, NIR546)   **PC** WT *SS*   OM

AN21 (RMB)   MINIATURE BUFFET CAR

Dia. AN203. Mark 1. –/44 2T. These vehicles are basically an open standard with two full window spaces removed to accommodate a buffet counter, and four seats removed to allow for a stock cupboard. All remaining vehicles now have fluorescent lighting. All vehicles have Commonwealth bogies except 1850 (B5). ETH 3.

1813–1832. Lot No. 30520 Wolverton 1960. 38 t.
1840–1842. Lot No. 30507 Wolverton 1960. 37 t.
1859–1863. Lot No. 30670 Wolverton 1961–62. 38 t.
1882. Lot No. 30702 Wolverton 1962. 38 t.

1842 has been refurbished and fitted with a microwave oven and payphone.
Dia. AN208.

1813	x	**M**	RS	*SS*	BN		1860	x	**M**	WC *SS*	CS
1832		**G**	RS	*SS*	BN		1861	x	**CH**	WC *SS*	TM
1840	v	**G**	MH	*SS*	RL		1863	x	**CH**	RV *SS*	CP
1842	x	**CH**	H	*SS*	CP		1882	x	**M**	WC *SS*	CS
1859	x	**M**	BK	*SS*	BT						

AJ41 (RBR) RESTAURANT BUFFET

Dia. AJ414. Mark 1. These vehicles were built as unclassified restaurant (RU).
They were rebuilt with buffet counters and 23 fixed polypropylene chairs (RBS),
then further refurbished by fitting fluorescent lighting and reclassified RBR. ETH
2X.

1953. Lot No. 30575 Swindon 1960. B4/B5 bogies. 36.5 t.
1961/1981. Lot No. 30632 Swindon 1961. Commonwealth bogies. 39 t.

1953	**VN**	VS	*SS*	CP
1961	x **G**	MH	*SS*	RL
1981	**M**	FR	*SS*	CS

AU51 CHARTER TRAIN STAFF COACHES

Dia. AU501. Mark 1. Converted from BCKs in 1988. Commonwealth bogies. ETH 2.

Lot No. 30732 Derby 1964. 37 t.

2833	(21270)	**BG**	RS	*SS*	BN		2834	(21267)	**GC** RS *SS* BN

AT5G HM THE QUEEN'S SALOON

Dia. AT525. Mark 3. Converted from a FO built 1972. Consists of a lounge,
bedroom and bathroom for HM The Queen, and a combined bedroom and
bathroom for the Queen's dresser. One entrance vestibule has double doors.
Air conditioned. BT10 bogies. ETH 9X.

Lot No. 30886 Wolverton 1977. 36 t.

2903	(11001)	**RP**	NR	*RP*	ZN

AT5G HRH THE DUKE OF EDINBURGH'S SALOON

Dia. AT526. Mark 3. Converted from a TSO built 1972. Consists of a combined
lounge/dining room, a bedroom and a shower room for the Duke, a kitchen and
a valet's bedroom and bathroom. Air conditioned. BT10 bogies. ETH 15X.

Lot No. 30887 Wolverton 1977. 36 t.

2904	(12001)	**RP**	NR	*RP*	ZN

AT5B — ROYAL HOUSEHOLD COUCHETTE

Dia. AT528. Mark 2B. Converted from a BFK built 1969. Consists of luggage accommodation, guards compartment and staff accommodation. Pressure ventilated. B5 bogies. ETH 4X.

Lot No. 30889 Wolverton 1977. 35.5 t.

2906   (14112)   **RP**   NR   DY

AT5G — ROYAL HOUSEHOLD SLEEPING CAR

Dia. AT531. Mark 3A. Built to similar specification as SLE 10646–732. 12 sleeping compartments for use of Royal Household with a fixed lower berth and a hinged upper berth. 2T plus shower room. Air conditioned. BT10 bogies. ETH 11X.

Lot No. 31002 Derby/Wolverton 1985. 44 t.

2915   **RP**   NR   *RP*   ZN

AT5G — ROYAL KITCHEN/DINING CAR

Dia. AT537. Mark 3. Converted from HST TRUK built 1976. Large kitchen retained, but dining area modified for Royal use seating up to 14 at central table(s). Air conditioned. BT10 bogies. ETH 13X.

Lot No. 31059 Wolverton 1988. 43 t.

2916   (40512)   **RP**   NR   *RP*   ZN

AT5G ROYAL HOUSEHOLD KITCHEN/DINING CAR

Dia. AT539. Mark 3. Converted from HST TRUK built 1977. Large kitchen retained and dining area slightly modified with seating for 22 Royal Household members. Air conditioned. BT10 bogies. ETH 13X.

Lot No. 31084 Wolverton 1990. 43 t.

2917   (40514)   **RP**   NR   *RP*   ZN

AT5G — ROYAL HOUSEHOLD CARS

Dia. AT538 (AT540*). Mark 3. Converted from HST TRUKs built 1976/7. Air conditioned. BT10 bogies. ETH 10X.

Lot Nos. 31083 (31085*) Wolverton 1989. 41.05 t.

2918   (40515)   **RP**   NR   ZN
2919   (40518)   * **RP**   NR   ZN

AT5B — ROYAL HOUSEHOLD COUCHETTES

Dia. AT536. Mark 2B. Converted from BFK built 1969. Consists of luggage accommodation, guard's compartment, workshop area, 350 kW diesel generator and staff sleeping accommodation. B5 bogies. ETH2X.

Lot No. 31044 Wolverton 1986. 48 t.

2920   (14109, 17109)   **RP**   NR   *RP*   ZN

Dia. AT541. Mark 2B. Converted from BFK built 1969. Consists of luggage accommodation, kitchen, brake control equipment and staff accommodation. B5 bogies. ETH7X.

Lot No. 31086 Wolverton 1990. 41.5 t.

2921   (14107, 17107)   **RP**   NR   *RP*   ZN

AT5G   HRH THE PRINCE OF WALES'S SLEEPING CAR

Dia. AT534. Mark 3B. BT10 bogies. Air conditioned.ETH 7X.

Lot No. 31035 Derby/Wolverton 1987.

2922   **RP**   NR   *RP*   ZN

AT5G   HRH THE PRINCE OF WALES'S SALOON

Dia. AT535. Mark 3B. BT10 bogies. Air conditioned. ETH 6X.

Lot No. 31036 Derby/Wolverton 1987.

2923   **RP**   NR   *RP*   ZN

AD11 (FO)   OPEN FIRST

Dia. AD103. Mark 1. 42/– 2T. ETH 3. Many now fitted with table lamps.

3063–3069. Lot No. 30169 Doncaster 1955. B4 bogies. 33 t.
3096–3100. Lot No. 30576 BRCW 1959. B4 bogies. 33 t.

3064 and 3068 were numbered DB 975607 and DB 975606 for a time when in departmental service for British Railways.

3063	**BG**	VS		SL		3096	× **M**	BK	*SS*	BT
3064	**BG**	VS		SL		3097	**GC**	RS	*SS*	BN
3066	**RV**	RV	*SS*	CP		3098	× **CH**	RV	*SS*	CP
3068	**RV**	RV	*SS*	CP		3100	× **M**	RS	*SS*	BN
3069	**RV**	RV	*SS*	CP						

Later design with fluorescent lighting, aluminium window frames and Commonwealth bogies.

3105–3128. Lot No. 30697 Swindon 1962–63. 36 t.
3130–3150. Lot No. 30717 Swindon 1963. 36 t.

3128/41/3/4/6/7/8 were renumbered 1058/63/5/6/8/9/70 when reclassified RUO, then 3600/8/9/2/6/4/10 when declassified, but have since regained their original numbers.

3105	x	**M**	WC	*SS*	CS		3127		**G**	RS	*SS*	BN
3107	x	**BG**	RV	*SS*	CP		3128	x	**M**	WC	*SS*	CS
3110	x	**M**	RS	*SS*	BN		3130	v	**M**	WC	*SS*	CS
3112	x	**CH**	RV	*SS*	CP		3131	x	**M**	RS	*SS*	BN
3113	x	**M**	WC	*SS*	CS		3132	x	**M**	RS	*SS*	BN
3114		**G**	RS	*SS*	BN		3133	x	**M**	RS	*SS*	BN
3115	x	**BG**	RS	*SS*	BN		3140	x	**CH**	RV	*SS*	CP
3117	x	**M**	WC	*SS*	CS		3141		**GC**	RS	*SS*	BN
3119	x	**G**	RS	*SS*	BN		3143		**M**	WC	*SS*	CS
3120		**GC**	RS	*SS*	BN		3144	x	**M**	RS	*SS*	BN
3121		**GC**	RS	*SS*	BN		3146		**GC**	RS	*SS*	BN
3122	x	**CH**	RV	*SS*	CP		3147		**GC**	RS	*SS*	BN
3123		**G**	RS	*SS*	BN		3148		**BG**	RV	*SS*	CP
3124		**G**	RS	*SS*	BN		3149		**GC**	RS	*SS*	BN
3125		**RV**	RV	*SS*	CP		3150		**G**	RS	*SS*	BN

AD1D (FO)   OPEN FIRST

Dia. AD105. Mark 2D. Air conditioned. 3172–88 have Stones equipment. 3202 has Temperature Ltd. 42/– 2T. B4 bogies. ETH 5.

† Table lights fitted and facelifted for VSOE "Northern Belle".

Lot No. 30821 Derby 1971–72. 34 t.

3172			NR	*SO*	DY		3182	†	**VN**	VS	*SS*	CP
3174	†	**VN**	VS	*SS*	CP		3186			MA		DY
3178			VS		CP		3188		**RV**	RV	*SS*	OM
3181		**RV**	RV	*SS*	OM		3192			NR	*SO*	DY

AD1E (FO)   OPEN FIRST

Dia. AD106. Mark 2E. Air conditioned. Stones equipment. 42/– 2T (41/– 2T 1W w, 36/– 2T p). B4 bogies. ETH 5.

r Refurbished with new seats.
u Fitted with power supply for Mk. 1 RBR.
† Table lights fitted and facelifted for VSOE "Northern Belle".

3255 was numbered 3525 for a time when fitted with a pantry.

Lot No. 30843 Derby 1972–73. 32.5 t. (35.8 t †).

Non-standard Livery: 3231 & 3246 are British racing green with gold lining.

Note: 3228, 3229 and 3244 are leased to Riviera Trains.

3223		**RV**	RV	*SS*	OM		3231	p	**0**	RA		CP
3225			E		KT		3232	dr	**FP**	H	*GW*	OO
3226			E		KT		3234	w		VS		CP
3228	du	**RV**	H	*SS*	OM		3235	u		H		PY
3229	d	**RV**	H	*SS*	CP		3239			VS		CP
3230			NR	*SO*	DY		3240		**RV**	RV	*SS*	OM

3241	dr	**FP**	H	*GW*	OO
3242	wu		H		PY
3244	d	**RV**	H	*SS*	OM
3246	p	**0**	RA		CP
3247	†	**VN**	VS	*SS*	CP
3248			NR	*SO*	DY
3252	w		H		PY
3255	dr	**FP**	H	*GW*	OO
3256	w		H		PY
3257	w		VS		CP

3258	n		E		KT
3261	dw	**FP**	H	*NW*	CP
3267	†	**VN**	VS	*SS*	CP
3268			RV		CP
3269	dr	**FP**	H	*GW*	OO
3270			VS		CP
3272			VS		CP
3273	†	**VN**	VS	*SS*	CP
3275	†	**VN**	VS	*SS*	CP

AD1F (FO)   OPEN FIRST

Dia. AD107. Mark 2F. Air conditioned. 3277–3318/58–81 have Stones equipment, others have Temperature Ltd. 42/– 2T. All now refurbished with power-operated vestibule doors, new panels and new seat trim. B4 bogies. d. ETH 5X.

3277–3318. Lot No. 30845 Derby 1973. 33.5 t.
3325–3428. Lot No. 30859 Derby 1973–74. 33.5 t.
3429–3438. Lot No. 30873 Derby 1974–75. 33.5 t.

r Further refurbished with table lamps, modified seats with burgundy seat trim and new m.a. sets.
s Further refurbished with table lamps and modified seats with burgundy seat trim.
u Fitted with power supply for Mk. 1 RBR.

3403 was numbered 6450 for a time when declassified.

3277		**AR**	H	*AR*	NC
3278	r	**V**	H	*VW*	OY
3279	u	**AR**	H	*AR*	NC
3285	s	**V**	H	*VW*	OY
3290		**AR**	H	*AR*	NC
3292			H	*AR*	NC
3293			H		CP
3295		**AR**	H	*AR*	NC
3299	r	**V**	H	*VW*	OY
3300	s	**V**	H	*VW*	OY
3303		**AR**	H	*AR*	NC
3304	r	**V**	H	*VW*	OY
3309			H	*AR*	NC
3312			H		DY
3313	r	**V**	H	*VW*	OY
3314	r	**V**	H	*VW*	OY
3318			H	*AR*	NC
3325	r	**V**	H	*VW*	OY
3326	r	**V**	H	*VW*	OY
3330	r	**V**	H	*VW*	OY
3331		**AR**	H	*AR*	NC
3333	r	**V**	H	*VW*	OY
3334		**AR**	H	*AR*	NC

3336	u	**AR**	H	*AR*	NC
3337	r	**V**	H	*VW*	OY
3338	u	**AR**	H	*AR*	NC
3340	r	**V**	H	*VW*	OY
3344	r	**V**	H	*VW*	OY
3345	r	**V**	H	*VW*	OY
3348	r	**V**	H	*VW*	OY
3350	r	**V**	H	*VW*	OY
3351		**AR**	H	*AR*	NC
3352	r	**V**	H	*VW*	OY
3353	s	**V**	H	*VW*	OY
3354	s	**V**	H	*VW*	OY
3356	r	**V**	H	*VW*	OY
3358		**AR**	H	*AR*	NC
3359	s	**V**	H	*VW*	OY
3360	s	**V**	H	*VW*	OY
3362	s	**V**	H	*VW*	OY
3363	s	**V**	H	*VW*	OY
3364	r	**V**	H	*VW*	OY
3366	s	**V**	H	*VW*	OY
3368		**AR**	H	*AR*	NC
3369	s	**V**	H	*VW*	OY
3373			H		MB

3374		H		DY		3402	s **V**	H	*VW*	OY
3375	**AR**	H	*AR*	NC		3403	s **V**	H	*VW*	OY
3379	u **AR**	H	*AR*	NC		3408	s **V**	H	*VW*	OY
3381		H		Bramley		3411	s **V**	H	*VW*	OY
3384	r **V**	H	*VW*	OY		3414	**AR**	H	*AR*	NC
3385	r **V**	H	*VW*	OY		3416		H	*AR*	NC
3386	r **V**	H	*VW*	OY		3417	**AR**	H	*AR*	NC
3387	s **V**	H	*VW*	OY		3424	**AR**	H	*AR*	NC
3388	**AR**	H	*AR*	NC		3425	s **V**	H	*VW*	OY
3389	s **V**	H	*VW*	OY		3426	r **V**	H	*VW*	OY
3390	r **V**	H	*VW*	OY		3428	s **V**	H	*VW*	OY
3392	r **V**	H	*VW*	OY		3429	r **V**	H	*VW*	OY
3395	r **V**	H	*VW*	OY		3431	r **V**	H	*VW*	OY
3397	r **V**	H	*VW*	OY		3433	r **V**	H	*VW*	OY
3399	u **AR**	H	*AR*	NC		3434	s **V**	H	*VW*	OY
3400	**AR**	H	*AR*	NC		3438	s **V**	H	*VW*	OY

AG1E (FO (T))   OPEN FIRST (PANTRY)

Dia. AG101. Mark 2E. Air conditioned. Converted from FO. Fitted with pantry containing microwave oven and space for a trolley. 36/– 2T. B4 bogies. p. d. ETH 5X.

Lot No. 30843 Derby 1972–73. 32.5 t.

3520	(3253)	**FP**	H	*NW*	CP		3523	(3238)	H		ZA
3521	(3271)	**AR**	H		ZA		3524	(3254)	H		IS
3522	(3236)	**FP**	H	*GW*	OO						

AC21 (TSO)   OPEN STANDARD

Dia. AC204. Mark 1. These vehicles have 2+2 seating and are classified TSO ('Tourist second open'– a former LNER designation). –/64 2T. Commonwealth bogies (originally built with BR Mark 1 bogies). ETH 4.

Lot No. 30079 York 1953. This coach has narrower seats than later vehicles. 36 t.

3766	x **M**	WC *SS*	CS		

AC21 (TSO)   OPEN STANDARD

Dia. AC201. Mark 1. These vehicles are a development of Dia. AC204 with fluorescent lighting and modified design of seat headrest. Built with BR Mark 1 bogies. –/64 2T. ETH 4.

4831–4836. Lot No. 30506 Wolverton 1959. Commonwealth bogies. 33 t.
4849–4880. Lot No. 30525 Wolverton 1959–60. B4 bogies. 33 t.

4831	x **M**	BK *SS*	BT		4854		**RR**	H	KT
4832	x **M**	BK *SS*	BT		4856	x **M**	BK *SS*	BT
4836	x **M**	BK *SS*	BT		4866		**RR**	H	KT
4849	**RR**	H	KT		4880		**RR**	H	KT

Lot No. 30646 Wolverton 1961. Built with Commonwealth bogies, but BR Mark 1 bogies substituted by the SR. All now re-rebogied. 34 t B4, 36 t C.

4902	x B4	**CH**	RV	*SS*	CP		4915	x B4	**M**	RS	*SS*	BN
4905	x C	**M**	WC	*SS*	CS		4916	x B4	**M**	RS	*SS*	BN
4912	x C	**M**	WC	*SS*	CS							

Lot No. 30690 Wolverton 1961–62. Commonwealth bogies and aluminium window frames. 37 t.

4925		**G**	RS	*SS*	BN		4994	x	**M**	WC	*SS*	CS
4927	x	**CH**	RV	*SS*	CP		4996	x	**M**	RS	*SS*	BN
4931	v	**M**	WC	*SS*	CS		4998		**BG**	RS	*SS*	BN
4938		**BG**	RS	*SS*	BN		4999		**BG**	RS	*SS*	BN
4940	x	**M**	WC	*SS*	CS		5002		**BG**	RS	*SS*	BN
4946	x	**M**	RS	*SS*	BN		5005		**BG**	RS	*SS*	BN
4949		**M**	RS	*SS*	BN		5007		**G**	RS	*SS*	BN
4951	x	**M**	WC	*SS*	CS		5008	x	**M**	RS	*SS*	BN
4954	v	**M**	WC	*SS*	CS		5009	x	**CH**	RV	*SS*	CP
4956		**BG**	RS	*SS*	BN		5023		**G**	RS	*SS*	BN
4958	v	**M**	WC	*SS*	CS		5027		**G**	RS	*SS*	BN
4959		**BG**	RS	*SS*	BN		5028	x	**BK**	*SS*		BT
4960		**M**	WC	*SS*	TM		5029	x	**CH**	RV	*SS*	CP
4963	x	**CH**	RV	*SS*	CP		5032	x	**M**	WC	*SS*	CS
4973	x	**M**	WC	*SS*	TM		5033	x	**M**	WC	*SS*	CS
4977		**G**	RS	*SS*	BN		5035	x	**M**	WC	*SS*	CS
4984	x	**M**	WC	*SS*	CS		5037		**G**	RS	*SS*	BN
4986		**G**	RS	*SS*	BN		5040	x	**CH**	RV	*SS*	CP
4991		**BG**	RS	*SS*	BN		5044	x	**M**	WC	*SS*	CS

AC2Z (TSO)   OPEN STANDARD

Dia. AC205. Mark 2. Pressure ventilated. –/64 2T. B4 bogies. ETH 4.

Lot No. 30751 Derby 1965–67. 32 t.

Note: 5157/77/91/98 are leased to Vintage Trains.

5125	v	**G**	MH	*SS*	RL		5186	v	**RR**	H		TM
5132	v	**LN**	H		LT		5191	v	**CH**	H	*SS*	TM
5135	v	**RR**	H		LT		5193	v	**LN**	H		TM
5148	v	**RR**	H		TM		5194	v	**RR**	H		TM
5157	v	**CH**	H	*SS*	TM		5198	v	**CH**	H	*SS*	TM
5161	v	**RR**	H		LT		5200	v	**G**	MH	*SS*	RL
5163	v	**RR**	H		LT		5207	v	**RR**	H		LT
5167	v	**RR**	H		LT		5212	v	**LN**	H		TM
5171	v	**G**	MH	*SS*	RL		5216	v	**G**	MH	*SS*	RL
5177	v	**CH**	H	*SS*	TM		5221	v	**RR**	H		TM
5179	v	**RR**	H		TM		5222	v	**G**	MH	*SS*	RL
5180	v	**RR**	H		LT		5226	v	**RR**	H		LT
5183	v	**RR**	H		TM							

AD2Z (SO)   OPEN STANDARD

Dia. AD203. Mark 2. Pressure ventilated. –/48 2T. B4 bogies. ETH 4.

Lot No. 30752 Derby 1966. 32 t.

5229	**PC**	WT	*SS*	OM		5239	**PC**	WT	*SS*	OM
5236	v **G**	MH	*SS*	RL		5249	v **G**	MH	*SS*	RL
5237	v **G**	MH	*SS*	RL						

AC2A (TSO)   OPEN STANDARD

Dia. AC206. Mark 2A. Pressure ventilated. –/64 2T (–/62 2T w). B4 bogies. ETH 4.

5265–5345. Lot No. 30776 Derby 1967–68. 32 t.
5350–5433. Lot No. 30787 Derby 1968. 32 t.

5265	**RR**	H		KT		5353	**RR**	H		KT
5266	**RR**	RV		CP		5354	**RR**	H		PY
5267	**RR**	H		KT		5364	**RV**	RV	*SS*	CP
5275	**RV**	RV	*SS*	CP		5365	**RV**	RV	*SS*	CP
5276	**RV**	RV	*SS*	OM		5366	**RV**	RV	*SS*	OM
5278	**PC**	WT	*SS*	OM		5373	**RV**	RV	*SS*	CP
5292	**RV**	RV	*SS*	OM		5376	**RV**	RV	*SS*	CP
5293	**NB**	H		KT		5378	**RV**	RV	*SS*	CP
5299	**M**	WC	*SS*	CS		5379	**RR**	H		KT
5304	**RR**	RV		CP		5381	w **RR**	RV		KT
5307	**RV**	RV	*SS*	CP		5384	**N**	RV		CP
5309	**CH**	RV	*SS*	CP		5386	w **RR**	RS		BN
5322	**RV**	RV	*SS*	OM		5389	w **PC**	WT	*SS*	OM
5331	**RR**	RS		BN		5410	**N**			KT
5335	**RR**	RV	*SS*	CP		5412	w **RR**	RV	*SS*	CP
5341	**RV**	RV	*SS*	OM		5419	w **PC**	WT	*SS*	OM
5345	**RR**	RV		KT		5420	w **PC**	WT	*SS*	OM
5350	**RV**	RV	*SS*	CP		5433	w **RR**	WT		TM

AC2B (TSO)   OPEN STANDARD

Dia. AC207. Mark 2B. Pressure ventilated. –/62 2T. B4 bogies. ETH 4.

Note: 5482 was numbered DB977936 for a time when in departmental service for British Railways.

Lot No. 30791 Derby 1969. 32 t.

5443	**N**	H		KT		5464	**N**	RV		CP
5446	**N**	H		KT		5471	**N**	H		KT
5447	**N**	RV		CP		5472	**N**	H		KT
5449	**N**	RV		CP		5475	**N**	H		KT
5450	**N**	RV		CP		5478	d **M**	WC	*VL*	CF
5453	d **M**	WC	*VL*	CF		5480	**N**	H		KT
5454	**N**	H		KT		5482	**G**	RS	*SS*	BN
5463	d **M**	WC	*VL*	CF		5487	d **M**	WC	*VL*	CF

| 5491 d | **M** | WC | *VL* | CF | | 5494 | **N** | RV | | CP |

AC2C (TSO)   OPEN STANDARD

Dia. AC208. Mark 2C. Pressure ventilated. –/62 2T. B4 bogies. ETH 4.

Lot No. 30795 Derby 1969–70. 32 t.

| 5569 d | **M** | WC | *VL* | CF | | 5600 | **M** | WC | *SS* | CS |

AC2D (TSO)   OPEN STANDARD

Dia. AC209. Mark 2D. Air conditioned. Stones equipment. –/62 2T. B4 bogies. ETH 5.

Non-Standard Livery: 5630, 5732 & 5739 are **WV** without lining.

r Refurbished with new seats and end luggage stacks. –/58 2T.

Lot No. 30822 Derby 1971. 33 t.

5616		RS		FP		5690		H		PY
5618		H		PY		5700 dr	**FP**	H	*GW*	OO
5620		H		PY		5704	**M**	WC	*SS*	CS
5623		H		PY		5710 dr	**FP**	H	*GW*	OO
5629		H		PY		5711		H		PY
5630	**0**	RV		CP		5714	**M**	WC	*SS*	CS
5631 dr	**FP**	H	*GW*	OO		5715		H		PY
5632 dr	**FP**	H	*GW*	OO		5724		H		PY
5636 dr	**FP**	H	*GW*	OO		5726		H		PY
5640		H		PY		5727	**M**	WC	*SS*	CS
5647	**RV**	RV	*SS*	CP		5728		H		PY
5650		H		PY		5732	**0**	RV		CP
5657 dr	**FP**	H	*GW*	OO		5737 dr	**FP**	H	*GW*	OO
5669 dr	**FP**	H	*GW*	OO		5739	**0**	RV		CP
5679 dr	**FP**	H	*GW*	OO		5740 dr	**FP**	H	*GW*	OO

AC2E (TSO)   OPEN STANDARD

Dia. AC210. Mark 2E. Air conditioned. Stones equipment. –/64 2T (w –/62 2T 1W). B4 bogies. d (except 5756 and 5879). ETH 5.

5744–5801. Lot No. 30837 Derby 1972. 33.5 t.
5810–5906. Lot No. 30844 Derby 1972–73. 33.5 t.

r Refurbished with new interior panelling.
s Refurbished with new interior panelling, modified design of seat headrest and centre luggage stack. –/60 2T (w –/58 2T 1W).
t Refurbished with new interior panelling and new seats.

Note: 5748/52/69/73/76/91/92/94/96, 5814/16/43 and 5905 are leased to Riviera Trains.

5744		**FP**	H	*GW*	OO		5750 s		**V**	H		KT
5745 s		**V**	H		KT		5752 wrpt			H	*SS*	OM
5746 r		**V**	H		KT		5754 ws		**V**	H		KT
5748 r pt			H	*SS*	OM		5756		**M**	WC	*SS*	CS

No.					
5769	r		H	SS	OM
5773	s pt	V	H	SS	CP
5775	s	V	H		KT
5776	r		H	SS	OM
5778		AR	H	AR	NC
5779	r		H		DY
5780		AR	H	AR	NC
5781		AR	H		NC
5784	r	V	H		KT
5787	s	V	H		KT
5788	r		H		DY
5789	r pt		H		BH
5791	wr		H	SS	OM
5792	r		H	SS	OM
5793	wspt	V	H		KT
5794	wr		H	SS	OM
5796	wr		H	SS	OM
5797	r		H		DY
5800		AR	H	AR	NC
5801	r	V	H		KT
5810	s	V	H		KT
5812	wr		H		DY
5814	r		H	SS	OM
5815	ws	V	H		KT
5816	r pt		H	SS	OM
5821	r pt	V	H		KT
5822	wspt	V	H		KT
5824	rw		H		BH
5827	r		H		BH
5828	ws	V	H		KT

No.					
5831		AR	H	AR	NC
5836		AR	H	AR	NC
5843	rw		H	SS	OM
5845	s	V	H		KT
5847	rw	V	H		KT
5852		AR	H	AR	NC
5853	t	M	WC	VL	CF
5859	s	V	H		KT
5863		AR	H	AR	NC
5866	r pt		H		DY
5868	s pt	V	H		KT
5869	t	M	WC	VL	CF
5874	t	M	WC	VL	CF
5876	s pt	V	H		KT
5879			RV		CP
5881	ws	V	H		KT
5886	s	V	H		KT
5887	wr	AR	H	AR	NC
5888	wr		H		DY
5889	s	V	H		KT
5893	s	V	H		KT
5897	r		H		BH
5899	s	V	H		KT
5900	wspt	V	H		KT
5901	s	V	H		KT
5902	s	V	H		KT
5903	s	V	H		KT
5905	s	V	H	SS	CP
5906	wspt		H		BH

AC2F (TSO)   OPEN STANDARD

Dia. AC211. Mark 2F. Air conditioned. Temperature Ltd. equipment. Inter-City 70 seats. All were refurbished in the 1980s with power-operated vestibule doors, new panels and new seat trim. –/64 2T. (w –/62 2T 1W) B4 bogies. d. ETH 5X.

5908–5958. Lot No. 30846 Derby 1973. 33 t.
5959–6170. Lot No. 30860 Derby 1973–74. 33 t.
6171–6184. Lot No. 30874 Derby 1974–75. 33 t.

* Early Mark 2 style seats.

These vehicles have undergone a second refurbishment with carpets and new seat trim .

Former Cross-Country vehicles:

r Standard refurbished vehicles with new m.a. sets.
s Also fitted with centre luggage stack. –/60 2T.
t Also fitted with centre luggage stack and wheelchair space. –/58 2T 1W.

West Coast vehicles:

r Standard refurbished vehicles with new seat trim and new m.a. sets.
u As 'r' but with two wheelchair spaces. –/60 2T 2W.
† Standard refurbished vehicles with new seat trim.

Notes: 5976, 6060/67 and 6157 are leased to Riviera Trains.
5925/58/81 and 6168 are fitted for blue star push-pull operation.

No.						No.					
5908	r	**V**	H	*VW*	OY	5955	r	**V**	H	*VW*	OY
5910	u	**V**	H	*VW*	OY	5956			H	*AR*	NC
5911	s	**V**	H		PY	5957	r	**V**	H	*VW*	OY
5912	s	**V**	H		KT	5958	s		H	*WX*	CF
5913	s	**M**	WC	*VL*	CF	5959	n	**AR**	H	*AR*	NC
5914	u	**V**	H	*VW*	OY	5960	s	**V**	H		KT
5915	r	**V**	H	*VW*	OY	5961	s pt	**V**	H		PY
5916	t		H		KT	5962	s pt	**V**	H		KT
5917	s	**V**	H		KT	5963	r	**V**	H	*VW*	OY
5918	t	**V**	H		KT	5964		**AR**	H	*AR*	NC
5919	s pt	**V**	H		KT	5965	t	**M**	WC	*VL*	CF
5920	†	**V**	H	*VW*	OY	5966		**AR**	H	*AR*	NC
5921		**AR**	H	*AR*	NC	5967	t	**V**	H		KT
5922		**AR**	H	*AR*	NC	5968		**AR**	H	*AR*	NC
5924		**AR**	H	*AR*	NC	5969	u	**V**	H	*VW*	OY
5925	s pt		H	*WX*	CF	5971	s		H		PY
5926			H	*AR*	NC	5973		**AR**	H	*AR*	NC
5927		**AR**	H	*AR*	NC	5975	s	**V**	H		KT
5928		**AR**	H	*AR*	NC	5976	t	**V**	H	*SS*	CP
5929		**AR**	H	*AR*	NC	5977	r	**V**	H	*VW*	OY
5930	t	**V**	H		KT	5978	r	**V**	H	*VW*	OY
5931	†w	**V**	H	*VW*	OY	5980	r	**V**	H	*VW*	OY
5932	r	**V**	H	*VW*	OY	5981	s		H	*WX*	CF
5933	r	**V**	H	*VW*	OY	5983	s	**V**	H		KT
5934	r	**V**	H	*VW*	OY	5984	r	**V**	H	*VW*	OY
5935		**AR**	H	*AR*	NC	5985		**AR**	H	*AR*	NC
5936		**AR**	H	*AR*	NC	5986	r	**V**	H	*VW*	OY
5937	r	**V**	H	*VW*	OY	5987	r	**V**	H	*VW*	OY
5939	r	**V**	H	*VW*	OY	5988	r	**V**	H	*VW*	OY
5940	u	**V**	H	*VW*	OY	5989	t	**V**	H		KT
5941	r	**V**	H	*VW*	OY	5991	s	**V**	H		KT
5943	rw	**V**	H	*VW*	OY	5993	*	**AR**	H	*AR*	NC
5944		**AR**	H	*AR*	NC	5994	r	**V**	H		KT
5945	r	**V**	H	*VW*	OY	5995	s		H		KT
5946	r	**V**	H	*VW*	OY	5996	s pt	**V**	H		KT
5947	s pt	**V**	H		KT	5997	r	**V**	H	*VW*	OY
5948	u	**V**	H	*VW*	OY	5998		**AR**	H	*AR*	NC
5949	u	**V**	H	*VW*	OY	5999	s	**V**	H		KT
5950		**AR**	H	*AR*	NC	6000	t	**V**	H		KT
5951	r	**V**	H		KT	6001	u	**V**	H		KT
5952	r	**V**	H	*VW*	OY	6002	†	**V**	H	*VW*	OY
5953	†	**V**	H	*VW*	OY	6005	r	**V**	H		KT
5954		**AR**	H	*AR*	NC	6006		**AR**	H	*AR*	NC

No.					
6008	s	**V**	H		PY
6009	r	**V**	H	*VW*	OY
6010	s	**V**	H		KT
6011	s	**V**	H		KT
6012	r	**V**	H	*VW*	OY
6013	s	**M**	WC	*VL*	CF
6014	s pt		H		KT
6015	t	**V**	H		KT
6016	r	**V**	H	*VW*	OY
6018	t	**V**	H		KT
6021	r	**V**	H	*VW*	OY
6022	s	**V**	H		KT
6024	s	**V**	H		PY
6025	t	**V**	H		KT
6026	s	**V**	H		KT
6027	u	**V**	H	*VW*	OY
6028		**AR**	H	*AR*	NC
6029	r	**V**	H	*VW*	OY
6030	t	**V**	H		PY
6031	r	**V**	H	*VW*	OY
6034		**AR**	H	*AR*	NC
6035	t		H		KT
6036	*	**AR**	H	*AR*	NC
6037		**AR**	H	*AR*	NC
6038	s	**V**	H		PY
6041	s	**V**	H		KT
6042		**AR**	H	*AR*	NC
6043	†	**V**	H	*VW*	OY
6045	†tw	**V**	H	*VW*	OY
6046	s	**V**	H		KT
6047	†n*	**V**	H	*VW*	OY
6049	r	**V**	H	*VW*	OY
6050	s		H		KT
6051	r	**V**	H	*VW*	OY
6052	tw		H		KT
6053	*	**AR**	H	*AR*	NC
6054	r	**V**	H	*VW*	OY
6055	†	**V**	H	*VW*	OY
6056	†	**V**	H	*VW*	OY
6057	r	**V**	H	*VW*	OY
6059	s	**V**	H		KT
6060	u	**V**	H	*VW*	OY
6061	s pt	**V**	H		KT
6062	†	**V**	H	*VW*	OY
6063	†tw	**V**	H	*VW*	OY
6064	s	**V**	H	*SS*	CP
6065	r	**V**	H	*VW*	OY
6066	s		H		KT
6067	s pt	**V**	H	*SS*	CP
6073	s	**V**	H		KT
6100	†*	**V**	H	*VW*	OY
6101	r	**V**	H	*VW*	OY
6102	r	**V**	H	*VW*	OY
6103		**AR**	H	*AR*	NC
6104	r	**V**	H	*VW*	OY
6105	tpt	**V**	H		PY
6106	r	**V**	H	*VW*	OY
6107	r	**V**	H	*VW*	OY
6110			H	*AR*	NC
6111	†	**V**	H	*VW*	OY
6112	s pt	**V**	H		KT
6113	†	**V**	H	*VW*	OY
6115	s		H		KT
6116	†	**V**	H	*VW*	OY
6117	t	**V**	H		BM
6119	s		H		PY
6120	s	**V**	H		KT
6121	†	**V**	H	*VW*	OY
6122	s	**V**	H		BM
6123		**AR**	H	*AR*	NC
6124	s pt		H		KT
6134	†	**V**	H	*VW*	OY
6135	s		H		KT
6136	r	**V**	H	*VW*	OY
6137	s pt	**V**	H		PY
6138	†	**V**	H	*VW*	OY
6139	n*		H	*AR*	NC
6141	u	**V**	H	*VW*	OY
6142	†*	**V**	H	*VW*	OY
6143	†*	**V**	H	*VW*	OY
6144	†*	**V**	H	*VW*	OY
6145	s pt	**V**	H		KT
6146	*	**AR**	H	*AR*	NC
6147	r	**V**	H	*VW*	OY
6148	s		H		KT
6149	u	**V**	H	*VW*	OY
6150	s		H		KT
6151	†*	**V**	H	*VW*	OY
6152	*	**AR**	H	*AR*	NC
6153	†	**V**	H	*VW*	OY
6154	r pt		H		KT
6155	*	**AR**	H	*AR*	NC
6157	s	**V**	H	*SS*	CP
6158	r	**V**	H	*VW*	OY
6159	s pt	**V**	H		KT
6160	*	**AR**	H	*AR*	NC
6161	†*	**V**	H	*VW*	OY
6162	s pt	**V**	H		PY
6163	r	**V**	H	*VW*	OY
6164	†	**V**	H	*VW*	OY
6165	r	**V**	H	*VW*	OY
6166			H	*AR*	NC
6167		**AR**	H	*AR*	NC

6168	s		H	WX	CF	6177	s	**V**	H		PY
6170	s	**V**	H		KT	6178	s		H		KT
6171	†	**V**	H	VW	OY	6179	r	**V**	H	VW	OY
6172	s	**V**	H		KT	6180	†w	**V**	H	VW	OY
6173	s	**V**	H		BM	6181	†wn	**V**	H	VW	OY
6174		**AR**	H	AR	NC	6182	s	**V**	H		KT
6175	r	**V**	H	VW	OY	6183	s	**V**	H		PY
6176	t	**V**	H		PY	6184	s	**V**	H		KT

AC2D (TSO)   OPEN STANDARD

Dia. AC217. Mark 2D. Air conditioned (Stones). Rebuilt from FO with new style 2+2 seats. –/58 2T. (–/58 1T*). B4 bogies. d. ETH 5X.

Lot No. 30821 Derby 1971–72. 33.5 t.

* One toilet converted to store room.

6200	(3198)		**FP**	H	NW	CP	6212	(3176)		**FP**	H	GW	OO
6202	(3191)*		**FP**	H	NW	CP	6213	(3208)		**FP**	H	NW	CP
6203	(3180)		**FP**	H	GW	OO	6219	(3213)		**FP**	H	GW	OO
6206	(3183)		**FP**	H	NW	CP	6221	(3173)		**FP**	H	NW	CP
6207	(3204)		**FP**	H	GW	OO	6226	(3203)		**FP**	H	GW	OO

AX51   BRAKE GENERATOR VAN

Dia. AX501. Mark 1. Renumbered 1989 from BR departmental series. Converted from NDA in 1973 to three-phase supply brake generator van for use with HST trailers. Modified 1999 for use with loco-hauled stock. B5 bogies.

Lot No. 30400 Pressed Steel 1958.

6310	(81448, 975325)	**CH**	RV	SS	CP

AX51   GENERATOR VAN

Dia. AX501. Mark 1. Converted from NDA in 1992 to generator vans for use on Anglo-Scottish sleeping car services. Now normally used on trains hauled by steam locomotives. B4 bogies. ETH75.

6311. Lot No. 30162 Pressed Steel 1958. 37.25 t.
6312. Lot No. 30224 Cravens 1956. 37.25 t.
6313. Lot No. 30484 Pressed Steel 1958. 37.25 t.

6313 is leased to the Venice Simplon Orient Express.

6311	(80903, 92911)	**B**	RS	SS	BN
6312	(81023, 92925)	**PC**	FS	SS	SO
6313	(81553, 92167)	**PC**	P	SS	SL

GS5 (HSBV)   HST BARRIER VEHICLE

Various diagrams. Renumbered from BR departmental series, or converted from various types. B4 bogies (Commonwealth bogies *).

6330. Dia. GS503. Mark 2A. Lot No. 30786 Derby 1968. 32 t.
6334. Dia. GS507. Mark 1. Lot No. 30400 Pressed Steel 1957–8. 31.5 t.
6336/38/44. Dia. GS507. Mark 1. Lot No. 30715 Gloucester 1962. 31 t.
6340. Dia. GS504. Mark 1. Lot No. 30669 Swindon 1962. 36 t.
6346. Dia. GS511. Mark 2A. Lot No. 30777 Derby 1967. 31.5 t.
6348. Dia. GS507. Mark 1. Lot No. 30163 Pressed Steel 1957. 31.5 t.

Non-standard Livery: 6344 & 6346 are GNER plain dark blue.

6330	(14084, 975629)	**G**	A	*GW*	LA
6334	(81478, 92128)	**P**	P	*VX*	NL
6336	(81591, 92185)	**G**	A	*GW*	LA
6338	(81581, 92180)	**G**	A	*GW*	LA
6340	(21251, 975678)	* **G**	A	*GW*	LA
6344	(81263, 92080)	**0**	A	*GN*	EC
6346	(9422)	**0**	A	*GN*	EC
6348	(81233, 92963)	**G**	A	*GW*	LA

AV5 (MFBV)   MARK 4 BARRIER VEHICLE

Various diagrams. Converted from FK* or BSO. B4 bogies.

6352/3. Dia. AV501/2 respectively. Mark 2A. Lot No. 30774 Derby 1968. 33 t.
6354/5. Dia. AV504. Mark 2C. Lot No. 30820 Derby 1970. 32 t.
6358/9. Dia. AV505. Mark 2A. Lot No. 30788 Derby 1968. 31.5 t.

Non-standard Livery: GNER plain dark blue.

6352	(13465, 19465)	* **0**	H	*GN*	BN
6353	(13478, 19478)	* **0**	H	*GN*	BN
6354	(9459)	**0**	H	*GN*	BN
6355	(9477)	**0**	H	*GN*	BN
6358	(9432)	**0**	H	*GN*	BN
6359	(9429)	**0**	H	*GN*	BN

AW5 (BV)   EMU TRANSLATOR VEHICLE

Dia. AW504. Mark 1. Converted 1992 from BG.

6364. Mark 1. Lot No. 30039 Derby 1954. BR Mark 1 bogies. 32 t.
6365. Mark 1. Lot No. 30323 Pressed Steel 1957. BR Mark 1 bogies. 32 t.

6364	(80565)	**RR**	P	*CT*	SI
6365	(81296, 84296)	**RR**	P	*CT*	SI

GS5 (HSBV)   HST BARRIER VEHICLE

Dia. GS507. Mark 1. Converted from BG in 1994–5. B4 bogies.

6392. Lot No. 30715 Gloucester 1962. 29.5 t.
6393/96/97. Lot No. 30716 Gloucester 1962. 29.5 t.
6394. Lot No. 30162 Pressed Steel 1956–57. 30.5 t.
6395. Lot No. 30484 Pressed Steel 1958. 30.5 t.
6398/99. Lot No. 30400 Pressed Steel 1957–58. 30.5 t.

6392	(81588, 92183)	**P**	P	*MM*	NL
6393	(81609, 92196)	**P**	P	*VX*	NL
6394	(80878, 92906)	**P**	P	*VX*	NL
6395	(81506, 92148)	**P**	P	*MM*	NL
6396	(81606, 92195)	**P**	P	*MM*	NL
6397	(81600, 92190)	**P**	P	*VX*	NL
6398	(81471, 92126)	**P**	P	*MM*	NL
6399	(81367, 92994)	**MA**	P	*MM*	NL

AG2C (TSOT)   OPEN STANDARD (TROLLEY)

Dia. AG201. Mark 2C. Converted from TSO by removal of one seating bay and replacing this by a counter with a space for a trolley. Adjacent toilet removed and converted to steward's washing area/store. Pressure ventilated. –/55 1T. B4 bogies. ETH 4.

Lot No. 30795 Derby 1969–70. 32.5 t.

6528	(5592)	**M**	WC	*SS*	CS

AN1F (RLO)   SLEEPER RECEPTION CAR

Dia. AN102 (AN101*). Mark 2F. Converted from FO, these vehicles consist of pantry, microwave cooking facilities, seating area for passengers, telephone booth and staff toilet. 6703–8 also have a bar. Converted at RTC, Derby (6700), Ilford (6701–5) and Derby (6706–8). Air conditioned. 6700/1/3/5/–8 have Stones equipment and 6702/4 have Temperature Ltd. equipment. 26/– 1T. B4 bogies. p. q. d. ETH 5X.

6700–2/4/8. Lot No. 30859 Derby 1973–74. 33.5 t.
6703/5–7. Lot No. 30845 Derby 1973. 33.5 t.

6700	(3347)		**CS**	H	*SR*	IS
6701	(3346)	*	**CS**	H	*SR*	IS
6702	(3421)	*	**CS**	H	*SR*	IS
6703	(3308)		**CS**	H	*SR*	IS
6704	(3341)		**CS**	H	*SR*	IS
6705	(3310, 6430)		**CS**	H	*SR*	IS
6706	(3283, 6421)		**CS**	H	*SR*	IS
6707	(3276, 6418)		**CS**	H	*SR*	IS
6708	(3370)		**CS**	H	*SR*	IS

AN1D (RMBF)   MINIATURE BUFFET CAR

Dia. AN103. Mark 2D. Converted from TSOT by the removal of another seating bay and fitting a proper buffet counter with boiler and microwave oven. Now converted to first class with new seating and end luggage stacks. Air conditioned. Stones equipment. 30/– 1T. B4 bogies. p. q. d. ETH 5.

Lot No. 30822 Derby 1971. 33 t.

6720	(5622, 6652)	**FP**	H	*GW*	OO
6721	(5627, 6660)	**FP**	H	*GW*	OO
6722	(5736, 6661)	**FP**	H	*GW*	OO
6723	(5641, 6662)	**FP**	H	*GW*	OO

6724	(5721, 6665)	**FP**	H	*GW*	OO

AC2F (TSO)   OPEN STANDARD

Dia. AC224. Mark 2F. Renumbered from FO and declassified in 1985–6. Converted 1990 to TSO with mainly unidirectional seating and power-operated sliding doors. Air conditioned. 6800–14 were converted by BREL Derby and have Temperature Ltd. air conditioning. 6815–29 were converted by RFS Industries Doncaster and have Stones air conditioning. –/74 2T. B4 bogies. d. ETH 5X.

6800–07. 6810–12. 6813–14. 6819/22/28. Lot No. 30859 Derby 1973–74. 33 t.
6808–6809. Lot No. 30873 Derby 1974–75. 33.5 t.
6815–18. 6820–21. 6823–27. 6829. Lot No. 30845 Derby 1973. 33 t.

6800	(3323, 6435)	**AR**	H	*AR*	NC
6801	(3349, 6442)	**AR**	H	*AR*	NC
6802	(3339, 6439)	**AR**	H	*AR*	NC
6803	(3355, 6443)	**AR**	H	*AR*	NC
6804	(3396, 6449)		H	*AR*	NC
6805	(3324, 6436)	**AR**	H	*AR*	NC
6806	(3342, 6440)	**AR**	H	*AR*	NC
6807	(3423, 6452)		H	*AR*	NC
6808	(3430, 6454)	**AR**	H	*AR*	NC
6809	(3435, 6455)	**AR**	H	*AR*	NC
6810	(3404, 6451)	**AR**	H	*AR*	NC
6811	(3327, 6437)	**AR**	H	*AR*	NC
6812	(3394, 6448)	**AR**	H	*AR*	NC
6813	(3410, 6463)		H	*AR*	NC
6814	(3422, 6465)	**AR**	H	*AR*	NC
6815	(3282, 6420)	**AR**	H	*AR*	NC
6816	(3316, 6461)	**AR**	H	*AR*	NC
6817	(3311, 6431)	**AR**	H	*AR*	NC
6818	(3298, 6427)	**AR**	H	*AR*	NC
6819	(3365, 6446)	**AR**	H	*AR*	NC
6820	(3320, 6434)	**AR**	H	*AR*	NC
6821	(3281, 6458)	**AR**	H	*AR*	NC
6822	(3376, 6447)	**AR**	H	*AR*	NC
6823	(3289, 6424)	**AR**	H	*AR*	NC
6824	(3307, 6429)	**AR**	H	*AR*	NC
6825	(3301, 6460)	**AR**	H	*AR*	NC
6826	(3294, 6425)	**AR**	H	*AR*	NC
6827	(3306, 6428)	**AR**	H	*AR*	NC
6828	(3380, 6464)	**AR**	H	*AR*	NC
6829	(3288, 6423)	**AR**	H	*AR*	NC

AH2Z (BSOT)
OPEN BRAKE STANDARD (MICRO-BUFFET)

Dia. AH203. Mark 2. Converted from BSO by removal of one seating bay and replacing this by a counter with a space for a trolley. Adjacent toilet removed and converted to a steward's washing area/store. –/23 0T. B4 bogies. ETH 4.

Lot No. 30757 Derby 1966. 31 t.

9101	(9398)	v	**RR**	H		TM
9104	(9401)	v	**G**	MH	*SS*	RL

AE2Z (BSO)   OPEN BRAKE STANDARD

Dia. AE203. Mark 2. These vehicles use the same body shell as the Mark 2 BFK and have first class seat spacing and wider tables. Pressure ventilated. –/31 1T. B4 bogies. ETH 4.

Lot No. 30757 Derby 1966. 31.5 t.

9385	v	**LN**	H		LT		9392	v	**G**	MH *SS*	RL
9391		**PC**	WT	*SS*	OM					

AE2A (BSO)   OPEN BRAKE STANDARD

Dia. AE204. Mark 2A. These vehicles use the same body shell as the Mark 2A BFK and have first class seat spacing and wider tables. Pressure ventilated. –/31 1T. B4 bogies. ETH 4.

9417. Lot No. 30777 Derby 1970. 31.5 t.
9428. Lot No. 30820 Derby 1970. 31.5 t.

9417		**RV**	RV *SS*	CP		9428	**DR**	DR *DR*	KM

AE2C (BSO)   OPEN BRAKE STANDARD

Dia. AE205. Mark 2C. Pressure ventilated. –/31 1T. B4 bogies. ETH 4.

Lot No. 30798 Derby 1970. 32 t.

9440	d	**M**	WC *VL*	CF		9448	d	**M**	WC *VL*	CF

AE2D (BSO)   OPEN BRAKE STANDARD

Dia. AE206 (AE210 r). Mark 2D. Air conditioned (Stones). –/31 1T. B4 bogies. pg. ETH 5.

b In use as a Pendolino barrier vehicle.
r Refurbished with new interior panelling.
s Refurbished with new seating –/22 1TD.
w Facelifted –/28 1W 1T.

Lot No. 30824 Derby 1971. 33 t.

9479	dr		H		DY		9489	drb	**V**	H *FL*	CP
9480	d	**FP**	H *NW*	CP		9490	ds	**FP**	H *GW*	OO
9481	ds	**FP**	H *GW*	OO		9492	dw	**FP**	H *GW*	OO
9483			H		PY		9493	ds	**FP**	H *GW*	OO
9486			H		PY		9494	ds	**FP**	H *GW*	OO
9488	ds	**FP**	H *GW*	OO						

AE2E (BSO)   OPEN BRAKE STANDARD

Dia. AE207 (AE209 w). Mark 2E. Air conditioned (Stones). –/32 1T. B4 bogies. d. pg. ETH 5.

Lot No. 30838 Derby 1972. 33 t.

r Refurbished with new interior panelling.
s Refurbished with modified design of seat headrest and new interior panelling.
w Facelifted –/28 1W 1T.

Notes: 9503 is leased to Riviera Trains.
9505 is fitted for blue star push-pull operation.

9496	r		H		DY	9504	s	V	H		KT
9497	r		H		ZA	9505	s		H	WX	CF
9498	r	V	H		KT	9506	s	V	H		BM
9500	r		H		BH	9507	s	V	H		KT
9501	w	FP	H	NW	CP	9508	s	V	H		KT
9502	s	V	H		KT	9509	s	V	H		KT
9503	s	V	H	SS	CP					

AE2F (BSO)   OPEN BRAKE STANDARD

Dia. AE208. Mark 2F. Air conditioned (Temperature Ltd.). All now refurbished with power-operated vestibule doors, new panels and seat trim. All now further refurbished with carpets and new m.a. sets. –/32 1T. B4 bogies. d. pg. ETH5X.

Lot No. 30861 Derby 1974. 34 t.

Note: 9520/26 are leased to Riviera Trains.

9513		V	H		KT	9526	n		H	SS	OM
9516	n	V	H		KT	9527	n	V	H		PY
9520	n	V	H	SS	OM	9529	n	V	H		PY
9521		V	H		KT	9531		V	H		PY
9522		V	H		KT	9537	n	V	H		KT
9523		V	H		KT	9538		V	H		KT
9524	n	V	H		KT	9539		M	WC	VL	CF
9525		V	H		BM						

AF2F (DBSO) DRIVING OPEN BRAKE STANDARD

Dia. AF201. Mark 2F. Air conditioned (Temperature Ltd.). Push & pull (t.d.m. system). Converted from BSO, these vehicles originally had half cabs at the brake end. They have since been refurbished and have had their cabs widened and the cab-end gangways removed. –/30 1W 1T. B4 bogies. d. pg. Cowcatchers. ETH 5X.

9701–9710. Lot No. 30861 Derby 1974. Converted Glasgow 1979. Disc brakes. 34 t.
9711–9713. Lot No. 30861 Derby 1974. Converted Glasgow 1985. 34 t.
9714. Lot No. 30861 Derby 1974. Converted Glasgow 1986. Disc brakes. 34 t.

9701	(9528)	**AR**	H *AR*	NC		9709	(9515)	**AR**	H *AR*	NC
9702	(9510)	**AR**	H *AR*	NC		9710	(9518)		H *AR*	NC
9703	(9517)	**AR**	H *AR*	NC		9711	(9532)	**AR**	H *AR*	NC
9704	(9512)	**AR**	H *AR*	NC		9712	(9534)	**AR**	H *AR*	NC
9705	(9519)	**AR**	H *AR*	NC		9713	(9535)	**AR**	H *AR*	NC
9707	(9511)	**AR**	H *AR*	NC		9714	(9536)	**AR**	H *AR*	NC
9708	(9530)	**AR**	H *AR*	NC						

AE4E (BUO) UNCLASSIFIED OPEN BRAKE

Dia. AE401. Mark 2E. Converted from TSO with new seating for use on Anglo-Scottish overnight services by Railcare, Wolverton. Air conditioned. Stones equipment. B4 bogies. d. –/31 1T. B4 bogies. ETH 4X.

9801–9803. Lot No. 30837 Derby 1972. 33.5 t.
9804–9810. Lot No. 30844 Derby 1972–73. 33.5 t.

9800	(5751)	**CS**	H *SR*	IS		9806	(5840)	**CS**	H *SR*	IS
9801	(5760)	**CS**	H *SR*	IS		9807	(5851)	**CS**	H *SR*	IS
9802	(5772)	**CS**	H *SR*	IS		9808	(5871)	**CS**	H *SR*	IS
9803	(5799)	**CS**	H *SR*	IS		9809	(5890)	**CS**	H *SR*	IS
9804	(5826)	**CS**	H *SR*	IS		9810	(5892)	**CS**	H *SR*	IS
9805	(5833)	**CS**	H *SR*	IS						

AJ1G (RFM)
RESTAURANT BUFFET FIRST (MODULAR)

Dia. AJ109 (AJ101*). Mark 3A. Air conditioned. Converted from HST TRFKs, RFBs and FOs. Refurbished with table lamps and burgundy seat trim (except *). 18/– plus two seats for staff use (*24/–). BT10 bogies. p. q. d. ETH 14X.

10200–10211. Lot No. 30884 Derby 1977. 39.8 t.
10212–10229. Lot No. 30878 Derby 1975–76. 39.8 t.
10230–10260. Lot No. 30890 Derby 1979. 39.8 t.

10200	(40519)	*	P *AR*	NC		10217	(11051)	**V**	P *VW*	MA
10201	(40520)	**V**	P *VW*	MA		10218	(11053)	**V**	P *VW*	MA
10202	(40504)	**V**	P *VW*	MA		10219	(11047)	**V**	P *VW*	MA
10203	(40506)	* **AR**	P *AR*	NC		10220	(11056)	**V**	P *VW*	OY
10204	(40502)	**V**	P *VW*	MA		10221	(11012)	**V**	P *VW*	MA
10205	(40503)	**V**	P *VW*	OY		10222	(11063)	**V**	P *VW*	MA
10206	(40507)	**V**	P *VW*	MA		10223	(11043)	* **AR**	P *AR*	NC
10207	(40516)	**V**	P *VW*	MA		10224	(11062)	**V**	P *VW*	MA
10208	(40517)	**V**	P *VW*	MA		10225	(11014)	**V**	P *VW*	OY
10209	(40508)	**V**	P *VW*	MA		10226	(11015)	**V**	P *VW*	MA
10210	(40509)	**V**	P *VW*	MA		10227	(11057)	**V**	P *VW*	MA
10211	(40510)	**V**	P *VW*	MA		10228	(11035)	* **AR**	P *AR*	NC
10212	(11049)	**V**	P *VW*	MA		10229	(11059)	**V**	P *VW*	OY
10213	(11050)	**V**	P *VW*	MA		10230	(10021)	**V**	P *VW*	MA
10214	(11034)	* **AR**	P *AR*	NC		10231	(10016)	**V**	P *VW*	OY
10215	(11032)	**V**	P *VW*	MA		10232	(10027)	**V**	P *VW*	OY
10216	(11041)	* **AR**	P *AR*	NC		10233	(10013)	**V**	P *VW*	MA

10234	(10004)	**V**	P	*VW*	MA	10249	(10012)	**V**	P	*VW*	MA
10235	(10015)	**V**	P	*VW*	OY	10250	(10020)	**V**	P	*VW*	OY
10236	(10018)	**V**	P	*VW*	MA	10251	(10024)	**V**	P	*VW*	OY
10237	(10022)	**V**	P	*VW*	MA	10252	(10008)	**V**	P	*VW*	OY
10238	(10017)	**V**	P	*VW*	OY	10253	(10026)	**V**	P	*VW*	OY
10240	(10003)	**V**	P	*VW*	OY	10254	(10006)	**V**	P	*VW*	MA
10241	(10009)	* **AR**	P	*AR*	NC	10255	(10010)	**V**	P	*VW*	OY
10242	(10002)	**V**	P	*VW*	OY	10256	(10028)	**V**	P	*VW*	MA
10245	(10019)	**V**	P	*VW*	MA	10257	(10007)	**V**	P	*VW*	MA
10246	(10014)	**V**	P	*VW*	MA	10258	(10023)	**V**	P	*VW*	MA
10247	(10011)	* **AR**	P	*AR*	NC	10259	(10025)	**V**	P	*VW*	OY
10248	(10005)	**V**	P	*VW*	OY	10260	(10001)	**V**	P	*VW*	MA

AJ1J (RFM)   RESTAURANT BUFFET FIRST (MODULAR)

Dia. AJ105. Mark 4. Air conditioned. 20/– 1T. BT41 bogies. ETH 6X.

Lot No. 31045 Metro-Cammell 1989 onwards. 45.5 t.

10300	**GN**	H	*GN*	BN	10316	**GN**	H	*GN*	BN
10301	**GN**	H	*GN*	BN	10317	**GN**	H	*GN*	BN
10302	**GN**	H	*GN*	BN	10318	**GN**	H	*GN*	BN
10303	**GN**	H	*GN*	BN	10319	**GN**	H	*GN*	BN
10304	**GN**	H	*GN*	BN	10320	**GN**	H	*GN*	BN
10305	**GN**	H	*GN*	BN	10321	**GN**	H	*GN*	BN
10306	**GN**	H	*GN*	BN	10323	**GN**	H	*GN*	BN
10307	**GN**	H	*GN*	BN	10324	**GN**	H	*GN*	BN
10308	**GN**	H	*GN*	BN	10325	**GN**	H	*GN*	BN
10309	**GN**	H	*GN*	BN	10326	**GN**	H	*GN*	BN
10310	**GN**	H	*GN*	BN	10328	**GN**	H	*GN*	BN
10311	**GN**	H	*GN*	BN	10329	**GN**	H	*GN*	BN
10312	**GN**	H	*GN*	BN	10330	**GN**	H	*GN*	BN
10313	**GN**	H	*GN*	BN	10331	**GN**	H	*GN*	BN
10314	**GN**	H	*GN*	BN	10332	**GN**	H	*GN*	BN
10315	**GN**	H	*GN*	BN	10333	**GN**	H	*GN*	BN

AU4G (SLEP)   SLEEPING CAR WITH PANTRY

Dia. AU401. Mark 3A. Air conditioned. Retention toilets. 12 compartments with a fixed lower berth and a hinged upper berth, plus an attendants compartment. 2T BT10 bogies. ETH 7X.

Lot No. 30960 Derby 1981–83. 41 t.

10500		SA		ZF	10513	d	**CS**	P	*SR*	IS
10501	d	**CS**	P	*SR*	IS	10514		SA		ZF
10502	d	**CS**	P	*SR*	IS	10515	d		P		IS
10503		SA		ZF	10516	d	**CS**	P	*SR*	IS
10504	d	**CS**	P	*SR*	IS	10519	d	**CS**	P	*SR*	IS
10506	d	**CS**	P	*SR*	IS	10520	d	**CS**	P	*SR*	IS
10507	d	**CS**	P	*SR*	IS	10522	d	**CS**	P	*SR*	IS
10508	d	**CS**	P	*SR*	IS	10523	d	**CS**	P	*SR*	IS
10510	d		P		IS	10526	d	**CS**	P	*SR*	IS

No.	d				
10527	d	CS	P	SR	IS
10529	d	CS	P	SR	IS
10530	d		P		MM
10531	d	CS	P	SR	IS
10532	d	FP	P	GW	PZ
10533			P		MM
10534	d	FP	P	GW	PZ
10536	d		P		KT
10537	d		P		MM
10538	d		P		KT
10539	d		P		KT
10540	d		P		MM
10542	d	CS	P	SR	IS
10543	d	CS	P	SR	IS
10544	d	CS	P	SR	IS
10546			P		MM
10547	d		P		IS
10548	d	CS	P	SR	IS
10549	d		P		MM
10550	d		P		MM
10551	d	CS	P	SR	IS
10553	d	CS	P	SR	IS
10554	d		P		MM
10555	d		P		KT
10557	d		P		MM
10559	d		P		KT
10560	d		P		MM
10561	d	CS	P	SR	IS
10562	d	CS	P	SR	IS
10563	d	FP	P	GW	PZ
10565	d	CS	P	SR	IS
10566	d		P		Eskmeals
10569	d	PC	VS	SS	SL
10570			P		KT
10571			SA			FP
10572	d		P			MM
10574			RS			OM
10575			SA			ZF
10577		BG	P		MM
10578			P		MM
10579		BG	P		KT
10580	d	CS	P	SR	IS
10582	d		P		MM
10583	d	FP	P		ZN
10584	d	FP	P	GW	PZ
10586	d		P		KT
10588	d	FP	P	GW	PZ
10589	d	FP	P	GW	PZ
10590	d	FP	P	GW	PZ
10592			P		KT
10593	d		P		KT
10594	d	FP	P	GW	PZ
10596	d		P		KT
10597	d	CS	P	SR	IS
10598	d	CS	P	SR	IS
10600	d	CS	P	SR	IS
10601	d	FP	P	GW	PZ
10602			P		MM
10604			P		MM
10605	d	CS	P	SR	IS
10607	d	CS	P	SR	IS
10610	d	CS	P	SR	IS
10612	d	FP	P	GW	PZ
10613	d	CS	P	SR	IS
10614	d	CS	P	SR	IS
10616	d	FP	P	GW	PZ
10617	d	CS	P	SR	IS

AS4G/AQ4G* (SLE/SLED*)   SLEEPING CAR

Dia. AS404 (AQ401*). Mark 3A. Air conditioned. Retention toilets. 13 compartments with a fixed lower berth and a hinged upper berth (* 11 compartments with a fixed lower berth and a hinged upper berth + one compartment for a disabled person). 2T. BT10 bogies. ETH 6X.

Notes:

10704 has Siemens bogies.
10729 is leased to Venice Simplon Orient Express.
10734 was originally 2914 and used as a Royal Train staff sleeping car and is Dia. AS405. It has 12 berths and a shower room and is ETH11X.

10646–10732. Lot No. 30961 Derby 1980–84. 43.5 t.
10734. Lot No. 31002 Derby/Wolverton 1985. 42.5 t.

10646		RS		OM	10699	d*CS	P	SR	IS
10647 d		P		KT	10701	d	P		KT
10648 d*CS		P	SR	IS	10702		SA		ZF
10649 d		P		KT	10703	d CS	P	SR	IS
10650 d*CS		P	SR	IS	10704	d	AE	AE	ZA
10651 d		P		MM	10706	d*CS	P	SR	IS
10653 d		P		MM	10709	d	P		MM
10654 d		P		MM	10710	d	P		KT
10655		SA		ZF	10711	d	P		MM
10657		SA		ZF	10712	d	P		MM
10658 d		P		KT	10713	d	P		MM
10660 d		P		MM	10714	d*CS	P	SR	IS
10662		P		MM	10715	d	P		MM
10663 d		P	SR	IS	10716	d	P		MM
10666 d*CS		P	SR	IS	10717	d	P		MM
10675 d CS		P	SR	IS	10718	d*CS	P	SR	IS
10678 BG		P		KT	10719	d*CS	P	SR	IS
10679 BG		P		KT	10720		P		KT
10680 d*CS		P	SR	IS	10722	d*CS	P	SR	IS
10682		P		MM	10723	d*CS	P	SR	IS
10683 d CS		P	SR	IS	10724		SA		FP
10686 d		P		MM	10725		SA		ZF
10687 d		P		Eskmeals	10726		SA		ZF
10688 d CS		P	SR	IS	10727		SA		ZF
10689 d*CS		P	SR	IS	10729	VN	SA	SS	CP
10690 d CS		P	SR	IS	10730	d	P		MM
10691 d		P		Eskmeals	10731	d	P		KT
10692 d		P		MM	10732	d	P		KT
10693 d CS		P	SR	IS	10734	RP	RV		ZN
10697 d		P		KT					

AD1G (FO)   OPEN FIRST

Dia. AD109. Mark 3A. Air conditioned. All now refurbished with table lamps and new seat cushions and trim. 48/– 2T (* 48/– 1T 1TD). BT10 bogies. d. ETH 6X.

11005–7 were open composites 11905–7 for a time.

Lot No. 30878 Derby 1975–76. 34.3 t.

11005		V	P	VW	MA	11024	V	P	VW	MA
11006		V	P	VW	MA	11026	V	P	VW	MA
11007		V	P	VW	MA	11027	V	P	VW	MA
11011	*	V	P	VW	MA	11028	V	P	VW	MA
11013		V	P	VW	MA	11029	V	P	VW	MA
11016		V	P	VW	MA	11030	V	P	VW	MA
11017		V	P	VW	MA	11031	V	P	VW	MA
11018		V	P	VW	MA	11033	V	P	VW	MA
11019		V	P	VW	MA	11036	V	P	VW	MA
11020		V	P	VW	MA	11037	V	P	VW	MA
11021		V	P	VW	MA	11038	V	P	VW	MA
11023		V	P	VW	MA	11039	V	P	VW	MA

11040	**V**	P	*VW*	MA		11052	**V**	P	*VW*	MA
11042	**V**	P	*VW*	MA		11054	**V**	P	*VW*	MA
11044	**V**	P	*VW*	MA		11055	**V**	P	*VW*	MA
11045	**V**	P	*VW*	MA		11058	**V**	P	*VW*	MA
11046	**V**	P	*VW*	MA		11060	**V**	P	*VW*	MA
11048	**V**	P	*VW*	MA						

AD1H (FO)   OPEN FIRST

Dia. AD114. Mark 3B. Air conditioned. Inter-City 80 seats. All now refurbished with table lamps and new seat cushions and trim. 48/– 2T. BT10 bogies. d. ETH 6X.

Lot No. 30982 Derby 1985. 36.5 t.

11064	**V**	P	*VW*	MA		11083 p	**V**	P	*VW*	MA
11065	**V**	P	*VW*	MA		11084 p	**V**	P	*VW*	MA
11066	**V**	P	*VW*	MA		11085 p	**V**	P	*VW*	MA
11067	**V**	P	*VW*	MA		11086 p	**V**	P	*VW*	MA
11068	**V**	P	*VW*	MA		11087 p	**V**	P	*VW*	MA
11069	**V**	P	*VW*	MA		11088 p	**V**	P	*VW*	MA
11070	**V**	P	*VW*	MA		11089 p	**V**	P	*VW*	MA
11071	**V**	P	*VW*	MA		11090 p	**V**	P	*VW*	MA
11072	**V**	P	*VW*	MA		11091 p	**V**	P	*VW*	MA
11073	**V**	P	*VW*	MA		11092 p	**V**	P	*VW*	MA
11074	**V**	P	*VW*	MA		11093 p	**V**	P	*VW*	MA
11075	**V**	P	*VW*	MA		11094 p	**V**	P	*VW*	MA
11076	**V**	P	*VW*	MA		11095 p	**V**	P	*VW*	MA
11077	**V**	P	*VW*	MA		11096 p	**V**	P	*VW*	MA
11078	**V**	P	*VW*	MA		11097 p	**V**	P	*VW*	MA
11079	**V**	P	*VW*	MA		11098 p	**V**	P	*VW*	MA
11080	**V**	P	*VW*	MA		11099 p	**V**	P	*VW*	MA
11081	**V**	P	*VW*	MA		11100 p	**V**	P	*VW*	MA
11082	**V**	P	*VW*	MA		11101 p	**V**	P	*VW*	MA

AD1J (FO)   OPEN FIRST

Dia. AD111. Mark 4. Air conditioned. 46/– 1T. BT41 bogies. ETH 6X.

Note: 11264–71 were cancelled.

Lot No. 31046 Metro-Cammell 1989–92. 39.7 t.

11200	**GN**	H	*GN*	BN		11210	**GN**	H	*GN*	BN
11201 p	**GN**	H	*GN*	BN		11211 p	**GN**	H	*GN*	BN
11202	**GN**	H	*GN*	BN		11212	**GN**	H	*GN*	BN
11203 p	**GN**	H	*GN*	BN		11214 p	**GN**	H	*GN*	BN
11204 p	**GN**	H	*GN*	BN		11215	**GN**	H	*GN*	BN
11205	**GN**	H	*GN*	BN		11216	**GN**	H	*GN*	BN
11206	**GN**	H	*GN*	BN		11217 p	**GN**	H	*GN*	BN
11207 p	**GN**	H	*GN*	BN		11218	**GN**	H	*GN*	BN
11208	**GN**	H	*GN*	BN		11219 p	**GN**	H	*GN*	BN
11209	**GN**	H	*GN*	BN		11220	**GN**	H	*GN*	BN

11221	p	**GN**	H	*GN*	BN			
11222	p	**GN**	H	*GN*	BN			
11223		**GN**	H	*GN*	BN			
11225	p	**GN**	H	*GN*	BN			
11226		**GN**	H	*GN*	BN			
11227	p	**GN**	H	*GN*	BN			
11228	p	**GN**	H	*GN*	BN			
11229	p	**GN**	H	*GN*	BN			
11230		**GN**	H	*GN*	BN			
11231	p	**GN**	H	*GN*	BN			
11232		**GN**	H	*GN*	BN			
11233	p	**GN**	H	*GN*	BN			
11234		**GN**	H	*GN*	BN			
11235	p	**GN**	H	*GN*	BN			
11236		**GN**	H	*GN*	BN			
11237	p	**GN**	H	*GN*	BN			
11238		**GN**	H	*GN*	BN			
11239	p	**GN**	H	*GN*	BN			
11240		**GN**	H	*GN*	BN			
11241		**GN**	H	*GN*	BN			
11242	p	**GN**	H	*GN*	BN			
11243	p	**GN**	H	*GN*	BN			
11244		**GN**	H	*GN*	BN			
11245	p	**GN**	H	*GN*	BN			

11246	p	**GN**	H	*GN*	BN
11247	p	**GN**	H	*GN*	BN
11248		**GN**	H	*GN*	BN
11249	p	**GN**	H	*GN*	BN
11250		**GN**	H	*GN*	BN
11251	p	**GN**	H	*GN*	BN
11252		**GN**	H	*GN*	BN
11253	p	**GN**	H	*GN*	BN
11254		**GN**	H	*GN*	BN
11255	p	**GN**	H	*GN*	BN
11256		**GN**	H	*GN*	BN
11257	p	**GN**	H	*GN*	BN
11258		**GN**	H	*GN*	BN
11259	p	**GN**	H	*GN*	BN
11260		**GN**	H	*GN*	BN
11261	p	**GN**	H	*GN*	BN
11262		**GN**	H	*GN*	BN
11263	p	**GN**	H	*GN*	BN
11272		**GN**	H	*GN*	BN
11273		**GN**	H	*GN*	BN
11274		**GN**	H	*GN*	BN
11275		**GN**	H	*GN*	BN
11276		**GN**	H	*GN*	BN

AC2G (TSO)   OPEN STANDARD

Dia. AC213 (AC218 s, AC220 z). Mark 3A. Air conditioned. All refurbished with modified seat backs and new layout and now further refurbished with new seat trim. –/76 2T (s –/70 2T 2W, z –/70 1TD 1T 2W). BT10 (* BREL T4) bogies. d. ETH 6X.

Note: 12169–72 were converted from open composites 11908–10/22, formerly FOs 11008–10/22.

Lot No. 30877 Derby 1975–77. 34.3 t.

12004		**V**	P	*VW*	MA		12021		**V**	P	*VW*	MA
12005		**V**	P	*VW*	MA		12022		**V**	P	*VW*	MA
12007		**V**	P	*VW*	MA		12023		**V**	P	*VW*	MA
12008		**V**	P	*VW*	MA		12024	s	**V**	P	*VW*	MA
12009		**V**	P	*VW*	MA		12025		**V**	P	*VW*	MA
12010		**V**	P	*VW*	MA		12026		**V**	P	*VW*	MA
12011		**V**	P	*VW*	MA		12027		**V**	P	*VW*	MA
12012		**V**	P	*VW*	MA		12028		**V**	P	*VW*	MA
12013		**V**	P	*VW*	MA		12029		**V**	P	*VW*	MA
12014		**V**	P	*VW*	MA		12030		**V**	P	*VW*	MA
12015		**V**	P	*VW*	MA		12031		**V**	P	*VW*	MA
12016		**V**	P	*VW*	MA		12032		**V**	P	*VW*	MA
12017		**V**	P	*VW*	MA		12033	z	**V**	P	*VW*	MA
12019		**V**	P	*VW*	MA		12034		**V**	P	*VW*	MA
12020		**V**	P	*VW*	MA		12035		**V**	P	*VW*	MA

12036 s	V	P	VW	MA	12089	V	P	VW	MA
12037	V	P	VW	MA	12090	V	P	VW	MA
12038	V	P	VW	MA	12091	V	P	VW	MA
12040	V	P	VW	MA	12092	V	P	VW	MA
12041	V	P	VW	MA	12093	V	P	VW	MA
12042 s	V	P	VW	MA	12094	V	P	VW	MA
12043	V	P	VW	MA	12095	V	P	VW	MA
12044	V	P	VW	MA	12096	V	P	VW	MA
12045	V	P	VW	MA	12097	V	P	VW	MA
12046	V	P	VW	MA	12098	V	P	VW	MA
12047 z	V	P	VW	MA	12099	V	P	VW	MA
12048	V	P	VW	MA	12100 z	V	P	VW	MA
12049	V	P	VW	MA	12101 s	V	P	VW	MA
12050 s	V	P	VW	MA	12102	V	P	VW	MA
12051	V	P	VW	MA	12103 s	V	P	VW	MA
12052	V	P	VW	MA	12104	V	P	VW	MA
12053	V	P	VW	MA	12105	V	P	VW	MA
12054 s	V	P	VW	MA	12106	V	P	VW	MA
12055	V	P	VW	MA	12107	V	P	VW	MA
12056	V	P	VW	MA	12108 s	V	P	VW	MA
12057	V	P	VW	MA	12109 s	V	P	VW	MA
12058	V	P	VW	MA	12110	V	P	VW	MA
12059 s	V	P	VW	MA	12111	V	P	VW	MA
12060	V	P	VW	MA	12112 z	V	P	VW	MA
12061 s	V	P	VW	MA	12113	V	P	VW	MA
12062	V	P	VW	MA	12114	V	P	VW	MA
12063	V	P	VW	MA	12115	V	P	VW	MA
12064	V	P	VW	MA	12116	V	P	VW	MA
12065	V	P	VW	MA	12117	V	P	VW	MA
12066	V	P	VW	MA	12118	V	P	VW	MA
12067	V	P	VW	MA	12119	V	P	VW	MA
12068	V	P	VW	MA	12120	V	P	VW	MA
12069	V	P	VW	MA	12121	V	P	VW	MA
12070	V	P	VW	MA	12122 z	V	P	VW	MA
12071	V	P	VW	MA	12123	V	P	VW	MA
12072	V	P	VW	MA	12124	V	P	VW	MA
12073	V	P	VW	MA	12125	V	P	VW	MA
12075	V	P	VW	MA	12126	V	P	VW	MA
12076	V	P	VW	MA	12127	V	P	VW	MA
12077	V	P	VW	MA	12128 s	V	P	VW	MA
12078	V	P	VW	MA	12129	V	P	VW	MA
12079	V	P	VW	MA	12130	V	P	VW	MA
12080	V	P	VW	MA	12131	V	P	VW	MA
12081	V	P	VW	MA	12132	V	P	VW	MA
12082	V	P	VW	MA	12133	V	P	VW	MA
12083	V	P	VW	MA	12134	V	P	VW	MA
12084	V	P	VW	MA	12135	V	P	VW	MA
12085 s	V	P	VW	MA	12136	V	P	VW	MA
12086 s	V	P	VW	MA	12137	V	P	VW	MA
12087 s	V	P	VW	MA	12138	V	P	VW	MA
12088 z	V	P	VW	MA	12139	V	P	VW	MA

12140 z*	**V**	P	*VW*	MA		12156	**V**	P	*VW*	MA
12141	**V**	P	*VW*	MA		12157	**V**	P	*VW*	MA
12142 z	**V**	P	*VW*	MA		12158	**V**	P	*VW*	MA
12143	**V**	P	*VW*	MA		12159	**V**	P	*VW*	MA
12144 s	**V**	P	*VW*	MA		12160 s	**V**	P	*VW*	MA
12145	**V**	P	*VW*	MA		12161 z	**V**	P	*VW*	MA
12146	**V**	P	*VW*	MA		12163	**V**	P	*VW*	MA
12147	**V**	P	*VW*	MA		12164	**V**	P	*VW*	MA
12148	**V**	P	*VW*	MA		12165	**V**	P	*VW*	MA
12149	**V**	P	*VW*	MA		12166	**V**	P	*VW*	MA
12150	**V**	P	*VW*	MA		12167	**V**	P	*VW*	MA
12151	**V**	P	*VW*	MA		12168 s	**V**	P	*VW*	MA
12152	**V**	P	*VW*	MA		12169 s	**V**	P	*VW*	MA
12153	**V**	P	*VW*	MA		12170 s	**V**	P	*VW*	MA
12154	**V**	P	*VW*	MA		12171 s	**V**	P	*VW*	MA
12155 s	**V**	P	*VW*	MA		12172 s	**V**	P	*VW*	MA

AL2J (TSOE)   OPEN STANDARD (END)

Dia. AL201. Mark 4. Air conditioned. –/74 2T. BT41 bogies. ETH 6X.

Lot No. 31047 Metro-Cammell 1989–91. 39.5 t.

Note: 12232 was converted from the original 12405.

12200	**GN**	H *GN*	BN		12216	**GN**	H *GN*	BN
12201	**GN**	H *GN*	BN		12217	**GN**	H *GN*	BN
12202	**GN**	H *GN*	BN		12218	**GN**	H *GN*	BN
12203	**GN**	H *GN*	BN		12219	**GN**	H *GN*	BN
12204	**GN**	H *GN*	BN		12220	**GN**	H *GN*	BN
12205	**GN**	H *GN*	BN		12222	**GN**	H *GN*	BN
12206	**GN**	H	ZF		12223	**GN**	H *GN*	BN
12207	**GN**	H *GN*	BN		12224	**GN**	H *GN*	BN
12208	**GN**	H *GN*	BN		12225	**GN**	H *GN*	BN
12209	**GN**	H *GN*	BN		12226	**GN**	H *GN*	BN
12210	**GN**	H *GN*	BN		12227	**GN**	H *GN*	BN
12211	**GN**	H *GN*	BN		12228	**GN**	H *GN*	BN
12212	**GN**	H *GN*	BN		12229	**GN**	H *GN*	BN
12213	**GN**	H *GN*	BN		12230	**GN**	H *GN*	BN
12214	**GN**	H *GN*	BN		12231	**GN**	H *GN*	BN
12215	**GN**	H *GN*	BN		12232	**GN**	H *GN*	BN

AL2J (TSOD) OPEN STANDARD (DISABLED ACCESS)

Dia. AL201. Mark 4. Air conditioned. –/72 1TD 1W. BT41 bogies. p. ETH 6X.

Lot No. 31048 Metro-Cammell 1989–91. 39.4 t.

12300	**GN**	H *GN*	BN		12305	**GN**	H *GN*	BN
12301	**GN**	H *GN*	BN		12307	**GN**	H *GN*	BN
12302	**GN**	H *GN*	BN		12308	**GN**	H *GN*	BN
12303	**GN**	H *GN*	BN		12309	**GN**	H *GN*	BN
12304	**GN**	H *GN*	BN		12310	**GN**	H *GN*	BN

12311	GN	H GN	BN		12322	GN	H GN	BN
12312	GN	H GN	BN		12323	GN	H GN	BN
12313	GN	H GN	BN		12324	GN	H GN	BN
12315	GN	H GN	BN		12325	GN	H GN	BN
12316	GN	H GN	BN		12326	GN	H GN	BN
12317	GN	H GN	BN		12327	GN	H GN	BN
12318	GN	H GN	BN		12328	GN	H GN	BN
12319	GN	H GN	BN		12329	GN	H GN	BN
12320	GN	H GN	BN		12330	GN	H GN	BN
12321	GN	H GN	BN					

AC2J (TSO)   OPEN STANDARD

Dia. AC214. Mark 4. Air conditioned. –/74 2T. BT41 bogies. ETH 6X.

Lot No. 31049 Metro-Cammell 1989–92. 39.9 t.

Note: 12405 is the second coach to carry that number. It was built from the bodyshell originally intended for 12221. The original 12405 is now 12232. 12490–12512 were cancelled.

12400	GN	H GN	BN		12432	GN	H GN	BN
12401	GN	H GN	BN		12433	GN	H GN	BN
12402	GN	H GN	BN		12434	GN	H GN	BN
12403	GN	H GN	BN		12435	GN	H GN	BN
12404	GN	H GN	BN		12436	GN	H GN	BN
12405	GN	H GN	BN		12437	GN	H GN	BN
12406	GN	H GN	BN		12438	GN	H GN	BN
12407	GN	H GN	BN		12439	GN	H GN	BN
12408	GN	H GN	BN		12440	GN	H GN	BN
12409	GN	H GN	BN		12441	GN	H GN	BN
12410	GN	H GN	BN		12442	GN	H GN	BN
12411	GN	H GN	BN		12443	GN	H GN	BN
12413	GN	H	ZF		12444	GN	H GN	BN
12414	GN	H GN	BN		12445	GN	H GN	BN
12415	GN	H GN	BN		12446	GN	H GN	BN
12416	GN	H GN	BN		12447	GN	H GN	BN
12417	GN	H GN	BN		12448	GN	H GN	BN
12418	GN	H GN	BN		12449	GN	H GN	BN
12419	GN	H GN	BN		12450	GN	H GN	BN
12420	GN	H GN	BN		12451	GN	H GN	BN
12421	GN	H GN	BN		12452	GN	H GN	BN
12422	GN	H GN	BN		12453	GN	H GN	BN
12423	GN	H GN	BN		12454	GN	H GN	BN
12424	GN	H GN	BN		12455	GN	H GN	BN
12425	GN	H GN	BN		12456	GN	H GN	BN
12426	GN	H GN	BN		12457	GN	H GN	BN
12427	GN	H GN	BN		12458	GN	H GN	BN
12428	GN	H GN	BN		12459	GN	H GN	BN
12429	GN	H GN	BN		12460	GN	H GN	BN
12430	GN	H GN	BN		12461	GN	H GN	BN
12431	GN	H GN	BN		12462	GN	H GN	BN

12463	**GN**	H *GN*	BN		12489	**GN**	H *GN*	BN
12464	**GN**	H *GN*	BN		12513	**GN**	H *GN*	BN
12465	**GN**	H *GN*	BN		12514	**GN**	H *GN*	BN
12466	**GN**	H *GN*	BN		12515	**GN**	H *GN*	BN
12467	**GN**	H *GN*	BN		12517	**GN**	H *GN*	BN
12468	**GN**	H *GN*	BN		12518	**GN**	H *GN*	BN
12469	**GN**	H *GN*	BN		12519	**GN**	H *GN*	BN
12470	**GN**	H *GN*	BN		12520	**GN**	H *GN*	BN
12471	**GN**	H *GN*	BN		12521	**GN**	H *GN*	BN
12472	**GN**	H *GN*	BN		12522	**GN**	H *GN*	BN
12473	**GN**	H *GN*	BN		12523	**GN**	H *GN*	BN
12474	**GN**	H *GN*	BN		12524	**GN**	H *GN*	BN
12475	**GN**	H *GN*	BN		12526	**GN**	H *GN*	BN
12476	**GN**	H *GN*	BN		12527	**GN**	H *GN*	BN
12477	**GN**	H *GN*	BN		12528	**GN**	H *GN*	BN
12478	**GN**	H *GN*	BN		12529	**GN**	H *GN*	BN
12479	**GN**	H *GN*	BN		12530	**GN**	H *GN*	BN
12480	**GN**	H *GN*	BN		12531	**GN**	H *GN*	BN
12481	**GN**	H *GN*	BN		12532	**GN**	H *GN*	BN
12482	**GN**	H *GN*	BN		12533	**GN**	H *GN*	BN
12483	**GN**	H *GN*	BN		12534	**GN**	H *GN*	BN
12484	**GN**	H *GN*	BN		12535	**GN**	H *GN*	BN
12485	**GN**	H *GN*	BN		12536	**GN**	H *GN*	BN
12486	**GN**	H *GN*	BN		12537	**GN**	H *GN*	BN
12487	**GN**	H *GN*	BN		12538	**GN**	H *GN*	BN
12488	**GN**	H *GN*	BN					

AA11 (FK)   CORRIDOR FIRST

Dia. AA101. Mark 1. 42/– 2T. ETH 3.

13225–13230. Lot No. 30381 Swindon 1959. B4 bogies. 33 t.
13321. Lot No. 30667 Swindon 1962. Commonwealth bogies. 36 t.

13225	k	**RR** H	EC		13230	xk	**M** BK *SS*	BT
13229	xk	**M** BK *SS*	BT		13321	x	**M** WC *SS*	CS

AA1A (FK)   CORRIDOR FIRST

Dia. AA106. Mark 2A. Pressure ventilated. 42/– 2T. B4 bogies. ETH 4.

13440. Lot No. 30774 Derby 1968. 33 t.
13474. Lot No. 30785 Derby 1968. 33 t.

13440	v	**G** MH *SS*	RL		13474	v	**G** MH *SS*	RL

AD1B (FO)   OPEN FIRST

Dia. AC2xx. Mark 2B. Pressure ventilated. 42/– 2T. B4 bogies. ETH 4.

Lot No. 30789 Derby 1968. 33 t.

These two vehicles were built as FKs, sold to Northern Ireland Railways 1980 and regauged to 5'3". NIR converted them to 56-seater TSOs. Since withdrawn, repatriated to Britain and converted back to standard gauge 2002. Under conversion to FO.

13498	(13498, NIR926)	**PC**	WT	LC
13508	(13508, NIR924)	**PC**	WT	LC

AA1D (FK) CORRIDOR FIRST

Dia. AA109. Mark 2D. Air conditioned (Stones). 42/– 2T. B4 bogies. ETH 5.

Lot No. 30825 Derby 1971–72. 34.5 t.

13582	E	KT		13607	RS	FP
13604	RS	FP				

AB11 (BFK) CORRIDOR BRAKE FIRST

Dia. AB101. Mark 1. 24/– 1T. Commonwealth bogies. ETH 2.

14007. Lot No. 30382 Swindon 1959. 35 t.
17013–17019. Lot No. 30668 Swindon 1961. 36 t.
17023. Lot No. 30718 Swindon 1963. Metal window frames. 36 t.

Originally numbered in 14xxx series and then renumberd in 17xxx series.

14007	x	**M**	B1	*LS*	Great Central	17018	v	**CH**	VT	*SS*	TM
17013		**PC**	FS	*LS*	SO	17019	x	**M**	NE	*LS*	BQ
17015	x	**G**	RS	*SS*	BN	17023	x	**G**	RS	*SS*	BN

AB1A (BFK) CORRIDOR BRAKE FIRST

Dia. AB103. Mark 2A. Pressure ventilated. 24/– 1T. B4 bogies. ETH 4.

17056–17077. Lot No. 30775 Derby 1967–8. 32 t.
17079–17102. Lot No. 30786 Derby 1968. 32 t.

Originally numbered 14056–102. 17079/90 were numbered 35515/03 for a time when declassified.

Non-standard Livery: 17079 is Brunswick green & cream.

Note: 17090 is leased to Vintage Trains.

* Cage removed from brake compartment.

17056		**CH**	RV	*SS*	CP	17090	v	**CH**	H	*SS*	TM
17058		**N**	H		KT	17091	v	**RR**	H		LT
17077		**RV**	RV	*SS*	CP	17096		**G**	MN	*LS*	SL
17079	*	**O**	RV	*SS*	CP	17102		**M**	WC	*SS*	CS
17086		**RV**	RV	*SS*	CP						

AX5B   COUCHETTE/GENERATOR COACH

Dia. AX504. Mark 2B. Formerly part of Royal Train. Converted from a BFK built 1969. Consists of luggage accommodation, guard's compartment, 350 kW diesel generator and staff sleeping accommodation. Pressure ventilated. B5 bogies. ETH 5X.

Non-standard Livery: 17105 is Oxford blue.

Lot No. 30888 Wolverton 1977. 46 t.

17105   (14105, 2905)   **0**   RV   *SS*   OM

AB1D (BFK)   CORRIDOR BRAKE FIRST

Dia. AB106. Mark 2D. Air conditioned (Stones equipment). 24/– 1T. B4 Bogies. ETH 5.

Lot No. 30823 Derby 1971–72. 33.5 t.

Non-Standard Livery: 17141 & 17164 are as **WV** without lining.

Originally numbered 14141–72.

17141	**0**	RS		FP	17163		VS		CO
17144		NR	*SO*	DY	17164	**0**	RV	*SS*	CP
17146		NR	*SO*	DY	17165		RS		FP
17151		VS		CP	17167	**VN**	VS	*SS*	CP
17153	**WR**	RS		CS	17168	**M**	WC	*VL*	CF
17156		MA		DY	17169		RS		CS
17159	**CH**	RV	*SS*	CP	17170		FR		DY
17161		E		OC	17172		RS		FP

AE1G (BFO)   OPEN BRAKE FIRST

Dia. AE101. Mark 3B. Air conditioned. Fitted with hydraulic handbrake. Refurbished with table lamps and burgundy seat trim. 36/– 1T (w 35/– 1T) BT10 bogies. pg. d. ETH 5X.

Lot No. 30990 Derby 1986. 35.81 t.

17173		**V**	P	*VW*	MA	17175	w	**V**	P	*VW*	MA
17174		**V**	P	*VW*	MA						

AA21 (SK)   CORRIDOR STANDARD

Dia. AA201 (AA202*). Mark 1. There are two variants depending upon whether the compartments have armrests. Each vehicle has eight compartments. All remaining vehicles have metal window frames and melamine interior panelling. Commonwealth bogies. –/48 2T (–/64 2T *). ETH 4.

18756–18893. Lot No. 30685 Derby 1961–62. 36 t.
18955. Lot No. 30686 Derby 1962. 36 t.
19013. Lot No. 30719 Derby 1962. 37 t.

Non-Standard Livery: 19013 is Pilkington's K (green with white/red chevron and light blue block).

f Facelifted with fluorescent lighting.
t Rebuilt internally as TSO using components from 4936. –/64 2T.

Originally numbered 25756–26013.

18756	x	**M**	WC	*SS*	CS		18862	x	**M**	WC	*SS*	CS
18767	x	**CH**	WC	*SS*	CS		18893	x	**CH**	WC	*SS*	CS
18806	xt	**M**	WC	*SS*	CS		18955	x*f	**M**	WC	*SS*	CS
18808	x	**M**	WC	*SS*	CS		19013	x	**0**	WC	*SS*	CS

AB31 (BCK)   CORRIDOR BRAKE COMPOSITE

Dia. AB301 (AB302*). Mark 1. There are two variants depending upon whether the standard class compartments have armrests. Each vehicle has two first class and three standard class compartments. 12/18 2T (12/24 2T *). ETH 2.

21224. Lot No. 30245. Metro-Cammell 1958. B4 bogies. 33 t.
21232. Lot No. 30574 GRCW 1960. B4 bogies. 34 t.
21236–21246. Lot No. 30669 Swindon 1961–62. Commonwealth bogies. 36 t.
21252–21256. Lot No. 30731 Derby 1963. Commonwealth bogies. 37 t.
21266–21272. Lot No. 30732 Derby 1964. Commonwealth bogies. 37 t.

21224		**VN**	RV	*SS*	CP		21252	v	**G**	MH	*SS*	RL
21232	x	**M**	62	*LS*	SK		21256	x	**M**	WC	*SS*	CS
21236	v	**M**	ER		ZG		21266	*	**M**	WC	*SS*	CS
21241	x	**M**	BK	*SS*	BT		21268	*		FS		SO
21245	x	**M**	RS	*SS*	BN		21269	*	**GC**	RS	*SS*	BN
21246		**BG**	RS	*SS*	BN		21272	x*	**CH**	RV	*SS*	CP

AB21 (BSK)   CORRIDOR BRAKE STANDARD

Dia. AB201 (AB202*). Mark 1. There are two variants depending upon whether the compartments have armrests. Each vehicle has four compartments. Lots 30699 and 30721 have metal window frames and melamine interior panelling. –/24 1T (–/32 1T*). ETH2.

b In use as a Pendolino barrier vehicle.
g Fitted with an e.t.s. generator.

34991. Lot No. 30229 Metro-Cammell 1956–57. Commonwealth bogies. 36 t.
35185. Lot No. 30427 Wolverton 1959. B4 bogies. 33 t.
35317–35333. Lot No. 30699 Wolverton 1962–63. Commonwealth bogies. 37 t.
35407, 35452–35486. Lot No. 30721 Wolverton 1963. Commonwealth bogies. 37 t.

Non-Standard Livery: 35322 and 35407 are in London & North Western Railway livery.

34991	*	**PC**	VS	*SS*	SL			
35185	x	**M**	BK	*SS*	BT			
35317	x	**G**	WT	*LS*	BQ			
35322	x	**O**	SH	*SS*	CJ			
35329	v	**G**	MH	*LS*	RL			
35333	x	**CH**	24	*LS*	DI			
35407	xg	**O**	SH	*SS*	CJ			
35452	xb	**RR**	LW	*FL*	CP			
35453	x	**CH**	GW	*LS*	DI			
35457	v	**M**	IE	*LS*	NY			
35459	x	**M**	WC	*SS*	CS			
35461	x	**CH**	RV	*LS*	OM			
35463	v	**M**	WC	*LS*	CS			
35465	x	**WV**	LW	*LS*	CP			
35468	v	**M**	NM	*LS*	YK			
35469	xg	**M**	RS	*SS*	BN			
35470	v	**CH**	VT	*LS*	TM			
35476	x	**M**	62	*LS*	SK			
35479	v	**M**	SV	*LS*	KR			
35486	x	**M**	SV	*LS*	KR			

AB1C (BFK)   CORRIDOR BRAKE FIRST

Dia. AB103. Mark 2C. Pressure ventilated. Renumbered when declassified. –/24 1T. B4 bogies. ETH 4.

Lot No. 30796 Derby 1969–70. 32.5 t.

35508	(14128, 17128)	**RR**	IR	BQ

AB5C   BRAKE/POWER KITCHEN

Dia. AB103. Mark 2C. Pressure ventilated. Converted from BFK (declassified to BSK) built 1970. Converted at West Coast Railway Company 2000–01. Consists of 60 kVA generator, guard's compartment and electric kitchen. B5 bogies. ETH 4.

Lot No. 30796 Derby 1969–70. 32.5 t.

Non-standard Livery: 35511 is British racing green with gold lining.

35511	(14130, 17130)	**O**	RA	CP

AB1A (BFK)   CORRIDOR BRAKE FIRST

Dia. AB105. Mark 2A. Pressure ventilated. Renumbered when declassified. –/24 1T. B4 bogies. ETH 4.

35512–13. Lot No. 30775 Derby 1967–68. 32 t.
35516–18. Lot No. 30786 Derby 1968. 32 t.

* Cage removed from brake compartment.

35512	(14057, 17057)	*	**RR**	H		CP
35513	(14063, 17063)	*	**RR**	H		KT
35516	(14080, 17080)	*	**RR**	H		KT
35517	(14088, 17088)	*	**M**	IR	*LS*	BQ
35518	(14097, 17097)	*	**PC**	WT	*LS*	OM

NAMED COACHES

The following miscellaneous coaches carry names:

1200	AMBER	5212	CAPERKAILZIE
1659	CAMELOT	5229	THE GREEN KNIGHT
1800	TINTAGEL	5239	THE RED KNIGHT
3105	JULIA	5275	Wendy
3113	JESSICA	5278	SIR GALAHAD
3117	CHRISTINA	5307	Beverley
3128	VICTORIA	5350	Dawn
3130	PAMELA	5364	Andrea
3143	PATRICIA	5365	Deborah
3174	GLAMIS	5373	Felicity
3181	TOPAZ	5376	Michaela
3182	WARWICK	5378	Sarah
3188	ONYX	5389	SIR LAUNCELOT
3223	DIAMOND	5419	MELISANDE
3228	AMETHYST	5420	LYONNESSE
3231	Apollo	9385	BALMACARA
3240	SAPPHIRE	9391	PENDRAGON
3244	EMERALD	9417	Ellen
3246	Aphrodite	10569	LEVIATHAN
3247	CHATSWORTH	10729	CREWE
3267	BELVOIR	13508	EXCALIBUR
3273	ALNWICK	17013	ALBANNACH SGIATHACH
3275	HARLECH	17077	Catherine
5132	CLAN MUNRO	17086	Georgina
5154	CLAN FRASER	35518	MERLIN
5193	CLAN MACLEOD		

2.2. HIGH SPEED TRAIN TRAILER CARS

HSTs normally run in formations of 7 or 8 trailer cars with a Class 43 power car at each end. All trailer cars are classified Mark 3 and have BT10 bogies with disc brakes and central door locking. Heating is by a 415 V three-phase supply and vehicles have air conditioning. Max. Speed is 125 m.p.h.

All vehicles underwent a mid-life refurbishment in the 1980s, and a further refurbishment programme was completed in November 2000, each train operating company having a different scheme as follows:

First Great Western. Green seat covers and extra partitions between seat bays.
Great North Eastern Railway. New ceiling lighting panels and brown seat covers. First class vehicles have table lamps and imitation walnut plastic end panels.
Virgin Cross-Country. Green seat covers. Standard class vehicles have four seats in the centre of each carriage replaced with a luggage stack.
Virgin West Coast. Similar to Virgin Cross-Country but without luggage stacks. These vehicles, owned by Angel Trains have now been transferred to Midland Mainline or Great North Eastern Railway.
Midland Mainline. Grey seat covers, redesigned seat squabs, side carpeting and two seats in the centre of each carriage replaced with a luggage stack.

All vehicles except TRFK 40501 and TRFM 40619 were included in this programme.

Tops Type Codes

TOPS type codes for HST trailer cars are made up as follows:

(1) Two letters denoting the layout of the vehicle as follows:

GH	Open
GJ	Open with Guard's compartment.
GK	Buffet
GL	Kitchen
GN	Buffet

(2) A digit for the class of passenger accommodation

1	First
2	Standard (formerly second)
4	Unclassified

(3) A suffix relating to the build of coach.

G	Mark 3

Operator Codes

The normal operator codes are given in brackets after the TOPS codes. These are as follows:

TF	Trailer First		TRFK	Trailer Kitchen First
TGS	Trailer Guard's Standard		TRFM	Trailer Modular Buffet First
TRB	Trailer Buffet First		TRSB	Trailer Buffet Standard
TRFB	Trailer Buffet First		TS	Trailer Standard

GN4G (TRB)   TRAILER BUFFET FIRST

Dia. GN401. Converted from TRSB by fitting first class seats. Renumbered from 404xx series by subtracting 200. 23/–. p. q.

40204–40228. Lot No. 30883 Derby 1976–77. 36.12 t.
40231. Lot No. 30899 Derby 1978–79. 36.12 t.

40204	FP	A	GW	PM	40209	FP	A	GW	PM
40205	FP	A	GW	PM	40210	FP	A	GW	PM
40206	FP	A	GW	PM	40221	FP	A	GW	PM
40207	FP	A	GW	PM	40228	FP	A	GW	PM
40208	FP	A	GW	PM	40231	FP	A	GW	PM

GK2G (TRSB)   TRAILER BUFFET STANDARD

Dia. GK202. Renumbered from 400xx series by adding 400. –/33 1W. p. q.

40401–40427. Lot No. 30883 Derby 1976–77. 36.12 t.
40429–40437. Lot No. 30899 Derby 1978–79. 36.12 t.

Note: 40411/2/32–4 were numbered 40211/2/32–4 for a time when fitted with first class seats.

40401	V	P	VX	LA	40423	V	P	VW	MA
40402	V	P	VW	MA	40424	V	P	VX	LA
40403	V	P	VX	LA	40425	V	P	VX	LA
40411	V	P	VX	LA	40426	V	P	VX	LA
40412	V	P	VX	LA	40427	V	P	VX	MA
40414	V	P	VX	MA	40429	V	P	VX	MA
40415	V	P	VX	MA	40430	V	P	VX	MA
40416	V	P	VX	LA	40432	V	P	VX	MA
40417	V	P	VX	LA	40433	V	P	VX	LA
40418	V	P	VX	MA	40434	V	P	VX	LA
40419	V	P	VX	MA	40435	V	P	VX	MA
40420	V	P	VX	MA	40436	V	P	VW	MA
40422	V	P	VX	MA	40437	V	P	VW	MA

GL1G (TRFK)   TRAILER KITCHEN FIRST

Dia. GL101. Reclassified from TRUK. p. q. 24/–.

Lot No. 30884 Derby 1976–77. 37 t.

40501		NR	Hunslet-Barclay, Kilmarnock

GK1G (TRFM) TRAILER MODULAR BUFFET FIRST

Dia. GK102. Converted to modular catering from TRFB 40719. 17/–. p. q.

Lot No. 30921 Derby 1978–79. 38.16 t.

40619		P	VX	LA

GK1G (TRFB)   TRAILER BUFFET FIRST

Dia. GK101. These vehicles have larger kitchens than the 402xx and 404xx series vehicles, and are used in trains where full meal service is required. They were renumbered from the 403xx series (in which the seats were unclassified) by adding 400 to previous number. 17/– (*12/– + one seat for staff use). p. q.

40700–40721. Lot No. 30921 Derby 1978–79. 38.16 t.
40722–40735. Lot No. 30940 Derby 1979–80. 38.16 t.
40736–40753. Lot No. 30948 Derby 1980–81. 38.16 t.
40754–40757. Lot No. 30966 Derby 1982. 38.16 t.

40700	**MM**	P	*MM*	NL	40730	**MM**	P	*MM*	NL
40701	**MM**	P	*MM*	NL	40731	**FP**	A	*GW*	LA
40702	**MM**	P	*MM*	NL	40732	**V**	A	*MM*	NL
40703	**FG**	A	*GW*	LA	40733	**FG**	A	*GW*	LA
40704	**GN**	A	*GN*	EC	40734	**FP**	A	*GW*	LA
40705	**GN**	A	*GN*	EC	40735	**GN**	A	*GN*	EC
40706	**GN**	A	*GN*	EC	40736	**FG**	A	*GW*	LA
40707	**FP**	A	*GW*	LA	40737	**GN**	A	*GN*	EC
40708	**MM**	P	*MM*	NL	40738	**FG**	A	*GW*	LA
40709	**FG**	A	*GW*	LA	40739	**FG**	A	*GW*	PM
40710	**FP**	A	*GW*	LA	40740	**GN**	A	*GN*	EC
40711	**GN**	A	*GN*	EC	40741	**MM**	P	*MM*	NL
40712	**FG**	A	*GW*	LA	40742	**V**	A	*GN*	EC
40713	**FG**	A	*GW*	LA	40743	**FP**	A	*GW*	LA
40714	**FG**	A	*GW*	PM	40744	**FG**	A	*GW*	LA
40715	**FP**	A	*GW*	LA	40745	**FP**	A	*GW*	LA
40716	**FP**	A	*GW*	PM	40746	**MM**	P	*MM*	NL
40717	**FP**	A	*GW*	PM	40747	**FP**	A	*GW*	PM
40718	**FG**	A	*GW*	LA	40748	**GN**	A	*GN*	EC
40720	**GN**	A	*GN*	EC	40749	**MM**	P	*MM*	NL
40721	**FG**	A	*GW*	LA	40750	**GN**	A	*GN*	EC
40722	**FG**	A	*GW*	LA	40751	**MM**	P	*MM*	NL
40723 *	**V**	A	*MM*	NL	40752	**FP**	A	*GW*	LA
40724	**FP**	A	*GW*	PM	40753	**MM**	P	*MM*	NL
40725	**FP**	A	*GW*	LA	40754	**MM**	P	*MM*	NL
40726	**FP**	A	*GW*	LA	40755	**FP**	A	*GW*	LA
40727	**FP**	A	*GW*	LA	40756	**MM**	P	*MM*	NL
40728	**MM**	P	*MM*	NL	40757	**FP**	A	*GW*	LA
40729	**MM**	P	*MM*	NL					

GH1G (TF)   TRAILER FIRST

Dia. GH102. 48/– 2T (w 47/– 2T 1W).

41003–41056. Lot No. 30881 Derby 1976–77. 33.66 t.
41057–41120. Lot No. 30896 Derby 1977–78. 33.66 t.
41121–41148. Lot No. 30938 Derby 1979–80. 33.66 t.
41149–41166. Lot No. 30947 Derby 1980. 33.66 t.

41167–41169. Lot No. 30963 Derby 1982. 33.66 t.
41170. Lot No. 30967 Derby 1982. Former prototype vehicle. 33.66 t.
41179/80. Lot No. 30884 Derby 1976–77. 33.60 t.

s Fitted with centre luggage stack. 46/– 1T 1TD 1W.
Note: 41170 was converted from 41001. 41179/80 have been converted from 40505 and 40511 respectively.

41003	p	**FP**	A	*GW*	LA	41052		**FP**	A	*GW*	LA
41004		**FP**	A	*GW*	PM	41055		**FG**	A	*GW*	LA
41005	p	**FG**	A	*GW*	LA	41056		**FG**	A	*GW*	LA
41006		**FG**	A	*GW*	LA	41057		**MM**	P	*MM*	NL
41007	p	**FP**	A	*GW*	PM	41058	s	**MM**	P	*MM*	NL
41008		**FP**	A	*GW*	PM	41059	w	**V**	P	*VW*	MA
41009	p	**FP**	A	*GW*	PM	41061		**MM**	P	*MM*	NL
41010		**FP**	A	*GW*	PM	41062	w	**MM**	P	*MM*	NL
41011	p	**FP**	A	*GW*	PM	41063		**MM**	P	*MM*	NL
41012		**FP**	A	*GW*	PM	41064	s	**MM**	P	*MM*	NL
41013	p	**FP**	A	*GW*	PM	41065		**FG**	A	*GW*	LA
41014		**FP**	A	*GW*	PM	41066	p	**V**	A	*GN*	EC
41015	p	**FP**	A	*GW*	PM	41067	s	**MM**	P	*MM*	NL
41016		**FP**	A	*GW*	PM	41068	s	**MM**	P	*MM*	NL
41017	p	**FP**	A	*GW*	PM	41069	s	**MM**	P	*MM*	NL
41018		**FP**	A	*GW*	PM	41070	s	**MM**	P	*MM*	NL
41019	p	**FP**	A	*GW*	PM	41071		**MM**	P	*MM*	NL
41020		**FP**	A	*GW*	PM	41072	s	**MM**	P	*MM*	NL
41021	p	**FP**	A	*GW*	PM	41075		**MM**	P	*MM*	NL
41022		**FP**	A	*GW*	PM	41076	s	**MM**	P	*MM*	NL
41023	p	**FP**	A	*GW*	LA	41077		**MM**	P	*MM*	NL
41024		**FP**	A	*GW*	LA	41078		**MM**	P	*MM*	NL
41025	p	**V**	A	*MM*	NL	41079		**MM**	P	*MM*	NL
41026		**V**	A	*MM*	NL	41080	s	**MM**	P	*MM*	NL
41027	p	**FP**	A	*GW*	LA	41081	w	**V**	P	*VX*	MA
41028		**FP**	A	*GW*	LA	41083		**MM**	P	*MM*	NL
41029	p	**FP**	A	*GW*	LA	41084	s	**MM**	P	*MM*	NL
41030		**FP**	A	*GW*	LA	41085	w	**V**	P	*VW*	MA
41031	p	**FP**	A	*GW*	LA	41086	w	**V**	P	*VW*	MA
41032		**FP**	A	*GW*	LA	41087		**GN**	A	*GN*	EC
41033	p	**FP**	A	*GW*	LA	41088		**GN**	A	*GN*	EC
41034		**FP**	A	*GW*	LA	41089		**FG**	A	*GW*	LA
41035	p	**V**	A	*MM*	NL	41090	w	**GN**	A	*GN*	EC
41036	w	**V**	A	*MM*	NL	41091		**GN**	A	*GN*	EC
41037	p	**FP**	A	*GW*	LA	41092	w	**GN**	A	*GN*	EC
41038		**FP**	A	*GW*	LA	41093		**FP**	A	*GW*	LA
41039		**GN**	A	*GN*	EC	41094		**FP**	A	*GW*	LA
41040		**GN**	A	*GN*	EC	41095	w	**V**	P	*VX*	MA
41041	ps	**MM**	P	*MM*	NL	41096	w	**V**	P	*VX*	MA
41043	w	**GN**	A	*GN*	EC	41097	w	**GN**	A	*GN*	EC
41044		**GN**	A	*GN*	EC	41098	w	**GN**	A	*GN*	EC
41045	w	**V**	P	*VW*	MA	41099		**GN**	A	*GN*	EC
41046	s	**MM**	P	*MM*	NL	41100	w	**GN**	A	*GN*	EC
41051		**FP**	A	*GW*	LA	41101		**FG**	A	*GW*	LA

41102		**FG**	A	*GW*	LA	41138		**FP**	A	*GW*	PM
41103		**FG**	A	*GW*	LA	41139	p	**FG**	A	*GW*	LA
41104		**FG**	A	*GW*	LA	41140		**FG**	A	*GW*	LA
41105		**FG**	A	*GW*	PM	41141	p	**FP**	A	*GW*	LA
41106		**FG**	A	*GW*	PM	41142		**FP**	A	*GW*	LA
41107	w	**V**	P	*VX*	MA	41143	p	**FG**	A	*GW*	LA
41108	w	**V**	P	*VX*	MA	41144		**FG**	A	*GW*	LA
41109	w	**V**	P	*VX*	MA	41145	p	**FP**	A	*GW*	LA
41110		**FP**	A	*GW*	PM	41146		**FP**	A	*GW*	LA
41111		**MM**	P	*MM*	NL	41147	w	**V**	P	*VX*	MA
41112		**MM**	P	*MM*	NL	41148	w	**V**	P	*VW*	MA
41113	s	**MM**	P	*MM*	NL	41149	w	**V**	P	*VX*	MA
41114	w	**V**	P	*VX*	LA	41150	w	**GN**	A	*GN*	EC
41115	w	**V**	P	*VX*	LA	41151		**GN**	A	*GN*	EC
41116		**FG**	A	*GW*	LA	41152		**GN**	A	*GN*	EC
41117		**MM**	P	*MM*	NL	41153		**MM**	P	*MM*	NL
41118	w	**GN**	A	*GN*	EC	41154	s	**MM**	P	*MM*	NL
41119	w	**V**	P	*VX*	MA	41155		**MM**	P	*MM*	NL
41120		**GN**	A	*GN*	EC	41156		**MM**	P	*MM*	NL
41121	p	**FG**	A	*GW*	LA	41157		**FP**	A	*GW*	LA
41122		**FG**	A	*GW*	LA	41158		**FP**	A	*GW*	LA
41123	p	**FG**	A	*GW*	PM	41159	w	**V**	P	*VX*	LA
41124		**FG**	A	*GW*	PM	41160	w	**V**	P	*VW*	MA
41125		**FG**	A	*GW*	PM	41161	w	**V**	P	*VX*	MA
41126	p	**FG**	A	*GW*	PM	41162	w	**V**	P	*VX*	LA
41127	p	**FP**	A	*GW*	PM	41163	w	**V**	P	*VX*	LA
41128		**FP**	A	*GW*	PM	41164	p	**V**	A	*GN*	EC
41129	p	**FP**	A	*GW*	PM	41165	w	**V**	P	*VX*	LA
41130		**FP**	A	*GW*	PM	41166	w	**V**	P	*VX*	LA
41131	p	**FG**	A	*GW*	LA	41167	w	**V**	P	*VW*	MA
41132		**FG**	A	*GW*	LA	41168	w	**V**	P	*VX*	MA
41133	p	**FG**	A	*GW*	LA	41169	w	**V**	P	*VW*	MA
41134		**FG**	A	*GW*	LA	41170		**GN**	A	*GN*	EC
41135		**FG**	A	*GW*	LA	41179		**FP**	A	*GW*	PM
41136		**FG**	A	*GW*	LA	41180		**FP**	A	*GW*	LA
41137	p	**FP**	A	*GW*	PM						

GH2G (TS)   TRAILER STANDARD

Dia. GH203. –/76 2T. (§ –/70 2T 2W).

42003–42090/42362. Lot No. 30882 Derby 1976–77. 33.60 t.
42091–42250. Lot No. 30897 Derby 1977–79. 33.60 t.
42251–42305. Lot No. 30939 Derby 1979–80. 33.60 t.
42306–42322. Lot No. 30969 Derby 1982. 33.60 t.
42323–42341. Lot No. 30983 Derby 1984–85. 33.60 t.
42342/60. Lot No. 30949 Derby 1982. 33.47 t. Converted from TGS.
42343/5. Lot No. 30970 Derby 1982. 33.47 t. Converted from TGS.
42344/61. Lot No. 30964 Derby 1982. 33.47 t. Converted from TGS.
42346/7/50/1. Lot No. 30881 Derby 1976–77. 33.66 t. Converted from TF.
42348/9/63. Lot No. 30896 Derby 1977–78. 33.66 t. Converted from TF.

42352/4. Lot No. 30897 Derby 1977. Were TF from 1983 to 1992. 33.66 t.
42353/5–7. Lot No. 30967 Derby 1982. Ex prototype vehicles. 33.66 t.

s Centre luggage stack –/72 2T.
t Centre luggage stack –/72 2T. Fitted with pt.
u Centre luggage stack –/74 2T (w –72 2T 1W).
* Disabled persons toilet and 5 tip-up seats. –/65 1T 1TD.
42158 was also numbered 41177 for a time when fitted with first class seats.

42003		**FP**	A	*GW*	PM	42047	**FP**	A	*GW*	LA
42004 *		**FP**	A	*GW*	LA	42048	**FP**	A	*GW*	LA
42005		**FP**	A	*GW*	PM	42049	**FP**	A	*GW*	LA
42006		**FP**	A	*GW*	PM	42050	**FP**	A	*GW*	LA
42007 *		**FP**	A	*GW*	LA	42051 §	**V**	A	*MM*	NL
42008 *		**FP**	A	*GW*	PM	42052	**V**	A	*MM*	NL
42009		**FP**	A	*GW*	PM	42053	**V**	A	*MM*	NL
42010		**FP**	A	*GW*	PM	42054	**FP**	A	*GW*	LA
42012 *		**FP**	A	*GW*	PM	42055	**FP**	A	*GW*	LA
42013		**FP**	A	*GW*	PM	42056	**GN**	A	*GN*	EC
42014		**FP**	A	*GW*	PM	42057	**GN**	A	*GN*	EC
42015 *		**FP**	A	*GW*	PM	42058	**GN**	A	*GN*	EC
42016		**FP**	A	*GW*	PM	42059	**GN**	A	*GN*	EC
42017		**FP**	A	*GW*	PM	42060	**FP**	A	*GW*	PM
42018 *		**FP**	A	*GW*	PM	42061	**FP**	A	*GW*	PM
42019		**FP**	A	*GW*	PM	42062 *	**FG**	A	*GW*	LA
42020		**FP**	A	*GW*	PM	42063	**GN**	A	*GN*	EC
42021 *		**FP**	A	*GW*	PM	42064	**GN**	A	*GN*	EC
42022		**FP**	A	*GW*	PM	42065	**GN**	A	*GN*	EC
42023		**FP**	A	*GW*	PM	42066 *	**FG**	A	*GW*	LA
42024 *		**FP**	A	*GW*	PM	42067	**FG**	A	*GW*	LA
42025		**FP**	A	*GW*	PM	42068	**FG**	A	*GW*	LA
42026		**FP**	A	*GW*	PM	42069 *	**FG**	A	*GW*	LA
42027		**FP**	A	*GW*	PM	42070	**FG**	A	*GW*	LA
42028		**FP**	A	*GW*	PM	42071	**FG**	A	*GW*	LA
42029		**FP**	A	*GW*	PM	42072	**FG**	A	*GW*	PM
42030 *		**FP**	A	*GW*	PM	42073	**FP**	A	*GW*	LA
42031		**FP**	A	*GW*	PM	42074	**FP**	A	*GW*	LA
42032		**FP**	A	*GW*	PM	42075	**FP**	A	*GW*	PM
42033		**FP**	A	*GW*	LA	42076	**FP**	A	*GW*	LA
42034		**FP**	A	*GW*	LA	42077	**FP**	A	*GW*	LA
42035		**FP**	A	*GW*	LA	42078	**FP**	A	*GW*	LA
42036		**V**	A	*MM*	NL	42079	**FP**	A	*GW*	PM
42037		**V**	A	*MM*	NL	42080	**FP**	A	*GW*	PM
42038		**V**	A	*MM*	NL	42081 *	**FG**	A	*GW*	LA
42039		**FP**	A	*GW*	LA	42083	**FG**	A	*GW*	LA
42040		**FP**	A	*GW*	LA	42084 s	**V**	P	*VX*	MA
42041		**FP**	A	*GW*	LA	42085 t	**V**	P	*VX*	MA
42042		**FP**	A	*GW*	LA	42086 s	**V**	P		DY
42043		**FP**	A	*GW*	LA	42087 s	**V**	P		DY
42044		**FP**	A	*GW*	LA	42088 s	**V**	P	*VX*	LA
42045		**FP**	A	*GW*	LA	42089	**FP**	A	*GW*	PM
42046		**FP**	A	*GW*	LA	42090 s	**V**	P		DY

No.					
42091	s	**V**	A	*GN*	EC
42092	s	**V**	P	*VX*	LA
42093	s	**V**	P	*VX*	LA
42094	s	**V**	P	*VX*	LA
42095	s	**V**	P	*VX*	LA
42096		**FG**	A	*GW*	LA
42097	§	**V**	A	*MM*	NL
42098		**FG**	A	*GW*	PM
42099		**FG**	A	*GW*	LA
42100	u	**MM**	P	*MM*	NL
42101	uw	**MM**	P	*MM*	NL
42102	u	**MM**	P	*MM*	NL
42103	s	**V**	P	*VW*	MA
42104		**GN**	A	*GN*	EC
42105	s	**V**	P	*VW*	MA
42106		**GN**	A	*GN*	EC
42107		**FP**	A	*GW*	LA
42108	s	**V**	P	*VX*	LA
42109	s	**V**	P	*VX*	LA
42110	s	**V**	P	*VX*	LA
42111	u	**MM**	P	*MM*	NL
42112	u	**MM**	P	*MM*	NL
42113	u	**MM**	P	*MM*	NL
42115	t	**V**	P	*VX*	MA
42116	s	**V**	A	*GN*	EC
42117	s	**V**	P		DY
42118		**FG**	A	*GW*	LA
42119	u	**MM**	P	*MM*	NL
42120	u	**MM**	P	*MM*	NL
42121	u	**MM**	P	*MM*	NL
42122		**V**	A	*GN*	EC
42123	u	**MM**	P	*MM*	NL
42124	u	**MM**	P	*MM*	NL
42125	u	**MM**	P	*MM*	NL
42126		**FG**	A	*GW*	LA
42127	s	**V**	A	*GN*	EC
42128	s	**V**	A	*GN*	EC
42129		**FP**	A	*GW*	LA
42130	t	**V**	P	*VX*	LA
42131	u	**MM**	P	*MM*	NL
42132	u	**MM**	P	*MM*	NL
42133	u	**MM**	P	*MM*	NL
42134		**V**	A	*GN*	EC
42135	u	**MM**	P	*MM*	NL
42136	u	**MM**	P	*MM*	NL
42137	u	**MM**	P	*MM*	NL
42138	*	**FP**	A	*GW*	PM
42139	u	**MM**	P	*MM*	NL
42140	u	**MM**	P	*MM*	NL
42141	u	**MM**	P	*MM*	NL
42143		**FP**	A	*GW*	LA
42144		**FP**	A	*GW*	LA
42145		**FP**	A	*GW*	LA
42146		**GN**	A	*GN*	EC
42147	u	**MM**	P	*MM*	NL
42148	u	**MM**	P	*MM*	NL
42149	u	**MM**	P	*MM*	NL
42150		**GN**	A	*GN*	EC
42151	uw	**MM**	P	*MM*	NL
42152	u	**MM**	P	*MM*	NL
42153	u	**MM**	P	*MM*	NL
42154		**GN**	A	*GN*	EC
42155	uw	**MM**	P	*MM*	NL
42156	u	**MM**	P	*MM*	NL
42157	u	**MM**	P	*MM*	NL
42158		**GN**	A	*GN*	EC
42159	s	**V**	P	*VX*	LA
42160	s	**V**	P	*VX*	LA
42161	s	**V**	A	*GN*	EC
42162	s	**V**	P	*VX*	MA
42163	uw	**MM**	P	*MM*	NL
42164	u	**MM**	P	*MM*	NL
42165	u	**MM**	P	*MM*	NL
42166	t	**V**	P	*VX*	MA
42167	s	**V**	P	*VW*	MA
42168	t	**V**	P	*VW*	MA
42169	s	**V**	P	*VW*	MA
42170	s	**V**	P	*VX*	LA
42171		**GN**	A	*GN*	EC
42172		**GN**	A	*GN*	EC
42173	s	**V**	P	*VX*	LA
42174	s	**V**	P	*VX*	LA
42175	t	**V**	P	*VW*	MA
42176	t	**V**	P	*VW*	MA
42177	s	**V**	P	*VW*	MA
42178	t	**V**	P	*VX*	MA
42179		**GN**	A	*GN*	EC
42180		**GN**	A	*GN*	EC
42181		**GN**	A	*GN*	EC
42182		**GN**	A	*GN*	EC
42183	*	**FP**	A	*GW*	LA
42184		**FP**	A	*GW*	LA
42185		**FP**	A	*GW*	LA
42186		**GN**	A	*GN*	EC
42187	t	**V**	P	*VX*	MA
42188	s	**V**	A	*GN*	EC
42189	s	**V**	A	*GN*	EC
42190		**GN**	A	*GN*	EC
42191		**GN**	A	*GN*	EC
42192		**GN**	A	*GN*	EC
42193		**GN**	A	*GN*	EC
42194	uw	**MM**	P	*MM*	NL

No.						No.					
42195	s	V	P	VX	MA	42246	s	V	P	VX	MA
42196		FG	A	GW	LA	42247	t	V	P	VX	MA
42197		FP	A	GW	PM	42248	s	V	P		DY	
42198		GN	A	GN	EC	42249	s	V	P		DY	
42199		GN	A	GN	EC	42250		FP	A	GW	LA
42200	*	FP	A	GW	LA	42251	*	FG	A	GW	PM
42201	*	FG	A	GW	LA	42252		FG	A	GW	LA
42202	*	FG	A	GW	LA	42253		FG	A	GW	LA
42203		FG	A	GW	LA	42254	s	V	P	VX	MA
42204		FG	A	GW	LA	42255	*	FG	A	GW	PM
42205	u	MM	P	MM	NL	42256		FG	A	GW	PM
42206	*	FP	A	GW	LA	42257		FG	A	GW	PM
42207	*	FG	A	GW	LA	42258	t	V	P	VX	MA
42208		FG	A	GW	LA	42259	*	FG	A	GW	PM
42209		FG	A	GW	LA	42260		FG	A	GW	PM
42210	u	MM	P	MM	NL	42261		FG	A	GW	PM
42211	*	FG	A	GW	PM	42262	s	V	P	VX	LA
42212		FG	A	GW	PM	42263		FG	A	GW	PM
42213		FG	A	GW	PM	42264	*	FG	A	GW	PM
42214		FG	A	GW	PM	42265		FG	A	GW	LA
42215		GN	A	GN	EC	42266	s	V	P	VX	LA
42216		FG	A	GW	LA	42267	*	FP	A	GW	PM
42217	t	V	P	VX	MA	42268	*	FP	A	GW	LA
42218	t	V	P	VX	LA	42269		FP	A	GW	PM
42219		GN	A	GN	EC	42270	s	V	P	VX	LA
42220	uw	MM	P	MM	NL	42271	*	FG	A	GW	LA
42221		FG	A	GW	LA	42272		FG	A	GW	LA
42222	t	V	P	VX	MA	42273		FG	A	GW	LA
42223	s	V	P	VX	LA	42274	t	V	P	VX	LA
42224	s	V	P	VX	LA	42275	*	FG	A	GW	LA
42225	u	MM	P	MM	NL	42276		FG	A	GW	LA
42226		GN	A	GN	EC	42277		FG	A	GW	LA
42227	u	MM	P	MM	NL	42278	s	V	P	VX	LA
42228	u	MM	P	MM	NL	42279	*	FG	A	GW	LA
42229	u	MM	P	MM	NL	42280		FG	A	GW	LA
42230	u	MM	P	MM	NL	42281		FG	A	GW	LA
42231	s	V	P	VX	LA	42282	s	V	P	VX	LA
42232	t	V	P	VX	LA	42283		FG	A	GW	LA
42233	s	V	P	VX	LA	42284		FP	A	GW	PM
42234	s	V	P	VX	LA	42285		FP	A	GW	PM
42235		GN	A	GN	EC	42286	s	V	P	VX	LA
42236		FP	A	GW	PM	42287	*	FG	A	GW	LA
42237	s	V	P	VX	MA	42288		FG	A	GW	LA
42238	s	V	A	GN	EC	42289		FG	A	GW	LA
42239	s	V	A	GN	EC	42290	t	V	P	VX	LA
42240		GN	A	GN	EC	42291	*	FP	A	GW	LA
42241		GN	A	GN	EC	42292	*	FP	A	GW	LA
42242		GN	A	GN	EC	42293		FP	A	GW	LA
42243		GN	A	GN	EC	42294	s	V	P	VX	LA
42244		GN	A	GN	EC	42295	*	FG	A	GW	LA
42245		FP	A	GW	LA	42296		FG	A	GW	LA

42297		**FG**	A	*GW*	LA
42298	s	**V**	P	*VX*	LA
42299	*	**FP**	A	*GW*	LA
42300		**FP**	A	*GW*	LA
42301		**FP**	A	*GW*	LA
42302	s	**V**	P	*VW*	MA
42303	t	**V**	P	*VW*	MA
42304	s	**V**	P	*VW*	MA
42305	s	**V**	P	*VW*	MA
42306	s	**V**	P	*VX*	LA
42307	s	**V**	P	*VX*	LA
42308	s	**V**	P	*VX*	LA
42309	s	**V**	P	*VX*	LA
42310	s	**V**	P	*VX*	LA
42311	t	**V**	P	*VX*	LA
42312	s	**V**	P	*VX*	LA
42313	s	**V**	P	*VX*	LA
42314	s	**V**	P	*VX*	MA
42315	t	**V**	P	*VX*	MA
42316	s	**V**	P	*VX*	LA
42317	s	**V**	P	*VX*	LA
42318	s	**V**	P	*VW*	MA
42319	t	**V**	P	*VW*	MA
42320	s	**V**	P	*VW*	MA
42321	s	**V**	P	*VW*	MA
42322	s	**V**	P	*VX*	LA
42323		**GN**	A	*GN*	EC
42324	uw	**MM**	P	*MM*	NL
42325		**FG**	A	*GW*	PM
42326	s	**V**	P	*VX*	MA
42327	uw	**MM**	P	*MM*	NL
42328	uw	**MM**	P	*MM*	NL
42329	uw	**MM**	P	*MM*	NL
42330	s	**V**	P	*VX*	MA
42331	uw	**MM**	P	*MM*	NL
42332		**FP**	A	*GW*	PM
42333		**FP**	A	*GW*	LA
42334	s	**V**	P	*VX*	MA
42335	uw	**MM**	P	*MM*	NL
42336	s	**V**	P	*VX*	MA
42337	uw	**MM**	P	*MM*	NL
42338	s	**V**	P	*VX*	MA
42339	uw	**MM**	P	*MM*	NL
42340		**GN**	A	*GN*	EC
42341	uw	**MM**	P	*MM*	NL

42342	(44082)		**V**	A	*MM*	NL
42343	(44095)		**FP**	A	*GW*	LA
42344	(44092)	*	**FG**	A	*GW*	PM
42345	(44096)	*	**FG**	A	*GW*	LA
42346	(41053)		**FP**	A	*GW*	PM
42347	(41054)	*	**FG**	A	*GW*	PM
42348	(41073)	*	**FG**	A	*GW*	LA
42349	(41074)		**FP**	A	*GW*	PM
42350	(41047)		**FG**	A	*GW*	LA
42351	(41048)		**FP**	A	*GW*	LA
42352	(42142, 41176)	u	**MM**	P	*MM*	NL
42353	(42001, 41171)	s	**V**	P	*VX*	MA
42354	(42114, 41175)		**GN**	A	*GN*	EC
42355	(42000, 41172)	§	**V**	A	*GN*	EC
42356	(42002, 41173)		**FP**	A	*GW*	PM
42357	(41002, 41174)		**V**	A	*GN*	EC
42360	(44084, 45084)		**FP**	A	*VW*	PM
42361	(44099)		**FG**	A	*GW*	LA
42362	(42011, 41178)		**FP**	A	*GW*	LA
42363	(41082)	s	**V**	A	*GN*	EC

GJ2G (TGS)   TRAILER GUARD'S STANDARD

Dia. GJ205. –/65 1T (w –/63 1T 1W). pg.
44000. Lot No. 30953 Derby 1980. 33.47 t.
44001–44090. Lot No. 30949 Derby 1980–82. 33.47 t.
44091–44094. Lot No. 30964 Derby 1982. 33.47 t.

▲ BR maroon liveried Mark 1 RBR 1730 is seen at Chester on 14/09/02.
Ivor Bufton

▼ BR Southern Railway green liveried Mark 1 FO 3127 at Blaneau Ffestiniog on 23/03/02.
Ivor Bufton

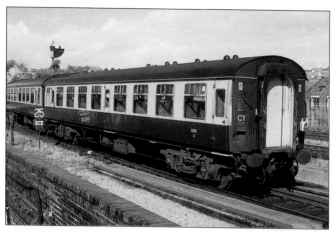

▲ BR blue and grey liveried Mark 1 TSO 4956 at Worcester Shrub Hill on 06/10/01.
Stephen Widdowson

▼ Mark 1 Open Standard (TSO) 5009 in BR Western Region chocolate and cream livery is seen at Holyhead on 01/06/02.
Ivor Bufton

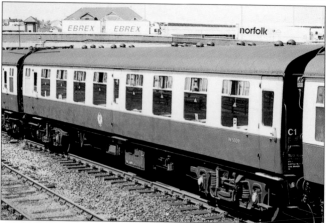

▲ Mark 1 BCK 21269 is seen at Reading on 11/09/01 in British racing green and cream livery. **Darren Ford**

▼ Mark 1 SK 18808 (99716) in BR maroon is seen stabled at Carnforth on 22/06/02. **Martyn Hilbert**

▲ Mark 2 TSO 5177 in BR Western Region chocolate and cream livery at Reading on 15/04/02. **Darren Ford**

▼ Mark 2A BFK 17086 in Riviera Trains livery at Llandrindod Wells on 19/05/01. **Ivor Bufton**

▲ Valley lines have four rakes of Mark 2s based at Cardiff Central for use on Cardiff–Rhymney services. On 31/08/02 Mark 2B TSO 5491 in BR maroon livery is seen at Rhymney behind train loco 37408. **Robert Pritchard**

▼ Mark 2D BSO 9480 in First Great Western livery at Reading on 23/05/01. **Mark Beal**

Mark 2E Unclassified Open Brake 9803 in Scotrail Caledonian Sleeper livery is seen at Glasgow Central on 12/05/02.

Darren Ford

▲ Mark 2F FO 3400 in Anglia Railways livery is seen at Norwich on 12/09/02.
Robert Pritchard

▼ Virgin Trains liveried Mark 2F 6179 (experimentally fitted with hopper window vents) seen at Wigan North Western on 13/04/02. **Martyn Hilbert**

DBSO 9707 in Anglia Railways livery at Ipswich on 15/07/02.

▲ Mark 3A First Great Western-liveried sleeping car with pantry 10588 at Long Rock, Penzance on 25/07/02. **Simon Wright**

▼ Mark 3A FO 11013 at Carlisle on 30/09/02 in the formation of the 11.40 Glasgow Central–London Euston. **Robert Pritchard**

▲ An "oddball" is HST Trailer Modular Buffet First 40619 which has seen most of 2002 out of use at Longsight and is still in Intercity livery. However on 02/08/01 it was in use on a Holyhead–Euston working, seen here at Stafford. **Simon Wright**

▼ Mark 4 Open Standard (End) 12230 in GNER livery stands at London King's Cross on 10/08/02. **Robert Pritchard**

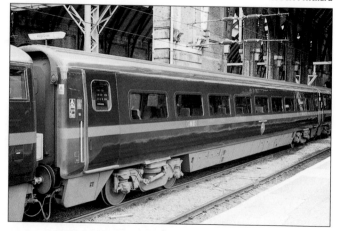

HST trailer standard 42196 in First Group Inter-City livery passes Abbotswood near Worcester on 01/06/02.

Stephen Widdowson

Former BR (LMR) General Manager's saloon 6320 (in BR maroon livery) is seen at Sheffield on 20/07/02.　　Peter Fox

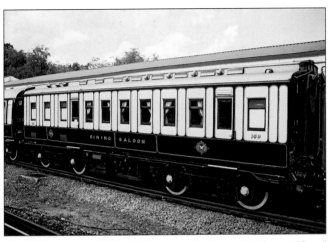

▲ LNWR dining saloon 159 (5159) is seen at Ascot as part of "Queen of Scots" rake on 21/06/02. **Darren Ford**

▼ Pullman parlour first 302 "PHOENIX" is seen at Cardiff in the VSOE British Pullman rake on 29/06/02. **Ivor Bufton**

Paul Chancellor

Virgin Trains liveried Mark 3 DVT 82114 leaves Crewe on 06/04/00.

▲ Mark 1 Gangwayed Brake van and Pendolino Barrier vehicle 92111 is seen at Wolverton as 390 001 is dragged by 47292 (out of sight) from Tebay to Wembley on 19/04/02.　　**Mark Beal**

▼ Mark 2 GNER liveried Mark 4 Barrier vehicle 6353 in Doncaster West Yard on 10/06/02.　　**Darren Ford**

▲ Royal Mail liveried Mark 1 Post Office sorting van 80366 is seen stabled at Carlisle on 30/09/02. **Robert Pritchard**

▼ Rail express systems-liveried Mark 1 High Security Brake van 94438 at Carlisle on 30/09/02. **Robert Pritchard**

44097–44101. Lot No. 30970 Derby 1982. 33.47 t.
s t Fitted with centre luggage stack s –/63 1T, t –/61 1T.

44000 t	**V**	P	*VX*	MA		44048 s	**MM**	P	*MM*	NL
44001 w	**FP**	A	*GW*	LA		44049 w	**FP**	A	*GW*	LA
44002 w	**FP**	A	*GW*	PM		44050 s	**MM**	P	*MM*	NL
44003 w	**FP**	A	*GW*	PM		44051 s	**MM**	P	*MM*	NL
44004 w	**FP**	A	*GW*	PM		44052 s	**MM**	P	*MM*	NL
44005 w	**FP**	A	*GW*	PM		44053 t	**V**	P	*VX*	LA
44006 w	**FP**	A	*GW*	PM		44054 s	**MM**	P	*MM*	NL
44007 w	**FP**	A	*GW*	PM		44055 t	**V**	P	*VW*	MA
44008 w	**FP**	A	*GW*	PM		44056 w	**GN**	A	*GN*	EC
44009 w	**FP**	A	*GW*	PM		44057 t	**V**	P	*VX*	LA
44010 w	**FP**	A	*GW*	PM		44058 w	**GN**	A	*GN*	EC
44011 w	**FP**	A	*GW*	PM		44059 w	**FP**	A	*GW*	LA
44012	**V**	A	*MM*	NL		44060 t	**V**	P	*VX*	MA
44013 w	**FP**	A	*GW*	LA		44061 w	**GN**	A	*GN*	EC
44014 w	**FP**	A	*GW*	LA		44062 t	**V**	P	*VX*	LA
44015 w	**FP**	A	*GW*	LA		44063 w	**GN**	A	*GN*	EC
44016 w	**FP**	A	*GW*	LA		44064 w	**FG**	A	*GW*	LA
44017	**V**	A	*MM*	NL		44065 t	**V**	P	*VX*	LA
44018 w	**FP**	A	*GW*	LA		44066 w	**FG**	A	*GW*	LA
44019 w	**GN**	A	*GN*	EC		44067 w	**FG**	A	*GW*	PM
44020 w	**FP**	A	*GW*	PM		44068 t	**V**	P	*VW*	MA
44021 t	**V**	P	*VX*	MA		44069 t	**V**	P	*VX*	MA
44022 w	**FG**	A	*GW*	LA		44070 s	**MM**	P	*MM*	NL
44023 w	**FG**	A	*GW*	LA		44071 s	**MM**	P	*MM*	NL
44024 w	**FP**	A	*GW*	LA		44072 t	**V**	P	*VX*	LA
44025 w	**FP**	A	*GW*	LA		44073 s	**MM**	P	*MM*	NL
44026 w	**FP**	A	*GW*	PM		44074 t	**V**	P	*VX*	LA
44027 s	**MM**	P	*MM*	NL		44075 t	**V**	P	*VX*	MA
44028 w	**FG**	A	*GW*	LA		44076 t	**V**	P	*VX*	LA
44029 w	**FG**	A	*GW*	PM		44077 w	**GN**	A	*GN*	EC
44030 w	**FG**	A	*GW*	PM		44078 t	**V**	P	*VX*	MA
44031	**V**	A	*GN*	EC		44079 t	**V**	P	*VX*	MA
44032 w	**FP**	A	*GW*	PM		44080 w	**GN**	A	*GN*	EC
44033 w	**FG**	A	*GW*	LA		44081 t	**V**	P	*VX*	LA
44034 w	**FG**	A	*GW*	LA		44083 s	**MM**	P	*MM*	NL
44035 w	**FG**	A	*GW*	LA		44085 s	**MM**	P	*MM*	NL
44036 w	**FP**	A	*GW*	PM		44086 w	**FP**	A	*GW*	LA
44037 w	**FG**	A	*GW*	LA		44087 t	**V**	P	*VX*	LA
44038 w	**FP**	A	*GW*	LA		44088 t	**V**	P	*VX*	LA
44039 w	**FG**	A	*GW*	LA		44089 t	**V**	P	*VX*	LA
44040 w	**FP**	A	*GW*	LA		44090 t	**V**	P	*VX*	MA
44041 s	**MM**	P	*MM*	NL		44091 t	**V**	P	*VW*	MA
44042 t	**V**	P	*VX*	MA		44093 w	**FP**	A	*GW*	LA
44043 w	**FG**	A	*GW*	LA		44094 w	**GN**	A	*GN*	EC
44044 s	**MM**	P	*MM*	NL		44097 t	**V**	P	*VX*	MA
44045 w	**GN**	A	*GN*	EC		44098 w	**GN**	A	*GN*	EC
44046 s	**MM**	P	*MM*	NL		44100 t	**V**	P	*VX*	LA
44047 s	**MM**	P	*MM*	NL		44101 t	**V**	P	*VX*	MA

2.3. SALOONS

Several specialist passenger carrying vehicles, normally referred to as saloons are permitted to run on the Network Rail system. Many of these are to pre-nationalisation designs.

LNER GENERAL MANAGERS SALOON

Dia. AO133. Built 1945 by LNER, York. Gangwayed at one end with a verandah at the other. The interior has a dining saloon seating twelve, kitchen, toilet, office and nine seat lounge. 21/– 1T. B4 bogies. 75 m.p.h. ETH3. 35.7 t.

1999	(902260)	**M**	GS	*SS*	EN

GNR FIRST CLASS SALOON

Dia. AO132. Built 1912 by GNR, Doncaster. Contains entrance vestibule, lavatory, two seperate saloons, library and luggage space. Gresley bogies. 19/– 1T. 75 m.p.h. 29.4 t.

Non-Standard Livery: Teak.

4807	(807)	x	**0**	SH	*SS*	CJ

LNWR DINING SALOON

Dia. AO131. Built 1890 by LNWR, Wolverton. Mounted on the underframe of LMS GUV 37908 in the 1980s. Contains kitchen and dining area seating 12 at tables for two. Gresley bogies. 10/–. 75 m.p.h. 25.4 t.

Non-Standard Livery: London & North Western Railway.

5159	(159)	x	**0**	SH	*SS*	CJ

GENERAL MANAGER'S SALOON

Dia. AZ501. Renumbered 1989 from London Midland Region departmental series. Formerly the LMR General Manager's saloon. Rebuilt from LMS period 1 BFK M 5033 M to dia. 1654 and mounted on the underframe of BR suburban BS M 43232. Screw couplings have been removed. B4 bogies. 100 m.p.h. ETH2X.

LMS Lot No. 326 Derby 1927. 27.5 t.

6320	(5033, DM 395707)	x	**M**	62	*SS*	SK

GWR FIRST CLASS SALOON

Dia. AO103. Built 1930 by GWR, Swindon. Contains saloons at either end with body end observation windows, staff compartment, central kitchen and pantry/bar. Numbered DE321011 when in departmental service with British Railways. 20/– 1T. GWR bogies. 75 m.p.h. 34 t.

GWR Lot No. 1431 1930.

9004   **CH**   RA   CS

WCJS OBSERVATION SALOON

Dia. AO102. Built 1892 by LNWR, Wolverton. Originally dining saloon mounted on six-wheel bogies. Rebuilt with new underframe with four-wheel bogies in 1927. Rebuilt 1960 as observation saloon with DMU end. Gangwayed at other end. The interior has a saloon, kitchen, guards vestibule and observation lounge. Gresley bogies. 19/– 1T. 28.5 t. 75 m.p.h.

Non-Standard Livery: London & North Western Railway.

45018 (484, 15555)   x **0**   SH   *SS*   CJ

LMS INSPECTION SALOONS

Dia. QX035 (*QX504). Built as engineers inspection saloons. Non-gangwayed. Observation windows at each end. The interior layout consists of two saloons interspersed by a central lavatory/kitchen/guards section. BR Mark 1 bogies. 80 m.p.h. 31.5 t.

45020–45026. Lot No. LMS 1356 Wolverton 1944.
45029. Lot No. LMS 1327 Wolverton 1942.
999503–999504. Lot No. BR Wagon Lot. 3093 Wolverton 1957.

45020	**E**	E	*SS*	TO
45026	v **M**	E		CL
45029	v **E**	E	*SS*	ML
999503	v* **M**	E		OC
999504	v* **E**	E	*SS*	TO

RAILFILMS KITCHEN/SLEEPING SALOON

Dia. AO. Converted from BR Mark 1 SK. Contains three sleeping cabins with showers and toilets and a large kitchen/pantry. Commonwealth bogies. 100 m.p.h. ETH 4.

Non-standard Livery: London & North Western Railway.

99884 (26208, 19208) **0**   RA   CS   State Car No. 84

ROYAL SCOTSMAN SALOONS

Built 1960 by Metro-Cammell as Pullman Parlour First (§Pullman Kitchen First) for East Coast Main Line services. Rebuilt 1990 as sleeping cars with four twin sleeping rooms (*§ three twin sleeping rooms and two single sleeping rooms at each end). Commonwealth bogies. 38.5 t.

99961	(324 AMBER) *	**M**	GS	*SS*	EN	STATE CAR 1
99962	(329 PEARL)	**M**	GS	*SS*	EN	STATE CAR 2
99963	(324 TOPAZ)	**M**	GS	*SS*	EN	STATE CAR 3
99964	(313 FINCH) §	**M**	GS	*SS*	EN	STATE CAR 4

Built 1960 by Metro-Cammell as Pullman Kitchen First for East Coast Main Line services. Rebuilt 1990 as observation car with open verandah seating 32. Commonwealth bogies. 38.5 t.

99965	(319 SNIPE)	**M**	GS	*SS*	EN	OBSERVATION CAR

Built 1960 by Metro-Cammell as Pullman Kitchen First for East Coast Main Line services. Rebuilt 1993 as dining car. Commonwealth bogies. 38.5 t.

99967	(317 RAVEN)	**M**	GS	*SS*	EN	DINING CAR

Mark 3A. Converted from SLEP at Carnforth Railway Restoration and Engineering Services in 1997. BT10 bogies. Attendant's and adjacent two sleeping compartments converted to generator room containing a 160 kW Volvo unit. In 99968 four sleeping compartments remain for staff use with another converted for use as a staff shower and toilet. The remaining five sleeping compartments have been replaced by two passenger cabins. In 99969 seven sleeping compartments remain for staff use. A further sleeping compartment, along with one toilet, have been converted to store rooms. The other two sleeping compartments have been combined to form a crew mess. ETH7X. 41.5 t.

Lot. No. 30960 Derby 1981–3.

99968	(10541)	**M**	GS	*SS*	EN	STATE CAR 5
99969	(10556)	**M**	GS	*SS*	EN	SERVICE CAR

RAILFILMS 'LMS CLUB CAR'

Dia. AO239. Converted from BR Mark 1 TSO at Carnforth Railway Restoration and Engineering Services in 1994. Contains kitchenette, pantry, coupé, lounge/reception area with two settees and two dining saloons. 24/– 1T. Commonwealth bogies. 100 m.p.h. ETH 4.

Lot. No. 30724 York 1963. 37 t.

99993	(5067)	**M**	RA	*SS*	TM	LMS CLUB CAR

BR INSPECTION SALOON

Dia. QX505. Mark 1. Short frames. Non-gangwayed. Observation windows at each end. The interior layout consists of two saloons interspersed by a central lavatory/kitchen/guards/luggage section. BR Mark 1 bogies. 90 m.p.h.

Lot No. BR Wagon Lot. 3379 Swindon 1960. 30.5 t.

999509	**E**	E	*SS*	ML

2.4. PULLMAN CAR COMPANY SERIES

Pullman cars have never generally been numbered as such, although many
have carried numbers, instead they have carried titles. However, a scheme of
schedule numbers exists which generally lists cars in chronological order. In
this section those numbers are shown followed by the car's title. Cars described
as 'kitchen' contain a kitchen in addition to passenger accommodation and
have gas cooking unless otherwise stated. Cars described as 'parlour' consist
entirely of passenger accomodation. Cars described as 'brake' contain a
compartment for the use of the guard and a luggage compartment in addition
to passenger accommodation.

PULLMAN PARLOUR FIRST

Built 1927 by Midland Carriage and Wagon Company. Gresley bogies. 26/– 2T.
ETH 2. 41 t.

213 MINERVA   **PC** VS *SS* SL

PULLMAN PARLOUR FIRST

Built 1928 by Metropolitan Carriage and Wagon Company. Gresley bogies.
24/– 2T. ETH 4. 40 t.

239 AGATHA   **PC** VS   SL
243 LUCILLE   **PC** VS *SS* SL

PULLMAN KITCHEN FIRST

Built 1925 by BRCW. Rebuilt by Midland Carriage & Wagon Company in 1928.
Gresley bogies. 20/– 1T. ETH 4. 41 t.

245 IBIS   **PC** VS *SS* SL

PULLMAN PARLOUR FIRST

Built 1928 by Metropolitan Carriage and Wagon Company. Gresley bogies.
24/– 2T. ETH 4.

254 ZENA   **PC** VS *SS* SL

PULLMAN KITCHEN FIRST

Built 1928 by Metropolitan Carriage and Wagon Company. Gresley bogies.
20/– 1T. ETH 4. 42 t.

255 IONE   **PC** VS *SS* SL

PULLMAN KITCHEN COMPOSITE

Built 1932 by Metropolitan Carriage and Wagon Company. Originally included in 6-Pul EMU. Electric cooking. EMU bogies. 12/16 1T.

264	RUTH		**PC**	VS		SL

PULLMAN KITCHEN FIRST

Built 1932 by Metopolitan Carriage and Wagon Company. Originally included in 'Brighton Belle' EMUs but now used as hauled stock. Electric cooking. B5 (SR) bogies (§ EMU bogies). 20/– 1T. ETH 2. 44 t.

280	AUDREY		**PC**	VS	*SS*	SL
281	GWEN		**PC**	VS	*SS*	SL
283	MONA	§	**PC**	VS		SL
284	VERA		**PC**	VS	*SS*	SL

PULLMAN PARLOUR THIRD

Built 1932 by Metropolitan Carriage and Wagon Company. Originally included in 'Brighton Belle' EMUs. EMU bogies. –/56 2T.

285	CAR No. 85	**PC**	VS	SL
286	CAR No. 86	**PC**	VS	SL

PULLMAN BRAKE THIRD

Built 1932 by Metropolitan Carriage and Wagon Company. Originally driving motor cars in 'Brighton Belle' EMUs. Traction and control equipment removed for use as hauled stock. EMU bogies. –/48 1T.

288	CAR No. 88	**PC**	VS	SL
292	CAR No. 92	**PC**	VS	SL
293	CAR No. 93	**PC**	VS	SL

PULLMAN PARLOUR FIRST

Built 1951 by Birmingham Railway Carriage and Wagon Company. Gresley bogies. 32/– 2T. ETH 3. 39 t.

301	PERSEUS	**PC**	VS	*SS*	SL

Dia. AO415. Built 1952 by Pullman Car Company, Preston Park using underframe and bogies from 176 RAINBOW, the body of which had been destroyed by fire. Gresley bogies. 26/– 2T. ETH 4. 38 t.

302	PHOENIX	**PC**	VS	*SS*	SL

PULLMAN PARLOUR FIRST

Built 1951 by Birmingham Railway Carriage & Wagon Company. Gresley bogies. 32/– 2T. ETH 3. 39 t.

308 CYGNUS   **PC** VS *SS* SL

PULLMAN FIRST BAR

Built 1951 by Birmingham Railway Carriage & Wagon Company. Rebuilt 1999 by Blake Fabrications, Edinburgh with original timber-framed body replaced by a new fabricated steel body. Contains kitchen, bar, dining saloon and coupé. Electric cooking. Gresley bogies. 14/– 1T. ETH 3.

310 PEGASUS   **PC** RA *SS* CP

Also carries "THE TRIANON BAR" branding.

2.5. PASSENGER COACHING STOCK AWAITING DISPOSAL

This list contains the last known locations of coaching stock awaiting disposal. The definition of which vehicles are "awaiting disposal" is somewhat vague, but generally speaking these are vehicles of types not now in normal service or vehicles which have been damaged by fire, vandalism or collision.

No.	Location		No.	Location
1644	CS		6361	NL
1650	CS		6362	LL
1652	CS		6363	LL
1653	FP		6390	ZB
1655	CS		6523	CS
1663	CS		6900	Cambridge Station Yard
1670	CS		6901	Cambridge Station Yard
1684	CS		9458	ZB
1688	CS		9482	NL
1697	CP		10322	ZF
1850	CP		10327	ZC
2127	CS		10664	ZN
4858	MB		10669	MM
4860	CS		10677	ZN
4932	CS		10694	MM
4997	CS		10695	ZN
5042	FP		10721	ZN
5476	HM		11213	ZF
5505	CS		11224	ZF
5533	HM		12306	ZF
5574	HM		12314	ZC
5585	HM		12412	ZF
5595	HM		12516	ZF
5645	CS		12525	ZF
5709	CS		13306	CS
5712	CS		13320	CS
6335	LA		13323	CS
6339	EC		17039	CD
6343	HT		17166	ZN
6345	EC		18837	CS
6347	ZN		21265	CS
6351	ZF		34525	CS
6356	ZF		34952	SL
6357	ZF		35509	ZH
6360	NL			

2.6. 99xxx RANGE NUMBER CONVERSION TABLE

The following table is presented to help readers identify vehicles which may carry numbers in the 99xxx range, the former private owner number series which is no longer in general use.

99xxx	BR No.	99xxx	BR No.	99xxx	BR No.	99xxx	BR No.
99035	35322	99322	5600	99539	255	99712	18893
99040	21232	99323	5704	99541	243	99713	19013
99041	35476	99324	5714	99542	889202	99716	18808
99052	45018	99325	5727	99543	284	99718	18862
99121	3105	99326	4954	99545	80207	99721	18756
99125	3113	99327	5044	99546	281	99722	18806
99127	3117	99328	5033	99670	546	99723	35459
99128	3130	99329	4931	99671	548	99792	17019
99131	1999	99371	3128	99672	549	99823	4832
99304	21256	99405	35486	99673	550	99826	13229
99311	1882	99530	301	99674	551	99827	3096
99312	35463	99531	302	99675	552	99830	5028
99315	18955	99532	308	99676	553	99880	5159
99316	13321	99534	245	99677	586	99881	4807
99317	3766	99535	213	99678	504	99886	35407
99318	4912	99536	254	99679	506	99953	35468
99319	17168	99537	280	99680	17102	99995	35457
99321	5299	99538	34991	99710	18767		

2.7. PRESERVED LOCOMOTIVE SUPPORT COACHES TABLE

The following table lists support coaches and the BR numbers of the locomotives which they normally support at present. These coaches can spend considerable periods of time off the Network Rail system when the locomotives they support are not being used on that system.

14007	61264	35329	RL locos	35465	46035	35486	SV locos
17013	60103*	35333	6024	35468	NR locos	35517	BQ locos
17019	46201	35453	5051	35470	TM locos	35518	34067
17096	35028	35457	62005	35476	46233	80204	WC locos
21232	46233	35461	5029	35479	SV locos	80217	75014
35317	34067	35463	WC locos				

* Carries former LNER number 4472.

3. DIESEL MULTIPLE UNITS

INTRODUCTION

DMU CLASSES

DMU Classes are listed in class number order. Principal details and dimensions are quoted for each class in metric and/or imperial units as considered appropriate bearing in mind common usage in the UK.

All dimensions and weights are quoted for vehicles in an 'as new' condition with all necessary supplies (e.g. oil, water, sand) on board. Dimensions are quoted in the order Length – Width. All lengths quoted are over buffers or couplers as appropriate. All width dimensions quoted are maxima.

NUMERICAL LISTINGS

DMUs are listed in numerical order of set – using current numbers as allocated by the RSL. Individual 'loose' vehicles are listed in numerical order after vehicles formed into fixed formations. Where numbers carried are different from those officially allocated these are noted in class headings where appropriate. Where sets or vehicles have been renumbered in recent years, former numbering detail is shown in parentheses. Each entry is laid out as in the following example:

Set No.   Detail Livery Owner Operation Depot   Formation
158 829   †   **WB**   A   WB   CF   52829   57829
Detail Differences. Detail differences which currently affect the areas and types of train which vehicles may work are shown, plus differences in interior layout. Where such differences occur within a class, these are shown either in the heading information or alongside the individual set or vehicle number. The following standard abbreviation is used:

r   Radio Electronic Token Block (RETB) equipment.

In all cases use of the above abbreviations indicates the equipment indicated is normally operable. Meaning of non-standard abbreviations is detailed in individual class headings.

Set Formations. Regular set formations are shown where these are normally maintained. Readers should note set formations might be temporarily varied from time to time to suit maintenance and/or operational requirements. Vehicles shown as 'Spare' are not formed in any regular set formation.

Codes. Codes used to denote the livery, owner, operation and depot of each unit. Details of these will be found in section 6 of this book. Where a unit or spare car is off-lease, the operation column will be left blank. (S) denotes stored.

Names. Only names carried with official sanction are listed. As far as possible names are shown in UPPER/lower case characters as actually shown on the name carried on the vehicle(s). Unless otherwise shown, complete units are regarded as named rather than just the individual car(s) which carry the name.

GENERAL INFORMATION

CLASSIFICATION AND NUMBERING

First generation ('Heritage') DMUs are classified in the series 100–139.
Second generation DMUs are classified in the series 140–199.
Diesel-electric multiple units are classified in the series 200–249.
Service units are classified in the series 930–999.
First and second generation individual cars are numbered in the series 50000–59999 and 79000–79999.

DEMU individual cars are numbered in the series 60000–60999, except for a few former EMU vehicles which retain their EMU numbers.

Service stock individual cars are numbered in the series 975000–975999 and 977000–977999, although this series is not exclusively used for DMU vehicles.

OPERATING CODES

These codes are used by train operating company staff to describe the various different types of vehicles and normally appear on data panels on the inner (i.e. non driving) ends of vehicles.

The first part of the code describes whether or not the car has a motor or a driving cab as follows:

DM Driving motor.
M   Motor
DT Driving trailer
T   Trailer

The next letter is a 'B' for cars with a brake compartment.

This is followed by the saloon details:

F   First
S   Standard
C   Composite
so denotes a semi-open vehicle (part compartments, part open). All other vehicles are assumed to consist solely of open saloons.

L denotes a vehicle with a lavatory compartment.

Finally vehicles with a buffet are suffixed RB or RMB for a miniature buffet.

Where two vehicles of the same type are formed within the same unit, the above codes may be suffixed by (A) and (B) to differentiate between the vehicles.

A composite is a vehicle containing both first and standard class accommodation, whilst a brake vehicle is a vehicle containing separate specific accommodation for the conductor.

Special Note: Where vehicles have been declassified, the correct operating code which describes the actual vehicle layout is quoted in this publication.

DESIGN CODES AND DIAGRAM CODES

For each type of vehicle the RSL issues a seven character 'Design Code' consisting of two letters plus four numbers and a suffix letter. (e.g. DP2010A). The first five characters of the Design Code are known as the 'Diagram Code' and these are quoted in this publication in sub-headings. The meaning of the various characters of the Design Code is as follows:

First Character
D   Diesel Multiple Unit vehicle.

Second Character
B   DEMU Driving motor passenger vehicle with brake compartment.
C   DEMU Driving motor passenger vehicle.
D   DEMU Non-driving motor passenger vehicle.
E   DEMU Driving trailer passenger vehicle.
F   DEMU Driving motor passenger vehicle (tilting).
G   DEMU Non-driving motor passenger vehicle (tilting).
H   DEMU Trailer passenger vehicle.
P   DMU (excl. DEMU) Driving motor passenger vehicle.
Q   DMU (excl. DEMU) Driving motor passenger vehicle with brake compartment.
R   DMU (excl. DEMU) Non-driving motor passenger vehicle.
S   DMU (excl. DEMU) Driving trailer passenger vehicle.
T   DMU (excl. DEMU) Trailer passenger vehicle.
X   DMU (excl. DEMU) Single unit railcar.
Z   All types of service vehicle.

Third Character
1   First class accommodation.
2   Standard class accommodation.
3   Composite accommodation.
5   No passenger accommodation.

Fourth & Fifth Characters
These distinguish between different designs of vehicle, each design being allocated a unique two digit number.

BUILD DETAILS

Lot Numbers

Vehicles ordered under the auspices of BR were allocated a Lot (batch) number when ordered and these are quoted in class headings and sub-headings.

ACCOMMODATION

The information given in class headings and sub-headings is in the form F/S nT (or TD) nW. For example 12/54 1T 1W denotes 12 first class and 54 standard class seats, 1 toilet and 1 wheelchair space. The seating layout of open saloons is shown as 2+1, 2+2 or 3+2 as the case may be. Where units have first class accommodation as well as standard and the layout is different for each class then these are shown separately prefixed by '1:' and '2:'. Compartments are always three seats a side in first class and four aside in standard class in DMUs. TD denotes a toilet suitable for a disabled person.

3.1. DIESEL MECHANICAL & DIESEL HYDRAULIC UNITS

3.1.1. FIRST GENERATION UNITS

CLASS 101   METRO-CAMMELL

First generation units still in service with First North Western.
DMBS–DMSL.
Construction: Aluminium alloy body on steel underframe.
Engines: Two Leyland 680/1 of 112 kW (150 h.p.) at 1800 r.p.m. per power car.
Transmission: Mechanical. Cardan shaft and freewheel to a four-speed epicyclic gearbox with a further cardan shaft to the final drive, each engine driving the inner axle of one bogie.
Brakes: Vacuum.
Gangways: British Standard (Midland scissors type). Within unit only.
Bogies: DD15 (motor) and DT11 (trailer).
Couplers: Screw couplings.
Dimensions: 18.49 x 2.82 m.
Seating Layout: 3+2 mainly unidirectional.
Doors: Manually-operated slam.
Multiple Working: 'Blue Square' coupling code. First generation vehicles may be coupled together to work in multiple up to a maximum of 6 motor cars or 12 cars in total in a formation. First generation vehicles may not be coupled in multiple with second generation vehicles.
Maximum Speed: 70 m.p.h.

51192/51205/51210. DMBS. Dia. DQ202. Lot No. 30467 1958–1959. –/52. 32.5 t.
53164. DMBS. Dia. DQ202. Lot No. 30546 1956. –/52. 32.5 t.
53204. DMBS. Dia. DQ202. Lot No. 30259 1957. –/52. 32.5 t.
53253. DMBS. Dia. DQ202. Lot No. 30266 1957. –/52. 32.5 t.
51511. DMSL. Dia. DP317. Lot No. 30501 1959. –/58. 32.5 t.
51803. DMSL. Dia. DP210. Lot No. 30588 1959. –/72 1T. 32.5 t.
53160. DMSL. Dia. DP214. Lot No. 30253 1956. –/72 1T. 32.5 t.
53170. DMSL. Dia. DP214. Lot No. 30255 1957. –/72 1T. 32.5 t.
53266. DMSL. Dia. DP210. Lot No. 30267 1957. –/72 1T. 32.5 t.
53746. DMSL. Dia. DP210. Lot No. 30271 1957. –/72 1T. 32.5 t.

Non-standard livery: 101 692 is in Caledonian style blue with yellow/orange stripes.

101 676	RR	A	NW	LO	51205	51803
101 678	RR	A	NW	LO	51210	53746
101 680	RR	A	NW	LO	53204	51511
101 685	G	A	NW	LO	53164	53160
101 692	O	A	NW	LO	53253	53170
101 693	S	A	NW	LO	51192	53266

CLASS 121   PRESSED STEEL SUBURBAN

First generation unit being refurbished for use by Chiltern on the Aylesbury–Princes Risborough services.

Construction: Steel.
Engines: Two Leyland 1595 of 112 kW (150 h.p.) at 1800 r.p.m.
Transmission: Mechanical. Cardan shaft and freewheel to a four-speed epicyclic gearbox and final drive.
Brakes: Vacuum.
Gangways: Non gangwayed single cars with cabs at each end.
Bogies: DD10.   **Couplers:** Screw couplings.
Dimensions: 20.45 x 2.82 m.   **Seating Layout:** 3+2 facing.
Doors: Manually-operated slam.   **Maximum Speed:** 70 m.p.h.
Multiple Working: As Class 101.

55020. DMBS. Dia. DX201. Lot No. 30518 1960. –/65. 38.0 t.

| 121 020 | N | CR *CR* | AL | 55020 |

3.1.2. SECOND GENERATION UNITS

All units in this section have air brakes and are equipped with public address, with transmission equipment on driving vehicles and flexible diaphragm gangways. Except where otherwise stated, transmission is Voith 211r hydraulic with a cardan shaft to a Gmeinder GM190 final drive.

CLASS 142   PACER   BREL DERBY/LEYLAND

DMS–DMSL.

Construction: Steel. Built from Leyland National bus parts on four-wheeled underframes.
Engines: One Cummins LTA10-R of 172 kW (230 h.p.) at 2100 r.p.m. (* One Perkins 2006-TWH of 172 kW (230 h.p.) at 2100 r.p.m.).
Couplers: BSI at outer ends, bar within unit.
Seating Layout: 3+2 mainly unidirectional bus/bench style unless stated.
Dimensions: 15.66 x 2.80 m.
Gangways: Within unit only.   **Wheel Arrangement:** 1-A A-1.
Doors: Twin-leaf inward pivoting.   **Maximum Speed:** 75 m.p.h.
Multiple Working: Within class and with Classes 143, 144, 150, 153, 155, 156, 158 and 159.

55542–55591. DMS. Dia. DP234 (s DP271). Lot No. 31003 1985–1986. –/62. (s –/58, t –/53 1W, u –/54, v –/52) 23.26 t.
55592–55641. DMSL. Dia. DP235 (s DP272). Lot No. 31004 1985–1986. –/59 1T. (s –/50 1T, u –/60 1T, v –/50 1T) 24.97 t.
55701–55746. DMS. Dia. DP234 (s DP271). Lot No. 31013 1986–1987. –/62. (s –/58, t –/53 1W, u –/54) 23.26 t.
55747–55792. DMSL. Dia. DP235 (s DP272). Lot No. 31014 1986–1987. –/59 1T. (s –/50 1T, u –/60 1T, v–/50 1T) 24.97 t.

s Fitted with 2+2 individual high-backed seating.
t First North Western facelifed units – DMS fitted with luggage rack and wheelchair space.
u Merseytravel units – Fitted with 3+2 individual low-back seating.
v Refurbished Valley Lines units. Fitted with 2+2 individual Chapman seating.

142 001	t	NW	A	NW	NH	55542	55592
142 002	v	VL	A	VL	CF	55543	55593
142 003		GM	A	NW	NH	55544	55594
142 004	t	NW	A	NW	NH	55545	55595
142 005	t	NW	A	NW	NH	55546	55596
142 006	v	VL	A	VL	CF	55547	55597
142 007	t	NW	A	NW	NH	55548	55598
142 009	t	NW	A	NW	NH	55550	55600	Newton Heath 125 1876–2001
142 010	v	VL	A	VL	CF	55551	55601
142 011	t	NW	A	NW	NH	55552	55602
142 012	t	NW	A	NW	NH	55553	55603
142 013		GM	A	NW	NH	55554	55604
142 014	t	NW	A	NW	NH	55555	55605
142 015	s	RR	A	AV	HT	55556	55606
142 016	s	RR	A	AV	HT	55557	55607
142 017	s	TW	A	AV	HT	55558	55608
142 018	s	TW	A	AV	HT	55559	55609
142 019	s	TW	A	AV	HT	55560	55610
142 020	s	TW	A	AV	HT	55561	55611
142 021	s	TW	A	AV	HT	55562	55612
142 022	s	TW	A	AV	HT	55563	55613
142 023	t	NW	A	NW	NH	55564	55614
142 024	s	RR	A	AV	HT	55565	55615
142 025	s	NS	A	AV	HT	55566	55616
142 026	s	NS	A	AV	HT	55567	55617
142 027	t	GM	A	NW	NH	55568	55618
142 028	t	NW	A	NW	NH	55569	55619
142 029		GM	A	NW	NH	55570	55620
142 030	t	NW	A	NW	NH	55571	55621
142 031	t	NW	A	NW	NH	55572	55622
142 032	t	NW	A	NW	NH	55573	55623
142 033	t	NW	A	NW	NH	55574	55624
142 034	t	NW	A	NW	NH	55575	55625
142 035	t	NW	A	NW	NH	55576	55626
142 036	t	NW	A	NW	NH	55577	55627
142 037	t	NW	A	NW	NH	55578	55628
142 038	t	NW	A	NW	NH	55579	55629
142 039	t	NW	A	NW	NH	55580	55630
142 040	t	GM	A	NW	NH	55581	55631
142 041	u	MY	A	NW	NH	55582	55632
142 042	u	MY	A	NW	NH	55583	55633
142 043	u	MY	A	NW	NH	55584	55634
142 044	u	MY	A	NW	NH	55585	55635
142 045	u	MY	A	NW	NH	55586	55636

142 046	u	**MY**	A	*NW*	NH	55587	55637
142 047	u	**MY**	A	*NW*	NH	55588	55638
142 048	u	**MY**	A	*NW*	NH	55589	55639
142 049	u	**MY**	A	*NW*	NH	55590	55640
142 050	s	**NS**	A	*AV*	HT	55591	55641
142 051	u	**MT**	A	*NW*	NH	55701	55747
142 052	u	**MT**	A	*NW*	NH	55702	55748
142 053	u	**MT**	A	*NW*	NH	55703	55749
142 054	u	**MT**	A	*NW*	NH	55704	55750
142 055	u	**MT**	A	*NW*	NH	55705	55751
142 056	u	**MT**	A	*NW*	NH	55706	55752
142 057	u	**MT**	A	*NW*	NH	55707	55753
142 058	u	**MT**	A	*NW*	NH	55708	55754
142 060	t	**NW**	A	*NW*	NH	55710	55756
142 061	t	**NW**	A	*NW*	NH	55711	55757
142 062	t	**NW**	A	*NW*	NH	55712	55758
142 063	t	**GM**	A	*NW*	NH	55713	55759
142 064	t	**NW**	A	*NW*	NH	55714	55760
142 065	s	**NS**	A	*AV*	HT	55715	55761
142 066	s	**NS**	A	*AV*	HT	55716	55762
142 067	t	**NW**	A	*NW*	NH	55717	55763
142 068	t	**NW**	A	*NW*	NH	55718	55764
142 069	v	**VL**	A	*VL*	CF	55719	55765
142 070	t	**NW**	A	*NW*	NH	55720	55766
142 071	s	**RR**	A	*AV*	HT	55721	55767
142 072	v	**VL**	A	*VL*	CF	55722	55768
142 073	v	**VL**	A	*VL*	CF	55723	55769
142 074	v	**VL**	A	*VL*	CF	55724	55770
142 075	v	**VL**	A	*VL*	CF	55725	55771
142 076	v	**VL**	A	*VL*	CF	55726	55772
142 077	v	**VL**	A	*VL*	CF	55727	55773
142 078	s	**RR**	A	*AV*	HT	55728	55774
142 079	s	**RR**	A	*AV*	HT	55729	55775
142 080	v	**VL**	A	*VL*	CF	55730	55776
142 081		**RR**	A	*VL*	CF	55731	55777
142 082	v	**VL**	A	*VL*	CF	55732	55778
142 083	v	**VL**	A	*VL*	CF	55733	55779
142 084	s*	**RR**	A	*AV*	HT	55734	55780
142 085	v	**VL**	A	*VL*	CF	55735	55781
142 086	s	**RR**	A	*AV*	HT	55736	55782
142 087	s	**RR**	A	*AV*	HT	55737	55783
142 088	s	**RR**	A	*AV*	HT	55738	55784
142 089	s	**RR**	A	*AV*	HT	55739	55785
142 090	s	**RR**	A	*AV*	HT	55740	55786
142 091	s	**RR**	A	*AV*	HT	55741	55787
142 092	s	**RR**	A	*AV*	HT	55742	55788
142 093	s	**RR**	A	*AV*	HT	55743	55789
142 094	s	**RR**	A	*AV*	HT	55744	55790
142 095	s	**RR**	A	*AV*	HT	55745	55791
142 096	s	**RR**	A	*AV*	HT	55746	55792

CLASS 143   PACER   ALEXANDER/BARCLAY

DMS–DMSL. Similar design to Class 142, but bodies built by W. Alexander with
Barclay underframes.

Construction: Steel. Alexander bus bodywork on four-wheeled underframes.
Engines: One Cummins LTA10-R of 172 kW (230 h.p.) at 2100 r.p.m.
Couplers: BSI at outer ends, bar couplers within unit.
Seating Layout: All units now fitted with 2+2 Chapman seating, mainly unidirectional.
Dimensions: 15.55 x 2.70 m.
Gangways: Within unit only.   **Wheel Arrangement:** 1-A A-1.
Doors: Twin-leaf inward pivoting.   **Maximum Speed:** 75 m.p.h.
Multiple Working: Within class and with Classes 142, 144, 150, 153, 155, 156,
158 and 159.

DMS. Dia. DP236 Lot No. 31005 Andrew Barclay 1985–1986. –/55. 24.5 t.
DMSL. Dia. DP237 Lot No. 31006 Andrew Barclay 1985–1986. –/51 1T. 25.0 t.

143 601	VL	RD	VL	CF	55642	55667	
143 602	VL	P	VL	CF	55651	55668	
143 603	BI	P	WX	CF	55658	55669	
143 604	VL	P	VL	CF	55645	55670	
143 605	VL	P	VL	CF	55646	55671	Crimestoppers
143 606	VL	P	VL	CF	55647	55672	
143 607	VL	P	VL	CF	55648	55673	
143 608	VL	P	VL	CF	55649	55674	
143 609	VL	BC	VL	CF	55650	55675	Tom Jones
143 610	VL	RD	VL	CF	55643	55676	
143 611	BI	P	WX	CF	55652	55677	
143 612	BI	P	WX	CF	55653	55678	
143 613	BI	P	WX	CF	55654	55679	
143 614	VL	RD	VL	CF	55655	55680	
143 615	VL	P	VL	CF	55656	55681	
143 616	VL	P	VL	CF	55657	55682	
143 617	BI	RI	WX	CF	55644	55683	
143 618	BI	RI	WX	CF	55659	55684	
143 619	BI	RI	WX	CF	55660	55685	
143 620	BI	P	WX	CF	55661	55686	
143 621	BI	P	WX	CF	55662	55687	
143 622	BI	P	WX	CF	55663	55688	
143 623	BI	P	WX	CF	55664	55689	
143 624	VL	P	VL	CF	55665	55690	
143 625	VL	P	VL	CF	55666	55691	Valley Kids

CLASS 144 PACER ALEXANDER/BREL DERBY

DMS–DMSL or DMS–MS–DMSL. As Class 143, but underframes built by BREL.

Construction: Steel. Alexander bus bodywork on four-wheeled underframes.
Engines: One Cummins LTA10-R of 172 kW (230 h.p.) at 2100 r.p.m.
Couplers: BSI at outer ends, bar couplers within unit.
Seating Layout: 3+2 mainly unidirectional bus/bench style unless stated.

Dimensions: 15.55 x 2.73 m.
Gangways: Within unit only.   **Wheel Arrangement:** 1-A A-1.
Doors: Twin-leaf inward pivoting.   **Maximum Speed:** 75 m.p.h.
Multiple Working: Wiyhin class and with Classes 142, 143, 150, 153, 155, 156, 158 and 159.

DMS. Dia. DP240 Lot No. 31015 BREL Derby 1986–1987. –/62 1W (s –48 1W) 24.2 t.
MS. Dia. DR205 Lot No. BREL Derby 31037 1987. –/73 22.6 t.
DMSL. Dia. DP241 Lot No. BREL Derby 31016 1986–1987. –/60 1T (s –45 1T) 25.0 t.

s Refurbished Arriva Trains Northern units. Fitted with 2+2 Richmond seating.

Note: The centre cars of the 3-car units are owned by West Yorkshire PTE, although managed by Porterbrook Leasing Company.

144 001	s	**YP**	P	AV	NL	55801		55824
144 002	s	**YP**	P	AV	NL	55802		55825
144 003	s	**YP**	P	AV	NL	55803		55826
144 004		**WY**	P	AV	NL	55804		55827
144 005		**WY**	P	AV	NL	55805		55828
144 006	s	**YP**	P	AV	NL	55806		55829
144 007		**WY**	P	AV	NL	55807		55830
144 008		**WY**	P	AV	NL	55808		55831
144 009		**WY**	P	AV	NL	55809		55832
144 010	s	**YP**	P	AV	NL	55810		55833
144 011	s	**YP**	P	AV	NL	55811		55834
144 012		**RR**	P	AV	NL	55812		55835
144 013	s	**YP**	P	AV	NL	55813		55836
144 014		**WY**	P	AV	NL	55814	55850	55837
144 015		**WY**	P	AV	NL	55815	55851	55838
144 016		**WY**	P	AV	NL	55816	55852	55839
144 017		**WY**	P	AV	NL	55817	55853	55840
144 018		**WY**	P	AV	NL	55818	55854	55841
144 019		**WY**	P	AV	NL	55819	55855	55842
144 020		**WY**	P	AV	NL	55820	55856	55843
144 021		**WY**	P	AV	NL	55821	55857	55844
144 022		**WY**	P	AV	NL	55822	55858	55845
144 023		**WY**	P	AV	NL	55823	55859	55846

CLASS 150/0   SPRINTER   BREL YORK

DMSL–MS–DMS. Prototype Sprinter.

Construction: Steel.
Engines: One Cummins NT-855-R4 of 213 kW (285 h.p.) at 2100 r.p.m.
Bogies: BX8P (powered), BX8T (non-powered).
Couplers: BSI at outer end of driving vehicles, bar non-driving ends.
Seating Layout: 3+2 mainly unidirectional.
Dimensions: 20.06/20.18 x 2.82 m.
Gangways: Within unit only.   **Wheel Arrangement:** 2-B – 2-B – B-2.
Doors: Single-leaf sliding.   **Maximum Speed:** 75 m.p.h.
Multiple Working: Within class and with Classes 142, 143, 144, 153, 155, 156, 158, 159 and 170.

DMSL. Dia. DP230. Lot No. 30984 1984. –/72 1T. 35.8 t.
MS. Dia. DR202. Lot No. 30986 1984. –/92. 34.4 t.
DMS. Dia. DP231. Lot No. 30985 1984. –/76. 35.6 t.

150 001	r	**CO**	A	*CT*	TS	55200	55400	55300
150 002	r	**CO**	A	*CT*	TS	55201	55401	55301

CLASS 150/1   SPRINTER   BREL YORK

DMSL–DMS or DMSL–DMSL–DMS or DMSL–DMS–DMS.

Construction: Steel.
Engines: One Cummins NT855R5 of 213 kW (285 h.p.) at 2100 r.p.m.
Bogies: BP38 (powered), BT38 (non-powered).
Couplers: BSI.
Seating Layout: 3+2 facing as built but 150 010–150 132 were reseated with mainly unidirectional seating.
Dimensions: 19.74 x 2.82 m.
Gangways: Within unit only.   **Wheel Arrangement:** 2-B (– 2–B) – B-2.
Doors: Single-leaf sliding.   **Maximum Speed:** 75 m.p.h.
Multiple Working: Within class and with Classes 142, 143, 144, 153, 155, 156, 158, 159 and 170.

DMSL. Dia. DP238. Lot No. 31011 1985–1986. –/72 1T (s –/59 1TD, t –/71 1W 1T, u –/71 1T). 36.5 t.
DMS. Dia. DP239. Lot No. 31012 1985–1986. –/76 (s –/65). 38.45 t.

Non-standard livery: 150 134 is in plain dark blue.

Notes: The centre cars of three-car units are Class 150/2 vehicles. For details see Class 150/2.
Units reliveried in **NW** livery have been refurbished with new Chapman seating.

150 003	ru	**CO**	A	*CT*	TS	52103	57210	57103
150 005	ru	**CO**	A	*CT*	TS	52105	57210	57105
150 010	ru	**CO**	A	*CT*	TS	52110	57226	57110
150 011	ru	**CO**	A	*CT*	TS	52111	52204	57111
150 012	ru	**CO**	A	*CT*	TS	52112	57206	57112
150 013	ru	**CO**	A	*CT*	TS	52113	52226	57113
150 014	ru	**CO**	A	*CT*	TS	52114	57204	57114
150 015	ru	**CO**	A	*CT*	TS	52115	52206	57115
150 016	ru	**CO**	A	*CT*	TS	52116	57212	57116
150 017	ru	**CO**	A	*CT*	TS	52117	57209	57117
150 018	ru	**CO**	A	*CT*	TS	52118	52220	57118
150 019	ru	**CO**	A	*CT*	TS	52119	57220	57119
150 101	ru	**CO**	A	*CT*	TS	52101	57102	
150 102	ru	**CO**	A	*CT*	TS	52102	57102	
150 104	ru	**CO**	A	*CT*	TS	52104	57104	
150 106	r	**CO**	A	*CT*	TS	52106	57106	
150 107	r	**CO**	A	*CT*	TS	52107	57107	
150 108	ru	**CO**	A	*CT*	TS	52108	57108	
150 109	ru	**CO**	A	*CT*	TS	52109	57109	
150 120	t	**SL**	A	*SL*	BY	52120	57120	
150 121	ru	**CO**	A	*CT*	TS	52121	57121	

150 122	ru	**CO**	A	*CT*	TS	52122	57122
150 123	t	**SL**	A	*SL*	BY	52123	57123
150 124	ru	**CO**	A	*CT*	TS	52124	57124
150 125	ru	**CO**	A	*CT*	TS	52125	57125
150 126	ru	**CO**	A	*CT*	TS	52126	57126
150 127	t	**SL**	A	*SL*	BY	52127	57127	Bletchley TMD
150 128	t	**SL**	A	*SL*	BY	52128	57128	Community Forest
150 129	t	**SL**	A	*SL*	BY	52129	57129	MARSTON VALE
150 130	t	**SL**	A	*SL*	BY	52130	57130	Bedford–Bletchley 150
150 131	t	**SL**	A	*SL*	BY	52131	57131	LESLIE CRABBE
150 132	r	**CO**	A	*CT*	TS	52132	57132
150 133	s	**NW**	A	*NW*	NH	52133	57133
150 134	s	**O**	A	*NW*	NH	52134	57134
150 135	s	**NW**	A	*NW*	NH	52135	57135
150 136	s	**NW**	A	*NW*	NH	52136	57136
150 137	s	**NW**	A	*NW*	NH	52137	57137
150 138	s	**NW**	A	*NW*	NH	52138	57138
150 139	s	**NW**	A	*NW*	NH	52139	57139
150 140	s	**NW**	A	*NW*	NH	52140	57140
150 141	s	**NW**	A	*NW*	NH	52141	57141
150 142	s	**NW**	A	*NW*	NH	52142	57142
150 143	s	**NW**	A	*NW*	NH	52143	57143
150 144	s	**NW**	A	*NW*	NH	52144	57144
150 145	s	**NW**	A	*NW*	NH	52145	57145
150 146	s	**NW**	A	*NW*	NH	52146	57146
150 147	s	**NW**	A	*NW*	NH	52147	57147
150 148	s	**NW**	A	*NW*	NH	52148	57148
150 149	s	**NW**	A	*NW*	NH	52149	57149
150 150	s	**NW**	A	*NW*	NH	52150	57150

CLASS 150/2   SPRINTER   BREL YORK

DMSL–DMS.

Construction: Steel.
Engines: One Cummins NT855R5 of 213 kW (285 h.p.) at 2100 r.p.m.
Bogies: BP38 (powered), BT38 (non-powered).
Couplers: BSI.
Seating Layout: 3+2 (v 2+2) mainly unidirectional seating.
Dimensions: 19.74 x 2.82 m.
Gangways: Throughout.   **Wheel Arrangement:** 2-B – B-2.
Doors: Single-leaf sliding.   **Maximum Speed:** 75 m.p.h.
Multiple Working: Within class and with Classes 142, 143, 144, 153, 155, 156, 158, 159 and 170.

DMSL. Dia. DP242. Lot No. 31017 1986–1987. –/73 1T (s –/70 1TD, v –/60 1T). 35.8 t.
DMS. Dia. DP243. Lot No. 31018 1986–1987. –/76 (* –/68, s –/62, v –/56). 34.9 t.
Units in **NW** livery have been refurbished with new Chapman seating.
v Refurbished Valley Lines/Wessex Trains units with 2+2 Chapman seating.

150 201	s	**NW**	A	*NW*	NH	52201	57201
150 202		**CO**	A	*CT*	TS	52202	57202

150 203	s	NW	A	NW	NH	52203	57203	
150 205	s	NW	A	NW	NH	52205	57205	
150 207	s	NW	A	NW	NH	52207	57207	
150 208		SR	P	SR	HA	52208	57208	
150 211	s	NW	A	NW	NH	52211	57211	
150 213	r*	AR	P	AR	NC	52213	57213	LORD NELSON
150 214		CO	A	CT	TS	52214	57214	
150 215	s	NW	A	NW	NH	52215	57215	
150 216		CO	A	CT	TS	52216	57216	
150 217	r*	AR	P	AR	NC	52217	57217	OLIVER CROMWELL
150 218	s	NW	A	NW	NH	52218	57218	
150 219	r	RR	P	WX	CF	52219	57219	
150 221	rv	WZ	P	WX	CF	52221	57221	
150 222	s	NW	A	NW	NH	52222	57222	
150 223	s	NW	A	WX	CF	52223	57223	
150 224	s	NW	A	NW	NH	52224	57224	
150 225	s	NW	A	NW	NH	52225	57225	
150 227	r*	AR	P	AR	NC	52227	57227	SIR ALF RAMSEY
150 228		RR	P	AV	NL	52228	57228	
150 229	r*	AR	P	AR	NC	52229	57229	GEORGE BORROW
150 230	r	RR	P	WX	CF	52230	57230	
150 231	r*	PS	P	AR	NC	52231	57231	KING EDMUND
150 232	r	RR	P	WX	CF	52232	57232	
150 233	r	RR	P	WX	CF	52233	57233	
150 234	r	RR	P	WX	CF	52234	57234	
150 235	r*	PS	P	AR	NC	52235	57235	CARDINAL WOLSEY
150 236	r	RR	P	WX	CF	52236	57236	
150 237	r*	AR	P	AR	NC	52237	57237	HEREWARD THE WAKE
150 238	r	RR	P	WX	CF	52238	57238	
150 239	rv	WZ	P	WX	CF	52239	57239	
150 240	r	RR	P	WX	CF	52240	57240	
150 241	rv	WZ	P	WX	CF	52241	57241	The Tarka Belle
150 242	rv	WZ	P	WX	CF	52242	57242	
150 243	rv	WZ	P	WX	CF	52243	57243	
150 244	rv	WZ	P	WX	CF	52244	57244	The West Cornwall Experience
150 245	r	AR	P	AR	NC	52245	57245	
150 246	r	RR	P	WX	CF	52246	57246	
150 247	rv	WZ	P	WX	CF	52247	57247	
150 248	r	RR	P	WX	CF	52248	57248	
150 249	r	RR	P	WX	CF	52249	57249	
150 250		SR	P	SR	HA	52250	57250	
150 251	rv	WZ	P	WX	CF	52251	57251	
150 252		SR	P	SR	HA	52252	57252	
150 253	r	RR	P	WX	CF	52253	57253	
150 254	r	RR	P	WX	CF	52254	57254	HENRY BLOGG
150 255	r*	AR	P	AR	NC	52255	57255	
150 256		SR	P	SR	HA	52256	57256	QUEEN BOADICEA
150 257	r*	AR	P	AR	NC	52257	57257	
150 258		SR	P	SR	HA	52258	57258	
150 259		SR	P	SR	HA	52259	57259	
150 260		SR	P	SR	HA	52260	57260	

150 261	r	**RR**	P	*WX*	CF	52261	57261
150 262		**SR**	P	*SR*	HA	52262	57262
150 263	r	**RR**	P	*WX*	CF	52263	57263
150 264		**SR**	P	*SR*	HA	52264	57264
150 265	r	**RR**	P	*WX*	CF	52265	57265
150 266	r	**RR**	P	*WX*	CF	52266	57266
150 267	rv	**VW**	P	*VL*	CF	52267	57267
150 268		**RR**	P	*AV*	NL	52268	57268
150 269		**RR**	P	*AV*	NL	52269	57269
150 270		**RR**	P	*AV*	NL	52270	57270
150 271		**RR**	P	*AV*	NL	52271	57271
150 272		**RR**	P	*AV*	NL	52272	57272
150 273		**RR**	P	*AV*	NL	52273	57273
150 274		**RR**	P	*AV*	NL	52274	57274
150 275		**RR**	P	*AV*	NL	52275	57275
150 276		**RR**	P	*AV*	NL	52276	57276
150 277		**RR**	P	*AV*	NL	52277	57277
150 278	rv	**VW**	P	*VL*	CF	52278	57278
150 279	v	**VW**	P	*VL*	CF	52279	57279
150 280	v	**VW**	P	*VL*	CF	52280	57280	University of Glamorgan/ Prifysgol Morgannwg
150 281	v	**VW**	P	*VL*	CF	52281	57281
150 282	v	**VW**	P	*VL*	CF	52282	57282
150 283		**SR**	P	*SR*	HA	52283	57283
150 284		**SR**	P	*SR*	HA	52284	57284
150 285		**SR**	P	*SR*	HA	52285	57285

CLASS 153   SUPER SPRINTER   LEYLAND BUS

DMSL. Converted by Hunslet-Barclay, Kilmarnock from Class 155 two-car units.

Construction: Steel. Built from Leyland National bus parts on bogied underframes.
Engine: One Cummins NT855R5 of 213 kW (285 h.p.) at 2100 r.p.m.
Bogies: One P3-10 (powered) and one BT38 (non-powered).
Couplers: BSI.
Seating Layout: 2+2 facing/unidirectional.
Dimensions: 23.21 x 2.70 m.
Gangways: Throughout.   **Wheel Arrangement:** 2-B.
Doors: Single-leaf sliding plug.   **Maximum Speed:** 75 m.p.h.
Multiple Working: Within class and with Classes 142, 143, 144, 150, 155, 156, 158, 159 and 170.

52301–52335. DMSL. Dia. DX203. Lot No. 31026 1987–1988. Converted under Lot No. 31115 1991–2. –/75 1T 1W (* –/66 1T 1W). 41.2 t.
57301–57335. DMSL. Dia. DX203. Lot No. 31027 1987–1988. Converted under Lot No. 31115 1991–2. –/75 1T (* –/66 1T). 41.2 t.
Advertising livery: 153 314 Norfolk and Norwich Festival (Black and orange).
Notes: Cars numbered in the 573XX series were renumbered by adding 50 to their original number so that the last two digits correspond with the set number. Central Trains and First North Western units have been fitted with new Chapman seating. Wales & Borders/Wessex Trains units have been reseated with seats

removed from that company's Class 158 units. Arriva units have been fitted with new Richmond seating.

153 301		AV	A	AV	NL	52301
153 302	r	DC	A	WX	CF	52302
153 303	r	HW	A	WB	CF	52303
153 304		AV	A	AV	NL	52304
153 305	r	WX	A	WX	CF	52305
153 306	r*	PS	P	AR	NC	52306	EDITH CAVELL
153 307		AV	A	AV	NL	52307
153 308	r	DC	A	WX	CF	52308
153 309	r*	PS	P	AR	NC	52309	GERARD FIENNES
153 310		NW	P	NW	NH	52310
153 311	r*	PS	P	AR	NC	52311	JOHN CONSTABLE
153 312		HW	A	WB	CF	52312
153 313		NW	P	NW	NH	52313
153 314	r*	AL	P	AR	NC	52314	DELIA SMITH
153 315		AV	A	AV	NL	52315
153 316		NW	P	NW	NH	52316
153 317		AV	A	AV	NL	52317
153 318	r	WX	A	WX	CF	52318
153 319		AV	A	AV	NL	52319
153 320	r	HW	P	WB	CF	52320
153 321	r	HW	P	WB	CF	52321
153 322	r*	AR	P	AR	NC	52322	BENJAMIN BRITTEN
153 323	r	HW	P	WB	CF	52323
153 324		NW	P	NW	NH	52324
153 325	r	RR	P	CT	TS	52325	TED ELLIS
153 326	r*	PS	P	AR	NC	52326
153 327	r	HW	A	WB	CF	52327
153 328		AV	A	AV	NL	52328
153 329	r	RR	P	CT	TS	52329
153 330		NW	P	NW	NH	52330
153 331		AV	A	AV	NL	52331
153 332		NW	P	NW	NH	52332
153 333	r	RR	P	CT	TS	52333
153 334	r	RR	P	CT	TS	52334
153 335	r*	PS	P	AR	NC	52335	MICHAEL PALIN
153 351		AV	A	AV	NL	57351
153 352		AV	A	AV	NL	57352
153 353	r	HW	A	WB	CF	57353
153 354	r	RR	P	CT	TS	57354
153 355	r	WX	A	WX	CF	57355
153 356	r	RR	P	CT	TS	57356
153 357		AV	A	AV	NL	57357
153 358		NW	P	NW	NH	57358
153 359		NW	P	NW	NH	57359
153 360		NW	P	NW	NH	57360
153 361		NW	P	NW	NH	57361
153 362	r	HW	A	WB	CF	57362
153 363		NW	P	NW	NH	57363

153 364	r	**RR**	P	*CT*	TS	57364
153 365	r	**RR**	P	*CT*	TS	57365
153 366	r	**RR**	P	*CT*	TS	57366
153 367		**NW**	P	*NW*	NH	57367
153 368	r	**WX**	A	*WX*	CF	57368
153 369	r	**RR**	P	*CT*	TS	57369
153 370	r	**WX**	A	*WX*	CF	57370
153 371	r	**RR**	P	*CT*	TS	57371
153 372	r	**WX**	A	*WX*	CF	57372
153 373	r	**WX**	A	*WX*	CF	57373
153 374	r	**DC**	A	*WX*	CF	57374
153 375	r	**RR**	P	*CT*	TS	57375
153 376	r	**RR**	P	*CT*	TS	57376
153 377	r	**DC**	A	*WX*	CF	57377
153 378		**AV**	A	*AV*	NL	57378
153 379	r	**RR**	P	*CT*	TS	57379
153 380	r	**DC**	A	*WX*	CF	57380
153 381	r	**RR**	P	*CT*	TS	57381
153 382	r	**DC**	A	*WX*	CF	57382
153 383	r	**RR**	P	*CT*	TS	57383
153 384	r	**RR**	P	*CT*	TS	57384
153 385	r	**RR**	P	*CT*	TS	57385

CLASS 155   SUPER SPRINTER   LEYLAND BUS

DMSL–DMS.

Construction: Steel. Built from Leyland National bus parts on bogied underframes.
Engines: One Cummins NT855R5 of 213 kW (285 h.p.) at 2100 r.p.m.
Bogies: One P3-10 (powered) and one BT38 (non-powered).
Couplers: BSI.
Seating Layout: 2+2 facing/unidirectional.
Dimensions: 23.21 x 2.70 m.
Gangways: Throughout.   **Wheel Arrangement:** 2-B – B-2.
Doors: Single-leaf sliding plug.   **Maximum Speed:** 75 m.p.h.
Multiple Working: Within class and with Classes 142, 143, 144, 150, 153, 156, 158, 159 and 170.

DMSL. Dia. DP248. Lot No. 31057 1988. –/80 1TD 1W. 39.0 t.
DMS. Dia. DP249. Lot No. 31058 1988. –/80. 38.7 t.

Note: These units are owned by West Yorkshire PTE, although managed by Porterbrook Leasing Company.

155 341	**WY**	P	*AV*	NL	52341	57341
155 342	**WY**	P	*AV*	NL	52342	57342
155 343	**WY**	P	*AV*	NL	52343	57343
155 344	**WY**	P	*AV*	NL	52344	57344
155 345	**WY**	P	*AV*	NL	52345	57345
155 346	**WY**	P	*AV*	NL	52346	57346
155 347	**WY**	P	*AV*	NL	52347	57347

CLASS 156 SUPER SPRINTER METRO-CAMMELL

DMSL–DMS.

Construction: Steel.
Engines: One Cummins NT855R5 of 213 kW (285 h.p.) at 2100 r.p.m.
Bogies: One P3-10 (powered) and one BT38 (non-powered).
Couplers: BSI.
Seating Layout: 2+2 facing/unidirectional.
Dimensions: 23.03 x 2.73 m.
Gangways: Throughout.   **Wheel Arrangement:** 2-B – B-2.
Doors: Single-leaf sliding plug.   **Maximum Speed:** 75 m.p.h.
Multiple Working: Within class and with Classes 142, 143, 144, 150, 153, 155, 158, 159 and 170.

DMSL. Dia. DP244 (q DP261). Lot No. 31028 1988–1989. –/74 (†* –/72, st –/70, u –/68) 1TD 1W. 36.1 t.
DMS. Dia. DP245 (q DP262). Lot No. 31029 1987–1989. –/76 (q –/78, † –/74, tu –/72) 35.5 t.

Notes: 156 500–156 514 are owned by Strathclyde PTE, although managed by Angel Trains.
Central Trains and First North Western units have been fitted with new Chapman seating.
Arriva Trains Northern units have been fitted with new Richmond seating.

156 401	r*	RE	P	CT	TS	52401 57401
156 402	r*	RE	P	CT	TS	52402 57402
156 403	r*	RE	P	CT	TS	52403 57403
156 404	r*	RE	P	CT	TS	52404 57404
156 405	r*	RE	P	CT	TS	52405 57405
156 406	r*	RE	P	CT	TS	52406 57406
156 407	r*	CT	P	CT	TS	52407 57407
156 408	r*	RE	P	CT	TS	52408 57408
156 409	r*	RE	P	CT	TS	52409 57409
156 410	r*	RE	P	CT	TS	52410 57410
156 411	r*	RE	P	CT	TS	52411 57411
156 412	r*	RE	P	CT	TS	52412 57412
156 413	r*	RE	P	CT	TS	52413 57413
156 414	r*	RE	P	CT	TS	52414 57414
156 415	r*	RE	P	CT	TS	52415 57415
156 416	r*	RE	P	CT	TS	52416 57416
156 417	r*	RE	P	CT	TS	52417 57417
156 418	r*	RE	P	CT	TS	52418 57418
156 419	r*	RE	P	CT	TS	52419 57419
156 420	s	RN	P	NW	NH	52420 57420
156 421	s	RN	P	NW	NH	52421 57421
156 422	r*	RE	P	CT	TS	52422 57422
156 423	s	RN	P	NW	NH	52423 57423
156 424	s	RN	P	NW	NH	52424 57424
156 425	s	RN	P	NW	NH	52425 57425
156 426	s	RN	P	NW	NH	52426 57426
156 427	s	RN	P	NW	NH	52427 57427

156 428	s	RN	P	NW	NH	52428	57428
156 429	s	RN	P	NW	NH	52429	57429
156 430	t	SC	A	SR	CK	52430	57430
156 431	t	SC	A	SR	CK	52431	57431
156 432	t	SC	A	SR	CK	52432	57432
156 433	t	SC	A	SR	CK	52433	57433
156 434	t	SC	A	SR	CK	52434	57434
156 435	t	SC	A	SR	CK	52435	57435
156 436	†	SC	A	SR	CK	52436	57436
156 437	rt	SC	A	SR	CK	52437	57437
156 438	q	NS	A	AV	NL	52438	57438
156 439	rt	SC	A	SR	CK	52439	57439
156 440	s	RN	P	NW	NH	52440	57440
156 441	s	RN	P	NW	NH	52441	57441
156 442	rt	SC	A	SR	CK	52442	57442
156 443	q	NS	A	AV	HT	52443	57443
156 444	q	NS	A	AV	HT	52444	57444
156 445	u	SC	A	SR	CK	52445	57445
156 446	rt	SR	A	SR	CK	52446	57446
156 447	ru	SR	A	SR	CK	52447	57447
156 448	q	NS	A	AV	HT	52448	57448
156 449	ru	SR	A	SR	CK	52449	57449
156 450	t	SR	A	SR	CK	52450	57450
156 451	q	NS	A	AV	HT	52451	57451
156 452	s	RN	P	NW	NH	52452	57452
156 453	ru	SR	A	SR	CK	52453	57453
156 454	q	NS	A	AV	HT	52454	57454
156 455	s	RN	P	NW	NH	52455	57455
156 456	rt	SR	A	SR	CK	52456	57456
156 457	rt	SR	A	SR	CK	52457	57457
156 458	rt	SR	A	SR	CK	52458	57458
156 459	s	RN	P	NW	NH	52459	57459
156 460	s	RN	P	NW	NH	52460	57460
156 461	s	RN	P	NW	NH	52461	57461
156 462		SR	A	SR	CK	52462	57462
156 463	q	NS	A	AV	HT	52463	57463
156 464	s	RN	P	NW	NH	52464	57464
156 465	u	SR	A	SR	CK	52465	57465
156 466	s	RN	P	NW	NH	52466	57466
156 467		SR	A	SR	CK	52467	57467
156 468	q	NS	A	AV	NL	52468	57468
156 469	q	NS	A	AV	HT	52469	57469
156 470	q	NS	A	AV	NL	52470	57470
156 471	q	NS	A	AV	NL	52471	57471
156 472	q	NS	A	AV	NL	52472	57472
156 473	q	NS	A	AV	NL	52473	57473
156 474	rt	SR	A	SR	CK	52474	57474
156 475	q	NS	A	AV	NL	52475	57475
156 476	rt	SR	A	SR	CK	52476	57476
156 477	rt	SR	A	SR	CK	52477	57477
156 478	t	SR	A	SR	CK	52478	57478

The Kilmarnock Edition

156 479	q	**NS**	A	*AV*	NL	52479	57479
156 480	q	**NS**	A	*AV*	NL	52480	57480
156 481	q	**NS**	A	*AV*	NL	52481	57481
156 482	q	**NS**	A	*AV*	NL	52482	57482
156 483	q	**NS**	A	*AV*	NL	52483	57483
156 484	q	**NS**	A	*AV*	NL	52484	57484
156 485	ru	**SR**	A	*SR*	CK	52485	57485
156 486	q	**NS**	A	*AV*	NL	52486	57486
156 487	q	**NS**	A	*AV*	NL	52487	57487
156 488	q	**NS**	A	*AV*	NL	52488	57488
156 489	q	**NS**	A	*AV*	NL	52489	57489
156 490	q	**NS**	A	*AV*	NL	52490	57490
156 491	q	**NS**	A	*AV*	NL	52491	57491
156 492	rt†	**SR**	A	*SR*	CK	52492	57492
156 493	rt	**SR**	A	*SR*	CK	52493	57493
156 494	§	**SC**	A	*SR*	CK	52494	57494
156 495	ru	**SC**	A	*SR*	CK	52495	57495
156 496	ru	**SR**	A	*SR*	CK	52496	57496
156 497	q	**NS**	A	*AV*	NL	52497	57497
156 498	q	**NS**	A	*AV*	NL	52498	57498
156 499	rt	**SR**	A	*SR*	CK	52499	57499
156 500	u	**SC**	A	*SR*	CK	52500	57500
156 501		**SC**	A	*SR*	CK	52501	57501
156 502		**SC**	A	*SR*	CK	52502	57502
156 503		**SC**	A	*SR*	CK	52503	57503
156 504		**SC**	A	*SR*	CK	52504	57504
156 505		**SC**	A	*SR*	CK	52505	57505
156 506		**SC**	A	*SR*	CK	52506	57506
156 507		**SC**	A	*SR*	CK	52507	57507
156 508		**SC**	A	*SR*	CK	52508	57508
156 509		**SC**	A	*SR*	CK	52509	57509
156 510		**SC**	A	*SR*	CK	52510	57510
156 511		**SC**	A	*SR*	CK	52511	57511
156 512		**SC**	A	*SR*	CK	52512	57512
156 513		**SC**	A	*SR*	CK	52513	57513
156 514		**SC**	A	*SR*	CK	52514	57514

CLASS 158/0   BREL

DMSL (B)–DMSL (A) or DMCL–DMSL or DMCL–MSL–DMSL.

Construction: Welded aluminium.
Engines: 158 701–158 814: One Cummins NTA855R of 260 kW (350 h.p.) at 1900 r.p.m.
158 863–158 872: One Cummins NTA855R of 300 kW (400 h.p.) at 2100 r.p.m.
158 815–158 862: One Perkins 2006-TWH of 260 kW (350 h.p.) at 1900 r.p.m. car.
Bogies: One BREL P4 (powered) and one BREL T4 (non-powered) per car.
Couplers: BSI.
Seating Layout: 2+2 facing/unidirectional in standard class and in ScotRail first class. 2+2 facing in Arriva Trains Northern first class, 2+1 facing/unidirectional in Virgin Cross-Country first class.

Dimensions: 22.57 x 2.70 m.
Gangways: Throughout.
Doors: Twin-leaf swing plug.
Multiple Working: Within class and with Classes 142, 143, 144, 150, 153, 155, 156, 159 and 170.

Wheel Arrangement: 2-B – B-2.
Maximum Speed: 90 m.p.h.

DMSL (B). Dia. DP252. Lot No. 31051 BREL Derby 1989–1992. –/68 1TD 1W. († –/66 1TD 1W, t –/64 1TD 1W). Public telephone and trolley space. 38.5 t.
MSL. Dia. DR207. Lot No. 31050 BREL Derby 1991. 37.1 t. –/70 2T. 37.1 t.
DMSL (A). Dia. DP251 Lot No. 31052 BREL Derby 1989–1992. –/70 1T († –/68 1T, t –/66 1T). 37.8 t.

The above details refer to the "as built" condition. The following DMSL(B) have now been converted to DMCL as follows:

52701–52744 (ScotRail/Arriva Trains Northern). Dia. DP318. 15/51 1TD 1W (*15/53 1TD 1W).
52747–52751. (Virgin Cross-Country/Arriva Trains Northern/Wessex Trains). Dia. DP323. 9/51 1TD 1W.
52760–779/781. (Arriva Trains Northern 2-car Units). Dia. DP331. 16/48 1TD 1W.
52798–814 (Arriva Trains Northern 3-car Units). Dia. DP332. 32/32 1TD 1W.

Note: All ScotRail Class 158s are "fitted" for RETB. When a unit arrives at Inverness the cab display unit is clipped on and plugged in.

s Arriva Trains Northern (Transpennine) and Central Trains units have been refurbished with new shape seat cushions. Arriva Transpennine units have also been fitted with table lamps in first class.
t Wales & Borders "Cambrian Line" units with some seats removed for additional luggage space. Central Trains style seats retained.
† Wessex Trains and Wales & Borders units fitted with new Chapman seating.

158 701	*	SR	P	SR	HA	52701	57701
158 702	*	SR	P	SR	HA	52702	57702	BBC Scotland – 75 Years
158 703	*	SR	P	SR	HA	52703	57703
158 704	*	SR	P	SR	HA	52704	57704
158 705	*	SR	P	SR	HA	52705	57705
158 706	*	SR	P	SR	HA	52706	57706
158 707	*	SR	P	SR	HA	52707	57707	Far North Line 125th ANNIVERSARY
158 708	*	SR	P	SR	HA	52708	57708
158 709	*	SR	P	SR	HA	52709	57709
158 710	*	SR	P	SR	HA	52710	57710
158 711	*	SR	P	SR	HA	52711	57711
158 712	*	SR	P	SR	HA	52712	57712
158 713	*	SR	P	SR	HA	52713	57713
158 714	*	SR	P	SR	HA	52714	57714
158 715	*	SR	P	SR	HA	52715	57715	Haymarket
158 716	*	SR	P	SR	HA	52716	57716
158 717	*	SR	P	SR	HA	52717	57717
158 718	*	SR	P	SR	HA	52718	57718
158 719	*	SR	P	SR	HA	52719	57719
158 720	*	SR	P	SR	HA	52720	57720
158 721	*	SR	P	SR	HA	52721	57721

158 722	*	**SR**	P	*SR*	HA	52722	57722
158 723	*	**SR**	P	*SR*	HA	52723	57723
158 724	*	**SR**	P	*SR*	HA	52724	57724
158 725	*	**SR**	P	*SR*	HA	52725	57725
158 726	*	**SR**	P	*SR*	HA	52726	57726
158 727	*	**SR**	P	*SR*	HA	52727	57727
158 728	*	**SR**	P	*SR*	HA	52728	57728
158 729	*	**SR**	P	*SR*	HA	52729	57729
158 730	*	**SR**	P	*SR*	HA	52730	57730
158 731	*	**SR**	P	*SR*	HA	52731	57731
158 732	*	**SR**	P	*SR*	HA	52732	57732
158 733	*	**SR**	P	*SR*	HA	52733	57733
158 734	*	**SR**	P	*SR*	HA	52734	57734
158 735	*	**SR**	P	*SR*	HA	52735	57735
158 736	*	**SR**	P	*SR*	HA	52736	57736
158 737		**TX**	P	*AV*	NL	52737	57737
158 738	*	**SR**	P	*SR*	HA	52738	57738
158 739	*	**SR**	P	*SR*	HA	52739	57739
158 740	*	**SR**	P	*SR*	HA	52740	57740
158 741	*	**SR**	P	*SR*	HA	52741	57741
158 742		**TX**	P	*AV*	NL	52742	57742
158 743		**TX**	P	*AV*	NL	52743	57743
158 744		**TX**	P	*AV*	NL	52744	57744
158 745	†	**WT**	P	*WX*	CF	52745	57745
158 746	†	**WT**	P	*WX*	CF	52746	57746	Spirit of the South West
158 747		**RE**	P	*VX*	NH	52747	57747
158 748		**RE**	P	*WX*	CF	52748	57748
158 749		**RE**	P	*VX*	NH	52749	57749
158 750		**RE**	P	*AV*	NL	52750	57750
158 751		**RE**	P	*VX*	NH	52751	57751
158 752		**NW**	P	*NW*	NH	52752	57752
158 753		**NW**	P	*NW*	NH	52753	57753
158 754		**NW**	P	*NW*	NH	52754	57754
158 755		**NW**	P	*NW*	NH	52755	57755
158 756		**NW**	P	*NW*	NH	52756	57756
158 757		**NW**	P	*NW*	NH	52757	57757
158 758		**NW**	P	*NW*	NH	52758	57758
158 759		**NW**	P	*NW*	NH	52759	57759
158 760		**TX**	P	*AV*	NL	52760	57760
158 761	s	**TX**	P	*AV*	NL	52761	57761
158 762	s	**TX**	P	*AV*	NL	52762	57762
158 763	s	**TX**	P	*AV*	NL	52763	57763
158 764	s	**TX**	P	*AV*	NL	52764	57764
158 765	s	**TX**	P	*AV*	NL	52765	57765
158 766	s	**TX**	P	*AV*	NL	52766	57766
158 767	s	**TX**	P	*AV*	NL	52767	57767
158 768	s	**TX**	P	*AV*	NL	52768	57768
158 769	s	**TX**	P	*AV*	NL	52769	57769
158 770	s	**TX**	P	*AV*	NL	52770	57770
158 771	s	**TX**	P	*AV*	HT	52771	57771
158 772	s	**TX**	P	*AV*	NL	52772	57772

158 773	s	**TX**	P	*AV*	NL	52773	57773	
158 774	s	**TX**	P	*AV*	NL	52774	57774	
158 775	s	**TX**	P	*AV*	HT	52775	57775	
158 776	s	**TX**	P	*AV*	HT	52776	57776	
158 777	s	**TX**	P	*AV*	HT	52777	57777	
158 778	s	**TX**	P	*AV*	HT	52778	57778	
158 779	s	**TX**	P	*AV*	HT	52779	57779	
158 780	s	**CT**	A	*CT*	TS	52780	57780	
158 781	s	**TX**	P	*AV*	HT	52781	57781	
158 782	s	**CT**	A	*CT*	TS	52782	57782	
158 783	s	**CT**	A	*CT*	TS	52783	57783	
158 784	s	**CT**	A	*CT*	TS	52784	57784	
158 785	s	**CT**	A	*CT*	TS	52785	57785	
158 786	s	**CT**	A	*CT*	TS	52786	57786	
158 787	s	**CT**	A	*CT*	TS	52787	57787	
158 788	s	**CT**	A	*CT*	TS	52788	57788	
158 789	s	**CT**	A	*CT*	TS	52789	57789	
158 790	s	**CT**	A	*CT*	TS	52790	57790	
158 791	s	**CT**	A	*CT*	TS	52791	57791	
158 792	s	**CT**	A	*CT*	TS	52792	57792	
158 793	s	**CT**	A	*CT*	TS	52793	57793	
158 794	s	**CT**	A	*CT*	TS	52794	57794	
158 795	s	**CT**	A	*CT*	TS	52795	57795	
158 796	s	**CT**	A	*CT*	TS	52796	57796	
158 797	s	**CT**	A	*CT*	TS	52797	57797	
158 798	s	**TX**	P	*AV*	HT	52798	58715	57798
158 799	s	**TX**	P	*AV*	HT	52799	58716	57799
158 800	s	**TX**	P	*AV*	HT	52800	58717	57800
158 801	s	**TX**	P	*AV*	HT	52801	58701	57801
158 802	s	**TX**	P	*AV*	HT	52802	58702	57802
158 803	s	**TX**	P	*AV*	HT	52803	58703	57803
158 804	s	**TX**	P	*AV*	HT	52804	58704	57804
158 805	s	**TX**	P	*AV*	HT	52805	58705	57805
158 806	s	**TX**	P	*AV*	HT	52806	58706	57806
158 807	s	**TX**	P	*AV*	HT	52807	58707	57807
158 808	s	**TX**	P	*AV*	HT	52808	58708	57808
158 809	s	**TX**	P	*AV*	HT	52809	58709	57809
158 810	s	**TX**	P	*AV*	HT	52810	58710	57810
158 811	s	**TX**	P	*AV*	HT	52811	58711	57811
158 812	s	**TX**	P	*AV*	HT	52812	58712	57812
158 813	s	**TX**	P	*AV*	HT	52813	58713	57813
158 814	s	**TX**	P	*AV*	HT	52814	58714	57814
158 815	†	**WT**	A	*WX*	CF	52815	57815	
158 816	†	**WT**	A	*WX*	CF	52816	57816	
158 817	†	**WB**	A	*WB*	CF	52817	57817	
158 818	†	**RE**	A	*WB*	CF	52818	57818	
158 819	†	**RE**	A	*WB*	CF	52819	57819	
158 820	†	**RE**	A	*WB*	CF	52820	57820	
158 821	†	**RE**	A	*WB*	CF	52821	57821	
158 822	†	**RE**	A	*WB*	CF	52822	57822	
158 823	†	**RE**	A	*WB*	CF	52823	57823	

158 824	†	**WB**	A	*WB*	CF	52824	57824
158 825	†	**RE**	A	*WB*	CF	52825	57825
158 826	†	**RE**	A	*WB*	CF	52826	57826
158 827	†	**GP**	A	*WB*	CF	52827	57827
158 828	†	**RE**	A	*WB*	CF	52828	57828
158 829	†	**WB**	A	*WB*	CF	52829	57829
158 830	†	**RE**	A	*WB*	CF	52830	57830
158 831	†	**WB**	A	*WB*	CF	52831	57831
158 832	†	**RE**	A	*WB*	CF	52832	57832
158 833	†	**WB**	A	*WB*	CF	52833	57833
158 834	†	**WB**	A	*WB*	CF	52834	57834
158 835	†	**WB**	A	*WB*	CF	52835	57835
158 836	†	**RE**	A	*WB*	CF	52836	57836
158 837	†	**RE**	A	*WB*	CF	52837	57837
158 838	†	**RE**	A	*WB*	CF	52838	57838
158 839	†	**RE**	A	*WB*	CF	52839	57839
158 840	†	**RE**	A	*WB*	CF	52840	57840
158 841	†	**GP**	A	*WB*	CF	52841	57841
158 842	†	**RE**	A	*WB*	CF	52842	57842
158 843	†	**WB**	A	*WB*	CF	52843	57843
158 844	rst	**CT**	A	*WB*	TS	52844	57844
158 845	rst	**CT**	A	*WB*	TS	52845	57845
158 846	rst	**CT**	A	*WB*	TS	52846	57846
158 847	rst	**CT**	A	*WB*	TS	52847	57847
158 848	rst	**CT**	A	*WB*	TS	52848	57848
158 849	rst	**CT**	A	*WB*	TS	52849	57849
158 850	rst	**CT**	A	*WB*	TS	52850	57850
158 851	rst	**CT**	A	*WB*	TS	52851	57851
158 852	rst	**CT**	A	*WB*	TS	52852	57852
158 853	rst	**CT**	A	*WB*	TS	52853	57853
158 854	rst	**CT**	A	*WB*	TS	52854	57854
158 855	rst	**CT**	A	*WB*	TS	52855	57855
158 856	s	**CT**	A	*CT*	TS	52856	57856
158 857	s	**CT**	A	*CT*	TS	52857	57857
158 858	s	**CT**	A	*CT*	TS	52858	57858
158 859	s	**CT**	A	*CT*	TS	52859	57859
158 860	s	**CT**	A	*CT*	TS	52860	57860
158 861	s	**CT**	A	*CT*	TS	52861	57861
158 862	s	**CT**	A	*CT*	TS	52862	57862
158 863	†	**WT**	A	*WX*	CF	52863	57863
158 864	†	**WT**	A	*WX*	CF	52864	57864
158 865	†	**WT**	A	*WX*	CF	52865	57865
158 866	†	**WT**	A	*WX*	CF	52866	57866
158 867	†	**WT**	A	*WX*	CF	52867	57867
158 868	†	**WT**	A	*WX*	CF	52868	57868
158 869	†	**WT**	A	*WX*	CF	52869	57869
158 870	†	**WT**	A	*WX*	CF	52870	57870
158 871	†	**WT**	A	*WX*	CF	52871	57871
158 872	†	**WT**	A	*WX*	CF	52872	57872

CLASS 158/9   BREL

DMSL–DMS. Units leased by West Yorkshire PTE. Details as for Class 158/0 except for seating layout and toilets.

DMSL. Dia. DP252. Lot No. 31051 BREL Derby 1990–1992. –/70 1TD 1W. Public telephone and trolley space. 38.1 t.
DMS. Dia. DP251. Lot No. 31052 BREL Derby 1990–1992. –/72 and parcels area. 37.8 t.

Note: These units are leased by West Yorkshire PTE and are managed by Porterbrook Leasing Company.

158 901	**WY**	P	*AV*	NL	52901	57901
158 902	**WY**	P	*AV*	NL	52902	57902
158 903	**WY**	P	*AV*	NL	52903	57903
158 904	**WY**	P	*AV*	NL	52904	57904
158 905	**WY**	P	*AV*	NL	52905	57905
158 906	**WY**	P	*AV*	NL	52906	57906
158 907	**WY**	P	*AV*	NL	52907	57907
158 908	**WY**	P	*AV*	NL	52908	57908
158 909	**YN**	P	*AV*	NL	52909	57909
158 910	**WY**	P	*AV*	NL	52910	57910

CLASS 159   BREL

DMCL–MSL–DMSL. Built as Class 158. Converted before entering passenger service to Class 159 by Rosyth Dockyard.

Construction: Welded aluminium.
Engines: One Cummins NTA855R of 300 kW (400 h.p.) at 2100 r.p.m.
Bogies: One BREL P4 (powered) and one BREL T4 (non-powered) per car.
Couplers: BSI.
Seating Layout: 1: 2+1 facing, 2: 2+2 facing/unidirectional.
Dimensions: 23.21 x 2.82 m.
Gangways: Throughout.   **Wheel Arrangement:** 2-B – B-2 – B-2.
Doors: Twin-leaf swing plug.   **Maximum Speed:** 90 m.p.h.
Multiple Working: Within class and with Classes 142, 143, 144, 150, 153, 155, 156, 158, and 170.

DMCL. Dia. DP322. Lot No. 31051 BREL Derby 1992–1993. 24/28 1TD 1W. 38.5 t.
MSL. Dia. DR209. Lot No. 31050 BREL Derby 1992–1993. 38 t. –/72 1T and parcels area.
DMSL. Dia. DP260. Lot No. 31052 BREL Derby 1992–1993. –/72 1T and parcels area. 37.8 t.

159 001	**SW**	P	*SW*	SA	52873	58718	57873 CITY OF EXETER
159 002	**SW**	P	*SW*	SA	52874	58719	57874 CITY OF SALISBURY
159 003	**SW**	P	*SW*	SA	52875	58720	57875 TEMPLECOMBE
159 004	**SW**	P	*SW*	SA	52876	58721	57876 BASINGSTOKE AND DEANE
159 005	**SW**	P	*SW*	SA	52877	58722	57877
159 006	**SW**	P	*SW*	SA	52878	58723	57878
159 007	**SW**	P	*SW*	SA	52879	58724	57879

159 008	**SW**	P	*SW*	SA	52880	58725	57880
159 009	**SW**	P	*SW*	SA	52881	58726	57881
159 010	**SW**	P	*SW*	SA	52882	58727	57882
159 011	**SW**	P	*SW*	SA	52883	58728	57883
159 012	**SW**	P	*SW*	SA	52884	58729	57884
159 013	**SW**	P	*SW*	SA	52885	58730	57885
159 014	**SW**	P	*SW*	SA	52886	58731	57886
159 015	**SW**	P	*SW*	SA	52887	58732	57887
159 016	**SW**	P	*SW*	SA	52888	58733	57888
159 017	**SW**	P	*SW*	SA	52889	58734	57889
159 018	**SW**	P	*SW*	SA	52890	58735	57890
159 019	**SW**	P	*SW*	SA	52891	58736	57891
159 020	**SW**	P	*SW*	SA	52892	58737	57892
159 021	**SW**	P	*SW*	SA	52893	58738	57893
159 022	**SW**	P	*SW*	SA	52894	58739	57894

CLASS 165/0   NETWORK TURBO   BREL

DMCL–DMS (Thames Trains units) or DMSL–DMS and DMSL–MS–DMS (Chiltern units). Chiltern Railways units are being refurbished and fitted with air-conditioning.

Construction: Welded aluminium.
Engines: One Perkins 2006-TWH of 260 kW (350 h.p.) at 1900 r.p.m.
Bogies: BREL P3-17 (powered), BREL T3-17 (non-powered).
Couplers: BSI.
Seating Layouts: 1: 2+2 facing (Thames Trains units only), 2: Thames Trains/ Chiltern unrefurbished units: 3+2 facing/unidirectional. 2: Refurbished Chiltern units: 2+2 facing/unidirectional (DMSL and DMS) and 3+2 facing/unidirectional (MS).
Dimensions: 23.50 x 2.85 m.
Gangways: Within unit only.
Doors: Twin-leaf swing plug.
Wheel Arrangement: 2-B (– B-2) – B-2.
Maximum Speed: 75 m.p.h.
Multiple Working: Within class and with Classes 166 and 168.

58801–58805. DMCL (Thames Trains units). Dia. DP319. Lot No. 31087 BREL York 1990. 16/72 1T. 37.0 t.
58806–58812, 58814–58822 and 58873–58878. DMSL (Chiltern 2-car units – First Class declassified). Dia. DP319. Lot No. 31087 BREL York 1990. 16/72 1T (* /89 1T). 37.0 t.
58823–58833. DMSL (Chiltern 3-car units – First Class declassified). Dia. DP320. Lot No. 31089 BREL York 1991–1992. 24/60 1T (* /89 1T). 37.0 t.
58813 DMSL (Trial refurbished Chiltern vehicle). Dia. DP286. Lot No. 31087 BREL York 1990. /82 1T. 37.0 t.
55404–55414. MS (Centre car for Chiltern 3-car units. Accomodation is unchanged by refurbishment). Dia. DR208. Lot No. 31090 BREL York 1991–1992. –/106. 37.0 t.
58834–58838. DMS (Thames Trains units). Dia. DP253. Lot No. 31088 BREL York 1991–1992. –/98. 37.0 t.
58839–58872. DMS (Chiltern units). Dia. DP253. Lot No. 31088 BREL York 1991–1992. –/98 (* /94). 37.0 t.

Notes:

† Trial refurbished Chiltern Railways unit.
* Fully refurbished Chiltern Railways units.
Chiltern Railways units 165 006–165 039 are fitted with tripcocks for working over London Underground tracks between Harrow-on-the-Hill and Amersham. Chiltern Railways units had their First Class seats declassified from 5 January 2003.

165 001		**NT**	A	*TT*	RG	58801	58834
165 002		**NT**	A	*TT*	RG	58802	58835
165 003		**NT**	A	*TT*	RG	58803	58836
165 004		**NT**	A	*TT*	RG	58804	58837
165 005		**NT**	A	*TT*	RG	58805	58838
165 006		**NT**	A	*CR*	AL	58806	58839
165 007		**NT**	A	*CR*	AL	58807	58840
165 008		**NT**	A	*CR*	AL	58808	58841
165 009		**NT**	A	*CR*	AL	58809	58842
165 010		**NT**	A	*CR*	AL	58810	58843
165 011		**NT**	A	*CR*	AL	58811	58844
165 012		**NT**	A	*CR*	AL	58812	58845
165 013	†	**CR**	A	*CR*	AL	58813	58846
165 014		**NT**	A	*CR*	AL	58814	58847
165 015		**NT**	A	*CR*	AL	58815	58848
165 016		**NT**	A	*CR*	AL	58816	58849
165 017		**NT**	A	*CR*	AL	58817	58850
165 018		**NT**	A	*CR*	AL	58818	58851
165 019		**NT**	A	*CR*	AL	58819	58852
165 020		**NT**	A	*CR*	AL	58820	58853
165 021		**NT**	A	*CR*	AL	58821	58854
165 022		**NT**	A	*CR*	AL	58822	58855
165 023		**NT**	A	*CR*	AL	58873	58867
165 024		**NT**	A	*CR*	AL	58874	58868
165 025		**NT**	A	*CR*	AL	58875	58869
165 026		**NT**	A	*CR*	AL	58876	58870
165 027		**NT**	A	*CR*	AL	58877	58871
165 028		**NT**	A	*CR*	AL	58878	58872
165 029		**NT**	A	*CR*	AL	58823	55404	58856
165 030		**NT**	A	*CR*	AL	58824	55405	58857
165 031		**NT**	A	*CR*	AL	58825	55406	58858
165 032		**NT**	A	*CR*	AL	58826	55407	58859
165 033		**NT**	A	*CR*	AL	58827	55408	58860
165 034		**NT**	A	*CR*	AL	58828	55409	58861
165 035		**NT**	A	*CR*	AL	58829	55410	58862
165 036	*	**CR**	A	*CR*	AL	58830	55411	58863
165 037		**NT**	A	*CR*	AL	58831	55412	58864
165 038		**NT**	A	*CR*	AL	58832	55413	58865
165 039		**NT**	A	*CR*	AL	58833	55414	58866

CLASS 165/1   NETWORK TURBO   BREL

Thames Trains units. DMCL–DMS or DMCL–MS–DMS.

Construction: Welded aluminium.
Engines: One Perkins 2006-TWH of 260 kW (350 h.p.) at 1900 r.p.m.
Bogies: BREL P3-17 (powered), BREL T3-17 (non-powered).
Couplers: BSI.
Seating Layout: 1: 2+2 facing, 2: 3+2 facing/unidirectional.
Dimensions: 23.50 x 2.85 m.
Gangways: Within unit only.   **Wheel Arrangement:** 2-B (– B-2) – B-2.
Doors: Twin-leaf swing plug.   **Maximum Speed:** 90 m.p.h.
Multiple Working: Within class and with Classes 166 and 168.

58953–58969. DMCL. Dia. DP320. Lot No. 31098 BREL York 1992. 16/66 1T. 37.0 t.
58879–58898. DMCL. Dia. DP319. Lot No. 31096 BREL York 1992. 16/72 1T. 37.0 t.
MS. Dia. DR208. Lot No. 31099 BREL 1992. –/106. 37.0 t.
DMS. Dia. DP253. Lot No. 31097 BREL 1992. –/98. 37.0 t.

165 101	TT	A	TT	RG	58953	55415	58916
165 102	TT	A	TT	RG	58954	55416	58917
165 103	TT	A	TT	RG	58955	55417	58918
165 104	TT	A	TT	RG	58956	55418	58919
165 105	TT	A	TT	RG	58957	55419	58920
165 106	TT	A	TT	RG	58958	55420	58921
165 107	TT	A	TT	RG	58959	55421	58922
165 108	TT	A	TT	RG	58960	55422	58923
165 109	TT	A	TT	RG	58961	55423	58924
165 110	TT	A	TT	RG	58962	55424	58925
165 111	TT	A	TT	RG	58963	55425	58926
165 112	TT	A	TT	RG	58964	55426	58927
165 113	TT	A	TT	RG	58965	55427	58928
165 114	TT	A	TT	RG	58966	55428	58929
165 116	TT	A	TT	RG	58968	55430	58931
165 117	NT	A	TT	RG	58969	55431	58932
165 118	NT	A	TT	RG	58879	58933	
165 119	NT	A	TT	RG	58880	58934	
165 120	NT	A	TT	RG	58881	58935	
165 121	NT	A	TT	RG	58882	58936	
165 122	NT	A	TT	RG	58883	58937	
165 123	NT	A	TT	RG	58884	58938	
165 124	NT	A	TT	RG	58885	58939	
165 125	NT	A	TT	RG	58886	58940	
165 126	NT	A	TT	RG	58887	58941	
165 127	NT	A	TT	RG	58888	58942	
165 128	NT	A	TT	RG	58889	58943	
165 129	NT	A	TT	RG	58890	58944	
165 130	NT	A	TT	RG	58891	58945	
165 131	NT	A	TT	RG	58892	58946	
165 132	NT	A	TT	RG	58893	58947	
165 133	NT	A	TT	RG	58894	58948	

165 134	**NT**	A	*TT*	RG	58895	58949
165 135	**NT**	A	*TT*	RG	58896	58950
165 136	**NT**	A	*TT*	RG	58897	58951
165 137	**NT**	A	*TT*	RG	58898	58952

CLASS 166   NETWORK EXPRESS TURBO   ABB

Thames Trains units, built for Paddington–Oxford/Newbury services. Air conditioned. DMCL (A)–MS–DMCL (B).

Construction: Welded aluminium.
Engines: One Perkins 2006-TWH of 260 kW (350 h.p.) at 1900 r.p.m.
Bogies: BREL P3-17 (powered), BREL T3-17 (non-powered).
Couplers: BSI.
Seating Layout: 1: 2+2 facing, 2: 3+2 facing/unidirectional. 20 standard class seats in 2+2 format in DMCL(B).
Dimensions: 23.50 x 2.85 m.
Gangways: Within unit only.   **Wheel Arrangement:** 2-B – B-2 – B-2.
Doors: Twin-leaf swing plug.   **Maximum Speed:** 90 m.p.h.
Multiple Working: Within class and with Classes 165 and 168.

DMCL (A). Dia. DP321. Lot No. 31116 ABB York 1992–1993. 16/75 1T. 40.62 t.
MS. Dia. DR209. Lot No. 31117 ABB York 1992–1993. –/96. 38.04 t.
DMCL (B). Dia. DP321. Lot No. 31116 ABB York 1992–1993. 16/72 1T. 40.64 t.

166 201	**TT**	A	*TT*	RG	58101	58601	58122
166 202	**TT**	A	*TT*	RG	58102	58602	58123
166 203	**TT**	A	*TT*	RG	58103	58603	58124
166 204	**TT**	A	*TT*	RG	58104	58604	58125
166 205	**TT**	A	*TT*	RG	58105	58605	58126
166 206	**TT**	A	*TT*	RG	58106	58606	58127
166 207	**TT**	A	*TT*	RG	58107	58607	58128
166 208	**TT**	A	*TT*	RG	58108	58608	58129
166 209	**TT**	A	*TT*	RG	58109	58609	58130
166 210	**TT**	A	*TT*	RG	58110	58610	58131
166 211	**TT**	A	*TT*	RG	58111	58611	58132
166 212	**TT**	A	*TT*	RG	58112	58612	58133
166 213	**TT**	A	*TT*	RG	58113	58613	58134
166 214	**TT**	A	*TT*	RG	58114	58614	58135
166 215	**TT**	A	*TT*	RG	58115	58615	58136
166 216	**TT**	A	*TT*	RG	58116	58616	58137
166 217	**TT**	A	*TT*	RG	58117	58617	58138
166 218	**TT**	A	*TT*	RG	58118	58618	58139
166 219	**TT**	A	*TT*	RG	58119	58619	58140
166 220	**TT**	A	*TT*	RG	58120	58620	58141
166 221	**TT**	A	*TT*	RG	58121	58621	58142

CLASS 168 CLUBMAN ADTRANZ/BOMBARDIER

DMSL(A)–MSL–MS–DMSL(B). Air conditioned.

Construction: Welded aluminium bodies with bolt-on steel ends.
Engines: One MTU 6R183TD13H of 315 kW (422 h.p.) at 1900 r.p.m.
Transmission: Hydraulic. Voith T211rzze to ZF final drive.
Bogies: One Adtranz P3–23 and one BREL T3–23 per car.
Couplers: BSI.
Seating Layout: 2+2 facing/unidirectional.
Dimensions: 23.62 x 2.69 m.
Gangways: Within unit only.   **Wheel Arrangement:** 2-B (– B-2 – B-2) – B-2.
Doors: Twin-leaf swing plug.   **Maximum Speed:** 100 m.p.h.
Multiple Working: Within class and with Classes 165 and 166.
Fitted with tripcocks for working over London Underground tracks between Harrow-on-the-Hill and Amersham.

Class 168/0. Original Design.

58151–58155. DMSL(A). Dia. DP270. Adtranz Derby 1997–1998. –/60 1TD 1W. 43.7 t.
58651–58655. MSL. Dia. DR211. Adtranz Derby 1998. –/73 1T. 41.0 t.
58451–58455. MS. Dia. DR211. Adtranz Derby 1998. –/77. 40.5 t.
58251–58255. DMSL(B). Dia. DP270. Adtranz Derby 1998. –/66 1T. 43.6 t.

Note: 58451–58455 were formerly numbered in 168 656–168 110.

168 001	**CR**	P	*CR*	AL	58151	58451	58651	58251
168 002	**CR**	P	*CR*	AL	58152	58452	58652	58252
168 003	**CR**	P	*CR*	AL	58153	58453	58653	58253
168 004	**CR**	P	*CR*	AL	58154	58454	58654	58254
168 005	**CR**	P	*CR*	AL	58155	58455	58655	58255

Class 168/1. These units are effectively Class 170s.

58156–58163. DMSL(A). Dia. DP280. Adtranz Derby 2000. –/59 1TD 2W. 43.7 t.
58756–58757. MSL. Dia. DR211. Bombardier Derby 2002. –/73 1T. 41.0 t.
58456–58460. MS. Dia. DR211. Bombardier Derby 2002. –/76. 40.5 t.
58461–58463. MS. Dia. DR211. Adtranz Derby 2000. –/76. 42.4 t.
58256–58263. DMSL(B). Dia. DP281. Adtranz Derby 2000. –/69 1T. 43.6 t.

Note: 58461–58463 have been renumbered from 58661–58663.
58756 and 58757 have been renumbered from 58656 and 58657.

168 106	**CR**	P	*CR*	AL	58156	58456	58756	58256
168 107	**CR**	P	*CR*	AL	58157	58457	58757	58257
168 108	**CR**	P	*CR*	AL	58158	58458		58258
168 109	**CR**	P	*CR*	AL	58159	58459		58259
168 110	**CR**	P	*CR*	AL	58160	58460		58260
168 111	**CR**	H	*CR*	AL	58161	58461		58261
168 112	**CR**	H	*CR*	AL	58162	58462		58262
168 113	**CR**	H	*CR*	AL	58163	58463		58263

Class 168/2. These units are effectively Class 170s. Fitted with databus system. On order.

58164–58167. DMSL(A). Dia. DP294. Bombardier Derby 2003. –/59 1TD 2W. 45.4 t.
58464. MS. Dia. DR222. Bombardier Derby 2003. –/76. 44.0 t.
58264–58267. DMSL(B). Dia. DP295. Bombardier Derby 2003. –/69 1T. 45.4 t.

168 214	**CR**	P	58164	58464	58264
168 215	**CR**	P	58165		58265
168 216	**CR**	P	58166		58266
168 217	**CR**	P	58167		58267

CLASS 170 TURBOSTAR ADTRANZ/BOMBARDIER

Various formations. Air conditioned.

Construction: Welded aluminium bodies with bolt-on steel ends.
Engines: One MTU 6R183TD13H of 315 kW (422 h.p.) at 1900 r.p.m.
Transmission: Hydraulic. Voith T211rzze to ZF final drive.
Bogies: One Adtranz P3–23 and one BREL T3–23 per car.
Couplers: BSI.
Seating Layout: 1: 2+1 facing/unidirectional (2+2 in first class in Class 170/1 end cars). 2: 2+2.
Dimensions: 23.62 x 2.69 m.
Gangways: Within unit only.   **Wheel Arrangement:** 2-B (– B-2) – B-2.
Doors: Twin-leaf swing plug.   **Maximum Speed:** 100 m.p.h.
Multiple Working: Within class and with Classes 150, 153, 155, 156, 158, 159.

Class 170/1. Midland Mainline units. DMCL–MCRMB–DMCL or DMCL–DMCL.

DMCL (A). Dia. DP324. Adtranz Derby 1998–1999. 12/45 1TD 2W. 45.19 t.
MCRMB. Dia. DR301. Adtranz Derby 2001. 24/24 and bar. 43.00 t.
DMCL (B). Dia. DP325. Adtranz Derby 1998–1999. 12/52 1T. Catering point. 45.22 t

Note: The DMCL (A) and DMCL (B) in the 3-car units have had their former first class end sections declassified.

170 101	**MM**	P	*MM*	DY	50101	55101	79101
170 102	**MM**	P	*MM*	DY	50102	55102	79102
170 103	**MM**	P	*MM*	DY	50103	55103	79103
170 104	**MM**	P	*MM*	DY	50104	55104	79104
170 105	**MM**	P	*MM*	DY	50105	55105	79105
170 106	**MM**	P	*MM*	DY	50106	55106	79106
170 107	**MM**	P	*MM*	DY	50107	55107	79107
170 108	**MM**	P	*MM*	DY	50108	55108	79108
170 109	**MM**	P	*MM*	DY	50109	55109	79109
170 110	**MM**	P	*MM*	DY	50110	55110	79110
170 111	**MM**	P	*MM*	DY	50111		79111
170 112	**MM**	P	*MM*	DY	50112		79112
170 113	**MM**	P	*MM*	DY	50113		79113
170 114	**MM**	P	*MM*	DY	50114		79114
170 115	**MM**	P	*MM*	DY	50115		79115
170 116	**MM**	P	*MM*	DY	50116		79116
170 117	**MM**	P	*MM*	DY	50117		79117

Class 170/2. Anglia Railways 3-car units. DMCL–MSLRB–DMSL.

DMCL. Dia. DP326. Adtranz Derby 1999. 30/3 1TD 2W. 44.30 t.
MSLRB. Dia. DR212. Adtranz Derby 1999. –/58 1T. Buffet and guard's office 42.76 t.
DMSL. Dia. DP274. Adtranz Derby 1999. –/66 1T. 44.70 t.

170 201	**AN**	P	*AR*	NC	50201	56201	79201
170 202	**AN**	P	*AR*	NC	50202	56202	79202
170 203	**AN**	P	*AR*	NC	50203	56203	79203
170 204	**AN**	P	*AR*	NC	50204	56204	79204
170 205	**AN**	P	*AR*	NC	50205	56205	79205
170 206	**AN**	P	*AR*	NC	50206	56206	79206
170 207	**AN**	P	*AR*	NC	50207	56207	79207
170 208	**AN**	P	*AR*	NC	50208	56208	79208

Class 170/2. Anglia Railways 2-car units. DMSL–DMCL.

DMSL. Dia. DP287. Bombardier Derby 2002. –/57 1TD 2W. 44.30 t.
DMCL. Dia. DP274. Bombardier Derby 2002. 9/53 1T. 44.70 t.

170 270	**AN**	P	*AR*	NC	50270	79270
170 271	**AN**	P	*AR*	NC	50271	79271
170 272	**AN**	P	*AR*	NC	50272	79272
170 273	**AN**	P	*AR*	NC	50273	79273

Class 170/3. South West Trains units. DMCL–DMCL.

50301–50308. DMCL(A). Dia. DP329. Adtranz Derby 2000. 9/43 1TD 2W. 45.80 t.
50392. DMCL(A). Dia. DP . Bombardier Derby 2003. Fitted with databus system. 9/43 1TD 2W. . t.
79301–79308. DMCL(B). Dia. DP330. Adtranz Derby 2000. 9/53 1T. 45.80 t.
79392. DMCL(B). Dia. DP . Bombardier Derby 2003. Fitted with databus system. 9/53 1T. . t.

170 301	**SW**	P	*SW*	SA	50301	79301
170 302	**SW**	P	*SW*	SA	50302	79302
170 303	**SW**	P	*SW*	SA	50303	79303
170 304	**SW**	P	*SW*	SA	50304	79304
170 305	**SW**	P	*SW*	SA	50305	79305
170 306	**SW**	P	*SW*	SA	50306	79306
170 307	**SW**	P	*SW*	SA	50307	79307
170 308	**SW**	P	*SW*	SA	50308	79308
170 392	**SW**	P			50392	79392

Class 170/3. Hull Trains units. On order. DMCL–MSLRB–DMSL.

DMCL. Dia. DP3 . Bombardier Derby 2003. 30/3 1TD 2W. 44.30 t.
MSLRB. Dia. DR2 . Bombardier Derby 2003. –/58 1T. Buffet and guard's office 42.76 t.
DMSL. Dia. DP2 . Bombardier Derby 2003. –/66 1T. 44.70 t.

170 393	P			50393	56393	79393
170 394	P			50394	56394	79394
170 395	P			50395	56395	79395
170 396	P			50396	56396	79396

Class 170/3. Porterbrook short lease units. DMCL–MC–DMCL.

DMCL(A). Dia. DP288. Bombardier Derby 2002. 12/43 1TD 1W. 45.40 t.
MC. Dia. DR302. Bombardier Derby 2002. 22/36. 41.60 t.
DMCL(B). Dia. DP289. Bombardier Derby 2002. –/66 1T. 45.80 t.

Advertising Liveries:

170 397 "Q-Jump". Sky blue with purple doors.
170 398 is all over white with large bodyside "BOMBARDIER" lettering in blue.

| 170 397 | **AL** | P | *MM* | DY | 50397 | 56397 | 79397 |
| 170 398 | **AL** | P | *CT* | TS | 50398 | 56398 | 79398 |

Class 170/3. Porterbrook short lease unit. DMCL–DMCL.

DMCL(A). Dia. DP329. Bombardier Derby 2001. 9/43 1TD 2W. 45.40 t.
DMCL(B). Dia. DP330. Bombardier Derby 2001. 9/53 1T. 45.80 t.

| 170 399 | **P** | P | *CT* | TS | 50399 | | 79399 |

Class 170/4. ScotRail units. DMCL–MS–DMCL.

DMCL(A). Dia. DP329. Adtranz Derby 1999–2001. 9/43 1TD 2W. 45.80 t.
MS. Dia. DR213. Adtranz Derby 1999–2001. –/76. 43.00 t.
DMCL(B). Dia. DP330. Adtranz Derby 1999–2001. 9/53 1T. 45.80 t.

170 401	**SR**	P	*SR*	HA	50401	56401	79401
170 402	**SR**	P	*SR*	HA	50402	56402	79402
170 403	**SR**	P	*SR*	HA	50403	56403	79403
170 404	**SR**	P	*SR*	HA	50404	56404	79404
170 405	**SR**	P	*SR*	HA	50405	56405	79405
170 406	**SR**	P	*SR*	HA	50406	56406	79406
170 407	**SR**	P	*SR*	HA	50407	56407	79407
170 408	**SR**	P	*SR*	HA	50408	56408	79408
170 409	**SR**	P	*SR*	HA	50409	56409	79409
170 410	**SR**	P	*SR*	HA	50410	56410	79410
170 411	**SR**	P	*SR*	HA	50411	56411	79411
170 412	**SR**	P	*SR*	HA	50412	56412	79412
170 413	**SR**	P	*SR*	HA	50413	56413	79413
170 414	**SR**	P	*SR*	HA	50414	56414	79414
170 415	**SR**	P	*SR*	HA	50415	56415	79415
170 416	**SR**	H	*SR*	HA	50416	56416	79416
170 417	**SR**	H	*SR*	HA	50417	56417	79417
170 418	**SR**	H	*SR*	HA	50418	56418	79418
170 419	**SR**	H	*SR*	HA	50419	56419	79419
170 420	**SR**	H	*SR*	HA	50420	56420	79420
170 421	**SR**	H	*SR*	HA	50421	56421	79421
170 422	**SR**	H	*SR*	HA	50422	56422	79422
170 423	**SR**	H	*SR*	HA	50423	56423	79423
170 424	**SR**	H	*SR*	HA	50424	56424	79424

Class 170/4. ScotRail units. On order. Fitted with databus system. DMCL–MS–DMSL.

Special note: The third cars of units 170 430–170 437 and 170 451–170 458 will be swapped when the latter units have been delivered.

DMCL(A). Dia. DP3 . Bombardier Derby 2003. 9/43 1TD 2W. 45.80 t.
MS. Dia. DR2 . Bombardier Derby 2003. –/76. 43.00 t.
DMSL. Dia. DP2 . Bombardier Derby 2003. –/67 1T. 45.80 t.

170 430	**SR**	P	50430	56430	79451
170 431	**SR**	P	50431	56431	79452
170 432	**SR**	P	50432	56432	79453
170 433	**SR**	P	50433	56433	79454
170 434	**SR**	P	50434	56434	79455
170 435	**SR**	P	50435	56435	79456
170 436	**SR**	P	50436	56436	79457
170 437	**SR**	P	50437	56437	79458

Class 170/4. ScotRail units. On order. Fitted with databus system. DMSL–MS–DMCL.

DMSL. Dia. DP2 . Bombardier Derby 2003–04. –/55 1TD 2W. 45.80 t.
MS. Dia. DR2 . Bombardier Derby 2003–04. –/76. 43.00 t.
DMCL. Dia. DP3 . Bombardier Derby 2003–04. 9/53 1T. 45.80 t.

170 438	**SR**	P	50438	56438	79438
170 439	**SR**	P	50439	56439	79439
170 451	**SR**	P	50451	56451	79430
170 452	**SR**	P	50452	56452	79431
170 453	**SR**	P	50453	56453	79432
170 454	**SR**	P	50454	56454	79433
170 455	**SR**	P	50455	56455	79434
170 456	**SR**	P	50456	56456	79435
170 457	**SR**	P	50457	56457	79436
170 458	**SR**	P	50458	56458	79437

Class 170/4. ScotRail units. On order. Fitted with databus system. DMSL–MS–DMCL.

DMSL. Dia. DP2 . Bombardier Derby 2003–04. –/55 1TD 2W. 45.80 t.
MS. Dia. DR2 . Bombardier Derby 2003–04. –/76. 43.00 t.
DMSL. Dia. DP3 . Bombardier Derby 2003–04. –/67 1T. 45.80 t.

170 459	**SR**	P	50459	56459	79459
170 460	**SR**	P	50460	56460	79460
170 461	**SR**	P	50461	56461	79461
170 462	**SR**	P	50462	56462	79462

Class 170/4. ScotRail units. Standard class only units for Strathclyde PTE. DMSL–MS–DMSL.

50470–50471. DMSL(A). Dia. DP284. Adtranz Derby 2001. –/55 1TD 2W. 45.80 t.
50474–50479. DMSL(A). Dia. DP2 . Bombardier Derby 2003. Fitted with databus system. –/55 1TD 2W.
56470–56471. MS. Dia. DR213. Adtranz Derby 2001. –/76. 43.00 t.
56474–56479. MS. Dia. DR2 . Bombardier Derby 2003. Fitted with databus system. . t.
79470–79471. DMSL(B). Dia. DP285. Adtranz Derby 2001. –/67 1T. 45.80 t.
79474–79479. DMSL(B). Dia. DP2 . Bombardier Derby 2003. Fitted with databus system. –/67 1T. . t.

170 470	**SP**	P	*SR*	HA	50470	56470	79470
170 471	**SP**	P	*SR*	HA	50471	56471	79471
170 474	**SP**	P			50474	56474	79474
170 475	**SP**	P			50475	56475	79475
170 476	**SP**	P			50476	56476	79476
170 477	**SP**	P			50477	56477	79477
170 478	**SP**	P			50478	56478	79478
170 479	**SP**	P			50479	56479	79479

Class 170/5. Central Trains 2-car units. DMSL–DMSL.

DMSL(A). Dia. DP275. Adtranz Derby 1999–2000. –/55 1TD 2W. 45.80 t.
DMSL(B). Dia. DP276. Adtranz Derby 1999–2000. –/67 1T. 46.80 t.

170 501	r	**CT**	P	*CT*	TS	50501	79501
170 502	r	**CT**	P	*CT*	TS	50502	79502
170 503	r	**CT**	P	*CT*	TS	50503	79503
170 504	r	**CT**	P	*CT*	TS	50504	79504
170 505	r	**CT**	P	*CT*	TS	50505	79505
170 506	r	**CT**	P	*CT*	TS	50506	79506
170 507	r	**CT**	P	*CT*	TS	50507	79507
170 508	r	**CT**	P	*CT*	TS	50508	79508
170 509	r	**CT**	P	*CT*	TS	50509	79509
170 510	r	**CT**	P	*CT*	TS	50510	79510
170 511	r	**CT**	P	*CT*	TS	50511	79511
170 512	r	**CT**	P	*CT*	TS	50512	79512
170 513	r	**CT**	P	*CT*	TS	50513	79513
170 514	r	**CT**	P	*CT*	TS	50514	79514
170 515	r	**CT**	P	*CT*	TS	50515	79515
170 516	r	**CT**	P	*CT*	TS	50516	79516
170 517	r	**CT**	P	*CT*	TS	50517	79517
170 518	r	**CT**	P	*CT*	TS	50518	79518
170 519	r	**CT**	P	*CT*	TS	50519	79519
170 520	r	**CT**	P	*CT*	TS	50520	79520
170 521	r	**CT**	P	*CT*	TS	50521	79521
170 522	r	**CT**	P	*CT*	TS	50522	79522
170 523	r	**CT**	P	*CT*	TS	50523	79523

Class 170/6. Central Trains 3-car units. DMSL–MS–DMSL.

DMSL(A). Dia. DP275. Adtranz Derby 2000. –/55 1TD 2W. 45.80 t.
MS. Dia. DR214. Adtranz Derby 2000. –/74. 43.00 t.
DMSL(B). Dia. DP276. Adtranz Derby 2000. –/67 1T. 46.80 t.

170 630	r	**CT**	P	*CT*	TS	50630	56630	79630
170 631	r	**CT**	P	*CT*	TS	50631	56631	79631
170 632	r	**CT**	P	*CT*	TS	50632	56632	79632
170 633	r	**CT**	P	*CT*	TS	50633	56633	79633
170 634	r	**CT**	P	*CT*	TS	50634	56634	79634
170 635	r	**CT**	P	*CT*	TS	50635	56635	79635
170 636	r	**CT**	P	*CT*	TS	50636	56636	79636
170 637	r	**CT**	P	*CT*	TS	50637	56637	79637
170 638	r	**CT**	P	*CT*	TS	50638	56638	79638
170 639	r	**CT**	P	*CT*	TS	50639	56639	79639

Class 170/7. GoVia South Central units. On order. Fitted with databus system.
DMCL–DMSL or DMCL–MS–MS–DMSL.

DMCL. Dia. DP . Bombardier Derby 2003. 9/43 1TD 2W. . t.
MS. Dia. DR . Bombardier Derby 2003. –/76. . t.
DMSL. Dia. DP . Bombardier Derby 2003. –/67 1T. . t.

170 721	SN	P		50721			79721
170 722	SN	P		50722			79722
170 723	SN	P		50723			79723
170 724	SN	P		50724			79724
170 725	SN	P		50725			79725
170 726	SN	P		50726			79726
170 731	SN	P		50731	56731	54731	79731
170 732	SN	P		50732	56732	54732	79732
170 733	SN	P		50733	56733	54733	79733
170 734	SN	P		50734	56734	54734	79734
170 735	SN	P		50735	56735	54735	79735
170 736	SN	P		50736	56736	54736	79736

CLASS 175   CORADIA 1000   ALSTOM

Air Conditioned.

Construction: Steel.
Engines: One Cummins N14 of 335 kW (450 h.p.).
Transmission: Hydraulic. Voith T211rzze to ZF final drive.
Bogies:
Couplers: Scharfenberg.
Seating Layout: 2+2 facing/unidirectional.
Dimensions: 23.71/23.03 x 2.73 m.
Gangways: Within unit only.   **Wheel Arrangement:** 2-B (– B-2) – B-2.
Doors: Single-leaf swing plug.   **Maximum Speed:** 100 m.p.h.
Multiple Working: Within class and with Class 180.

Class 175/0. DMSL–DMSL. 2-car units.

DMSL(A). Dia. DP278. Alstom Birmingham 1999–2000. –/54 1TD 2W. 51.00 t.
DMSL(B). Dia. DP279. Alstom Birmingham 1999–2000. –/64 1T. 51.00 t.

175 001	FS	A	NW	CH	50701	79701
175 002	FS	A	NW	CH	50702	79702
175 003	FS	A	NW	CH	50703	79703
175 004	FS	A	NW	CH	50704	79704
175 005	FS	A	NW	CH	50705	79705
175 006	FS	A	NW	CH	50706	79706
175 007	FS	A	NW	CH	50707	79707
175 008	FS	A	NW	CH	50708	79708
175 009	FS	A	NW	CH	50709	79709
175 010	FS	A	NW	CH	50710	79710
175 011	FS	A	NW	CH	50711	79711

Names (carried on one side of each DMSL):

175 004   MENCAP National Colleges Pengwern College
175 008   Valhalla Blackpool Pleasure Beach

Class 175/1. DMSL–MSL–DMSL. 3-car units.

DMSL(A). Dia. DP278. Alstom Birmingham 1999–2001. –/54 1TD 2W. 51.00 t.
MSL. Dia. DR216. Alstom Birmingham 1999–2001. –/68 1T. 43 t 68 1T. 47.50 t.
DMSL(B). Dia. DP279. Alstom Birmingham 1999–2001. –/64 1T. 51.00 t.

175 101	**FS**	A	NW	CH	50751	56751	79751
175 102	**FS**	A	NW	CH	50752	56752	79752
175 103	**FS**	A	NW	CH	50753	56753	79753
175 104	**FS**	A	NW	CH	50754	56754	79754
175 105	**FS**	A	NW	CH	50755	56755	79755
175 106	**FS**	A	NW	CH	50756	56756	79756
175 107	**FS**	A	NW	CH	50757	56757	79757
175 108	**FS**	A	NW	CH	50758	56758	79758
175 109	**FS**	A	NW	CH	50759	56759	79759
175 110	**FS**	A	NW	CH	50760	56760	79760
175 111	**FS**	A	NW	CH	50761	56761	79761
175 112	**FS**	A	NW	CH	50762	56762	79762
175 113	**FS**	A	NW	CH	50763	56763	79763
175 114	**FS**	A	NW	CH	50764	56764	79764
175 115	**FS**	A	NW	CH	50765	56765	79765
175 116	**FS**	A	NW	CH	50766	56766	79766

Names (carried on one side of each DMSL):

175 103   Mum
175 111   Brief Encounter
175 112   South Lakes Wild Animal Park SUMATRAN TIGER
175 114   Commonwealth Cruiser

CLASS 180   CORADIA 1000   ALSTOM

New units for First Great Western.

Construction: Steel.
Engines: One Cummins QSK19 of 560 kW (750 h.p.) at 2100 r.p.m.
Transmission: Hydraulic. Voith T312br to Voith final drive.
Bogies: Alstom MB2.
Couplers: Scharfenberg.
Seating Layout: 1: 2+1 facing/unidirectional, 2: 2+2 facing/unidirectional.
Dimensions: 23.71/23.03 x 2.73 m.
Gangways: Within unit only.   **Wheel Arrangement:** 2-B–B-2–B-2–B-2–B-2.
Doors: Single-leaf swing plug.   **Maximum Speed:** 125 m.p.h.
Multiple Working: Within class and with Class 175.

DMSL(A). Dia. DP282. Alstom Birmingham 2000–2001. –/46 2W 1TD. 53.00 t.
MFL. Dia. DR101. Alstom Birmingham 2000–2001. 42/– 1T 1W + catering point. 51.50 t.
MSL. Dia. DR217. Alstom Birmingham 2000–2001. –/68 1T. 51.50 t.

MSLRB. Dia. DR218. Alstom Birmingham 2000–2001. –/56 1T. 51.50 t.
DMSL(B). Dia. DP283. Alstom Birmingham 2000–2001. –/56 1T. 53.00 t.

180 101	FG	W			50901	54901	55901	56901	59901
180 102	FG	W	GW	OM	50902	54902	55902	56902	59902
180 103	FG	W	GW	OM	50903	54903	55903	56903	59903
180 104	FG	W	GW	OM	50904	54904	55904	56904	59904
180 105	FG	W	GW	OM	50905	54905	55905	56905	59905
180 106	FG	W	GW	OM	50906	54906	55906	56906	59906
180 107	FG	W	GW	OM	50907	54907	55907	56907	59907
180 108	FG	W	GW	OM	50908	54908	55908	56908	59908
180 109	FG	W	GW	OM	50909	54909	55909	56909	59909
180 110	FG	W	GW	OM	50910	54910	55910	56910	59910
180 111	FG	W	GW	OM	50911	54911	55911	56911	59911
180 112	FG	W	GW	OM	50912	54912	55912	56912	59912
180 113	FG	W	GW	OM	50913	54913	55913	56913	59913
180 114	FG	W	GW	OM	50914	54914	55914	56914	59914

3.2. DIESEL ELECTRIC UNITS

The following features are standard to ex-BR Southern Region diesel-electric multiple unit power cars (Classes 201–207):

Construction: Steel.
Engine: One English Electric 4SRKT Mk. 2 of 450 kW (600 h.p.) at 850 r.p.m.
Main Generator: English Electric EE824.
Traction Motors: Two English Electric EE507 mounted on the inner bogie.

Bogies: SR Mk. 4. (Former EMU TSL vehicles have Commonwealth bogies).
Couplers: Drophead buckeye.
Doors: Manually operated slam.
Brakes: Electro-pneumatic and automatic air.
Maximum Speed: 75 m.p.h.
Multiple Working: Other ex-BR Southern Region DEMU vehicles.

CLASS 201/202 PRESERVED 'HASTINGS' UNIT BR

DMBS–2TSL–TSRB–TSL–DMBS.

Preserved unit made up from 2 Class 201 short-frame cars and 2 Class 202 long-frame cars. The 'Hastings' units were made with narrow body-profiles for use on the section between Tonbridge and Battle which had tunnels of restricted loading gauge. These tunnels were converted to single track operation in the 1980s thus allowing standard loading gauge stock to be used. The set also contains a Class 411 EMU trailer (not Hastings line gauge).

Gangways: Within unit only.
Seating Layout: 2+2 facing.
Dimensions: 18.36 x 2.50 m (60000/60501), 20.34 x 2.50 m. (60118/60529) 20.34 x 2.82 m (69337/70262).

60000. DMBS. Dia DB201. Lot No. 30329 Eastleigh 1957. –/22. 54 t.
60501. TSL. Dia DH201. Lot No. 30331 Eastleigh 1957. –/52 2T. 29 t.
70262. TSL (ex Class 411/5 EMU). Dia. DH208. Lot No. 30455 Eastleigh 1958–1959. –/64 2T. 33.78 t.
69337. TSRB (ex Class 422 EMU). Dia. DH209. Lot No. 30805 York 1970. –/40. 35 t.
60529. TSL. Dia DH202. Lot No. 30397 Eastleigh 1957. –/60 2T. 30 t.
60118. DMBS. Dia DB202. Lot No. 30395 Eastleigh 1957. –/30. 55 t.

| 201 001 | **G** | HD *SS* | SE | 60000 | 60529 | 70262 | 69337 | 60501 | 60118 |

Names:

60000	Hastings	60118	Tunbridge Wells

CLASS 205/0 (3H) BR 'HAMPSHIRE'

DMBS–TSL–DTCsoL or DMBS–DTCsoL.

Gangways: Non-gangwayed.
Seating Layout: 3+2 facing or compartments.
Dimensions: 20.33 x 2.82 m (DMBS), 20.28 x 2.82 m (TS), 20.36 x 2.82 m (DTCsoL).

60111/60117/60154. DMBS. Dia DB203. Lot No. 30332 Eastleigh 1957. –/52. 56 t.
60122–60124. DMBS. Dia DB203. Lot No. 30540 Eastleigh 1958–1959. –/52. 56 t.
60146–60151. DMBS. Dia DB204. Lot No. 30671 Eastleigh 1960–1962. –/42. 56 t.
60650–60670. TS. Dia DH203. Lot No. 30542 Eastleigh 1958–1959. –/104. 30 t.
60673–60678. TS. Dia DH203. Lot No. 30672 Eastleigh 1960–1962. –/104. 30 t.
60800–60808. DTCsoL. Dia DE301. Lot No. 30333 Eastleigh 1956–1957. 13/50 2T. 32 t.
60811. DTCsoL. Dia DE302. Lot No. 30333 Eastleigh 1956–1957. 19/50 2T. 32 t.
60820. DTCsoL. Dia DE301. Lot No. 30399 Eastleigh 1957–1958. 13/50 2T. 32 t.
60823/60824. DTCsoL. Dia DE301. Lot No. 30541 Eastleigh 1958–1959. 13/50 2T. 32 t.
60827–60832. DTCsoL. Dia DE303. Lot No. 30673 Eastleigh 1960–1962. 13/62 2T. (13/60 2T 60827 (DE304), 13/57 2T 60831 (DE305)) 32 t.

205 001	**CX**	P	*SC*	SU	60154		60800
205 009	**CX**	P	*SC*	SU	60108	60658	60808
205 012	**CX**	P	*SC*	SU	60111		60811
205 018	**CX**	P	*SC*	SU	60117	60674	60828
205 025	**CX**	P	*SC*	SU	60124		60824
205 028	**CX**	P	*SC*	SU	60146	60673	60827
205 032	**CX**	P	*SC*	SU	60150	60677	60831
205 033	**CX**	P	*SC*	SU	60151	60678	60832
Spare	**CX**	P		ZG		60650	
Spare	**N**	P		SU	60123		60823
Spare	**N**	P		SU		60670	
Spare	**G**	HD		SE	60122	60668	

CLASS 205/2 (3H) BR 'HAMPSHIRE'

DMBS–TSL (ex Class 411/5 EMU)–DTSL. Refurbished 1980. Fluorescent lighting.

Details as for Class 205/0 except:

Gangways: Within unit only.
Seating Layout: 3+2 facing.

DMBS. Dia. DB203. Lot No. 30332 Eastleigh 1957. –/39. 57 t.
TSL. Dia. DH207. Converted from loco-hauled TS 4059 Lot No. 30149 Swindon 1955–1957. –/64 2T. 33.78 t.
DTSL. Dia. DE204. Lot No. 30333 Eastleigh 1957. –/76 2T. 32 t.

Note: This unit operates as a two-car set in winter.

205 205	**CX**	P	*SC*	SU	60110	71634	60810

CLASS 207/0 (2D)   BR 'OXTED'

DMBS–DTS (formerly DMBS–TCsoL–DTS).

This class was built for the Oxted line and therefore referred to as 'Oxted' units.
They were made with a narrower body-profile which also allowed them to be
used through the restricted loading-gauge Somerhill Tunnel between Tonbridge
and Grove Junction (Tunbridge Wells). This tunnel was converted to single track
operation in the 1980s thus allowing standard loading gauge stock to be used.

Gangways: Non-gangwayed.
Seating Layout: 3+2 facing or compartments.
Dimensions: 20.33 x 2.74 m (DMBS/TCsoL), 20.32 x 2.74 m. (DTS).

DMBS. Dia DB205. Lot No. 30625 Eastleigh 1962. –/42. 56 t.
60616. TCsoL. Dia DH301. Lot No. 30626 Eastleigh 1962. 24/42 1T. 31 t.
60916. DTS. Dia DE201. Lot No. 30627 Eastleigh 1962. –/76. 32 t.

207 017	**CX**	P	*SC*	SU	60142	60916
Spare	**G**	HD		SE	60138 60616	

CLASS 207/2 (3D)   BR 'OXTED'

DMBS–TSL–DTS.
Gangwayed sets with an ex-Class 411 EMU trailer in the centre.

Gangways: Within unit only.
Seating Layout: 2+2 facing.
Dimensions: 20.34 x 2.74 m (DMBS), 20.32 x 2.74 m. (DTS).

DMBS. Dia DB205. Lot No. 30625 Eastleigh 1962. –/40. 56 t.
70286. TSL. Dia DH206. Lot No. 30455 Eastleigh 1958–1959. –/64 2T. 33.78 t.
70547/70549. TSL. Dia DH206. Lot No. 30620 Eastleigh 1960–1961 –/64 2T. 33.78 t.
DTS. Dia DE201. Lot No. 30627 Eastleigh 1962. –/75. 32 t.

Note: These units operate as two-car sets in winter.

207 201	**CX**	P	*SC*	SU (S)	60129	70286	60903
207 202	**CX**	P	*SC*	SU	60130	70549	60904
207 203	**CX**	P	*SC*	SU	60127	70547	60901

Names (carried on DMBS):

207 201 Ashford Fayre | 207 202 Brighton Royal Pavilion

CLASS 220   VOYAGER   BOMBARDIER

DMS–MSRMB–MS–DMF.

Construction: Steel.
Engine: Cummins of 750 h.p. (560 kW) at 1800 r.p.m.
Transmission: Two Alstom Onix 800 three-phase traction motors of 275 kW.
Braking: Rheostatic and electro-pneumatic.
Bogies: Bombardier B5005.
Couplers: Dellner.
Seating Layout: 1: 2+1 facing/unidirectional, 2: 2+2 mainly unidirectional.
Dimensions: 23.85/22.82 x 2.73 m.
Gangways: Within unit only.
Wheel Arrangement: 1A-A1 – 1A-A1 – 1A-A1 – 1A-A1.
Doors: Single-leaf swing plug.
Maximum Speed: 125 m.p.h.
Multiple Working: Within class and with Classes 221 and 222.

DMS. Dia DC201. Bombardier Brugge/Wakefield 2000–2001. –/42 1TD 1W. 48.10 t.
MSRMB. Dia. DD201. Bombardier Brugge/Wakefield 2000–2001. –/58. 48.00 t.
MS. Dia. DD202. Bombardier Brugge/Wakefield 2000–2001. –/62 1TD 1W. 45.00 t.
DMF. Dia DC101. Bombardier Brugge/Wakefield 2000–2001. 26/– 1TD 1W. 44.50 t.

220 001	**VT**	HX	*VX*	CZ	60301	60701	60201	60401
220 002	**VT**	HX	*VX*	CZ	60302	60702	60202	60402
220 003	**VT**	HX	*VX*	CZ	60303	60703	60203	60403
220 004	**VT**	HX	*VX*	CZ	60304	60704	60204	60404
220 005	**VT**	HX	*VX*	CZ	60305	60705	60205	60405
220 006	**VT**	HX	*VX*	CZ	60306	60706	60206	60406
220 007	**VT**	HX	*VX*	CZ	60307	60707	60207	60407
220 008	**VT**	HX	*VX*	CZ	60308	60708	60208	60408
220 009	**VT**	HX	*VX*	CZ	60309	60709	60209	60409
220 010	**VT**	HX	*VX*	CZ	60310	60710	60210	60410
220 011	**VT**	HX	*VX*	CZ	60311	60711	60211	60411
220 012	**VT**	HX	*VX*	CZ	60312	60712	60212	60412
220 013	**VT**	HX	*VX*	CZ	60313	60713	60213	60413
220 014	**VT**	HX	*VX*	CZ	60314	60714	60214	60414
220 015	**VT**	HX	*VX*	CZ	60315	60715	60215	60415
220 016	**VT**	HX	*VX*	CZ	60316	60716	60216	60416
220 017	**VT**	HX	*VX*	CZ	60317	60717	60217	60417
220 018	**VT**	HX	*VX*	CZ	60318	60718	60218	60418
220 019	**VT**	HX	*VX*	CZ	60319	60719	60219	60419
220 020	**VT**	HX	*VX*	CZ	60320	60720	60220	60420
220 021	**VT**	HX	*VX*	CZ	60321	60721	60221	60421
220 022	**VT**	HX	*VX*	CZ	60322	60722	60222	60422
220 023	**VT**	HX	*VX*	CZ	60323	60723	60223	60423
220 024	**VT**	HX	*VX*	CZ	60324	60724	60224	60424
220 025	**VT**	HX	*VX*	CZ	60325	60725	60225	60425
220 026	**VT**	HX	*VX*	CZ	60326	60726	60226	60426
220 027	**VT**	HX	*VX*	CZ	60327	60727	60227	60427
220 028	**VT**	HX	*VX*	CZ	60328	60728	60228	60428

220 029	**VT**	HX	*VX*	CZ	60329	60729	60229	60429
220 030	**VT**	HX	*VX*	CZ	60330	60730	60230	60430
220 031	**VT**	HX	*VX*	CZ	60331	60731	60231	60431
220 032	**VT**	HX	*VX*	CZ	60332	60732	60232	60432
220 033	**VT**	HX	*VX*	CZ	60333	60733	60233	60433
220 034	**VT**	HX	*VX*	CZ	60334	60734	60234	60434

Names (carried on MS):

220 001	Maiden Voyager		220 018	Dorset Voyager
220 002	Forth Voyager		220 019	Mersey Voyager
220 003	Solent Voyager		220 020	Wessex Voyager
220 004	Cumbrian Voyager		220 021	Blackpool Voyager
220 005	Guildford Voyager		220 022	Brighton Voyager
220 006	Clyde Voyager		220 023	Mancunian Voyager
220 007	Thames Voyager		220 024	Sheffield Voyager
220 008	Draig Gymreig/Welsh Dragon		220 025	Severn Voyager
220 009	Gatwick Voyager		220 026	Stagecoach Voyager
220 010	Ribble Voyager		220 027	Avon Voyager
220 011	Tyne Voyager		220 028	Black Country Voyager
220 012	Lanarkshire Voyager		220 029	Vyajer Kernewek/
220 013	Gwibiwr De Cymru/			Cornish Voyager
	South Wales Voyager		220 030	Devon Voyager
220 014	South Yorkshire Voyager		220 031	Tay Voyager
220 015	Solway Voyager		220 032	Grampian Voyager
220 016	Midland Voyager		220 033	Fife Voyager
220 017	BOMBARDIER Voyager		220 034	Yorkshire Voyager

CLASS 221   SUPER VOYAGER   BOMBARDIER

DMS–MSRMB–MS(–MS)–DMF. Tilting units.

Construction: Steel.
Engine: Cummins of 750 h.p. (560 kW) at 1800 r.p.m.
Transmission: Two Alstom Onix 800 three-phase traction motors of 275 kW.
Braking: Rheostatic and electro-pneumatic.
Bogies: Bombardier HVP.
Couplers: Dellner.
Seating Layout: 1: 2+1 facing/unidirectional, 2: 2+2 mainly unidirectional.
Dimensions: 23.85/22.82 x 2.73 m.
Gangways: Within unit only.
Wheel Arrangement: 1A-A1 – 1A-A1 – 1A-A1 (– 1A-A1) – 1A-A1.
Doors: Single-leaf swing plug.
Maximum Speed: 125 m.p.h.
Multiple Working: Within class and with Classes 220 and 222.

DMS. Dia DF201. Bombardier Brugge/Wakefield 2001–2002. –/42 1TD 1W. 58.30 t.
MSRMB. Dia. DG201. Bombardier Brugge/Wakefield 2001–2002. –/58. 58.00 t.
MS. Dia. DG202. Bombardier Brugge/Wakefield 2001–2002. –/62 1TD 1W. 55.80 t.
DMF. Dia DF101. Bombardier Brugge/Wakefield 2001–2002. 26/– 1TD 1W. 54.90 t.

221 101	**VT**	HX			60351	60751	60951	60851	60451
221 102	**VT**	HX	*VX*	CZ	60352	60782	60952	60852	60452
221 103	**VT**	HX	*VX*	CZ	60353	60783	60953	60853	60453
221 104	**VT**	HX	*VX*	CZ	60354	60785	60954	60854	60454
221 105	**VT**	HX	*VX*	CZ	60355	60755	60955	60855	60455
221 106	**VT**	HX	*VX*	CZ	60356	60756	60956	60856	60456
221 107	**VT**	HX	*VX*	CZ	60357	60757	60957	60857	60457
221 108	**VT**	HX	*VX*	CZ	60358	60758	60958	60858	60458
221 109	**VT**	HX	*VX*	CZ	60359	60759	60959	60859	60459
221 110	**VT**	HX	*VX*	CZ	60360	60760	60960	60860	60460
221 111	**VT**	HX	*VX*	CZ	60361	60761	60961	60861	60461
221 112	**VT**	HX	*VX*	CZ	60362	60762	60962	60862	60462
221 113	**VT**	HX	*VX*	CZ	60363	60763	60963	60863	60463
221 114	**VT**	HX	*VX*	CZ	60364	60764	60964	60864	60464
221 115	**VT**	HX	*VX*	CZ	60365	60765	60965	60865	60465
221 116	**VT**	HX	*VX*	CZ	60366	60766	60966	60866	60466
221 117	**VT**	HX	*VX*	CZ	60367	60767	60967	60867	60467
221 118	**VT**	HX	*VX*	CZ	60368	60768	60968	60868	60468
221 119	**VT**	HX	*VX*	CZ	60369	60769	60969	60869	60469
221 120	**VT**	HX	*VX*	CZ	60370	60770	60970	60870	60470
221 121	**VT**	HX	*VX*	CZ	60371	60771	60971	60871	60471
221 122	**VT**	HX	*VX*	CZ	60372	60772	60972	60872	60472
221 123	**VT**	HX	*VX*	CZ	60373	60773	60973	60873	60473
221 124	**VT**	HX	*VX*	CZ	60374	60774	60974	60874	60474
221 125	**VT**	HX	*VX*	CZ	60375	60775	60975	60875	60475
221 126	**VT**	HX	*VX*	CZ	60376	60776	60976	60876	60476
221 127	**VT**	HX	*VX*	CZ	60377	60777	60977	60877	60477
221 128	**VT**	HX	*VX*	CZ	60378	60778	60978	60878	60478
221 129	**VT**	HX	*VX*	CZ	60379	60779	60979	60879	60479
221 130	**VT**	HX	*VX*	CZ	60380	60780	60980	60880	60480
221 131	**VT**	HX	*VX*	CZ	60381	60781	60981	60881	60481
221 132	**VT**	HX	*VX*	CZ	60382	60782	60982	60882	60482
221 133	**VT**	HX	*VX*	CZ	60383	60783	60983	60883	60483
221 134	**VT**	HX	*VX*	CZ	60384	60784	60984	60884	60484
221 135	**VT**	HX	*VX*	CZ	60385	60785	60985	60885	60485
221 136	**VT**	HX	*VX*	CZ	60386	60786	60986	60886	60486
221 137	**VT**	HX	*VX*	CZ	60387	60787	60987	60887	60487
221 138	**VT**	HX	*VX*	CZ	60388	60788	60988	60888	60488
221 139	**VT**	HX	*VX*	CZ	60389	60789	60989	60889	60489
221 140	**VT**	HX	*VX*	CZ	60390	60790	60990	60890	60490
221 141	**VT**	HX	*VX*	CZ	60391	60791	60991		60491
221 142	**VT**	HX	*VX*	CZ	60392	60792	60992		60492
221 143	**VT**	HX	*VX*	CZ	60393	60793	60993		60493
221 144	**VT**	HX	*VX*	CZ	60394	60794	60994		60494

Names (carried on MS No. 609xx):

221 101	Louis Bleriot	221 123	Henry Hudson
221 102	John Cabot	221 124	Charles Lindbergh
221 103	Christopher Columbus	221 125	Henry the Navigator
221 104	Sir John Franklin	221 126	Captain Robert Scott
221 105	William Baffin	221 127	Wright Brothers
221 106	Willem Barents	221 128	Captain John Smith
221 107	Sir Martin Frobisher	221 129	George Vancouver
221 108	Sir Ernest Shackleton	221 130	Michael Palin
221 109	Marco Polo	221 131	Edgar Evans
221 110	James Cook	221 132	William Speirs Bruce
221 111	Roald Amundsen	221 133	Alexander Selkirk
221 112	Ferdinand Magellan	221 134	Mary Kingsley
221 113	Sir Walter Raleigh	221 135	Donald Campbell
221 114	Sir Francis Drake	221 136	Yuri Gagarin
221 115	Sir Francis Chichester	221 137	Mayflower Pilgrims
221 116	David Livingstone	221 138	Thor Heyerdahl
221 117	Sir Henry Morton Stanley	221 139	Leif Erikson
221 118	Mungo Park	221 140	Vasco da Gama
221 119	Amelia Earhart	221 141	Amerigo Vespucci
221 120	Amy Johnson	221 142	Mathew Flinders
221 121	Charles Darwin	221 143	Auguste Picard
221 122	Doctor Who	221 144	Prince Madoc

CLASS 222   MERIDIAN   BOMBARDIER

Various formations. New 9-car and 4-car units on order for Midland Mainline.

Construction: Steel.
Engine: Cummins of 750 h.p. (560 kW) at 1800 r.p.m.
Transmission: Two Alstom Onix 800 three-phase traction motors of 275 kW.
Braking: Rheostatic and electro-pneumatic.
Bogies: Bombardier B5005.
Couplers: Dellner.
Seating Layout: 1: 2+1 facing/unidirectional, 2: 2+2 facing/unidirectional.
Dimensions: 23.85/22.82 x 2.73 m.
Gangways: Within unit only.
Wheel Arrangement: All cars 1A-A1.
Doors: Single-leaf swing plug.
Maximum Speed: 125 m.p.h.
Multiple Working: Within class and with Classes 220 and 221.

DMRFO. Dia DD1 . Bombardier Brugge/Wakefield 2002–2004. 22/– 1TD 1W.   . t.
MFO. Dia. DC1 . Bombardier Brugge/Wakefield 2002–2004. 42/– 1T.   . t.
MCO. Dia. DC3 . Bombardier Brugge/Wakefield 2002–2004. 28/20 1T.   . t.
MSORMB. Dia. DC2 . Bombardier Brugge/Wakefield 2002–2004. –/62.   . t.
MSO. Dia. DC2 . Bombardier Brugge/Wakefield 2002–2004. –/70 1T.   . t.
DMSO. Dia DD2 . Bombardier Brugge/Wakefield 2002–2004. –/36 1TD 2W.   . t.

222 001–007. 9-car units. DMRFO–MFO–MFO–MSO–MSO–MSORMB–MSO–
MSO–DMSO.

222 001	**MN**	H	60161	60531	60541	60551	60561
			60621	60341	60441	60241	
222 002	**MN**	H	60162	60532	60542	60552	60562
			60622	60342	60442	60242	
222 003	**MN**	H	60163	60533	60543	60553	60563
			60623	60343	60443	60243	
222 004	**MN**	H	60164	60534	60544	60554	60564
			60624	60344	60444	60244	
222 005	**MN**	H	60165	60535	60545	60555	60565
			60625	60345	60445	60245	
222 006	**MN**	H	60166	60536	60546	60556	60566
			60626	60346	60446	60246	
222 007	**MN**	H	60167	60537	60547	60557	60567
			60627	60347	60447	60247	

222 008–023. 4-car units. DMRFO–MCO–MSORMB–DMSO.

222 008	**MN**	H	60168	60918	60628	60248
222 009	**MN**	H	60169	60919	60629	60249
222 010	**MN**	H	60170	60920	60630	60250
222 011	**MN**	H	60171	60921	60631	60251
222 012	**MN**	H	60172	60922	60632	60252
222 013	**MN**	H	60173	60923	60633	60253
222 014	**MN**	H	60174	60922	60634	60254
222 015	**MN**	H	60175	60925	60635	60255
222 016	**MN**	H	60176	60926	60636	60256
222 017	**MN**	H	60177	60927	60637	60257
222 018	**MN**	H	60178	60928	60638	60258
222 019	**MN**	H	60179	60929	60639	60259
222 020	**MN**	H	60180	60930	60640	60260
222 021	**MN**	H	60181	60931	60641	60261
222 022	**MN**	H	60182	60932	60642	60262
222 023	**MN**	H	60183	60933	60643	60263

3.3 SERVICE DMUS

This section lists vehicles not used for passenger-carrying purposes. Some vehicles are numbered in the special service stock number series.

CLASS 114/1   ROUTE LEARNING UNIT

DMB–DT. Converted 1992 from Class 114/1. Gangwayed within unit.

Construction: Steel.
Engines: Two Leyland TL11/40 of 153 kW (205 h.p.) at 1950 r.p.m.
Transmission: Mechanical. Cardan shaft and freewheel to a four-speed epicyclic gearbox with a further cardan shaft to the final drive, each engine driving the inner axle of one bogie.

Maximum Speed: 70 m.p.h.	**Couplings:** Screw.
Bogies: DD9 + DT9.	**Multiple Working:** Blue Square.
Brakes: Twin pipe vacuum.	**Dimensions:** 20.45 x 2.82 m.

Doors: Manually operated slam/roller shutter.
Non-Standard Livery: Grey, red and yellow.

977775. DMB. Dia. DZ518. Lot No. 30209 Derby 1957. 38.0 t.
977776. DT. Dia. DZ516. Lot No. 30210 Derby 1957. 30.0 t.

-		**0**	E		TE	977775	(55928)	977776	(54904)

CLASS 122   ROUTE LEARNING UNIT

DM. Converted 1995 from DMBS. Non gangwayed single car with cab at each end.

Construction: Steel.
Engines: Two Leyland 1595 of 112 kW (150 h.p.) at 1800 r.p.m.
Transmission: Mechanical. Cardan shaft and freewheel to a four-speed epicyclic gearbox with a further cardan shaft to the final drive, each engine driving the inner axle of one bogie.

Maximum Speed: 75 m.p.h.	**Couplings:** Screw.
Bogies: DD10.	**Multiple Working:** Blue Square.
Brakes: Twin pipe vacuum.	**Dimensions:** 20.45 x 2.82 m.

Doors: Manually operated slam.

55012. DM. Dia. DX202. Lot No. 30419 Gloucester 1958. Converted by ABB Doncaster 1995. 36.5 t.

-		**LH**	E		TE	55012

CLASS 930   SANDITE/DE-ICING UNIT

DMB–T–DMB. Converted 1993 from Class 205. Gangwayed within unit. Sandite trailer 977870 is replaced by de-icing trailer 977364 as required.

Construction: Steel.
Engine: One English Electric 4SRKT Mk. 2 of 450 kW (600 h.p.) at 850 r.p.m.
Transmission: Electric. Two English Electric EE507 traction motors mounted on the bogie at the non-driving end of each power car.
Maximum Speed: 75 m.p.h.   **Bogies:** SR Mk. 4.
Brakes: Electro-pneumatic and automatic air.
Doors: Manually operated slam.   **Couplings:** Drophead buckeye.
Multiple Working: Classes 201–207.
Dimensions: 20.33 x 2.82 x 3.87 m. (DMB); 20.28 x 2.82 m.

977939–977940. DMB. Dia. DZ537. Lot No. 30671 Eastleigh 1962. 56.0 t.
977870. T. Dia. DZ533. Lot No. 30542 Eastleigh 1960. 30.5 t.

930 301	**RO**	NR	*SC*	SU	977939	(60145)	977870	(60660)
					977940	(60149)		

CLASS 960   ULTRASONIC TESTING/TRACTOR UNIT

DM–DM. Converted 1986 from Class 101. Gangwayed within unit. Often operates with either 975091 or 999602 as a centre car.

For detail see page 173 except:

Brakes: Air.

977391. DM. Dia. DZ503. Lot No. 30500 Metro-Cammell. 1959. 32.5 t.
977392. DM. Dia. DZ503. Lot No. 30254 Metro-Cammell. 1956. 32.5 t.

-	**RK**	NR	*SO*	RG	977391	(51433)	977392	(53167)

CLASS 960   TEST UNIT (Iris 2)

DM–DM. Converted 1991 from Class 101. Gangwayed within unit.

For details see page 173.

977693. DM. Dia. DZ503. Lot No. 30261 Metro-Cammell. 1957. 32.5 t.
977694. DM. Dia. DZ503. Lot No. 30276 Metro-Cammell. 1958. 32.5 t.

-	**SO**	NR	*SO*	BY	977693	(53222)	977694	(53338)

CLASS 960   SANDITE UNITS

DMB. Converted 1991/1993 from Class 121. Non gangwayed.

For details see page 174.

977723. DMB. Dia. DX515. Lot No. 30518 Pressed Steel 1960. 38.0 t.
977858–60/66/73. DMB. Dia. DZ526. Lot No. 30518 Pressed Steel 1960. 38.0 t.

960 010	**M**	NR	*CR*	AL	977858	(55024)

960 011	**RK**	NR	*BB*	AP	977859	(55025)
960 012	**N**	NR		AP	977860	(55028)
960 013	**RO**	NR		DY	977866	(55030)
960 014	**N**	NR		DY	977873	(55022)
960 021	**RO**	NR	*CR*	AL	977723	(55021)

CLASS 960   EMERGENCY TRAIN UNITS

Under conversion from Class 121 for Severn Tunnel emergency train.
For details see page 174.

DMB. Dia. DX515. Lot No. 30518 Pressed Steel 1960. 38.5 t.

| 960 0 | **SL** | NR | | CP | 977975 | (55027) |
| 960 0 | **N** | NR | | CP | 977975 | (55031) |

CLASS 960   TRACK ASSESSMENT UNIT

Converted from Class 121. **For details see page 174.**

977968. DMB. Dia. DZ542.

| 977968 | **ES** | ES | *CA* | RU | 55029 |

CLASS 960   SANDITE UNIT

DMB. Converted 1991 from Class 122. Non gangwayed.

Construction: Steel.
Engines: Two Leyland 1595 of 112 kW (150 h.p.) at 1800 r.p.m.
Transmission: Mechanical. Cardan shaft and freewheel to a four-speed epicyclic gearbox with a further cardan shaft to the final drive, each engine driving the inner axle of one bogie.
Maximum Speed: 70 m.p.h.
Bogies: DD10.   **Couplings:** Screw.
Brakes: Twin pipe vacuum.   **Multiple Working:** Blue Square.
Doors: Manually operated slam.   **Dimensions:** 20.45 x 2.82 m.

975042. DMB. Dia. DX516. Lot No. 30419 Gloucester 1958. 36.5 t.

| 960 015 | **RO** | NR | *CR* | AL | 975042 | (55019) |

UNCLASSIFIED   DE-ICING UNIT

T. Converted 1960 from 4-Sub EMU vehicle. Non gangwayed. Operates with 977939/40.

Construction: Steel.
Maximum Speed: 70 m.p.h.   **Couplings:** Drophead buckeye.
Bogies: Central 43 inch.   **Multiple Working:** SR system.
Brakes: Electro-pneumatic and automatic air.
Doors: Manually operated slam.   **Dimensions:**

977364. T. Dia. EZ520. Southern Railway Eastleigh 1946. 29.0 t.

| - | **RO** | NR | *SC* | SU | 977364 | (10400) |

CLASS 960   TRACK ASSESSMENT UNIT

DM–DM. Purpose built service unit. Gangwayed within unit.

Construction: Steel.
Engine: One Cummins NT-855-RT5 of 213 kW (285 h.p.) at 2100 r.p.m. per power car.
Transmission: Hydraulic. Voith T211r with cardan shafts to Gmeinder GM190 final drive.
Maximum Speed: 75 m.p.h.   **Couplers:** BSI automatic.
Bogies: BP38 (powered), BT38 (non-powered).
Brakes: Electro-pneumatic.   **Dimensions:** 20.06 x 2.82 m.
Doors: Manually operated slam & power operated sliding.
Multiple Working: Classes 142, 143, 144, 150, 153, 155, 156, 158, 159, 170.

999600. DM. Dia. DZ536. Lot No. 4060 BREL York 1987. 36.5 t.
999601. DM. Dia. DZ536. Lot No. 4061 BREL York 1987. 36.5 t.

-      RK   NR *SO*   ZA   999600 999601

CLASS 960   ULTRASONIC TEST UNIT

T. Converted 1986 from Class 432 EMU. Gangwayed. Operates with 977391/2.

Construction: Steel.   **Maximum Speed:** 70 m.p.h.
Bogies: SR Mk. 6.   **Couplings:** Screw.
Brakes: Twin pipe vacuum.   **Multiple Working:** Blue Square.
Doors: Manually operated slam.   **Dimensions:** 19.66 x 2.82 m.

999602. T. Dia. DZ531. Lot No. 30862 York 1974. 55.5 t.

-      RK   SO *SO*   ZA   999602 (62483)

CLASS 960   TRACK ASSESSMENT/RECORDING UNIT

DM–DM. Universal track recording unit for video inspections, for measuring rail profiles etc. Plasser type UFM 160-1. Full details awaited.

Construction: **Engine:**
Transmission:
Maximum Speed: 100 m.p.h.   **Weight:** 70 t.
Brakes: **Dimensions:** 20.06 x 2.82 m.

999700. DM.
999701. DM.

-      ES   ES *CA*   RU   999700 999701

CLASS 960 TRACK ASSESSMENT/RECORDING UNIT

DM. On order. Full details awaited.

Construction:	**Engine:**
Transmission:	
Maximum Speed: 100 m.p.h.	**Weight:** 70 t.
Brakes:	**Dimensions:** 20.06 x 2.82 m.

DM.

-            ES   ES   *CA*   RU   999800

3.4. DMUS AWAITING DISPOSAL

The list below comprises vehicles awaiting disposal which are stored on the
Network Rail network, together with vehicles stored at other locations (e.g.
repair facilites) which, although awaiting disposal, remain Network Rail
registered. This includes vehicles for which sales have been agreed, but
collection by the new owner had not been made at the time of going to press.

Class 100

977191	**B**	LW	ZC	

Class 101

101 654	**RR**	A	PY	51800	54408			
101 656	**RR**	A	LO	51230	54056			
101 657	**RR**	A	LO	53211	54085			
101 658	**RR**	A	LO	51175	54091			
101 659	**RR**	A	PY	51213	54352			
101 660	**RR**	A	PY	51189	54343			
101 662	**RR**	A	PY	53228	54055			
101 664	**RR**	A	PY	51442	54061			
101 665	**RR**	A	PY	51429	54393			
101 677	**RR**	A	PY	51179	51496			
101 681	**RR**	A	PY	51228	51506			
101 682	**RR**	A	PY	53256	51505			
101 683	**RR**	A	LO	51177	53269			
101 684	**S**	A	PY	51187	51509			
101 686	**S**	A	PY	51231	51500			
101 687	**S**	A	PY	51247	51512			
101 690	**S**	A	PY	51435	53177			
101 691	**S**	A	LO	51253	53171			
101 694	**S**	A	PY	51188	53268			
101 695	**S**	A	PY	51226	51499			
101 835	**RR**	A	PY	51432	51498			
101 840	**N**	A	LO	53311	53322			
960 991	**N**	NR	DY	977895	(53308)	977896	(53331)	
960 992	**BG**	NR	DY	977897	(53203)	977898	(53193)	
960 993	**BG**	NR	DY	977899	(51427)	977900	(53321)	
960 994	**BG**	NR	DY	977901	(53200)	977902	(53231)	
960 995	**BG**	NR	DY	977903	(53208)	977904	(53291)	
Spare	**RR**	A	PY	51463	54062	54347	54358	54365
Spare	**BG**	A	PY	54350				
Spare	**RR**	A	ZH	51224	51428	53163		
Spare	**S**	A	ZH	51185				
Spare	**RR**	A	LO	51533				
Spare	**BG**	A	NL	54342				
Spare	**RR**	A	BP	59303				
Spare	**G**	A	BP	59539				

Class 117

117 301	**RR**	A	PY	51353		51395	
117 308	**RR**	A	PY	51371		51413	
117 310	**RR**	A	PY	51373	59486	51381	
117 313	**RR**	A	PY	51339		51382	
117 701	**N**	A	PY	51350		51392	
117 702	**N**	A	PY	51356		51398	
117 704	**N**	A	PY	51341		51383	
117 706	**N**	A	AL	51366		51408	
117 707	**N**	A	PY	51335		51377	
Spare	**RR**	A	AL	51369			
Spare	**N**	A	PY	51358			
Spare	**RR**	A	PY	51411			
Spare	**RR**	A	PY	59492	59500	59509	59521

Class 141

141 101	**WY**	CD	ZF	55501	55521
141 105	**WY**	CD	ZF	55505	55525
141 106	**WY**	CD	ZF	55506	55526
141 112	**WY**	CD	ZF	55512	55532
141 116	**WY**	CD	MM	55516	55536
141 118	**SO**	CD	ZF	55518	55538

Note: 141 101, 141 105 and 141 116 are pending sale to Iran.

Class 165

Spare	**NT**	A	ZC	58930

Class 951

977696	**N**	NR	ZG

4. ELECTRIC MULTIPLE UNITS

INTRODUCTION

EMU CLASSES

Principal details and dimensions are quoted for each class in metric and/or imperial units as considered appropriate bearing in mind common UK usage.

All dimensions and weights are quoted for vehicles in an 'as new' condition with all necessary supplies on board. Dimensions are quoted in the order length x overall width. All lengths quoted are over buffers or couplers as appropriate. Where two lengths are quoted, the first refers to outer vehicles in a set and the second to inner vehicles.

Bogie Types are quoted in the format motored/non-motored (e.g BP20/BT13 denotes BP20 motored bogies and BT non-motored bogies).

Unless noted to the contrary, all vehicles listed have bar couplings at non-driving ends.

NUMERICAL LISTINGS

25 kV AC 50 Hz overhead Electric Multiple Units (EMUs) and dual voltage EMUs are listed in numerical order of of set numbers. Individual 'loose' vehicles are listed after vehicles formed into fixed formations. Where numbers carried are different to those officially allocated, these are noted in class headings where appropriate.

750 V DC third rail EMUs are listed in numerical order of class number, then in numerical order of set number. **NOTE: This is a change from previous editions.** Some of these use the former Souther Region four-digit set numbers. These are derived from theoretical six digit set numbers which are the four-digit set number prefixed by the first two numbers of the class.

Where sets or vehicles have been renumbered in recent years, former numbering detail is shown alongside current detail. Each entry is laid out as in the following example:

Set No.	Detail	Livery	Owner	Operation	Allocation	Formation			
315 815	**GE**	H	*GE*	IL		64489	71295	71403	64490

Detail Differences. Only detail differences which currently affect the areas and types of train which vehicles may work are shown. All other detail differences are specifically excluded. Where such differences occur within a class or part class, these are shown alongside the individual set or vehicle number. Meaning of abbreviations is detailed in individual class headings.

Set Formations. Set formations shown are those normally maintained. Readers should note some set formations might be temporarily varied from time to time to suit maintenance and/or operational requirements. Vehicles shown as 'Spare' are not formed in any regular set formation.

Codes. Codes are used to denote the livery, owner, operation and depot of each unit. Details of these will be found in section 6 of this book. Where a unit or spare car is off-lease, the operation column will be left blank.

Names. Only names carried with official sanction are listed. As far as possible names are shown in UPPER/lower case characters as actually shown on the name carried on the vehicle(s). Unless otherwise shown, complete units are regarded as named rather than just the individual car(s) which carry the name.

GENERAL INFORMATION

CLASSIFICATION AND NUMBERING

25 kV AC 50 Hz overhead and 'Versatile' EMUs are classified in the series 300–399.

750 V DC third rail EMUs are classified in the series 400–599.
Service units are classified in the series 900–949.

EMU individual cars are numbered in the series 61000–78999, except for vehicles used on the Isle of Wight – which are numbered in a separate series.

Prior to privatisation, Service Stock individual cars were numbered in the series 975000–975999 and 977000–977999, although this series was not used exclusively for EMU vehicles. Since privatisation, use of these series has been sporadic, vehicles often now retaining their former numbers.

Where a vehicle carries an incorrect number which duplicates another correct number, the actual number carried is shown followed by ⁱⁱ to indicate a duplicate number. Correct number details are noted in the class heading.

Any vehicle constructed or converted to replace another vehicle following accident damage and carrying the same number as the original vehicle is denoted by the superscript ⁱⁱ in this publication.

OPERATING CODES

These codes are used by train operating company staff to describe the various different types of vehicles and normally appear on data panels on the inner (i.e. non driving) ends of vehicles.

A 'B' prefix indicates a battery vehicle.

A 'P' prefix indicates a trailer vehicle on which is mounted the pantograph, instead of the default case where the pantograph is mounted on a motor vehicle.

The first part of the code describes whether or not the car has a motor or a driving cab as follows:

DM Driving motor.

M   Motor
DT   Driving trailer
T   Trailer

The next letter is a 'B' for cars with a brake compartment.
This is followed by the saloon details:

F   First
S   Standard
C   Composite

The next letter denotes the style of accommodation as follows:

O   Open
K   Side compartment with lavatory
so   Semi-open (part compartments, part open). All other vehicles are assumed
     to consist solely of open saloons.

Finally vehicles with a buffet are suffixed RB or RMB for a miniture buffet.

Where two vehicles of the same type are formed within the same unit, the
above codes may be suffixed by (A) and (B) to differentiate between the
vehicles.

A composite is a vehicle containing both first and standard class
accommodation, whilst a brake vehicle is a vehicle containing separate specific
accommodation for the conductor.

Special Note: Where vehicles have been declassified, the correct opearting
code which describes the actual vehicle layout is quoted in this publication.

The following codes are used to denote special types of vehicle:

DMLF   Driving Motor Lounge First
DMLV   Driving Motor Luggage Van
TFH   Trailer First with Handbrake
TRBS   Trailer Restaurant Buffet Standard

DESIGN CODES AND DIAGRAM CODES

For each type of vehicle the Rolling Stock Library issues a seven character
'Design Code' consisting of two letters plus four numbers and a suffix letter.
(e.g. EF2110A). The first five characters of the Design Code are known as the
'Diagram Code' and these are quoted in this publication in sub-headings. The
meaning of the various characters of the Design Code is as follows:

First Character
E   Electric Multiple Unit
L   Eurostar Unit

Second Character
A   Driving Motor
B   Driving Motor Brake
C   Non-driving Motor
D   Non-driving Motor Brake
E   Driving Trailer

F   Battery Driving Trailer
G   Driving Trailer Brake
H   Trailer
I   Battery Driving Motor
J   Trailer Brake
N   Trailer Buffet
O   Battery Driving Trailer Brake
P   Trailer with Handbrake
X   Driving Motor Van
Z   All types of service vehicle

Third Character
1   First class accommodation
2   Standard class accommodation
3   Composite accommodation
4   Unclassified accommodation
5   No passenger accommodation

Fourth & Fifth Characters
These distinguish between different designs of vehicle, each design being allocated a unique two digit number.

ACCOMMODATION

The information given in class headings and sub-headings is in the form F/S nT (or TD) nW. For example 12/54 1T 1W denotes 12 first class and 54 standard class seats, 1 toilet and 1 wheelchair space. The seating layout of open saloons is shown as 2+1, 2+2 or 3+2 as the case may be. Where units have first class accommodation as well as standard and the layout is different for each class then these are shown separately prefixed by '1:' and '2:'. Compartments are always three seats a side in first class and four aside in standard class in EMUs.

▲ "Heritage" Class 101s are still at work in the Manchester area for First North Western. On 02/07/02 101 676 arrives at Manchester Piccadilly with the 13.52 from Rose Hill. **Chris Booth**

▼ Several 142s now sport the Valley Lines livery. On 10/09/02 142 085 pauses at Taffs Well with a Barry Island service. **Bob Sweet**

All Wessex Trains Class 143s are now in the deep blue "Visit Bristol" livery. On 25/04/02 143 620 approaches Lawrence Hill with the 10.30 Bristol Temple Meads–Avonmouth.

Hugh Ballantyne

▲ All Class 144s are operated by Arriva Trains Northern and are undergoing refurbishment at Neville Hill during which sets are being repainted into a new West Yorkshire PTE livery. The first unit so painted, 144 006 is seen arriving at Meadowhall with the 10.08 Bridlington–Sheffield on 20/06/02. **Peter Fox**

▼ ScotRail liveried 150 262 is seen at Haymarket with a service to Edinburgh Waverley from Bathgate on 21/05/01. **Jason Rogers**

North Western Trains / First North Western liveried 150 150 is seen with a Class 156 approaching Manchester Oxford Road with a Buxton–Blackpool North service on 08/09/02.

Jason **Rogers**

▲ Anglia's Class 153s are now being painted into their corporate livery. On 04/09/02 153 322 is seen near Whittlesea with a Peterborough–Ipswich service.
John Rudd

▼ 155 345 passes Colton Bridge with the 10.23 York–Manchester Victoria on 28/08/01.
John Teasdale

▲ Carmine and Cream liveried 156 495 arrives at Glasgow Central on 14/05/02.
Gavin Morrison

▼ All First North Western 156s still carry the old Regional Railways North West 'green stripe' livery, albeit with FNW branding. On 14/09/02 156 452 is seen leaving Workington with the 09.15 Whitehaven–Carlisle.   **Robert Pritchard**

ScotRail liveried 158 728 passes Greenhill Lower Junction with the 18.19 Stirling–Glasgow Queen Street on 05/08/02.

Paul Robertson

▲ Wessex Trains are painting their 158s into a silver livery with purple doors (Wales & Borders' 158s are in a similar livery with blue doors). On 02/08/02 158 869 arrives at Bath with the 14.24 Portsmouth–Cardiff. **Hugh Ballantyne**

▼ South West Trains liveried 159 016 + 159 010 leave Newton Abbot on 06/07/02 with the 10.00 Brighton–Paignton. **Paul Robertson**

▲ Newly repainted Thames Trains liveried 165 106 is seen near Salfords with the 07.12 Reading–Gatwick Airport on 23/06/02. **Alex Dasi-Sutton**

▼ 166 213 passes Shallesbrook on the Great Western main line with a Reading–Paddington service on 01/09/01. Note the variation in the Thames Trains Class 165 and 166 liveries. **Rodney Lissenden**

▲ Chiltern Railways liveried 168 108 passes Tyseley on 28/07/02 with a Marylebone–Birmingham Moor Street service. **Jason Rogers**

▼ Central Trains' 170s are one of the most travelled classes of DMU. Most services on the Liverpool–Norwich corridor are booked for the class and on 12/09/02 170 507 is seen pausing at Wymondham with the 08.52 Liverpool–Norwich. **Robert Pritchard**

Midland Mainline liveried 170 110 leaves Wellingborough on 24/09/02 with the 08.52 Nottingham–St. Pancras.

Dick Crane

▲ 175 102 is seen leaving Abergele & Pensarn with a Llandudno–Chester service on 31/08/02.　**Jason Rogers**

▼ "Adelante" unit 180 107 passes Manor Farm on the GWML with the 15.30 Paddington–Cardiff on 14/08/02.　**Anthony Kay**

"Hastings" DEMU Class 201 No. 201 001 pulls away from Crowhurst whilst working a Tonbridge–Hastings service during the line's 150th anniversary day - 01/09/01.

Ian Feather

▲ South Central operated 205 025, still in Connex livery, arrives at Rye on an Ashford–Hastings service on 02/08/02. These units are to be replaced on this line and on the Uckfield line by Class 170s. **John Chalcraft**

▼ 3-car 207 203 is seen here approaching May Cross with the 12.52 Ashford–Hastings service. **Ian Feather**

▲ All of Virgin Cross-Country's Class 220 and 221 "Voyager" fleet is now in operation, working services the length and breadth of the country. On 28/07/02 220 029 "Cornish Voyager" and 220 004 "New Dawn" (since re-named "Cumbrian Voyager") pass Whitacre Junction with the diverted 10.04 Birmingham–Manchester. **Hugh Ballantyne**

▼ 221 140 "Vasco da Gama" leaves Sheffield on 26/10/02 with the 09.58 Newcastle–Cardiff Central. **Robert Pritchard**

▲ Class 960 (ex-class 121) "Bubble-car" 977 968 is seen at Rugby on 01/05/02. This unit is operated by Eurailscout GB and is used as a track recording unit.
Andy Flowers

▼ BR maroon liveried sandite "Bubble-car" No. 960 010 (55024) is seen at Marylebone on 09/10/01. **Paul Chancellor**

4.1. 25 kV AC 50 Hz OVERHEAD & DUAL VOLTAGE UNITS.

Note: Except where otherwise stated, all units in this section operate on 25 kV AC 50 Hz overhead only.

CLASS 306   METRO-CAMMELL/BRCW

Museum unit which is not used in normal service. Originally built as 1500 V DC, but converted to AC in 1960/61.
Formation: DMSO–TBSO–DTSO.
Construction: Steel.   **Doors:** Power-operated sliding.
Traction Motors: Four Crompton-Parkinson 155 kW.
Gangways: None.   **Bogies:** LNER ED6/ET6.
Couplers: Screw.   **Maximum Speed:** 70 m.p.h.
Seating Layout: 2+2 facing.   **Dimensions:** 19.24/17.40 x 2.89 m.
Braking: Tread brakes.   **Multiple Working:** Within class.

DMSO. Dia. EA203. Lot No. 363 Metro-Cammell 1949. –/62. 51.7 t.
TBSO. Dia. EJ201. Lot No. 365 BRCW 1949. –/46. 25.4 t.
DTSO. Dia. EE211. Lot No. 364 Metro-Cammell 1949. –/60. 27.9 t.

306 017   **G**   H   *SS*   IL   65217   65417   65617

CLASS 312   BREL YORK

Formation: BDTSO–MBSO–TSO–DTCO (* declassified).
Construction: Steel.   **Doors:** Slam.
Traction Motors: Four English Electric 546 of 201.5 kW.
Gangways: Within unit.   **Bogies:** B4.
Couplers: Buckeye.   **Maximum Speed:** 90 m.p.h.
Seating Layout: 1: 2+2 facing, 2: 3+2 facing.
Dimensions: 20.18 x 2.82 m.   **Braking:** Disc brakes.
Multiple Working: Within class.

Class 312/0. Built to operate on 25 kV 50 Hz overhead only.

76949–74 BDTSO. Dia. EF213. Lot No. 30863 1977–1978. –/84 1T. 34.9 t.
76994–97 BDTSO. Dia. EF213. Lot No. 30891 1976. –/84 1T. 34.9 t.
62484–509 MBSO. Dia. ED212. Lot No. 30864 1977–1978. –/68. 56 t.
62657–60 MBSO. Dia. ED214. Lot No. 30892 1976. –/68. 56 t.
71168–93 TSO. Dia. EH209. Lot No. 30865 1977–1978. –/98. 30.5 t.
71277–80 TSO. Dia. EH209. Lot No. 30893 1976. –/98. 30.5 t.
78000–25 DTCO. Dia. EE305. Lot No. 30866 1977–1978. 25/47 1T. 33.0 t.
78045–48 DTCO. Dia. EE305. Lot No. 30894 1976. 25/47 1T. 33.0 t.

312 701	GE	A	*GE*	IL	76949	62484	71168	78000
312 702	GE	A	*GE*	IL	76950	62485	71169	78001
312 703	GE	A	*GE*	IL	76951	62486	71170	78002
312 704	GE	A	*GE*	IL	76952	62487	71171	78003
312 705	GE	A	*GE*	IL	76953	62488	71172	78004

312 706	**GE**	A	*GE*	IL	76954	62489	71173	78005
312 707	**GE**	A	*GE*	IL	76955	62490	71174	78006
312 708	**GE**	A	*GE*	IL	76956	62491	71175	78007
312 709	**GE**	A	*GE*	IL	76957	62492	71176	78008
312 710	**GE**	A	*GE*	IL	76958	62493	71177	78009
312 711	**GE**	A	*GE*	IL	76959	62494	71178	78010
312 712	**GE**	A	*GE*	IL	76960	62495	71179	78011
312 713	**GE**	A	*GE*	IL	76961	62496	71180	78012
312 714	**GE**	A	*GE*	IL	76962	62497	71181	78013
312 715	**GE**	A	*GE*	IL	76963	62498	71182	78014
312 716	**GE**	A	*GE*	IL	76964	62499	71183	78015
312 717	**GE**	A	*GE*	IL	76965	62500	71184	78016
312 718	**GE**	A	*GE*	IL	76966	62501	71185	78017
312 719	**GE**	A	*GE*	IL	76967	62502	71186	78018
312 720	**GE**	A	*GE*	IL	76968	62503	71187	78019
312 721	**GE**	A	*GE*	IL	76969	62504	71188	78020
312 722	**GE**	A	*GE*	IL	76970	62505	71189	78021
312 723	**GE**	A	*GE*	IL	76971	62506	71190	78022
312 724	**GE**	A	*GE*	IL	76972	62507	71191	78023
312 725	* **N**	A		PY	76973	62509	71192	78025
312 726	* **N**	A		PY	76974	62508	71193	78024
312 727	* **N**	A		PY	76994	62657	71277	78045
312 728	* **N**	A	*GE*	IL	76995	62658	71278	78046
312 729	* **N**	A		PY	76996	62659	71279	78047
312 730	* **N**	A		PY	76997	62660	71280	78048

Class 312/1. Built to operate on 25 kV or 6.25 kV 50 Hz overhead.

BDTSO. Dia. EF213. Lot No. 30867 1975–1976. –/84 2T. 34.9 t.
MBSO. Dia. ED213. Lot No. 30868 1975–1976. –/68. 56 t.
TSO. Dia. EH209. Lot No. 30869 1975–1976. –/98. 30.5 t.
DTCO. Dia. EE305. Lot No. 30870 1975–1976. 25/47 2T. 33.0 t.

312 781	* **N**	A	*C2*	EM	76975	62510	71194	78026
312 782	* **N**	A		PY	76976	62511	71195	78027
312 783	* **N**	A	*C2*	EM	76977	62512	71196	78028
312 784	* **N**	A	*C2*	EM	76978	62513	71197	78029
312 785	* **N**	A		PY	76979	62514	71198	78030
312 786	* **N**	A		PY	76980	62515	71199	78031
312 787	* **N**	A		PY	76981	62516	71200	78032
312 788	* **N**	A		PY	76982	62517	71201	78033
312 789	* **N**	A		PY	76983	62518	71202	78034
312 790	* **N**	A		PY	76984	62519	71203	78035
312 791	* **N**	A		PY	76985	62520	71204	78036
312 792	* **N**	A	*C2*	EM	76986	62521	71205	78037
312 793	* **N**	A		PY	76987	62522	71206	78038
312 794	* **N**	A		PY	76988	62523	71207	78039
312 795	* **N**	A		PY	76989	62524	71208	78040
312 796	* **N**	A		PY	76990	62525	71209	78041
312 797	* **N**	A	*C2*	EM	76991	62526	71210	78042
312 798	* **N**	A		PY	76992	62527	71211	78043
312 799	* **N**	A		PY	76993	62528	71212	78044

CLASS 313   BREL YORK

WAGN/Silverlink inner suburban units.
Formation: DMSO–PTSO–BDMSO.
Systems: 25 kV AC overhead/750 V DC third rail.
Construction: Steel underframe, aluminium alloy body and roof.
Traction Motors: Four GEC G310AZ of 82.125 kW.

Doors: Sliding.	**Control System:** Camshaft.
Gangways: Within unit + end doors.	**Bogies:** BX1.
Couplers: Tightlock	**Maximum Speed:** 75 m.p.h.
Seating Layout: 3+2 facing.	**Dimensions:** 20.18 x 2.82 m.
Braking: Disc and rheostatic.	
Multiple Working: Within class.	

DMSO. Dia. EA204. Lot No. 30879 1976–1977. –/74. 36.4 t.
PTSO. Dia. EH210. Lot No. 30880 1976–1977. –/84 (313/0). –/80 (313/1). 30.5 t.
BDMSO. Dia. EI201. Lot No. 30885 1976–1977. –/74. 37.6 t.

Advertising Liveries: 313 027, 313 043, 313 057, 313 064 WAGN Family
Travelcard ("Go to town with WAGN") – White.
313 050 WAGN Daytripper Ticket – White.
313 060, 313 063 WAGN "Intalink" livery – White with a yellow and green
bodyside stripe.

Class 313/0. Standard Design. All now refurbished with high back seats.

313 018	**WP**	H	*WN*	HE	62546	71230	62610
313 024	**WP**	H	*WN*	HE	62552	71236	62616
313 025	**N**	H	*WN*	HE	62553	71237	62617
313 026	**N**	H	*WN*	HE	62554	71238	62618
313 027	**AL**	H	*WN*	HE	62555	71239	62619
313 028	**WP**	H	*WN*	HE	62556	71240	62620
313 029	**U**	H	*WN*	HE	62557	71241	62621
313 030	**WP**	H	*WN*	HE	62558	71242	62622
313 031	**WP**	H	*WN*	HE	62559	71243	62623
313 032	**U**	H	*WN*	HE	62560	71244	62643
313 033	**U**	H	*WN*	HE	62561	71245	62625
313 035	**U**	H	*WN*	HE	62563	71247	62627
313 036	**U**	H	*WN*	HE	62564	71248	62628
313 037	**U**	H	*WN*	HE	62565	71249	62629
313 038	**U**	H	*WN*	HE	62566	71250	62630
313 039	**U**	H	*WN*	HE	62567	71251	62631
313 040	**U**	H	*WN*	HE	62568	71252	62632
313 041	**U**	H	*WN*	HE	62569	71253	62633
313 042	**N**	H	*WN*	HE	62570	71254	62634
313 043	**AL**	H	*WN*	HE	62571	71255	62635
313 044	**U**	H	*WN*	HE	62572	71256	62636
313 045	**U**	H	*WN*	HE	62573	71257	62637
313 046	**U**	H	*WN*	HE	62574	71258	62638
313 047	**U**	H	*WN*	HE	62575	71259	62639
313 048	**N**	H	*WN*	HE	62576	71260	62640
313 049	**U**	H	*WN*	HE	62577	71261	62641

313 050	**AL**	H	*WN*	HE	62578	71262	62649
313 051	**U**	H	*WN*	HE	62579	71263	62624
313 052	**N**	H	*WN*	HE	62580	71264	62644
313 053	**N**	H	*WN*	HE	62581	71265	62645
313 054	**N**	H	*WN*	HE	62582	71266	62646
313 055	**N**	H	*WN*	HE	62583	71267	62647
313 056	**WP**	H	*WN*	HE	62584	71268	62648
313 057	**AL**	H	*WN*	HE	62585	71269	62642
313 058	**N**	H	*WN*	HE	62586	71270	62650
313 059	**N**	H	*WN*	HE	62587	71271	62651
313 060	**AL**	H	*WN*	HE	62588	71272	62652
313 061	**N**	H	*WN*	HE	62589	71273	62653
313 062	**N**	H	*WN*	HE	62590	71274	62654
313 063	**AL**	H	*WN*	HE	62591	71275	62655
313 064	**AL**	H	*WN*	HE	62592	71276	62656

Class 313/1. Extra shoegear for Silverlink services.

313 101	**SL**	H	*SL*	BY	62529	71213	62593
313 102	**SL**	H	*SL*	BY	62530	71214	62594
313 103	**SL**	H	*SL*	BY	62531	71215	62595
313 104	**SL**	H	*SL*	BY	62532	71216	62596
313 105	**SL**	H	*SL*	BY	62533	71217	62597
313 106	**SL**	H	*SL*	BY	62534	71218	62598
313 107	**SL**	H	*SL*	BY	62535	71219	62599
313 108	**SL**	H	*SL*	BY	62536	71220	62600
313 109	**SL**	H	*SL*	BY	62537	71221	62601
313 110	**SL**	H	*SL*	BY	62538	71222	62602
313 111	**SL**	H	*SL*	BY	62539	71223	62603
313 112	**SL**	H	*SL*	BY	62540	71224	62604
313 113	**SL**	H	*SL*	BY	62541	71225	62605
313 114	**SL**	H	*SL*	BY	62542	71226	62606
313 115	**SL**	H	*SL*	BY	62543	71227	62607
313 116	**SL**	H	*SL*	BY	62544	71228	62608
313 117	**SL**	H	*SL*	BY	62545	71229	62609
313 119	**SL**	H	*SL*	BY	62547	71231	62611
313 120	**SL**	H	*SL*	BY	62548	71232	62612
313 121	**SL**	H	*SL*	BY	62549	71233	62613
313 122	**SL**	H	*SL*	BY	62550	71234	62614
313 123	**SL**	H	*SL*	BY	62551	71235	62615
313 134	**SL**	H	*SL*	BY	62562	71246	62626

Names (carried on PTSO):

| 313 109 | Arnold Leah | | 313 116 | Nikola Teslar |
| 313 120 | PARLIAMENT HILL. | | | |

CLASS 314   BREL YORK

ScotRail inner suburban units.
Formation: DMSO–PTSO–DMSO.
Construction: Steel underframe, aluminium alloy body and roof.
Traction Motors: Four GEC G310AZ (* Brush TM61-53) of 82.125 kW.
Doors: Sliding.   **Control System:** Thyristor.
Gangways: Within unit + end doors.   **Bogies:** BX1.
Couplers: Tightlock   **Maximum Speed:** 75 m.p.h.
Seating Layout: 3+2 facing.   **Dimensions:** 20.18 x 2.82 m.
Braking: Disc and rheostatic.
Multiple Working: Within class and with Class 315.

64583–64614. DMSO. Dia. EA206. Lot No. 30912 1979. –/68. 34.5 t.
64588". DMSO. Dia. EA207. Lot No. 30908 1978–1980. Rebuilt Railcare Glasgow
1996 from Class 507 No. 64426. The original 64588 has been scrapped.
This vehicle has an experimental seating layout. –/74. 35.63 t.
PTSO. Dia. EH211. Lot No. 30913 1979. –/76. 33.0 t.

314 201	*	**S**	A	*SR*	GW	64583	71450	64584
314 202	*	**S**	A	*SR*	GW	64585	71451	64586
314 203	*	**SC**	A	*SR*	GW	64587	71452	64588"
314 204	*	**SC**	A	*SR*	GW	64589	71453	64590
314 205	*	**SC**	A	*SR*	GW	64591	71454	64592
314 206	*	**SC**	A	*SR*	GW	64593	71455	64594
314 207		**S**	A	*SR*	GW	64595	71456	64596
314 208		**SC**	A	*SR*	GW	64597	71457	64598
314 209		**S**	A	*SR*	GW	64599	71458	64600
314 210		**SC**	A	*SR*	GW	64601	71459	64602
314 211		**SC**	A	*SR*	GW	64603	71460	64604
314 212		**SC**	A	*SR*	GW	64605	71461	64606
314 213		**SC**	A	*SR*	GW	64607	71462	64608
314 214		**S**	A	*SR*	GW	64609	71463	64610
314 215		**SC**	A	*SR*	GW	64611	71464	64612
314 216		**SC**	A	*SR*	GW	64613	71465	64614

Names (carried on PTSO):

314 203   European Union

CLASS 315   BREL YORK

FGE/WAGN inner suburban units.
Formation: DMSO–TSO–PTSO–DMSO.
Construction: Steel underframe, aluminium alloy body and roof.
Traction Motors: Four Brush TM61-53 (* GEC G310AZ) of 82.125 kW.
Doors: Sliding.   **Control System:** Thyristor.
Gangways: Within unit + end doors.   **Bogies:** BX1.
Couplers: Tightlock   **Maximum Speed:** 75 m.p.h.
Seating Layout: 3+2 facing.   **Dimensions:** 20.18 x 2.82 m.
Braking: Disc and rheostatic.

Multiple Working: Within class and with Class 314.

64461–64582. DMSO. Dia. EA207. Lot No. 30902 1980–1981. –/74. 35 t.
71281–71341. TSO. Dia. EH216. Lot No. 30904 1980–1981. –/86. 25.5 t.
71389–71449. PTSO. Dia. EH217. Lot No. 30903 1980–1981. –/84. 32 t.

Advertising Liveries: 315 844, 315 845 WAGN Family Travelcard ("Go to town with WAGN") – White.
315 857 WAGN "Intalink" livery – White with a yellow and green bodyside stripe.

315 801	**GE**	H	*GE*	IL	64461	71281	71389	64462
315 802	**GE**	H	*GE*	IL	64463	71282	71390	64464
315 803	**GE**	H	*GE*	IL	64465	71283	71391	64466
315 804	**GE**	H	*GE*	IL	64467	71284	71392	64468
315 805	**GE**	H	*GE*	IL	64469	71285	71393	64470
315 806	**GE**	H	*GE*	IL	64471	71286	71394	64472
315 807	**GE**	H	*GE*	IL	64473	71287	71395	64474
315 808	**GE**	H	*GE*	IL	64475	71288	71396	64476
315 809	**GE**	H	*GE*	IL	64477	71289	71397	64478
315 810	**GE**	H	*GE*	IL	64479	71290	71398	64480
315 811	**GE**	H	*GE*	IL	64481	71291	71399	64482
315 812	**GE**	H	*GE*	IL	64483	71292	71400	64484
315 813	**GE**	H	*GE*	IL	64485	71293	71401	64486
315 814	**GE**	H	*GE*	IL	64487	71294	71402	64488
315 815	**GE**	H	*GE*	IL	64489	71295	71403	64490
315 816	**GE**	H	*GE*	IL	64491	71296	71404	64492
315 817	**GE**	H	*GE*	IL	64493	71297	71405	64494
315 818	**GE**	H	*GE*	IL	64495	71298	71406	64496
315 819	**GE**	H	*GE*	IL	64497	71299	71407	64498
315 820	**GE**	H	*GE*	IL	64499	71300	71408	64500
315 821	**GE**	H	*GE*	IL	64501	71301	71409	64502
315 822	**GE**	H	*GE*	IL	64503	71302	71410	64504
315 823	**GE**	H	*GE*	IL	64505	71303	71411	64506
315 824	**GE**	H	*GE*	IL	64507	71304	71412	64508
315 825	**GE**	H	*GE*	IL	64509	71305	71413	64510
315 826	**GE**	H	*GE*	IL	64511	71306	71414	64512
315 827	**GE**	H	*GE*	IL	64513	71307	71415	64514
315 828	**GE**	H	*GE*	IL	64515	71308	71416	64516
315 829	**GE**	H	*GE*	IL	64517	71309	71417	64518
315 830	**GE**	H	*GE*	IL	64519	71310	71418	64520
315 831	**GE**	H	*GE*	IL	64521	71311	71419	64522
315 832	**GE**	H	*GE*	IL	64523	71312	71420	64524
315 833	**GE**	H	*GE*	IL	64525	71313	71421	64526
315 834	**GE**	H	*GE*	IL	64527	71314	71422	64528
315 835	**GE**	H	*GE*	IL	64529	71315	71423	64530
315 836	**GE**	H	*GE*	IL	64531	71316	71424	64532
315 837	**GE**	H	*GE*	IL	64533	71317	71425	64534
315 838	**GE**	H	*GE*	IL	64535	71318	71426	64536
315 839	**GE**	H	*GE*	IL	64537	71319	71427	64538
315 840	**GE**	H	*GE*	IL	64539	71320	71428	64540
315 841	**GE**	H	*GE*	IL	64541	71321	71429	64542
315 842	* **GE**	H	*GE*	IL	64543	71322	71430	64544

315 843	*	**GE**	H	*GE*	IL	64545	71323	71431	64546
315 844	*	**AL**	H	*WN*	HE	64547	71324	71432	64548
315 845	*	**AL**	H	*WN*	HE	64549	71325	71433	64550
315 846	*	**U**	H	*WN*	HE	64551	71326	71434	64552
315 847	*	**U**	H	*WN*	HE	64553	71327	71435	64554
315 848	*	**U**	H	*WN*	HE	64555	71328	71436	64556
315 849	*	**U**	H	*WN*	HE	64557	71329	71437	64558
315 850	*	**U**	H	*WN*	HE	64559	71330	71438	64560
315 851	*	**U**	H	*WN*	HE	64561	71331	71439	64562
315 852	*	**U**	H	*WN*	HE	64563	71332	71440	64564
315 853	*	**U**	H	*WN*	HE	64565	71333	71441	64566
315 854	*	**U**	H	*WN*	HE	64567	71334	71442	64568
315 855	*	**U**	H	*WN*	HE	64569	71335	71443	64570
315 856	*	**U**	H	*WN*	HE	64571	71336	71444	64572
315 857	*	**AL**	H	*WN*	HE	64573	71337	71445	64574
315 858	*	**U**	H	*WN*	HE	64579	71338	71446	64580
315 859	*	**WP**	H	*WN*	HE	64577	71339	71447	64578
315 860	*	**WP**	H	*WN*	HE	64575	71340	71448	64576
315 861	*	**WP**	H	*WN*	HE	64581	71341	71449	64582

CLASS 317   BREL

WAGN outer suburban units.
Formations: Various.
Construction: Steel.
Traction Motors: Four GEC G315BZ of 247.5 kW.
Doors: Sliding.   **Control System:** Thyristor.
Gangways: Throughout   **Bogies:** BP20 (MSO), BT13 (others).
Couplers: Tightlock.   **Maximum Speed:** 100 m.p.h.
Seating Layout: Various.   **Dimensions:** 20.13/20.18 x 2.82 m.
Braking: Disc.
Multiple Working: Within class and with Classes 318–323.

Class 317/1. Pressure ventilated.

Formation: DTSO(A)–MSO–TCO–DTSO(B).
Seating Layout: 1: 2+2 facing, 2: 3+2 facing.

DTSO(A) Dia. EE216. Lot No. 30955 York 1981–1982. –/74. 29.44 t.
MSO. Dia. EC202. Lot No. 30958 York 1981–1982. –/79. 49.76 t.
TCO. Dia. EH307. Lot No. 30957 Derby 1981–1982. 22/46 2T. 28.80 t. Retention
toilets (decommisioned).
DTSO(B) Dia. EE235 (* EE232). Lot No. 30956 York 1981–1982. –/70. (* –/71). 29.28 t.

Non-standard livery: 317 301–317 306 are in the former LTS Rail livery (white &
blue with grey & green bands).

Note: Four (unspecified) Class 317/1s are hired to Thameslink every day for
Bedford–Moorgate services.

317 301	**0**	A	*WN*	HE	77024	62661	71577	77048
317 302	**0**	A	*WN*	HE	77001	62662	71578	77049
317 303	**0**	A	*WN*	HE	77002	62663	71579	77050

317 304	0	A	WN	HE	77003	62664	71580	77051
317 305	0	A	WN	HE	77004	62665	71581	77052
317 306	0	A	WN	HE	77005	62666	71582	77053
317 307	WP	A	WN	HE	77006	62667	71583	77054
317 311	WP	A	WN	HE	77010	62697	71587	77058
317 312	WP	A	WN	HE	77011	62672	71588	77059
317 313	WP	A	WN	HE	77012	62673	71589	77060
317 315	WP	A	WN	HE	77014	62675	71591	77062
317 316	N	A	WN	HE	77015	62676	71592	77063
317 317	WP	A	WN	HE	77016	62677	71593	77064
317 318	WP	A	WN	HE	77017	62678	71594	77065
317 320	WP	A	WN	HE	77019	62680	71596	77067
317 321	WP	A	WN	HE	77020	62681	71597	77068
317 324	N	A	WN	HE	77023	62684	71600	77071
317 325	N	A	WN	HE	77000	62685	71601	77072
317 326	N	A	WN	HE	77025	62686	71602	77073
317 327	N	A	WN	HE	77026	62687	71603	77074
317 328	N	A	WN	HE	77027	62688	71604	77075
317 330	WP	A	WN	HE	77043	62704	71606	77077
317 331	WP	A	WN	HE	77030	62691	71607	77078
317 333	WP	A	WN	HE	77032	62693	71609	77080
317 334	WP	A	WN	HE	77033	62694	71610	77081
317 335	WP	A	WN	HE	77034	62695	71611	77082
317 336	WP	A	WN	HE	77035	62696	71612	77083
317 337	* N	A	WN	HE	77036	62671	71613	77084
317 338	* N	A	WN	HE	77037	62698	71614	77085
317 339	* N	A	WN	HE	77038	62699	71615	77086
317 340	* WP	A	WN	HE	77039	62700	71616	77087
317 341	* N	A	WN	HE	77040	62701	71617	77088
317 342	* N	A	WN	HE	77041	62702	71618	77089
317 343	* WP	A	WN	HE	77042	62703	71619	77090
317 344	* N	A	WN	HE	77029	62690	71620	77091
317 345	* N	A	WN	HE	77044	62705	71621	77092
317 346	* N	A	WN	HE	77045	62706	71622	77093
317 347	* N	A	WN	HE	77046	62707	71623	77094
317 348	* N	A	WN	HE	77047	62708	71624	77095

Class 317/6. Convection heating. Units converted from Class 317/2 by Railcare Wolverton 1998–99 with new seating layouts.

Formation: DTSO–MSO–TSO–DTCO.
Seating Layout: 2+2 facing.

77200–19. DTSO. Dia. EE247. Lot No. 30994 York 1985–1986. –/64. 29.31 t.
77280–83. DTSO. Dia. EE247. Lot No. 31007 York 1987. –/64. 29.31 t.
62846–65. MSO. Dia. EC222. Lot No. 30996 York 1985–1986. –/70. 50.08 t.
62886–89. MSO. Dia. EC222. Lot No. 31009 York 1987. –/70. 50.08 t.
71734–53. TSO. Dia. EH247. Lot No. 30997 York 1985–1986. –/62 2T. 28.28 t.
71762–65. TSO. Dia. EH247. Lot No. 31010 York 1987. –/62 2T. 28.28 t.
77220–39. DTCO. Dia. EE375. Lot No. 30995 York 1985–1986. 24/48. 29.28 t.
77284–87. DTCO. Dia. EE375. Lot No. 31008 York 1987. 24/48. 29.28 t.

317 649	(317 349)	**WN**	A	*WN*	HE	77200	62846	71734	77220
317 650	(317 350)	**WN**	A	*WN*	HE	77201	62847	71735	77221
317 651	(317 351)	**WN**	A	*WN*	HE	77202	62848	71736	77222
317 652	(317 352)	**WN**	A	*WN*	HE	77203	62849	71739	77223
317 653	(317 353)	**WN**	A	*WN*	HE	77204	62850	71738	77224
317 654	(317 354)	**WN**	A	*WN*	HE	77205	62851	71737	77225
317 655	(317 355)	**WN**	A	*WN*	HE	77206	62852	71740	77226
317 656	(317 356)	**WN**	A	*WN*	HE	77207	62853	71742	77227
317 657	(317 357)	**WN**	A	*WN*	HE	77208	62854	71741	77228
317 658	(317 358)	**WN**	A	*WN*	HE	77209	62855	71743	77229
317 659	(317 359)	**WN**	A	*WN*	HE	77210	62856	71744	77230
317 660	(317 360)	**WN**	A	*WN*	HE	77211	62857	71745	77231
317 661	(317 361)	**WN**	A	*WN*	HE	77212	62858	71746	77232
317 662	(317 362)	**WN**	A	*WN*	HE	77213	62859	71747	77233
317 663	(317 363)	**WN**	A	*WN*	HE	77214	62860	71748	77234
317 664	(317 364)	**WN**	A	*WN*	HE	77215	62861	71749	77235
317 665	(317 365)	**WN**	A	*WN*	HE	77216	62862	71750	77236
317 666	(317 366)	**WN**	A	*WN*	HE	77217	62863	71752	77237
317 667	(317 367)	**WN**	A	*WN*	HE	77218	62864	71751	77238
317 668	(317 368)	**WN**	A	*WN*	HE	77219	62865	71753	77239
317 669	(317 369)	**WN**	A	*WN*	HE	77280	62886	71762	77284
317 670	(317 370)	**WN**	A	*WN*	HE	77281	62887	71763	77285
317 671	(317 371)	**WN**	A	*WN*	HE	77282	62888	71764	77286
317 672	(317 372)	**WN**	A	*WN*	HE	77283	62889	71765	77287

Class 317/7. Units converted from Class 317/1 by Railcare Wolverton 2000 for Stansted Express services from London Liverpool Street to Stansted Airport. Fitted with air conditioning and extra luggage stacks.

Formation: DTSO–MSO–TSO–DTCO.
Seating Layout: 1: 2+1 facing, 2: 2+2 facing.

DTSO Dia. EE285. Lot No. 30955 York 1981–1982. –/52 + catering point. 29.44 t.
MSO. Dia. EC232. Lot No. 30958 York 1981–1982. –/62. 49.76 t.
TSO. Dia. EH256. Lot No. 30957 Derby 1981–1982. –/42 1W 1T 1TD. 28.80 t. Retention toilets (decommisioned).
DTCO Dia. EE301. Lot No. 30956 York 1981–1982. 22/16 + catering point. 29.28 t.

317 708	(317 308)	**SX**	A	*WN*	HE	77007	62668	71584	77055
317 709	(317 309)	**SX**	A	*WN*	HE	77008	62669	71585	77056
317 710	(317 310)	**SX**	A	*WN*	HE	77009	62670	71586	77057
317 714	(317 314)	**SX**	A	*WN*	HE	77013	62674	71590	77061
317 719	(317 319)	**SX**	A	*WN*	HE	77018	62679	71595	77066
317 722	(317 392)	**SX**	A	*WN*	HE	77021	62682	71598	77069
317 723	(317 393)	**SX**	A	*WN*	HE	77022	62683	71599	77070
317 729	(317 329)	**SX**	A	*WN*	HE	77028	62689	71605	77076
317 732	(317 332)	**SX**	A	*WN*	HE	77031	62692	71608	77079

CLASS 318   BREL YORK

ScotRail outer suburban units.
Formation: DTSO–MSO–DTSO.
Construction: Steel.
Traction Motors: Four Brush TM 2141 of 268 kW.
Doors: Sliding.   **Control System:** Thyristor.
Gangways: Throughout.   **Bogies:** BP20 (MSO), BT13 (others).
Couplers: Tightlock   **Maximum Speed:** 90 m.p.h.
Seating Layout: 3+2 facing.   **Dimensions:** 20.18 x 2.82 m.
Braking: Disc.
Multiple Working: Within class and with Classes 317, 319, 320, 321, 322 and 323.

77240–59. DTSO. Dia. EE227. Lot No. 30999 1985–1986. –/66 1T. 30.01 t.
77288. DTSO. Dia. EE227. Lot No. 31020 1986–1987. –/66 1T. 30.01 t.
62866–85. MSO. Dia. EC207. Lot No. 30998 1985–1986. –/79. 50.90 t.
62890. MSO. Dia. EC207. Lot No. 31019 1987. –/79. 50.90 t.
77260–79. DTSO. Dia. EE228. Lot No. 31000 1985–1986. –/71. 26.60 t.
77289. DTSO. Dia. EE228. Lot No. 31021 1987. –/71. 26.60 t.

318 250	**SC**	H	*SR*	GW	77260	62866	77240
318 251	**SC**	H	*SR*	GW	77261	62867	77241
318 252	**SC**	H	*SR*	GW	77262	62868	77242
318 253	**SC**	H	*SR*	GW	77263	62869	77243
318 254	**SC**	H	*SR*	GW	77264	62870	77244
318 255	**SC**	H	*SR*	GW	77265	62871	77245
318 256	**SC**	H	*SR*	GW	77266	62872	77246
318 257	**SC**	H	*SR*	GW	77267	62873	77247
318 258	**SC**	H	*SR*	GW	77268	62874	77248
318 259	**SC**	H	*SR*	GW	77269	62875	77249
318 260	**SC**	H	*SR*	GW	77270	62876	77250
318 261	**SC**	H	*SR*	GW	77271	62877	77251
318 262	**SC**	H	*SR*	GW	77272	62878	77252
318 263	**SC**	H	*SR*	GW	77273	62879	77253
318 264	**SC**	H	*SR*	GW	77274	62880	77254
318 265	**SC**	H	*SR*	GW	77275	62881	77255
318 266	**SC**	H	*SR*	GW	77276	62882	77256
318 267	**SC**	H	*SR*	GW	77277	62883	77257
318 268	**SC**	H	*SR*	GW	77278	62884	77258
318 269	**SC**	H	*SR*	GW	77279	62885	77259
318 270	**SC**	H	*SR*	GW	77289	62890	77288

Names (carried on MSO):

318 259   Citizens' Network | 318 266   STRATHCLYDER.

CLASS 319   BREL YORK

System: 25 kV AC overhead/750 V DC third rail.
Formation: Various.
Construction: Steel.
Traction Motors: Four GEC G315BZ of 268 kW.
Doors: Sliding.   **Control System:** GTO chopper.
Gangways: Within unit + end doors. **Bogies:** P7-4 (MSO), T3-7 (others).
Couplers: Tightlock   **Maximum Speed:** 100 m.p.h.
Seating Layout: Various.   **Dimensions:** 20.18 x 2.82 m.
Braking: Disc.
Multiple Working: Within class and with Classes 317, 318, 320, 321, 322 and 323.

Class 319/0. DTSO(A)–MSO–TSO–DTSO(B). South Central units.
Seating Layout: 3+2 facing.

DTSO(A). Dia. EE233. Lot No. 31022 (odd nos.) 1987–1988. –/82. 30.12 t.
MSO. Dia. EC209. Lot No. 31023 1987–1988. –/82. 51 t.
TSO. Dia. EH234. Lot No. 31024 1987–1988. –/77 2T. 51 t.
DTSO(B). Dia. EE234. Lot No. 31025 (even nos.) 1987–1988. –/78. 30 t.

Note: Two (unspecified) Class 319/0s are hired to Thameslink every day.

319 001	**CX**	P	*SC*	SU	77291	62891	71772	77290
319 002	**CX**	P	*SC*	SU	77293	62892	71773	77292
319 003	**CX**	P	*SC*	SU	77295	62893	71774	77294
319 004	**CX**	P	*SC*	SU	77297	62894	71775	77296
319 005	**CX**	P	*SC*	SU	77299	62895	71776	77298
319 006	**CX**	P	*SC*	SU	77301	62896	71777	77300
319 007	**CX**	P	*SC*	SU	77303	62897	71778	77302
319 008	**CX**	P	*SC*	SU	77305	62898	71779	77304
319 009	**CX**	P	*SC*	SU	77307	62899	71780	77306
319 010	**CX**	P	*SC*	SU	77309	62900	71781	77308
319 011	**CX**	P	*SC*	SU	77311	62901	71782	77310
319 012	**CX**	P	*SC*	SU	77313	62902	71783	77312
319 013	**CX**	P	*SC*	SU	77315	62903	71784	77314

Names (carried on TSO):

319 008 Cheriton	319 011 John Ruskin College
319 009 Coquelles	319 013 The Surrey Hills

Class 319/2. DTSO–MSO–TSO–DTCO. Units converted from Class 319/0 for South Central express services from London to Brighton. 25 kV supply isolated.
Seating Layout: 1: 2+1 facing, 2: 2+2 facing.

DTSO. Dia. EE244. Lot No. 31022 (odd nos.) 1987–1988. –/64. 30.2 t.
MSO. Dia. EN262. Lot No. 31023 1987–1988. –/60 2T. (including 12 seats in a "snug" under the pantograph area). External sliding doors sealed adjacent to this area. 51.0 t.
TSO. Dia. EH212. Lot No. 31024 1987–1988. –/52 1T 1TD. 34 t.
DTCO. Dia. EE374. Lot No. 31025 (even nos.) 1987–1988. 18/36. 30 t.

Advertising Livery: 319 214, 319 215, 319 218, 319 220 Connex Days out/"Family Zone" (Yellow, green and red with various images).

319 214	(319 014)	**AL**	P	*SC*	SU	77317	62904	71785	77316
319 215	(319 015)	**AL**	P	*SC*	SU	77319	62905	71786	77318
319 216	(319 016)	**CX**	P	*SC*	SU	77321	62906	71787	77320
319 217	(319 017)	**CX**	P	*SC*	SU	77323	62907	71788	77322
319 218	(319 018)	**AL**	P	*SC*	SU	77325	62908	71789	77324
319 219	(319 019)	**CX**	P	*SC*	SU	77327	62909	71790	77326
319 220	(319 020)	**AL**	P	*SC*	SU	77329	62910	71791	77328

Names (carried on TSO):

319 215	London	319 218	Croydon.
319 217	Brighton		

Class 319/3. DTSO (A)–MSO–TSO–DTSO(B). Thameslink units. Converted from Class 319/1 by replacing first class seats with standard class seats. Used mainly on the Luton–Sutton route.
Seating layout: 3+2 facing

DTSO(A). Dia. EE240. Lot No. 31063 1990. –/70. 29.0 t.
MSO. Dia. EC214. Lot No. 31064 1990. –/78. 50.6 t.
TSO. Dia. EH238. Lot No. 31065 1990. –/74 2T. 31.0 t.
DTSO(B). Dia. EE240. Lot No. 31066 1990. –/78. 29.7 t.

319 361	(319 161)	**TR**	P	*TR*	SU	77459	63043	71929	77458
319 362	(319 162)	**TR**	P	*TR*	SU	77461	63044	71930	77460
319 363	(319 163)	**TR**	P	*TR*	SU	77463	63045	71931	77462
319 364	(319 164)	**TR**	P	*TR*	SU	77465	63046	71932	77464
319 365	(319 165)	**TR**	P	*TR*	SU	77467	63047	71933	77466
319 366	(319 166)	**TR**	P	*TR*	SU	77469	63048	71934	77468
319 367	(319 167)	**TR**	P	*TR*	SU	77471	63049	71935	77470
319 368	(319 168)	**TR**	P	*TR*	SU	77473	63050	71936	77472
319 369	(319 169)	**TR**	P	*TR*	SU	77475	63051	71937	77474
319 370	(319 170)	**TR**	P	*TR*	SU	77477	63052	71938	77476
319 371	(319 171)	**TR**	P	*TR*	SU	77479	63053	71939	77478
319 372	(319 172)	**TR**	P	*TR*	SU	77481	63054	71940	77480
319 373	(319 173)	**TR**	P	*TR*	SU	77483	63055	71941	77482
319 374	(319 174)	**TR**	P	*TR*	SU	77485	63056	71942	77484
319 375	(319 175)	**TR**	P	*TR*	SU	77487	63057	71943	77486
319 376	(319 176)	**TR**	P	*TR*	SU	77489	63058	71944	77488
319 377	(319 177)	**TR**	P	*TR*	SU	77491	63059	71945	77490
319 378	(319 178)	**TR**	P	*TR*	SU	77493	63060	71946	77492
319 379	(319 179)	**TR**	P	*TR*	SU	77495	63061	71947	77494
319 380	(319 180)	**TR**	P	*TR*	SU	77497	63062	71948	77496
319 381	(319 181)	**TR**	P	*TR*	SU	77973	63093	71979	77974
319 382	(319 182)	**TR**	P	*TR*	SU	77975	63094	71980	77976
319 383	(319 183)	**TR**	P	*TR*	SU	77977	63095	71981	77978
319 384	(319 184)	**TR**	P	*TR*	SU	77979	63096	71982	77980
319 385	(319 185)	**TR**	P	*TR*	SU	77981	63097	71983	77982
319 386	(319 186)	**TR**	P	*TR*	SU	77983	63098	71984	77984

Class 319/4. DTCO–MSO–TSO–DTSO. Thameslink units. Converted from Class 319/0. Refurbished with carpets. DTSO(A) converted to composite. Used mainly on the Bedford–Gatwick–Brighton route.

Seating Layout: 1: 2+2 facing, 2: 3+2 facing.

77331–81. DTCO. Dia. EE314. Lot No. 31022 (odd nos.) 1987–1988. 12/54. 30.1 t.
77431–57. DTCO. Dia. EE314. Lot No. 31038 (odd nos.) 1988. 12/54. 30.1 t.
62911–36. MSO. Dia. EC209. Lot No. 31023 1987–1988. –/77. 51.0 t.
62961–74. MSO. Dia. EC209. Lot No. 31039 1988. –/77. 51.0 t.
71792–817. TSO. Dia. EH234. Lot No. 31024 1987–1988. –/72 2T. 51.0 t.
71866–79. TSO. Dia. EH234. Lot No. 31040 1988. –/72 2T. 51.0 t.
77330–80. DTSO. Dia. EE234. Lot No. 31025 (even nos.) 1987–1988. –/74. 30.0 t.
77430–56. DTSO. Dia. EE234. Lot No. 31041 (even nos.) 1988. –/74. 30.0 t.

319 421	(319 021)	**TR**	P	*TR*	SU	77331	62911	71792	77330
319 422	(319 022)	**TR**	P	*TR*	SU	77333	62912	71793	77332
319 423	(319 023)	**TR**	P	*TR*	SU	77335	62913	71794	77334
319 424	(319 024)	**TR**	P	*TR*	SU	77337	62914	71795	77336
319 425	(319 025)	**TR**	P	*TR*	SU	77339	62915	71796	77338
319 426	(319 026)	**TR**	P	*TR*	SU	77341	62916	71797	77340
319 427	(319 027)	**TR**	P	*TR*	SU	77343	62917	71798	77342
319 428	(319 028)	**TR**	P	*TR*	SU	77345	62918	71799	77344
319 429	(319 029)	**TR**	P	*TR*	SU	77347	62919	71800	77346
319 430	(319 030)	**TR**	P	*TR*	SU	77349	62920	71801	77348
319 431	(319 031)	**TR**	P	*TR*	SU	77351	62921	71802	77350
319 432	(319 032)	**TR**	P	*TR*	SU	77353	62922	71803	77352
319 433	(319 033)	**TR**	P	*TR*	SU	77355	62923	71804	77354
319 434	(319 034)	**TR**	P	*TR*	SU	77357	62924	71805	77356
319 435	(319 035)	**TR**	P	*TR*	SU	77359	62925	71806	77358
319 436	(319 036)	**TR**	P	*TR*	SU	77361	62926	71807	77360
319 437	(319 037)	**TR**	P	*TR*	SU	77363	62927	71808	77362
319 438	(319 038)	**TR**	P	*TR*	SU	77365	62928	71809	77364
319 439	(319 039)	**TR**	P	*TR*	SU	77367	62929	71810	77366
319 440	(319 040)	**TR**	P	*TR*	SU	77369	62930	71811	77368
319 441	(319 041)	**TR**	P	*TR*	SU	77371	62931	71812	77370
319 442	(319 042)	**TR**	P	*TR*	SU	77373	62932	71813	77372
319 443	(319 043)	**TR**	P	*TR*	SU	77375	62933	71814	77374
319 444	(319 044)	**TR**	P	*TR*	SU	77377	62934	71815	77376
319 445	(319 045)	**TR**	P	*TR*	SU	77379	62935	71816	77378
319 446	(319 046)	**TR**	P	*TR*	SU	77381	62936	71817	77380
319 447	(319 047)	**TR**	P	*TR*	SU	77431	62961	71866	77430
319 448	(319 048)	**TR**	P	*TR*	SU	77433	62962	71867	77432
319 449	(319 049)	**TR**	P	*TR*	SU	77435	62963	71868	77434
319 450	(319 050)	**TR**	P	*TR*	SU	77437	62964	71869	77436
319 451	(319 051)	**TR**	P	*TR*	SU	77439	62965	71870	77438
319 452	(319 052)	**TR**	P	*TR*	SU	77441	62966	71871	77440
319 453	(319 053)	**TR**	P	*TR*	SU	77443	62967	71872	77442
319 454	(319 054)	**TR**	P	*TR*	SU	77445	62968	71873	77444
319 455	(319 055)	**TR**	P	*TR*	SU	77447	62969	71874	77446
319 456	(319 056)	**TR**	P	*TR*	SU	77449	62970	71875	77448
319 457	(319 057)	**TR**	P	*TR*	SU	77451	62971	71876	77450
319 458	(319 058)	**TR**	P	*TR*	SU	77453	62972	71877	77452

| 319 459 | (319 059) | **TR** | P | *TR* | SU | 77455 | 62973 | 71878 | 77454 |
| 319 460 | (319 060) | **TR** | P | *TR* | SU | 77457 | 62974 | 71879 | 77456 |

CLASS 320   BREL YORK

Formation: DTSO–MSO–DTSO.
Construction: Steel
Traction Motors: Four Brush TM2141B of 268 kW.
Doors: Sliding.   **Control System:** Thyristor.
Gangways: Within unit.   **Bogies:** P7-4 (MSO), T3-7 (others).
Couplers: Tightlock   **Maximum Speed:** 75 m.p.h.
Seating Layout: 3+2 facing.   **Dimensions:** 20.18 x 2.82 m.
Braking: Disc.
Multiple Working: Within class and with Classes 317, 318, 319, 321, 322 and 323.

DTSO (A). Dia. EE238. Lot No. 31060 1990. –/77. 30.7 t.
MSO. Dia. EC212. Lot No. 31062 1990. –/77. 52.1 t.
DTSO (B). Dia. EE239. Lot No. 31061 1990. –/76 31.7 t.

320 301	**S**	H	*SR*	GW	77899	63021	77921
320 302	**SC**	H	*SR*	GW	77900	63022	77922
320 303	**SC**	H	*SR*	GW	77901	63023	77923
320 304	**SC**	H	*SR*	GW	77902	63024	77924
320 305	**S**	H	*SR*	GW	77903	63025	77925
320 306	**SC**	H	*SR*	GW	77904	63026	77926
320 307	**SC**	H	*SR*	GW	77905	63027	77927
320 308	**SC**	H	*SR*	GW	77906	63028	77928
320 309	**SC**	H	*SR*	GW	77907	63029	77929
320 310	**SC**	H	*SR*	GW	77908	63030	77930
320 311	**SC**	H	*SR*	GW	77909	63031	77931
320 312	**SC**	H	*SR*	GW	77910	63032	77932
320 313	**SC**	H	*SR*	GW	77911	63033	77933
320 314	**SC**	H	*SR*	GW	77912	63034	77934
320 315	**SC**	H	*SR*	GW	77913	63035	77935
320 316	**SC**	H	*SR*	GW	77914	63036	77936
320 317	**SC**	H	*SR*	GW	77915	63037	77937
320 318	**SC**	H	*SR*	GW	77916	63038	77938
320 319	**SC**	H	*SR*	GW	77917	63039	77939
320 320	**SC**	H	*SR*	GW	77918	63040	77940
320 321	**SC**	H	*SR*	GW	77919	63041	77941
320 322	**SC**	H	*SR*	GW	77920	63042	77942

Names (carried on MSO):

320 305	GLASGOW SCHOOL OF ART 1844–150–1994
320 306	Model Rail Scotland
320 308	High Road 20th Anniversary 2000
320 309	Radio Clyde 25th Anniversary
320 311	Royal College of Physicians and Surgeons of Glasgow
320 321	The Rt. Hon. John Smith, QC, MP
320 322	Festive Glasgow Orchid

CLASS 321   BREL YORK

Formation: DTCO (DTSO on Class 321/9)–MSO–TSO–DTSO.
Construction: Steel.
Traction Motors: Four Brush TM2141C (268 kW).
Doors: Sliding.   **Control System:** Thyristor.
Gangways: Within unit.   **Bogies:** P7-4 (MSO), T3-7 (others).
Couplers: Tightlock   **Maximum Speed:** 100 m.p.h.
Seating Layout: 1: 2+2 facing, 2: 3+2 facing.
Dimensions: 20.18 x 2.82 m.
Braking: Disc.
Multiple Working: Within class and with Classes 317, 318, 319, 320, 322 and 323.

Class 321/3. First Great Eastern units.

DTCO. Dia. EE308. Lot No. 31053 1988–1990. 12/56 (*16/57). 29.3 t.
MSO. Dia. EC210. Lot No. 31054 1988–1990. –/79 (*–/82). 51.5 t.
TSO. Dia. EH235. Lot No. 31055 1988–1990. –/74 2T (*–/75 2T). 28 t.
DTSO. Dia. EE236. Lot No. 31056 1988–1990. –/78. 29.1 t.

Advertising Livery: 321 366 "East of England" promotional livery (Lime green with dark green doors).

321 301	*	GE	H	GE	IL	78049	62975	71880	77853
321 302	*	GE	H	GE	IL	78050	62976	71881	77854
321 303	*	GE	H	GE	IL	78051	62977	71882	77855
321 304	*	GE	H	GE	IL	78052	62978	71883	77856
321 305	*	GE	H	GE	IL	78053	62979	71884	77857
321 306	*	GE	H	GE	IL	78054	62980	71885	77858
321 307	*	GE	H	GE	IL	78055	62981	71886	77859
321 308	*	GE	H	GE	IL	78056	62982	71887	77860
321 309	*	GE	H	GE	IL	78057	62983	71888	77861
321 310	*	GE	H	GE	IL	78058	62984	71889	77862
321 311	*	GE	H	GE	IL	78059	62985	71890	77863
321 312	*	GE	H	GE	IL	78060	62986	71891	77864
321 313	*	GE	H	GE	IL	78061	62987	71892	77865
321 314	*	GE	H	GE	IL	78062	62988	71893	77866
321 315		GE	H	GE	IL	78063	62989	71894	77867
321 316		GE	H	GE	IL	78064	62990	71895	77868
321 317		GE	H	GE	IL	78065	62991	71896	77869
321 318		GE	H	GE	IL	78066	62992	71897	77870
321 319		GE	H	GE	IL	78067	62993	71898	77871
321 320		GE	H	GE	IL	78068	62994	71899	77872
321 321	*	GE	H	GE	IL	78069	62995	71900	77873
321 322		GE	H	GE	IL	78070	62996	71901	77874
321 323		GE	H	GE	IL	78071	62997	71902	77875
321 324		GE	H	GE	IL	78072	62998	71903	77876
321 325		GE	H	GE	IL	78073	62999	71904	77877
321 326		GE	H	GE	IL	78074	63000	71905	77878
321 327		GE	H	GE	IL	78075	63001	71906	77879
321 328		GE	H	GE	IL	78076	63002	71907	77880
321 329		GE	H	GE	IL	78077	63003	71908	77881

321 330	GE	H	*GE*	IL		78078	63004	71909	77882
321 331	GE	H	*GE*	IL		78079	63005	71910	77883
321 332	GE	H	*GE*	IL		78080	63006	71911	77884
321 333	GE	H	*GE*	IL		78081	63007	71912	77885
321 334	GE	H	*GE*	IL		78082	63008	71913	77886
321 335	GE	H	*GE*	IL		78083	63009	71914	77887
321 336	GE	H	*GE*	IL		78084	63010	71915	77888
321 337	GE	H	*GE*	IL		78085	63011	71916	77889
321 338	GE	H	*GE*	IL		78086	63012	71917	77890
321 339	GE	H	*GE*	IL		78087	63013	71918	77891
321 340	GE	H	*GE*	IL		78088	63014	71919	77892
321 341	GE	H	*GE*	IL		78089	63015	71920	77893
321 342	GE	H	*GE*	IL		78090	63016	71921	77894
321 343	GE	H	*GE*	IL		78091	63017	71922	77895
321 344	GE	H	*GE*	IL		78092	63018	71923	77896
321 345	GE	H	*GE*	IL		78093	63019	71924	77897
321 346	GE	H	*GE*	IL		78094	63020	71925	77898
321 347	GE	H	*GE*	IL		78131	63105	71991	78280
321 348	GE	H	*GE*	IL		78132	63106	71992	78281
321 349	GE	H	*GE*	IL		78133	63107	71993	78282
321 350	GE	H	*GE*	IL		78134	63108	71994	78283
321 351	GE	H	*GE*	IL		78135	63109	71995	78284
321 352	GE	H	*GE*	IL		78136	63110	71996	78285
321 353	GE	H	*GE*	IL		78137	63111	71997	78286
321 354	GE	H	*GE*	IL		78138	63112	71998	78287
321 355	GE	H	*GE*	IL		78139	63113	71999	78288
321 356	GE	H	*GE*	IL		78140	63114	72000	78289
321 357	GE	H	*GE*	IL		78141	63115	72001	78290
321 358	GE	H	*GE*	IL		78142	63116	72002	78291
321 359	GE	H	*GE*	IL		78143	63117	72003	78292
321 360	GE	H	*GE*	IL		78144	63118	72004	78293
321 361	GE	H	*GE*	IL		78145	63119	72005	78294
321 362	GE	H	*GE*	IL		78146	63120	72006	78295
321 363	GE	H	*GE*	IL		78147	63121	72007	78296
321 364	GE	H	*GE*	IL		78148	63122	72008	78297
321 365	GE	H	*GE*	IL		78149	63123	72009	78298
321 366	AL	H	*GE*	IL		78150	63124	72010	78299

Names (carried on TSO):

321 312	Southend-on-Sea
321 321	NSPCC ESSEX FULL STOP
321 334	Amsterdam
321 336	GEOFFREY FREEMAN ALLEN
321 343	RSA–RAILWAY STUDY ASSOCIATION
321 351	GURKHA

Class 321/4. Silverlink and First Great Eastern units.

DTCO. Dia. EE309. Lot No. 31067 1989–1990. 28/40. 29.3 t.
MSO. Dia. EC210. Lot No. 31068 1989–1990. –/79. 51.5 t.
TSO. Dia. EH235. Lot No. 31069 1989–1990. –/74 2T. 28 t.
DTSO. Dia. EE236. Lot No. 31070 1989–1990. –/78. 29.1 t.

Advertising livery: 321 428 For Silverlink Travel and the "Birmingham day-tripper" ticket (Grey with various images).

Note: The DTCOs of FGE units have had 12 first class seats declassified.

321 401	**SL**	H	*SL*	BY	78095	63063	71949	77943
321 402	**SL**	H	*SL*	BY	78096	63064	71950	77944
321 403	**SL**	H	*SL*	BY	78097	63065	71951	77945
321 404	**SL**	H	*SL*	BY	78098	63066	71952	77946
321 405	**SL**	H	*SL*	BY	78099	63067	71953	77947
321 406	**SL**	H	*SL*	BY	78100	63068	71954	77948
321 407	**SL**	H	*SL*	BY	78101	63069	71955	77949
321 408	**SL**	H	*SL*	BY	78102	63070	71956	77950
321 409	**SL**	H	*SL*	BY	78103	63071	71957	77951
321 410	**SL**	H	*SL*	BY	78104	63072	71958	77952
321 411	**SL**	H	*SL*	BY	78105	63073	71959	77953
321 412	**SL**	H	*SL*	BY	78106	63074	71960	77954
321 413	**SL**	H	*SL*	BY	78107	63075	71961	77955
321 414	**SL**	H	*SL*	BY	78108	63076	71962	77956
321 415	**SL**	H	*SL*	BY	78109	63077	71963	77957
321 416	**SL**	H	*SL*	BY	78110	63078	71964	77958
321 417	**SL**	H	*SL*	BY	78111	63079	71965	77959
321 418	**N**	H	*SL*	BY	78112	63080	71968	77962
321 419	**SL**	H	*SL*	BY	78113	63081	71967	77961
321 420	**SL**	H	*SL*	BY	78114	63082	71966	77960
321 421	**SL**	H	*SL*	BY	78115	63083	71969	77963
321 422	**SL**	H	*SL*	BY	78116	63084	71970	77964
321 423	**SL**	H	*SL*	BY	78117	63085	71971	77965
321 424	**SL**	H	*SL*	BY	78118	63086	71972	77966
321 425	**N**	H	*SL*	BY	78119	63087	71973	77967
321 426	**SL**	H	*SL*	BY	78120	63088	71974	77968
321 427	**SL**	H	*SL*	BY	78121	63089	71975	77969
321 428	**AL**	H	*SL*	BY	78122	63090	71976	77970
321 429	**SL**	H	*SL*	BY	78123	63091	71977	77971
321 430	**SL**	H	*SL*	BY	78124	63092	71978	77972
321 431	**SL**	H	*SL*	BY	78151	63125	72011	78300
321 432	**SL**	H	*SL*	BY	78152	63126	72012	78301
321 433	**SL**	H	*SL*	BY	78153	63127	72013	78302
321 434	**SL**	H	*SL*	BY	78154	63128	72014	78303
321 435	**SL**	H	*SL*	BY	78155	63129	72015	78304
321 436	**SL**	H	*SL*	BY	78156	63130	72016	78305
321 437	**SL**	H	*SL*	BY	78157	63131	72017	78306
321 438	**GE**	H	*GE*	IL	78158	63132	72018	78307
321 439	**GE**	H	*GE*	IL	78159	63133	72019	78308
321 440	**GE**	H	*GE*	IL	78160	63134	72020	78309
321 441	**GE**	H	*GE*	IL	78161	63135	72021	78310
321 442	**GE**	H	*GE*	IL	78162	63136	72022	78311
321 443	**GE**	H	*GE*	IL	78125	63099	71985	78274
321 444	**GE**	H	*GE*	IL	78126	63100	71986	78275
321 445	**GE**	H	*GE*	IL	78127	63101	71987	78276
321 446	**GE**	H	*GE*	IL	78128	63102	71988	78277
321 447	**GE**	H	*GE*	IL	78129	63103	71989	78278

| 321 448 | **GE** | H | *GE* | IL | 78130 | 63104 | 71990 | 78279 |

Names (carried on TSO):

321 407	HERTFORDSHIRE WRVS
321 413	Bill Green
321 427	Major Tim Warr
321 439	Chelmsford Cathedral Festival
321 444	Essex Lifeboats

Class 321/9. DTSO(A)–MSO–TSO–DTSO(B). Units leased by West Yorkshire PTE from International Bank of Scotland. Managed by Porterbrook Leasing Company.

DTSO(A). Dia. EE277. Lot No. 31108 1991. –/77. 29.3 t.
MSO. Dia. EC216. Lot No. 31109 1991. –/79. 51.5 t.
TSO. Dia. EH240. Lot No. 31110 1991. –/74 2T. 28 t.
DTSO(B). Dia. EE277. Lot No. 31111 1991. –/77. 29.1 t.

321 901	**WY**	P	*AV*	NL	77991	63153	72128	77993
321 902	**WY**	P	*AV*	NL	77990	63154	72129	77994
321 903	**WY**	P	*AV*	NL	77992	63155	72130	77995

CLASS 322   BREL YORK

Units built for use on Stansted Airport services. Now working with ScotRail on the Edinburgh–North Berwick line.

Formation: DTCO–MSO–TSO–DTSO.
Construction: Steel.
Traction Motors: Four Brush TM2141C (268 kW).
Doors: Sliding.   **Control System:** Thyristor.
Gangways: Within unit.   **Bogies:** P7-4 (MSO), T3-7 (others).
Couplers: Tightlock   **Maximum Speed:** 100 m.p.h.
Seating Layout: 1: 2+1 facing, 2: 2+2 facing.
Dimensions: 20.18 x 2.82 m.
Braking: Disc.
Multiple Working: Within class and with Classes 317, 318, 319, 320, 321 and 323.

DTCO. Dia. EE313. Lot No. 31094 1990. 35/22. 30.4 t.
MSO. Dia. EC215. Lot No. 31092 1990. –/70. 52.3 t.
TSO. Dia. EH239. Lot No. 31093 1990. –/60 2T. 29.5 t.
DTSO. Dia. EE242. Lot No. 31091 1990. –/65. 29.8 t.

Non-Standard livery: Stansted Skytrain livery (light grey with a yellow stripe, now also with ScotRail brandings).

322 481	**0**	H	*SR*	GW	78163	72023	63137	77985
322 482	**0**	H	*SR*	GW	78164	72024	63138	77986
322 483	**0**	H	*SR*	GW	78165	72025	63139	77987
322 484	**NW**	H	*SR*	GW	78166	72026	63140	77988
322 485	**0**	H	*SR*	GW	78167	72027	63141	77989

Name (carried on MSO):

| 322 485 | North Berwick Flyer 1850–2000. |

CLASS 323 HUNSLET TRANSPORTATION PROJECTS

Formation: DMSO(A)–PTSO–DMSO(B).
Construction: Welded aluminium alloy.
Doors: Sliding plug.
Traction Motors: Four Holec DMKT 52/24 of 146 kW.
Gangways: Within unit.
Bogies: SRP BP62 (DMSO), BT52 (PTSO).
Couplers: Tightlock   **Maximum Speed:** 100 m.p.h.
Seating Layout: 1: 2+1 facing, 2: 2+2 facing.
Dimensions: 23.37/23.44 x 2.80 m.
Braking: Disc.
Multiple Working: Within class and with Classes 317, 318, 319, 320, 321 and 322.

DMSO(A). Dia. EA272. Lot No. 31112 Hunslet 1992–1993. –/98 (* –/82). 41.0 t.
TSO. Dia. EH296. Lot No. 31113 Hunslet 1992–1993. –/88 1T. (* –/80 1T). 23.37 t.
DMSO(B). Dia. EA272. Lot No. 31114 Hunslet 1992–1993. –/98 (* –/82). 39.4t.

323 201		CO	P	CT	SI	64001	72201	65001
323 202		CO	P	CT	SI	64002	72202	65002
323 203		CO	P	CT	SI	64003	72203	65003
323 204		CO	P	CT	SI	64004	72204	65004
323 205		CO	P	CT	SI	64005	72205	65005
323 206		CO	P	CT	SI	64006	72206	65006
323 207		CO	P	CT	SI	64007	72207	65007
323 208		CO	P	CT	SI	64008	72208	65008
323 209		CO	P	CT	SI	64009	72209	65009
323 210		CO	P	CT	SI	64010	72210	65010
323 211		CO	P	CT	SI	64011	72211	65011
323 212		CO	P	CT	SI	64012	72212	65012
323 213		CO	P	CT	SI	64013	72213	65013
323 214		CO	P	CT	SI	64014	72214	65014
323 215		CO	P	CT	SI	64015	72215	65015
323 216		CO	P	CT	SI	64016	72216	65016
323 217		CO	P	CT	SI	64017	72217	65017
323 218		CO	P	CT	SI	64018	72218	65018
323 219		CO	P	CT	SI	64019	72219	65019
323 220		CO	P	CT	SI	64020	72220	65020
323 221		CO	P	CT	SI	64021	72221	65021
323 222		CO	P	CT	SI	64022	72222	65022
323 223	*	GM	P	NW	LG	64023	72223	65023
323 224	*	NW	P	NW	LG	64024	72224	65024
323 225	*	GM	P	NW	LG	64025	72225	65025
323 226		FS	P	NW	LG	64026	72226	65026
323 227		FS	P	NW	LG	64027	72227	65027
323 228		FS	P	NW	LG	64028	72228	65028
323 229		FS	P	NW	LG	64029	72229	65029
323 230		GM	P	NW	LG	64030	72230	65030
323 231		GM	P	NW	LG	64031	72231	65031
323 232		FS	P	NW	LG	64032	72232	65032
323 233		NW	P	NW	LG	64033	72233	65033

323 234	GM	P	NW	LG	64034	72234	65034
323 235	FS	P	NW	LG	64035	72235	65035
323 236	FS	P	NW	LG	64036	72236	65036
323 237	GM	P	NW	LG	64037	72237	65037
323 238	GM	P	NW	LG	64038	72238	65038
323 239	GM	P	NW	LG	64039	72239	65039
323 240	CO	P	CT	SI	64040	72340	65040
323 241	CO	P	CT	SI	64041	72341	65041
323 242	CO	P	CT	SI	64042	72342	65042
323 243	CO	P	CT	SI	64043	72343	65043

CLASS 325   ABB DERBY

Postal units based on Class 319. Compatible with diesel locomotive haulage.
Formation: DTPMV–MPMV–TPMV–DTPMV.
System: 25 kV a.c. overhead/750 V d.c. third rail.
Construction: Steel.
Traction Motors: Four GEC G315BZ of 268 kW.
Doors: Roller shutter.
Gangways: None.
Couplers: Drop-head buckeye.
Braking: Disc.
Multiple Working: Within class.

Control System: GTO chopper.
Bogies: P7-4 (MSO), T3-7 (others).
Maximum Speed: 100 m.p.h.
Dimensions: 20.18 x 2.82 m.

DTPMV. Dia. EE501. Lot No. 31144 1995.
MPMV. Dia. EC501. Lot No. 31145 1995.
TPMV. Dia. EH501. Lot No. 31146 1995.

325 001	RM	RM	E	CE	68300	68340	68360	68301
325 002	RM	RM	E	CE	68302	68341	68361	68303
325 003	RM	RM	E	CE	68304	68342	68362	68305
325 004	RM	RM	E	CE	68306	68343	68363	68307
325 005	RM	RM	E	CE	68308	68344	68364	68309
325 006	RM	RM	E	CE	68310	68345	68365	68311
325 007	RM	RM	E	CE	68312	68346	68366	68313
325 008	RM	RM	E	CE	68314	68347	68367	68315
325 009	RM	RM	E	CE	68316	68348	68368	68317
325 010	RM	RM	E	CE	68318	68349	68369	68319
325 011	RM	RM	E	CE	68320	68350	68370	68321
325 012	RM	RM	E	CE	68322	68351	68371	68323
325 013	RM	RM	E	CE	68324	68352	68372	68325
325 014	RM	RM	E	CE	68326	68353	68373	68327
325 015	RM	RM	E	CE	68328	68354	68374	68329
325 016	RM	RM	E	CE	68330	68355	68375	68331

Names (carried on one side of each DTPMV):

325 002	Royal Mail North Wales & North West
325 006	John Grierson
325 008	Peter Howarth C.B.E.

CLASS 332   HEATHROW EXPRESS   SIEMENS

Dedicated Heathrow Express units. Five units were increased from 4-car to 5-car in late 2002/early 2003. Usually operate in coupled pairs.

Formations: Various.
Construction: Steel.   **Doors:** Sliding plug.
Traction Motors: Two Siemens monomotors of 350 kW.
Gangways: Within unit.   **Bogies:** CAF.
Couplers: Scharfenberg   **Maximum Speed:** 100 m.p.h.
Seating Layout: 1: 2+1 facing/unidirectional, 2: 2+2 mainly unidirectional.
Dimensions: 23.74/23.15 x 2.80 m.   **Braking:** Disc.
Multiple Working: Within class and with Class 333.

332 001–332 007. DMFO–TSO–PTSO–(TSO)–DMSO.

DMFO. Dia. EA244. CAF 1997–1998. 26/–. 48.8 t.
TSO. Dia. EH245. CAF 1997–1998. –/56 35.8 t.
PTSO. Dia. EH243. CAF 1997–1998. –/44 1TD 1W. 45.6 t.
TSO. Dia. EH245. CAF 2002. –/56 35.8 t. (new TSOs being fitted to 332 005–332 007).
DMSO. Dia. EA243. CAF 1997–1998. –/48. 48.8 t.

Advertising Livery: Vehicles 78401, 78402, 78405, 78406, 78408, 78410, 78412 carry Royal Bank of Scotland advertising livery (deep blue).

332 001	**HE**	HE	*HE*	OH	78400	72412	63400		78401
332 002	**HE**	HE	*HE*	OH	78402	72409	63401		78403
332 003	**HE**	HE	*HE*	OH	78404	72407	63402		78405
332 004	**HE**	HE	*HE*	OH	78406	72405	63403		78407
332 005	**HE**	HE	*HE*	OH	78408	72411	63404	72417	78409
332 006	**HE**	HE	*HE*	OH	78410	72410	63405	72415	78411
332 007	**HE**	HE	*HE*	OH	78412	72401	63406	72414	78413

332 008–332 014. DMSO–TSO–PTSO–(TSO)–DMLFO.

DMSO. Dia. EA244. CAF 1997–1998. –/48. 48.8 t.
TSO. Dia. EH245. CAF 1997–1998. –/56 35.8 t.
PTSO. Dia. EH243. CAF 1997–1998. –/44 1TD 1W. 45.6 t.
TSO. Dia. EH245. CAF 2002. –/56 35.8 t. (new TSOs being fitted to 332 008–332 009).
DMLFO. Dia. EA243. CAF 1997–1998. 14/– 1W. 48.8 t.

Advertising Livery: Vehicles 78414, 78416, 78419, 78421, 78423, 78425, 78427 carry Royal Bank of Scotland advertising livery (deep blue).

332 008	**HE**	HE	*HE*	OH	78414	72413	63407	72418	78415
332 009	**HE**	HE	*HE*	OH	78416	72400	63408	72416	78417
332 010	**HE**	HE	*HE*	OH	78418	72402	63409		78419
332 011	**HE**	HE	*HE*	OH	78420	72403	63410		78421
332 012	**HE**	HE	*HE*	OH	78422	72404	63411		78423
332 013	**HE**	HE	*HE*	OH	78424	72408	63412		78425
332 014	**HE**	HE	*HE*	OH	78426	72406	63413		78427

CLASS 333   SIEMENS

Formation: DMSO–PTSO–TSO–DMSO.
Construction: Steel.   **Doors:** Sliding plug.
Traction Motors: Two Siemens monomotors of 350 kW.
Gangways: Within unit.   **Bogies:** CAF.
Couplers: Scharfenberg   **Maximum Speed:** 100 m.p.h.
Seating Layout: 3+2 facing/unidirectional.
Dimensions: 23.74/23.15 x 2.80 m.
Multiple Working: Within class and with Class 332.

DMSO(A). (Odd Nos.) Dia. EA278. CAF 2001. –/90. 50.0 t.
PTSO. Dia. EH264. CAF 2001. –/73 1TD 2W. 46.0 t.
TSO. Dia. EH264. CAF 2002–2003. –/100. 38.5 t.
DMSO(B). (Even Nos.) Dia. EA279. CAF 2001. –/90. 50.0 t.

Note: 333 001–333 008 were made up to 4-car units from 3-car units in 2002.
New TSOs (74485–74492) are on order from CAF to make 333 009–333 016 up
to 4-car units in 2003. Unit formations are shown as they should be later in 2003.

333 001	**YN**	A	*AV*	NL	78451	74461	74477	78452
333 002	**YN**	A	*AV*	NL	78453	74462	74478	78454
333 003	**YN**	A	*AV*	NL	78455	74463	74479	78456
333 004	**YN**	A	*AV*	NL	78457	74464	74480	78458
333 005	**YN**	A	*AV*	NL	78459	74465	74481	78460
333 006	**YN**	A	*AV*	NL	78461	74466	74482	78462
333 007	**YN**	A	*AV*	NL	78463	74467	74483	78464
333 008	**YN**	A	*AV*	NL	78465	74468	74484	78466
333 009	**YN**	A	*AV*	NL	78467	74469	74485	78468
333 010	**YN**	A	*AV*	NL	78469	74470	74486	78470
333 011	**YN**	A	*AV*	NL	78471	74471	74487	78472
333 012	**YN**	A	*AV*	NL	78473	74472	74488	78474
333 013	**YN**	A	*AV*	NL	78475	74473	74489	78476
333 014	**YN**	A	*AV*	NL	78477	74474	74490	78478
333 015	**YN**	A	*AV*	NL	78479	74475	74491	78480
333 016	**YN**	A	*AV*	NL	78481	74476	74492	78482

CLASS 334 JUNIPER ALSTOM BIRMINGHAM

New ScotRail units.
Formations: DMSO–PTSO–DMSO.
Construction: Steel.   **Doors:** Sliding plug.
Traction Motors: Two Alstom ONIX 800 of 270 kW.
Gangways: Within unit.   **Bogies:** Alstom LTB3/TBP3.
Couplers: Tightlock.   **Maximum Speed:** 100 m.p.h.
Seating Layout: 2+2 facing/unidirectional (2+3 in PTSO).
Dimensions: 21.16/19.94 x 2.80 m.   **Braking:** Disc.
Multiple Working: Within class.

64101–64140. DMSO. Dia. EA215. 1999–2001. –/64. 42.6 t.
PTSO. Dia. EH255. 1999–2001. –/55 1TD 1W. 39.4 t.
65101–65140. DMSO. Dia. EA215. 1999–2001. –/64. 42.6 t.

334 001	**SP**	H	*SR*	GW	64101	74301	65101
334 002	**SP**	H	*SR*	GW	64102	74302	65102
334 003	**SP**	H	*SR*	GW	64103	74303	65103
334 004	**SP**	H	*SR*	GW	64104	74304	65104
334 005	**SP**	H	*SR*	GW	64105	74305	65105
334 006	**SP**	H	*SR*	GW	64106	74306	65106
334 007	**SP**	H	*SR*	GW	64107	74307	65107
334 008	**SP**	H	*SR*	GW	64108	74308	65108
334 009	**SP**	H	*SR*	GW	64109	74309	65109
334 010	**SP**	H	*SR*	GW	64110	74310	65110
334 011	**SP**	H	*SR*	GW	64111	74311	65111
334 012	**SP**	H	*SR*	GW	64112	74312	65112
334 013	**SP**	H	*SR*	GW	64113	74313	65113
334 014	**SP**	H	*SR*	GW	64114	74314	65114
334 015	**SP**	H	*SR*	GW	64115	74315	65115
334 016	**SP**	H	*SR*	GW	64116	74316	65116
334 017	**SP**	H	*SR*	GW	64117	74317	65117
334 018	**SP**	H	*SR*	GW	64118	74318	65118
334 019	**SP**	H	*SR*	GW	64119	74319	65119
334 020	**SP**	H	*SR*	GW	64120	74320	65120
334 021	**SP**	H	*SR*	GW	64121	74321	65121
334 022	**SP**	H	*SR*	GW	64122	74322	65122
334 023	**SP**	H	*SR*	GW	64123	74323	65123
334 024	**SP**	H	*SR*	GW	64124	74324	65124
334 025	**SP**	H	*SR*	GW	64125	74325	65125
334 026	**SP**	H	*SR*	GW	64126	74326	65126
334 027	**SP**	H	*SR*	GW	64127	74327	65127
334 028	**SP**	H	*SR*	GW	64128	74328	65128
334 029	**SP**	H	*SR*	GW	64129	74329	65129
334 030	**SP**	H	*SR*	GW	64130	74330	65130
334 031	**SP**	H	*SR*	GW	64131	74331	65131
334 032	**SP**	H	*SR*	GW	64132	74332	65132
334 033	**SP**	H	*SR*	GW	64133	74333	65133
334 034	**SP**	H	*SR*	GW	64134	74334	65134
334 035	**SP**	H	*SR*	GW	64135	74335	65135
334 036	**SP**	H	*SR*	GW	64136	74336	65136
334 037	**SP**	H	*SR*	GW	64137	74337	65137
334 038	**SP**	H	*SR*	GW	64138	74338	65138
334 039	**SP**	H	*SR*	GW	64139	74339	65139
334 040	**SP**	H	*SR*	GW	64140	74340	65140

CLASS 357 ELECTROSTAR
ADTRANZ/BOMBARDIER DERBY

New c2c units. Provision for 750 V DC supply if required.
Formation: DMSO(A)–MSO–PTSO–DMSO(B).
Construction: Welded aluminium alloy underframe, sides and roof with steel ends. All sections bolted together.
Traction Motors: Two Adtranz 250 kW. **Doors:** Sliding plug.
Gangways: Within unit.   **Bogies:** Adtranz P3-25/T3-25.

Couplers: Tightlock.
Seating Layout: 3+2 facing/unidirectional.
Braking: Disc & regenerative.
Maximum Speed: 100 m.p.h.
Dimensions: 20.40/19.99 x 2.80 m.
Multiple Working: Within class.

Class 357/0. Owned by Porterbrook Leasing.

DMSO(A). Dia. EA273. 1999–2001. –/71. 40.7 t.
MSO. Dia. EC225. 1999–2001. –/78. 39.5 t.
PTSO. Dia. EH215. 1999–2001. –/62 1TD 2W. 36.7 t.
DMSO(B). Dia. EA214. 1999–2001. –/71. 40.7 t.

357 001	C2	P	C2	EM	67651	74151	74051	67751
357 002	C2	P	C2	EM	67652	74152	74052	67752
357 003	C2	P	C2	EM	67653	74153	74053	67753
357 004	C2	P	C2	EM	67654	74154	74054	67754
357 005	C2	P	C2	EM	67655	74155	74055	67755
357 006	C2	P	C2	EM	67656	74156	74056	67756
357 007	C2	P	C2	EM	67657	74157	74057	67757
357 008	C2	P	C2	EM	67658	74158	74058	67758
357 009	C2	P	C2	EM	67659	74159	74059	67759
357 010	C2	P	C2	EM	67660	74160	74060	67760
357 011	C2	P	C2	EM	67661	74161	74061	67761
357 012	C2	P	C2	EM	67662	74162	74062	67762
357 013	C2	P	C2	EM	67663	74163	74063	67763
357 014	C2	P	C2	EM	67664	74164	74064	67764
357 015	C2	P	C2	EM	67665	74165	74065	67765
357 016	C2	P	C2	EM	67666	74166	74066	67766
357 017	C2	P	C2	EM	67667	74167	74067	67767
357 018	C2	P	C2	EM	67668	74168	74068	67768
357 019	C2	P	C2	EM	67669	74169	74069	67769
357 020	C2	P	C2	EM	67670	74170	74070	67770
357 021	C2	P	C2	EM	67671	74171	74071	67771
357 022	C2	P	C2	EM	67672	74172	74072	67772
357 023	C2	P	C2	EM	67673	74173	74073	67773
357 024	C2	P	C2	EM	67674	74174	74074	67774
357 025	C2	P	C2	EM	67675	74175	74075	67775
357 026	C2	P	C2	EM	67676	74176	74076	67776
357 027	C2	P	C2	EM	67677	74177	74077	67777
357 028	C2	P	C2	EM	67678	74178	74078	67778
357 029	C2	P	C2	EM	67679	74179	74079	67779
357 030	C2	P	C2	EM	67680	74180	74080	67780
357 031	C2	P	C2	EM	67681	74181	74081	67781
357 032	C2	P	C2	EM	67682	74182	74082	67782
357 033	C2	P	C2	EM	67683	74183	74083	67783
357 034	C2	P	C2	EM	67684	74184	74084	67784
357 035	C2	P	C2	EM	67685	74185	74085	67785
357 036	C2	P	C2	EM	67686	74186	74086	67786
357 037	C2	P	C2	EM	67687	74187	74087	67787
357 038	C2	P	C2	EM	67688	74188	74088	67788
357 039	C2	P	C2	EM	67689	74189	74089	67789
357 040	C2	P	C2	EM	67690	74190	74090	67790
357 041	C2	P	C2	EM	67691	74191	74091	67791

357 042	C2	P	C2	EM	67692	74192	74092	67792
357 043	C2	P	C2	EM	67693	74193	74093	67793
357 044	C2	P	C2	EM	67694	74194	74094	67794
357 045	C2	P	C2	EM	67695	74195	74095	67795
357 046	C2	P	C2	EM	67696	74196	74096	67796

Class 357/2. Owned by Angel Trains.

DMSO(A). Dia. EA279. 2001–2002. –/71. 40.7 t.
MSO. Dia. EC257. 2001–2002. –/78. 39.5 t.
PTSO. Dia. EH233. 2001–2002. –/62 1TD 2W. 36.7 t.
DMSO(B). Dia. EA280. 2001–2002. –/71. 40.7 t.

357 201	C2	A	C2	EM	68601	74701	74601	68701
357 202	C2	A	C2	EM	68602	74702	74602	68702
357 203	C2	A	C2	EM	68603	74703	74603	68703
357 204	C2	A	C2	EM	68604	74704	74604	68704
357 205	C2	A	C2	EM	68605	74705	74605	68705
357 206	C2	A	C2	EM	68606	74706	74606	68706
357 207	C2	A	C2	EM	68607	74707	74607	68707
357 208	C2	A	C2	EM	68608	74708	74608	68708
357 209	C2	A	C2	EM	68609	74709	74609	68709
357 210	C2	A	C2	EM	68610	74710	74610	68710
357 211	C2	A	C2	EM	68611	74711	74611	68711
357 212	C2	A	C2	EM	68612	74712	74612	68712
357 213	C2	A	C2	EM	68613	74713	74613	68713
357 214	C2	A	C2	EM	68614	74714	74614	68714
357 215	C2	A	C2	EM	68615	74715	74615	68715
357 216	C2	A	C2	EM	68616	74716	74616	68716
357 217	C2	A	C2	EM	68617	74717	74617	68717
357 218	C2	A	C2	EM	68618	74718	74618	68718
357 219	C2	A	C2	EM	68619	74719	74619	68719
357 220	C2	A	C2	EM	68620	74720	74620	68720
357 221	C2	A	C2	EM	68621	74721	74621	68721
357 222	C2	A	C2	EM	68622	74722	74622	68722
357 223	C2	A	C2	EM	68623	74723	74623	68723
357 224	C2	A	C2	EM	68624	74724	74624	68724
357 225	C2	A	C2	EM	68625	74725	74625	68725
357 226	C2	A	C2	EM	68626	74726	74626	68726
357 227	C2	A	C2	EM	68627	74727	74627	68727
357 228	C2	A	C2	EM	68628	74728	74628	68728

Names (carried on DMSO(A) and DMSO(B) (one plate on each)):

357 201   KEN BIRD | 357 202   KENNY MITCHELL

CLASS 360   DESIRO UK   SIEMENS

New units on order from Siemens for First Great Eastern.
Formation: DMCO(A)–PTSO–TSO–DMCO(B).
Systems: 25 kV AC overhead.
Construction: Welded aluminium.   **Doors:** Sliding plug.
Traction Motors: 4 Siemens 1TB2016-0GB02 asynchronous.
Gangways: Within unit only.   **Bogies:** SGP SF5000.

Couplers: Dellner 12.　　　　　　**Maximum Speed:** 100 m.p.h.
Seating Layout: 1: 2+2 facing, 2: 3+2 facing/unidirectional.
Dimensions: 20.40 x 2.79 m.　　　**Multiple Working:** Within class.
Braking: Disc & regenerative.

DMCO(A). Dia. EA304. Siemens Uerdingen 2002–2003. 8/59. 45.0 t.
PTSO. Dia. EH273. Siemens Wien 2002–2003. –/68 1TD 2W. 43.0 t.
TSO. Dia. EH200. Siemens Wien 2002–2003. –/78 . 35.0 t.
DMCO(B). Dia. EA305. Siemens Uerdingen 2002–2003. 8/59. 45.0 t.

360 101	**FS**	A	65551	72551	74551	68551
360 102	**FS**	A	65552	72552	74552	68552
360 103	**FS**	A	65553	72553	74553	68553
360 104	**FS**	A	65554	72554	74554	68554
360 105	**FS**	A	65555	72555	74555	68555
360 106	**FS**	A	65556	72556	74556	68556
360 107	**FS**	A	65557	72557	74557	68557
360 108	**FS**	A	65558	72558	74558	68558
360 109	**FS**	A	65559	72559	74559	68559
360 110	**FS**	A	65560	72560	74560	68560
360 111	**FS**	A	65561	72561	74561	68561
360 112	**FS**	A	65562	72562	74562	68562
360 113	**FS**	A	65563	72563	74563	68563
360 114	**FS**	A	65564	72564	74564	68564
360 115	**FS**	A	65565	72565	74565	68565
360 116	**FS**	A	65566	72566	74566	68566
360 117	**FS**	A	65567	72567	74567	68567
360 118	**FS**	A	65568	72568	74568	68568
360 119	**FS**	A	65569	72569	74569	68569
360 120	**FS**	A	65570	72570	74570	68570
360 121	**FS**	A	65571	72571	74571	68571

CLASS 365　NETWORKER EXPRESS　ABB YORK

Formation: DMCO(A)–TSO–PTSO–DMCO(B).
Systems: 25 kV AC overhead/750 V DC third rail. WAGN units have no shoegear, i.e. 750 V DC cannot be used, whilst Connex South Eastern units have their pantograph apertures covered over so that the 25 kV AC system cannot be used.
Construction: Welded aluminium alloy.
Traction Motors: Four GEC-Alsthom G354CX 157 kW.
Doors: Sliding plug.
Gangways: Within unit.
Couplers: Tightlock.　　　　　　**Bogies:** ABB P3-16/T3-16.
Seating Layout: 1: 2+2 facing, 2: 3+2 facing.　**Maximum Speed:** 100 m.p.h.
Dimensions: 20.89/20.06 x 2.80 m.
Braking: Disc, rheostatic & regenerative.
Multiple Working: Within class and with Classes 465 and 466.

DMCO(A). Dia. EA301. Lot No. 31133 1994–1995. 12/56. 46.7 t.
TSO. Dia. EH298. Lot No. 31134 1994–1995. –/59 1TD. 32.9 t.
PTSO. Dia. EH298. Lot No. 31135 1994–1995. –/68 1T. 34.6 t.

DMCO(B). Dia. EA301. Lot No. 31136 1994–1995. 12/56. 46.7 t.

365 501	**CB**	H	*SE*	RM	65894	72241	72240	65935
365 502	**CB**	H	*SE*	RM	65895	72243	72242	65936
365 503	**CB**	H	*SE*	RM	65896	72245	72244	65937
365 504	**CB**	H	*SE*	RM	65897	72247	72246	65938
365 505	**CB**	H	*SE*	RM	65898	72249	72248	65939
365 506	**CB**	H	*SE*	RM	65899	72251	72250	65940
365 507	**CB**	H	*SE*	RM	65900	72253	72252	65941
365 508	**CB**	H	*SE*	RM	65901	72255	72254	65942
365 509	**CB**	H	*SE*	RM	65902	72257	72256	65943
365 510	**CB**	H	*SE*	RM	65903	72259	72258	65944
365 511	**CB**	H	*SE*	RM	65904	72261	72260	65945
365 512	**CB**	H	*SE*	RM	65905	72263	72262	65946
365 513	**CB**	H	*SE*	RM	65906	72265	72264	65947
365 514	**CB**	H	*SE*	RM	65907	72267	72266	65948
365 515	**CB**	H	*SE*	RM	65908	72269	72268	65949
365 516	**CB**	H	*SE*	RM	65909	72271	72270	65950
365 517	**NT**	H	*WN*	HE	65910	72273	72272	65951
365 518	**NT**	H	*WN*	HE	65911	72275	72274	65952
365 519	**NT**	H	*WN*	HE	65912	72277	72276	65953
365 520	**NT**	H	*WN*	HE	65913	72279	72278	65954
365 521	**NT**	H	*WN*	HE	65914	72281	72280	65955
365 522	**NT**	H	*WN*	HE	65915	72283	72282	65956
365 523	**NT**	H	*WN*	HE	65916	72285	72284	65957
365 524	**NT**	H	*WN*	HE	65917	72287	72286	65958
365 525	**NT**	H	*WN*	HE	65918	72289	72288	65959
365 526	**NT**	H		ZC	65919	72291	72290	65960
365 527	**NT**	H	*WN*	HE	65920	72293	72292	65961
365 528	**NT**	H	*WN*	HE	65921	72295	72294	65962
365 529	**NT**	H	*WN*	HE	65922	72297	72296	65963
365 530	**NT**	H	*WN*	HE	65923	72299	72298	65964
365 531	**NT**	H	*WN*	HE	65924	72301	72300	65965
365 532	**NT**	H	*WN*	HE	65925	72303	72302	65966
365 533	**NT**	H	*WN*	HE	65926	72305	72304	65967
365 534	**NT**	H	*WN*	HE	65927	72307	72306	65968
365 535	**NT**	H	*WN*	HE	65928	72309	72308	65969
365 536	**NT**	H	*WN*	HE	65929	72311	72310	65970
365 537	**NT**	H	*WN*	HE	65930	72313	72312	65971
365 538	**NT**	H	*WN*	HE	65931	72315	72314	65972
365 539	**NT**	H	*WN*	HE	65932	72317	72316	65973
365 540	**NT**	H	*WN*	HE	65933	72319	72318	65974
365 541	**NT**	H	*WN*	HE	65934	72321	72320	65975

Names (Carried on one side of each DMCO):

365 505	Spirit of Ramsgate
365 515	Spirit of Dover

CLASS 375 ELECTROSTAR
ADTRANZ/BOMBARDIER DERBY

New units being delivered for Connex South Eastern.
Systems: 25 kV AC overhead/750 V DC third rail (some third rail only with provision for retro-fitting of AC equipment).
Formations: Various.
Construction: Welded aluminium alloy underframe, sides and roof with steel ends. All sections bolted together.
Traction Motors: Two Adtranz 250 kW. **Doors:** Sliding plug.
Gangways: Throughout.   **Bogies:** Adtranz P3-25/T3-25.
Couplers: Tightlock.   **Maximum Speed:** 100 m.p.h.
Seating Layout: 2+2 facing/unidirectional (express units), 3+2 facing/unidirectional (outer suburban units).
Dimensions: 20.40/19.99 x 2.80 m.
Braking: Disc & regenerative.   **Multiple Working:** Within class.

Class 375/3. Express units. 750 V DC only. DMSO(A)–TSO–DMSO(B).

DMSO(A). Dia. EA277. 2001–2002. –/60. 43.8 t.
TSO. Dia. EH254 2001–2002. –/56 1TD 2W. 34.1 t.
DMSO(B). Dia. EA277. 2001–2002. –/60. 43.8 t.

375 301	**CN**	H	*SE*	AF	67921	74351	67931
375 302	**CN**	H	*SE*	AF	67922	74352	67932
375 303	**CN**	H	*SE*	AF	67923	74353	67933
375 304	**CN**	H	*SE*	AF	67924	74354	67934
375 305	**CN**	H	*SE*	AF	67925	74355	67935
375 306	**CN**	H	*SE*	AF	67926	74356	67936
375 307	**CN**	H	*SE*	AF	67927	74357	67937
375 308	**CN**	H	*SE*	AF	67928	74358	67938
375 309	**CN**	H	*SE*	AF	67929	74359	67939
375 310	**CN**	H	*SE*	AF	67930	74360	67940

Class 375/6. Express units. 25 kV AC/750 V DC DMSO(A)–MSO–PTSO–DMSO(B).

DMSO(A). Dia. EA277. 1999–2001. –/60. 43.8 t.
MSO. Dia. EC230 1999–2001. –/66 1T. 40.5 t.
PTSO. Dia. EH252 1999–2001. –/56 1TD 2W. 34.1 t.
DMSO(B). Dia. EA277. 1999–2001. –/60. 43.8 t.

Non-Standard livery: 375 610 is as **CN** but with blue doors instead of yellow and a gold band instead of a grey band on the lower bodyside (a special "Golden Jubilee" livery).

375 601	**CN**	H	*SE*	AF	67801	74251	74201	67851
375 602	**CN**	H	*SE*	AF	67802	74252	74202	67852
375 603	**CN**	H	*SE*	AF	67803	74253	74203	67853
375 604	**CN**	H	*SE*	AF	67804	74254	74204	67854
375 605	**CN**	H	*SE*	AF	67805	74255	74205	67855
375 606	**CN**	H	*SE*	AF	67806	74256	74206	67856
375 607	**CN**	H	*SE*	AF	67807	74257	74207	67857

375 608	CN	H	*SE*	AF	67808	74258	74208	67858
375 609	CN	H	*SE*	AF	67809	74259	74209	67859
375 610	O	H	*SE*	AF	67810	74260	74210	67860
375 611	CN	H	*SE*	AF	67811	74261	74211	67861
375 612	CN	H	*SE*	AF	67812	74262	74212	67862
375 613	CN	H	*SE*	AF	67813	74263	74213	67863
375 614	CN	H	*SE*	AF	67814	74264	74214	67864
375 615	CN	H	*SE*	AF	67815	74265	74215	67865
375 616	CN	H	*SE*	AF	67816	74266	74216	67866
375 617	CN	H	*SE*	AF	67817	74267	74217	67867
375 618	CN	H	*SE*	AF	67818	74268	74218	67868
375 619	CN	H	*SE*	AF	67819	74269	74219	67869
375 620	CN	H	*SE*	AF	67820	74270	74220	67870
375 621	CN	H	*SE*	AF	67821	74271	74221	67871
375 622	CN	H	*SE*	AF	67822	74272	74222	67872
375 623	CN	H	*SE*	AF	67823	74273	74223	67873
375 624	CN	H	*SE*	AF	67824	74274	74224	67874
375 625	CN	H	*SE*	AF	67825	74275	74225	67875
375 626	CN	H	*SE*	AF	67826	74276	74226	67876
375 627	CN	H	*SE*	AF	67827	74277	74227	67877
375 628	CN	H	*SE*	AF	67828	74278	74228	67878
375 629	CN	H	*SE*	AF	67829	74279	74229	67879
375 630	CN	H	*SE*	AF	67830	74280	74230	67880

Names (carried on one side of each DMSO):

375 608	BROMLEY TRAVELWISE	375 610	Royal Tunbridge Wells
375 619	DRIVER JOHN NEVE	375 623	HOSPICE IN THE WEALD
375 624	White Cliffs Country		

Class 375/7. Express units. 750 V DC only. DMSO(A)–MSO–TSO–DMSO(B).

DMSO(A). Dia. EA276. 2001–2002. –/60. 43.8 t.
MSO. Dia. EC231 2001–2002. –/66 1T. 40.5 t.
TSO. Dia. EH253 2001–2002. –/56 1TD 2W. 34.1 t.
DMSO(B). Dia. EA276. 2001–2002. –/60. 43.8 t.

375 701	CN	H	*SE*	AF	67831	74281	74231	67881
375 702	CN	H	*SE*	AF	67832	74282	74232	67882
375 703	CN	H	*SE*	AF	67833	74283	74233	67883
375 704	CN	H	*SE*	AF	67834	74284	74234	67884
375 705	CN	H	*SE*	AF	67835	74285	74235	67885
375 706	CN	H	*SE*	AF	67836	74286	74236	67886
375 707	CN	H	*SE*	AF	67837	74287	74237	67887
375 708	CN	H	*SE*	AF	67838	74288	74238	67888
375 709	CN	H	*SE*	AF	67839	74289	74239	67889
375 710	CN	H	*SE*	AF	67840	74290	74240	67890
375 711	CN	H	*SE*	AF	67841	74291	74241	67891
375 712	CN	H	*SE*	AF	67842	74292	74242	67892
375 713	CN	H	*SE*	AF	67843	74293	74243	67893
375 714	CN	H	*SE*	AF	67844	74294	74244	67894
375 715	CN	H	*SE*	AF	67845	74295	74245	67895

Class 375/8. Express units. 750 V DC only. DMSO(A)–MSO–TSO–DMSO(B). Similar to Class 375/7 but with modified shoegear.

DMSO(A). Dia. EA288. 2003–2004. –/ . . t.
MSO. Dia. EC239. 2003–2004. –/ 1T. . t.
TSO. Dia. EH262. 2003–2004. –/ 1TD 2W. . t.
DMSO(B). Dia. EA288. 2003–2004. –/ . . t.

375 801	**CN**	H		73301	79001	78201	73701
375 802	**CN**	H		73302	79002	78202	73702
375 803	**CN**	H		73303	79003	78203	73703
375 804	**CN**	H		73304	79004	78204	73704
375 805	**CN**	H		73305	79005	78205	73705
375 806	**CN**	H		73306	79006	78206	73706
375 807	**CN**	H		73307	79007	78207	73707
375 808	**CN**	H		73308	79008	78208	73708
375 809	**CN**	H		73309	79009	78209	73709
375 810	**CN**	H		73310	79010	78210	73710
375 811	**CN**	H		73311	79011	78211	73711
375 812	**CN**	H		73312	79012	78212	73712
375 813	**CN**	H		73313	79013	78213	73713
375 814	**CN**	H		73314	79014	78214	73714
375 815	**CN**	H		73315	79015	78215	73715
375 816	**CN**	H		73316	79016	78216	73716
375 817	**CN**	H		73317	79017	78217	73717
375 818	**CN**	H		73318	79018	78218	73718
375 819	**CN**	H		73319	79019	78219	73719
375 820	**CN**	H		73320	79020	78220	73720
375 821	**CN**	H		73321	79021	78221	73721
375 822	**CN**	H		73322	79022	78222	73722
375 823	**CN**	H		73323	79023	78223	73723
375 824	**CN**	H		73324	79024	78224	73724
375 825	**CN**	H		73325	79025	78225	73725
375 826	**CN**	H		73326	79026	78226	73726
375 827	**CN**	H		73327	79027	78227	73727
375 828	**CN**	H		73328	79028	78228	73728
375 829	**CN**	H		73329	79029	78229	73729
375 830	**CN**	H		73330	79030	78230	73730

Class 375/9. Outer suburban units. 750 V DC only. DMSO(A)–MSO–TSO–DMSO(B).

DMSO(A). Dia. EA289. 2003–2004. –/ . . t.
MSO. Dia. EC240. 2003–2004. –/ 1T. . t.
TSO. Dia. EH263. 2003–2004. –/ 1TD 2W. . t.
DMSO(B). Dia. EA289. 2003–2004. –/ . . t.

375 901	**CN**	H		73331	79031	79061	73731
375 902	**CN**	H		73332	79032	79062	73732
375 903	**CN**	H		73333	79033	79063	73733
375 904	**CN**	H		73334	79034	79064	73734
375 905	**CN**	H		73335	79035	79065	73735
375 906	**CN**	H		73336	79036	79066	73736

375 907	CN	H	73337	79037	79067	73737
375 908	CN	H	73338	79038	79068	73738
375 909	CN	H	73339	79039	79069	73739
375 910	CN	H	73340	79040	79070	73740
375 911	CN	H	73341	79041	79071	73741
375 912	CN	H	73342	79042	79072	73742
375 913	CN	H	73343	79043	79073	73743
375 914	CN	H	73344	79044	79074	73744
375 915	CN	H	73345	79045	79075	73745
375 916	CN	H	73346	79046	79076	73746
375 917	CN	H	73347	79047	79077	73747
375 918	CN	H	73348	79048	79078	73748
375 919	CN	H	73349	79049	79079	73749
375 920	CN	H	73350	79050	79080	73750
375 921	CN	H	73351	79051	79081	73751
375 922	CN	H	73352	79052	79082	73752
375 923	CN	H	73353	79053	79083	73753
375 924	CN	H	73354	79054	79084	73754
375 925	CN	H	73355	79055	79085	73755
375 926	CN	H	73356	79056	79086	73756
375 927	CN	H	73357	79057	79087	73757

CLASS 377 ELECTROSTAR BOMBARDIER DERBY

New units being delivered for South Central. Expected to enter service in large numbers in 2003.

Systems: 25 kV AC overhead/750 V DC third rail or third rail only with provision for retro-fitting of AC equipment.
Formations: Various.
Construction: Welded aluminium alloy underframe, sides and roof with steel ends. All sections bolted together.

Traction Motors: Two Bombardier 250 kW.	**Doors:** Sliding plug.
Gangways: Throughout.	**Bogies:** Bombardier P3-25/T3-25.
Couplers: Dellner 12.	**Maximum Speed:** 100 m.p.h.
Seating Layout: Various.	**Dimensions:** 20.40/19.99 x 2.80 m.
Braking: Disc & regenerative.	**Multiple Working:** Within class.

Class 377/1. 750 V DC only. DMSO(A)–MSO–TSO–DMSO(B).
Seating layout: 2+2.

DMSO(A). Dia. EA276. 2002–2003. –/60. 43.4 t.
MSO. Dia. EC231. 2002–2003. –/66. 1T. 39.0 t.
TSO. Dia. EH253. 2002–2003. –/56 1TD 2W. 35.4 t.
DMSO(B). Dia. EA276 . 2002–2003. –/60. 43.4 t.

377 101	SN	P	78501	77101	78901	78701
377 102	SN	P	78502	77102	78902	78702
377 103	SN	P	78503	77103	78903	78703
377 104	SN	P	78504	77104	78904	78704
377 105	SN	P	78505	77105	78905	78705
377 106	SN	P	78506	77106	78906	78706
377 107	SN	P	78507	77107	78907	78707

377 108	SN	P		78508	77108	78908	78708
377 109	SN	P		78509	77109	78909	78709
377 110	SN	P		78510	77110	78910	78710
377 111	SN	P		78511	77111	78911	78711
377 112	SN	P		78512	77112	78912	78712
377 113	SN	P		78513	77113	78913	78713
377 114	SN	P		78514	77114	78914	78714
377 115	SN	P		78515	77115	78915	78715
377 116	SN	P		78516	77116	78916	78716
377 117	SN	P		78517	77117	78917	78717
377 118	SN	P		78518	77118	78918	78718
377 119	SN	P		78519	77119	78919	78719
377 120	SN	P		78520	77120	78920	78720
377 121	SN	P		78521	77121	78921	78721
377 122	SN	P		78522	77122	78922	78722
377 123	SN	P		78523	77123	78923	78723
377 124	SN	P		78524	77124	78924	78724
377 125	SN	P		78525	77125	78925	78725
377 126	SN	P		78526	77126	78926	78726
377 127	SN	P		78527	77127	78927	78727
377 128	SN	P		78528	77128	78928	78728
377 129	SN	P		78529	77129	78929	78729
377 130	SN	P		78530	77130	78930	78730
377 131	SN	P		78531	77131	78931	78731
377 132	SN	P		78532	77132	78932	78732
377 133	SN	P		78533	77133	78933	78733
377 134	SN	P		78534	77134	78934	78734
377 135	SN	P		78535	77135	78935	78735
377 136	SN	P		78536	77136	78936	78736
377 137	SN	P		78537	77137	78937	78737
377 138	SN	P		78538	77138	78938	78738
377 139	SN	P		78539	77139	78939	78739
377 140	SN	P		78540	77140	78940	78740
377 141	SN	P		78541	77141	78941	78741
377 142	SN	P		78542	77142	78942	78742
377 143	SN	P		78543	77143	78943	78743
377 144	SN	P		78544	77144	78944	78744
377 145	SN	P		78545	77145	78945	78745
377 146	SN	P		78546	77146	78946	78746
377 147	SN	P		78547	77147	78947	78747
377 148	SN	P		78548	77148	78948	78748
377 149	SN	P		78549	77149	78949	78749
377 150	SN	P		78550	77150	78950	78750
377 151	SN	P		78551	77151	78951	78751
377 152	SN	P		78552	77152	78952	78752
377 153	SN	P		78553	77153	78953	78753
377 154	SN	P		78554	77154	78954	78754
377 155	SN	P		78555	77155	78955	78755
377 156	SN	P		78556	77156	78956	78756
377 157	SN	P		78557	77157	78957	78757
377 158	SN	P		78558	77158	78958	78758

377 159	SN	P		78559	77159	78959	78759
377 160	SN	P		78560	77160	78960	78760
377 161	SN	P		78561	77161	78961	78761
377 162	SN	P		78562	77162	78962	78762
377 163	SN	P		78563	77163	78963	78763
377 164	SN	P		78564	77164	78964	78764

Class 377/2. 25 kV AC/750 V DC. DMSO(A)–MSO–PTSO–DMSO(B).

DMSO(A). Dia. EA289. 2002–2003. –/60. 43.8 t.
MSO. Dia. EC289 2002–2003. –/66 1T. 40.5 t.
PTSO. Dia. EH273 2002–2003. –/56 1TD 2W. 34.1 t.
DMSO(B). Dia. EA289. 2002–2003. –/60. 43.8 t.

377 201	SN	P		78571	77171	78971	78771
377 202	SN	P		78572	77172	78972	78772
377 203	SN	P		78573	77173	78973	78773
377 204	SN	P		78574	77174	78974	78774
377 205	SN	P		78575	77175	78975	78775
377 206	SN	P		78576	77176	78976	78776
377 207	SN	P		78577	77177	78977	78777
377 208	SN	P		78578	77178	78978	78778
377 209	SN	P		78579	77179	78979	78779
377 210	SN	P		78580	77180	78980	78780
377 211	SN	P		78581	77181	78981	78781
377 212	SN	P		78582	77182	78982	78782
377 213	SN	P		78583	77183	78983	78783
377 214	SN	P		78584	77184	78984	78784
377 215	SN	P		78585	77185	78985	78785

Class 377/3. 750 V DC only. DMSO(A)–TSO–DMSO(B).

Units built as Class 375, to be renumbered in the Class 377/3 range when the couplers are changed from Tightlock to Dellner.
Seating Layout: 2+2 facing/undirectional.

DMSO(A). Dia. EA275. 2001–2002. –/60. 45.3 t.
TSO. Dia. EH252 2001–2002. –/56 1TD 2W. 40.2 t.
DMSO(B). Dia. EA275. 2001–2002. –/60. 45.3 t.

377 301	(375 311)	SN	P	*SC*	BI	68201	74801	68401
377 302	(375 312)	SN	P	*SC*	BI	68202	74802	68402
377 303	(375 313)	SN	P	*SC*	BI	68203	74803	68403
377 304	(375 314)	SN	P	*SC*	BI	68204	74804	68404
377 305	(375 315)	SN	P	*SC*	BI	68205	74805	68405
377 306	(375 316)	SN	P	*SC*	BI	68206	74806	68406
377 307	(375 317)	SN	P	*SC*	BI	68207	74807	68407
377 308	(375 318)	SN	P	*SC*	BI	68208	74808	68408
377 309	(375 319)	SN	P	*SC*	BI	68209	74809	68409
377 310	(375 320)	SN	P	*SC*	BI	68210	74810	68410
377 311	(375 321)	SN	P	*SC*	BI	68211	74811	68411
377 312	(375 322)	SN	P	*SC*	BI	68212	74812	68412
377 313	(375 323)	SN	P	*SC*	BI	68213	74813	68413
377 314	(375 324)	SN	P	*SC*	BI	68214	74814	68414

377 315	(375 325)	**SN**	P	*SC*	BI	68215	74815	68415
377 316	(375 326)	**SN**	P	*SC*	BI	68216	74816	68416
377 317	(375 327)	**SN**	P	*SC*	BI	68217	74817	68417
377 318	(375 328)	**SN**	P	*SC*	BI	68218	74818	68418
377 319	(375 329)	**SN**	P	*SC*	BI	68219	74819	68419
377 320	(375 330)	**SN**	P	*SC*	BI	68220	74820	68420
377 321	(375 331)	**SN**	P	*SC*	BI	68221	74821	68421
377 322	(375 332)	**SN**	P	*SC*	BI	68222	74822	68422
377 323	(375 333)	**SN**	P	*SC*	BI	68223	74823	68423
377 324	(375 334)	**SN**	P	*SC*	BI	68224	74824	68424
377 325	(375 335)	**SN**	P	*SC*	BI	68225	74825	68425
377 326	(375 336)	**SN**	P	*SC*	BI	68226	74826	68426
377 327	(375 337)	**SN**	P	*SC*	BI	68227	74827	68427
377 328	(375 338)	**SN**	P	*SC*	BI	68228	74828	68428

Class 377/4. Details awaited. 4-car units.
Seating Layout: 2+2 outer cars, 3+2 inner cars.

377 401	**SN**	P	73401	78801	78601	73801
377 402	**SN**	P	73402	78802	78602	73802
377 403	**SN**	P	73403	78803	78603	73803
377 404	**SN**	P	73404	78804	78604	73804
377 405	**SN**	P	73405	78805	78605	73805
377 406	**SN**	P	73406	78806	78606	73806
377 407	**SN**	P	73407	78807	78607	73807
377 408	**SN**	P	73408	78808	78608	73808
377 409	**SN**	P	73409	78809	78609	73809
377 410	**SN**	P	73410	78810	78610	73810
377 411	**SN**	P	73411	78811	78611	73811
377 412	**SN**	P	73412	78812	78612	73812
377 413	**SN**	P	73413	78813	78613	73813
377 414	**SN**	P	73414	78814	78614	73814
377 415	**SN**	P	73415	78815	78615	73815
377 416	**SN**	P	73416	78816	78616	73816
377 417	**SN**	P	73417	78817	78617	73817
377 418	**SN**	P	73418	78818	78618	73818
377 419	**SN**	P	73419	78819	78619	73819
377 420	**SN**	P	73420	78820	78620	73820
377 421	**SN**	P	73421	78821	78621	73821
377 422	**SN**	P	73422	78822	78622	73822
377 423	**SN**	P	73423	78823	78623	73823
377 424	**SN**	P	73424	78824	78624	73824
377 425	**SN**	P	73425	78825	78625	73825
377 426	**SN**	P	73426	78826	78626	73826
377 427	**SN**	P	73427	78827	78627	73827
377 428	**SN**	P	73428	78828	78628	73828
377 429	**SN**	P	73429	78829	78629	73829
377 430	**SN**	P	73430	78830	78630	73830
377 431	**SN**	P	73431	78831	78631	73831
377 432	**SN**	P	73432	78832	78632	73832
377 433	**SN**	P	73433	78833	78633	73833
377 434	**SN**	P	73434	78834	78634	73834

377 435	SN	P	73435	78835	78635	73835
377 436	SN	P	73436	78836	78636	73836
377 437	SN	P	73437	78837	78637	73837
377 438	SN	P	73438	78838	78638	73838
377 439	SN	P	73439	78839	78639	73839
377 440	SN	P	73440	78840	78640	73840
377 441	SN	P	73441	78841	78641	73841
377 442	SN	P	73442	78842	78642	73842
377 443	SN	P	73443	78843	78643	73843
377 444	SN	P	73444	78844	78644	73844
377 445	SN	P	73445	78845	78645	73845
377 446	SN	P	73446	78846	78646	73846
377 447	SN	P	73447	78847	78647	73847
377 448	SN	P	73448	78848	78648	73848
377 449	SN	P	73449	78849	78649	73849
377 450	SN	P	73450	78850	78650	73850
377 451	SN	P	73451	78851	78651	73851
377 452	SN	P	73452	78852	78652	73852
377 453	SN	P	73453	78853	78653	73853
377 454	SN	P	73454	78854	78654	73854
377 455	SN	P	73455	78855	78655	73855
377 456	SN	P	73456	78856	78656	73856
377 457	SN	P	73457	78857	78657	73857
377 458	SN	P	73458	78858	78658	73858
377 459	SN	P	73459	78859	78659	73859
377 460	SN	P	73460	78860	78660	73860
377 461	SN	P	73461	78861	78661	73861
377 462	SN	P	73462	78862	78662	73862
377 463	SN	P	73463	78863	78663	73863
377 464	SN	P	73464	78864	78664	73864
377 465	SN	P	73465	78865	78665	73865
377 466	SN	P	73466	78866	78666	73866
377 467	SN	P	73467	78867	78667	73867
377 468	SN	P	73468	78868	78668	73868
377 469	SN	P	73469	78869	78669	73869
377 470	SN	P	73470	78870	78670	73870
377 471	SN	P	73471	78871	78671	73871
377 472	SN	P	73472	78872	78672	73872
377 473	SN	P	73473	78873	78673	73873
377 474	SN	P	73474	78874	78674	73874
377 475	SN	P	73475	78875	78675	73875

CLASS 390 PENDOLINO ALSTOM BIRMINGHAM

New tilting units for Virgin West Coast.
Formation: DMRFO–MFO–PTFO–MFO–(TSO)–MSO–PTSRMB–MSO–DMSO.
Construction: Welded aluminium alloy.
Traction Motors: Two Alstom ONIX 800 of 425 kW.
Doors: Sliding plug.
Gangways: Within unit.   **Bogies:** Fiat-SIG.
Couplers: Dellner.   **Maximum Speed:** 140 m.p.h.

Seating Layout: 1: 2+1 facing/unidirectional, 2: 2+2 mainly unidirectional.
Dimensions: 23.05 (outer) 23.90 (inner) x 2.73 m.
Braking: Disc, rheostatic & regenerative.
Multiple Working: Within class.

DMRFO: Dia. EA102. 2001–2003. 18/–. 55.6 t.
MFOD: Dia. EC101. 2001–2003. 39/– 1TD 1W. 52.0 t.
PTFO: Dia. EH162. 2001–2003. 44/– 1T. 50.1 t.
MFO: Dia. EC103. 2001–2003. 46/– 1T. 51.8 t.
TSO: Dia. EH258. 2001–2003. –/76 1T. 45.5 t.
MSO(A): Dia. EC234. 2001–2003. –/66 1TD 1W. 50.0 t.
PTSRMB: Dia. EH259. 2001–2003. –/48. 52.0 t.
MSO(B): Dia. EC235. 2001–2003. –/64 1TD 1W. 51.7 t.
DMSO: Dia. EA281. 2001–2003. –/46 1T. 51.0 t.

Note: These units are being delivered as 8-car units, without the TSO (688xx). These are expected to be added to the units to make them up to 9-car upon delivery of the final unit.

390 001	**VT** A			69101	69401	69501	69601	68801
				69701	69801	69901	69201	
390 002	**VT** A			69102	69402	69502	69602	68802
				69702	69802	69902	69202	
390 003	**VT** A			69103	69403	69503	69603	68803
				69703	69803	69903	69203	
390 004	**VT** A			69104	69404	69504	69604	68804
				69704	69804	69904	69204	
390 005	**VT** A			69105	69405	69505	69605	68805
				69705	69805	69905	69205	
390 006	**VT** A	*VW* MA		69106	69406	69506	69606	68806
				69706	69806	69906	69206	
390 007	**VT** A	*VW* MA		69107	69407	69507	69607	68807
				69707	69807	69907	69207	
390 008	**VT** A			69108	69408	69508	69608	68808
				69708	69808	69908	69208	
390 009	**VT** A			69109	69409	69509	69609	68809
				69709	69809	69909	69209	
390 010	**VT** A	*VW* MA		69110	69410	69510	69610	68810
				69710	69810	69910	69210	
390 011	**VT** A	*VW* MA		69111	69411	69511	69611	68811
				69711	69811	69911	69211	
390 012	**VT** A	*VW* MA		69112	69412	69512	69612	68812
				69712	69812	69912	69212	
390 013	**VT** A	*VW* MA		69113	69413	69513	69613	68813
				69713	69813	69913	69213	
390 014	**VT** A	*VW* MA		69114	69414	69514	69614	68814
				69714	69814	69914	69214	
390 015	**VT** A			69115	69415	69515	69615	68815
				69715	69815	69915	69215	
390 016	**VT** A			69116	69416	69516	69616	68816
				69716	69816	69916	69216	
390 017	**VT** A			69117	69417	69517	69617	68817
				69717	69817	69917	69217	

390 018	**VT** A	69118	69418	69518	69618	68818
		69718	69818	69918	69218	
390 019	**VT** A	69119	69419	69519	69619	68819
		69719	69819	69919	69219	
390 020	**VT** A	69120	69420	69520	69620	68820
		69720	69820	69920	69220	
390 021	**VT** A	69121	69421	69521	69621	68821
		69721	69821	69921	69221	
390 022	**VT** A	69122	69422	69522	69622	68822
		69722	69822	69922	69222	
390 023	**VT** A	69123	69423	69523	69623	68823
		69723	69823	69923	69223	
390 024	**VT** A	69124	69424	69524	69624	68824
		69724	69824	69924	69224	
390 025	**VT** A	69125	69425	69525	69625	68825
		69725	69825	69925	69225	
390 026	**VT** A	69126	69426	69526	69626	68826
		69726	69826	69926	69226	
390 027	**VT** A	69127	69427	69527	69627	68827
		69727	69827	69927	69227	
390 028	**VT** A	69128	69428	69528	69628	68828
		69728	69828	69928	69228	
390 029	**VT** A	69129	69429	69529	69629	68829
		69729	69829	69929	69229	
390 030	**VT** A	69130	69430	69530	69630	68830
		69730	69830	69930	69230	
390 031	**VT** A	69131	69431	69531	69631	68831
		69731	69831	69931	69231	
390 032	**VT** A	69132	69432	69532	69632	68832
		69732	69832	69932	69232	
390 033	**VT** A	69133	69433	69533	69633	68833
		69733	69833	69933	69233	
390 034	**VT** A	69134	69434	69534	69634	68834
		69734	69834	69934	69234	
390 035	**VT** A	69135	69435	69535	69635	68835
		69735	69835	69935	69235	
390 036	**VT** A	69136	69436	69536	69636	68836
		69736	69836	69936	69236	
390 037	**VT** A	69137	69437	69537	69637	68837
		69737	69837	69937	69237	
390 038	**VT** A	69138	69438	69538	69638	68838
		69738	69838	69938	69238	
390 039	**VT** A	69139	69439	69539	69639	68839
		69739	69839	69939	69239	
390 040	**VT** A	69140	69440	69540	69640	68840
		69740	69840	69940	69240	
390 041	**VT** A	69141	69441	69541	69641	68841
		69741	69841	69941	69241	
390 042	**VT** A	69142	69442	69542	69642	68842
		69742	69842	69942	69242	

390 043	**VT** A	69143	69443	69543	69643	68843
		69743	69843	69943	69243	
390 044	**VT** A	69144	69444	69544	69644	68844
		69744	69844	69944	69244	
390 045	**VT** A	69145	69445	69545	69645	68845
		69745	69845	69945	69245	
390 046	**VT** A	69146	69446	69546	69646	68846
		69746	69846	69946	69246	
390 047	**VT** A	69147	69447	69547	69647	68847
		69747	69847	69947	69247	
390 048	**VT** A	69148	69448	69548	69648	68848
		69748	69848	69948	69248	
390 049	**VT** A	69149	69449	69549	69649	68849
		69749	69849	69949	69249	
390 050	**VT** A	69150	69450	69550	69650	68850
		69750	69850	69950	69250	
390 051	**VT** A	69151	69451	69551	69651	68851
		69751	69851	69951	69251	
390 052	**VT** A	69152	69452	69552	69652	68852
		69752	69852	69952	69252	
390 053	**VT** A	69153	69453	69553	69653	68853
		69753	69853	69953	69253	

Names (carried on MFO No. 696xx):

390 001	Virgin Pioneer	390 028	
390 002	Red Revolution	390 029	
390 003	Virgin Enterprise	390 030	
390 004		390 031	
390 005		390 032	
390 006	Mission Possible	390 033	
390 007	Virgin Lady	390 034	
390 008	Virgin King	390 035	
390 009	Virgin Queen	390 036	
390 010	Commonwealth Games 2002	390 037	
390 011	City of Preston	390 038	
390 012	Virgin Star	390 039	
390 013	Virgin Spirit	390 040	
390 014	City of Manchester	390 041	
390 015		390 042	
390 016	Virgin Champion	390 043	
390 017		390 044	
390 018		390 045	
390 019		390 046	
390 020		390 047	
390 021		390 048	
390 022		390 049	
390 023		390 050	
390 024		390 051	
390 025		390 052	
390 026		390 053	
390 027			

4.2. 750 V DC THIRD RAIL EMUs

These classes use the third rail system at 750–850 V DC. Buffet cars have electric cooking. In addition to the class number, the old SR designations e.g. 4 Cig are quoted. Outer couplings are buckeyes on units built before 1982 with bar couplings within the units. Newer units have tightlock outer couplers.

CLASS 411   BR EASTLEIGH

Units built for the Kent Coast Electrification. Refurbished and fitted with hopper ventilators, Inter-City 70 seats and fluorescent lighting. Connex South Eastern units were due to finish work with the company in 2003, many are now being moved to Immingham Railfreight Terminal for scrapping.

SR designation: 3 Cep or 4 Cep.
Formation: DMSO(A)–TBCK–TSO–DMSO(B).
Construction: Steel.   **Doors:** Slam.
Gangways: Throughout.   **Electrical Equipment:** 1966-type.
Traction Motors: Two EE507 of 185 kW.
Bogies: One Mk. 4 (* Mark 3B, † Mark 6) motor bogie (DMSO). Commonwealth († B5 (SR)) trailer bogies.
Maximum Speed: 90 m.p.h.   **Dimensions:** 20.18 x 2.82 m.
Seating Layout: 1: Compartments, 2: 2+2 facing.
Braking: Tread brakes.   **Couplers:** Buckeye.
Multiple Working: Within Class and with Classes 412, 421, 422, 423, 438 and locos of Classes 33/1 and 73.

DMSO (A). Dia. EA263. –/64. 44.2 t.
TBCK. Dia. EJ361. 24/6 2T. 36.2 t.
TSOL. Dia. EH282. –/64 2T. 33.8 t.
DMSO (B). Dia. EA264. –/64. 43.5 t.

Lot numbers are as follows, all cars being built at Eastleigh:

61229–61237. 30449 1958.	**70261–70268.** 30455 1958–1959.
61307–61407. 30454 1958–1959.	**70304–70354.** 30456 1958–1959.
61698–61808. 30619 1960–1961.	**70503–70550.** 30620 1960–1961.
61950–61959. 30708 1963.	**70552–70609.** 30621 1960–1961.
70229–70233. 30450 1958.	**70654–70657.** 30709 1963.
70235–70239. 30451 1958.	**70664.** 30710 1963.
70241. 30640 1961.	

71626–71636. Converted at Swindon 1981–1983 from loco-hauled TSO of various lots.
71711. Converted at Swindon 1981–1983 from loco-hauled TSO. Former numbers as follows:

71626 (3916)	71627 (3921)	71629 (3992)	71632 (4063)
71636 (4065)	71711 (3994)		

Former number of converted buffet car:

69343 (69018)

Class 411/9. Units with TSO removed (DMSO–TBCK–DMSO).

1101		**N**	P	*SE*	RM	61331	70316	61330
1102		**N**	P	*SE*	RM	61231	70604	61232
1103	*	**N**	P	*SE*	RM	61750	70580	61751
1105	*	**N**	P	*SE*	RM	61952	70655	61953
1107		**N**	P	*SE*	RM	61343	70327	61380
1108		**N**	P	*SE*	RM	61399	70350	61398
1112		**N**	P	*SE*	RM	61369	70335	61368
1113		**N**	P	*SE*	RM	61371	70336	61370
1114		**N**	P	*SE*	RM	61377	70339	61376
1116	*	**N**	P	*SE*	RM	61756	70589	61757
1117	*	**N**	P	*SE*	RM	61704	70557	61705
1118	*	**N**	P	*SE*	RM	61708	70559	61709

Class 411/5. Standard units.

1507		**ST**	P		FR	61363	70332		61362
1512		**ST**	P		BM	61321	70311	70268	61320
1517		**ST**	P	*SW*	FR	61317	70309	70266	61316
1518		**N**	P		ZG	61333	70317	70274	61332
1519		**ST**	P	*SW*	FR	61403	70352	70536	61402
1527		**N**	P		BM	61237	70239	70233	61238
1531		**ST**	P	*SW*	FR	61233	70237	70231	61234
1533		**ST**	P	*SW*	FR	61393	70347	71627	61385
1534		**ST**	P	*SW*	FR	61405	70353	71626	61404
1535		**ST**	P	*SW*	FR	61397	70349	71629	61396
1539		**ST**	P	*SW*	FR	61401	70351	71632	61400
1544		**ST**	P	*SW*	FR	61315	70308	70265	61349
1550		**ST**	P	*SW*	FR	61313	70307	70264	61312
1553		**ST**	P	*SW*	FR	61728	70306	70263	61350
1555		**ST**	P	*SW*	FR	61311	70326	70283	61310
1562		**N**	P	*SE*	RM	61407	70236	70241	61406
1563	*	**ST**	P	*SW*	FR	61740	70575	70526	61741
1564	*	**N**	P	*SE*	RM	61788	70599	70550	61789
1565	*	**ST**	P	*SW*	FR	61762	70586	71711	61763
1571	*	**ST**	P	*SW*	FR	61806	70608	70289	61807
1573	*	**ST**	P	*SW*	FR	61726	70568	70519	61727
1578	*	**ST**	P	*SW*	FR	61700	70555	70506	61701
1581	*	**ST**	P	*SW*	FR	61784	70597	70548	61785
1586	*	**N**	P	*SE*	RM	61714	70562	70513	61715
1590	*	**N**	P	*SE*	RM	61696	70553	70504	61697
1592	*	**G**	P	*SE*	RM	61778	70594	70545	61779
1593	*	**N**	P	*SE*	RM	61730	70570	70521	61731
1594	*	**N**	P	*SE*	RM	61754	70582	70533	61755
1602	*	**CX**	P	*SE*	RM	61958	70565	70279	61959
1606	*	**N**	P		AF	61694	70552		61695
1607	*	**N**	P	*SE*	RM	61698	70554	70505	61699
1612	*	**ST**	P	*SW*	FR	61794	70602	70535	61795
1614	*	**N**	P	*SE*	RM	61702	70556	70507	61703
1615	*	**N**	P	*SE*	RM	61956	70657	70664	61957
1616	*	**N**	P	*SE*	RM	61323	70654	70543	61951

1697	†	**ST**	P	*SW*	FR	61373	70337	70294	61372
1698	†	**ST**	P	*SW*	FR	61355	70343	70300	61384
1699	†	**ST**	P	*SW*	FR	61712	70561	70512	61713
Spare	*	**N**	P		BM	61734			61735
Spare		**ST**	P		FR			69343	
Spare		**N**	P		ZG			70503	

CLASS 412   BR EASTLEIGH

All Reformed in 2002. For details see Class 411 above except **69341–69347**.

Class 412/1. "Greyhound" 4 Cep. These are former Beps which were reformed in 2002. They have had their buffet cars removed and replaced by TSOs.

Formation: DMSO(A)–TBCK–TSO–DMSO(B).

2311	(2301)	**ST**	P	*SW*	FR	61804	70607	70539	61805
2312	(2302)	**ST**	P	*SW*	FR	61774	70592	70295	61809
2313	(2303)	**ST**	P	*SW*	FR	61954	70656	71636	61955
2314	(2304)	**ST**	P	*SW*	FR	61736	70573	70517	61737
2315	(2305)	**ST**	P	*SW*	FR	61798	70354	70229	61799
2316	(2306)	**ST**	P	*SW*	FR	61808	70609	70272	61775
2317	(2307)	**ST**	P	*SW*	FR	61802	70606	70261	61803

Class 412/2. 4 Bep. These are former Ceps which were reformed in 2002. They have had their TSOs removed and replaced by buffet cars.

Formation: DMSO(A)–TBCK–TSRB–DMSO(B).

69341–69347. TSRB. Dia. EN261. Lot No. 30622 1961. Converted from TRB to TSRB at BREL Swindon 1982–84. –/24 1T + 9 longitudinal buffet chairs. 35.5 t.

2321	(1568)	**ST**	P	*SW*	FR	61766	70588	69341	61767
2322	(1548)	**ST**	P	*SW*	FR	61375	70338	69342	61374
2324	(1566)	**ST**	P	*SW*	FR	61722	70566	69344	61723
2325	(1537)	**ST**	P	*SW*	FR	61229	70235	69345	61230
2326	(1547)	**ST**	P	*SW*	FR	61329	70578	69346	61328
2327	(1538)	**ST**	P	*SW*	FR	61307	70304	69347	61306

Former numbers of converted buffet cars:

| 69341 (69014) | 69342 (69019) | 69344 (69012) | 69345 (69013) |
| 69346 (69016) | 69347 (69015) | | |

CLASS 421   BR YORK

Units built for Portsmouth and Brighton lines. Facelifted with new trim and fluorescent lighting in saloons.

SR designation: 4 Cig.
Formation: DTCso(A)–MBSO–TSO–DTCso(B).
Construction: Steel.   **Doors:** Slam.
Gangways: Throughout.   **Electrical Equipment:** 1966-type.
Traction Motors: Four EE507 of 185 kW. **Couplers:** Buckeye.
Bogies: Two Mk. 4 or Mk. 6 motor bogies (MBSO). B5 (SR) bogies (trailer cars).
Maximum Speed: 90 m.p.h.   **Dimensions:** 20.18 x 2.82 m.

Seating Layout: 1: Compartments, 2: 2+2 facing.
Braking: Tread brakes.
Multiple Working: Within class and with Classes 411, 412, 423, 438 and locos of Classes 33/1 and 73.

Phase 1 Sets. These have SR Mark 4 motor bogies.

76076–76129. DTCsoL(A). Dia. EE364. Lot No. 30741 1964–1965. 18/36 2T (–/54 2T†, –/60 2T§). 35.5 t.
62017–62070.MBSO. Dia. ED260. Lot No. 30742 1964–1965. –/56. 49 t.
70695–70730. TSO. Dia. EH275. Lot No. 30730 1964–1965. –/72. 31.5 t.
71044–71097. TSO. Dia. EH275. Lot No. 30817 1970. –/72. 31.5 t.
71766–71770. TSO. Dia. EH275. Lot No. 30784 1964–1965. –/72. 31.5 t.
76022–76075. DTCsoL(B). Dia. EE363. Lot No. 30740 1964–1965. 24/28 2T.

Phase 2 Sets. These have SR Mark 6 motor bogies.

76561–76570. DTCso(A). Dia. EE369. Lot No. 30802 1970. 18/36 2T (–/54 2T†, –/60 2T§). 35.5 t.
76581–76610. DTCso(A). Dia. EE369. Lot No. 30806 1970. 18/36 2T (–/54 2T†, –/60 2T§). 35.5 t.
76717–76787. DTCso(A). Dia. EE369. Lot No. 30814 1970–1972. 18/36 2T (–/54 2T†, –/60 2T§). 35.5 t.
76859. DTCso(A). Dia. EE369. Lot No. 30827 1972. 12/42 2T. 35.5 t.
62277–62286. MBSO. Dia. ED264. Lot No. 30804 1970. –/56. 49 t.
62287–62316. MBSO. Dia. ED264. Lot No. 30808 1970. –/56. 49 t.
62355–62425. MBSO. Dia. ED264. Lot No. 30816 1970. –/56. 49 t.
62430. MBSO. Dia. ED264. Lot No. 30829 1972. –/56. 49 t.
70967–70996. TSO. Dia. EH287. Lot No. 30809 1970–1971. –/72. 31.5t.
71035–71105. TSO. Dia. EH287. Lot No. 30817 1970. –/72. 31.5t.
71106. TSO. Dia. EH287. Lot No. 30830 1972. –/72. 31.5t.
71926–71928. TSO. Dia. EH287. Lot No. 30805 1970. –/72. 31.5t.
76571–76580. DTCso(B). Dia. EE369. Lot No. 30802 1970. 24/28 2T. 35 t.
76611–76640. DTCso(B). Dia. EE369. Lot No. 30807 1970. 24/28 2T. 35 t.
76788–76858. DTCso(B). Dia. EE369. Lot No. 30815 1970–1972. 24/28 2T. 35 t.
76860. DTCso(B). Dia. EE369. Lot No. 30828 1972. 18/36 2T. 35 t.

Notes: DTCso(A) were built with three first class compartments and one standard class compartment. On units marked † the three first class compartments have been declassified, whilst on units marked § all they have been converted to standard.
d Fitted with central door locking (unit 1812). This unit was also the "guinea pig" for the cup and cone device system.

Class 421/5. Phase 2 units.These sets are known as 'Greyhound' units and are fitted with an additional stage of field weakening to improve the maximum attainable speed. This term is traditional on the lines of the former London & South Western railway, as it was formerly applied to their Class T9 4–4–0 express steam locomotives.

1301	**ST**	H	*SW*	FR	76595	62301	70981	76625
1302	**ST**	H	*SW*	FR	76584	62290	70970	76614
1303	**ST**	H	*SW*	FR	76581	62287	70967	76611
1304	**ST**	H	*SW*	FR	76583	62289	70969	76613

1305	**ST**	H	*SW*	FR	76717	62355	71035	76788
1306	**ST**	H	*SW*	FR	76723	62361	71041	76794
1307	**ST**	H	*SW*	FR	76586	62292	70972	76616
1308	**ST**	H	*SW*	FR	76627	62298	70978	76622
1309	**ST**	H	*SW*	FR	76594	62300	70980	76624
1310	**ST**	H	*SW*	FR	76567	62283	71926	76577
1311	**ST**	H	*SW*	FR	76561	62277	71927	76571
1312	**ST**	H	*SW*	FR	76562	62278	71928	76572
1313	**ST**	H	*SW*	FR	76596	62302	70982	76626
1314	**ST**	H	*SW*	FR	76588	62294	70974	76618
1315	**ST**	H	*SW*	FR	76608	62314	70994	76638
1316	**ST**	H	*SW*	FR	76585	62291	70971	76615
1317	**ST**	H	*SW*	FR	76597	62303	70983	76592
1318	**ST**	H	*SW*	FR	76590	62296	70976	76620
1319	**ST**	H	*SW*	FR	76591	62297	70977	76621
1320	**ST**	H	*SW*	FR	76593	62299	70979	76623
1321	**ST**	H	*SW*	FR	76589	62295	70975	76619
1322	**ST**	H	*SW*	FR	76587	62293	70973	76617

Former numbers of converted buffet cars:

71926 (69315) | 71927 (69330) | 71928 (69331)

Note: No new Lot Nos were issued for the above conversions.

Class 421/8. 'Greyhound' units formed of former Class 422 units with the TRSB replaced by a Class 411/5 TSO.

1392	**ST**	P	*SW*	FR	76811	62378	70273	76740
1393	**ST**	P	*SW*	FR	76746	62384	70527	76817
1394	**ST**	P	*SW*	FR	76726	62364	70663	76797
1395	**ST**	P	*SW*	FR	76850	62417	70662	76779
1396	**ST**	P	*SW*	FR	76803	62370	70531	76732
1397	**ST**	P	*SW*	FR	76749	62387	70515	76820
1398	**ST**	P	*SW*	FR	76819	62386	70292	76748
1399	**ST**	P	*SW*	FR	76747	62385	70508	76818

Class 421/7. Phase 2 units rebuilt at Wessex Traincare/Alstom Eastleigh 1997–1998 for Brighton–Portsmouth "Coastway" line. Compartments opened out, first class seating replaced by standard with a TSO removed.
SR designation: 3 Cop.
Formation: DTSso(A)–MBSO–DTSso(B).
Diagram Numbers: EE245 + ED264 + EE245.
Accommodation: –/60 1T + –/56 1W + 18/36 1T.

1401	§	**CX**	P	*SC*	BI	76568	62284	76578
1402	§	**CX**	P		ZG	76564	62280	76574
1403	§	**CX**	P	*SC*	BI	76563	62279	76573
1404	§	**CX**	P	*SC*	BI	76602	62308	76632
1405	§	**CX**	P	*SC*	BI	76565	62281	76575
1406	§	**CX**	P	*SC*	BI	76728	62366	76799
1407	§	**CX**	P	*SC*	BI	76729	62367	76800
1408	§	**CX**	P	*SC*	BI	76750	62388	76821
1409	§	**CX**	P	*SC*	BI	76569	62285	76579

| 1410 | § | **CX** | P | *SC* | BI | 76734 | 62372 | 76805 |
| 1411 | § | **CX** | P | *SC* | BI | 76570 | 62286 | 76580 |

Names (carried on MBS):

| 1408 | Littlehampton Progress 2000 |
| 1409 | Operation Perseus |

Class 421/3. Phase 1 units.

1701		**U**	A		RM	76087	62028	70706	76033
1702	†	**CX**	A		PY	76101	62042	70720	76047
1703	†	**CX**	A		PY	76097	62038	70716	76043
1704	†	**CX**	A	*SC*	BI	76092	62033	70711	76038
1705	†	**CX**	A	*SC*	BI	76076	62017	70695	76022
1706	†	**CX**	A		PY	76094	62035	70713	76040
1707	†	**CX**	A	*SC*	BI	76084	62025	70703	76030
1708	†	**CX**	A	*SC*	BI	76110	62051	70729	76056
1709	†	**CX**	A	*SC*	BI	76103	62044	70722	76049
1710	†	**CX**	A	*SC*	BI	76078	62019	70697	76024
1711	§	**CX**	A	*SC*	BI	76114	62055	71766	76060
1712	†	**CX**	A	*SC*	BI	76079	62020	70698	76025
1713	§	**CX**	A	*SC*	BI	76128	62069	71767	76074
1714	†	**CX**	A	*SC*	BI	76077	62018	70696	76023
1717	†	**CX**	A	*SC*	BI	76083	62024	70702	76029
1719	†	**CX**	A	*SC*	BI	76116	62057	70719	76062
1720	†	**CX**	A	*SC*	BI	76098	62039	71769	76044
1721	§	**CX**	A	*SC*	BI	76090	62031	70709	76036
1722	§	**CX**	A	*SC*	BI	76106	62047	70725	76052
1724	†	**CX**	A	*SC*	BI	76120	62061	71770	76066
1725	†	**CX**	A	*SC*	BI	76088	62029	70707	76034
1726	§	**CX**	A	*SC*	BI	76109	62050	70728	76055
1727	†	**CX**	A	*SC*	BI	76111	62052	70730	76057
1731	†	**CX**	A	*SC*	BI	76095	62036	70714	76041
1733	†	**CX**	A	*SC*	BI	76122	62063	71047	76068
1734	†	**U**	A	*SC*	BI	76063	62054	71044	76059
1735	†	**GA**	A	*SC*	BI	76117	62058	71050	76051
1736	†	**U**	A	*SC*	BI	76124	62065	71052	76070
1737	†	**U**	A	*SC*	BI	76121	62062	71058	76067
1738	†	**GA**	A	*SC*	BI	76129	62064	71046	76069
1739	†	**CX**	A	*SC*	BI	76123	62070	71066	76075
1740	†	**GA**	A	*SC*	BI	76126	62067	71097	76072
1741	†	**CX**	A	*SC*	BI	76089	62030	70708	76035
1742		**U**	A	*SE*	RM	76086	62027	70705	76032
1743	†	**CX**	A	*SC*	BI	76118	62059	71065	76064
1744	†	**CX**	A	*SC*	BI	76127	62068	71064	76073
1745	§	**CX**	A	*SC*	BI	76085	62026	70704	76031
1746	§	**CX**	A	*SC*	BI	76091	62032	70710	76037
1747	§	**CX**	A	*SC*	BI	76093	62034	70712	76026
1748		**U**	A	*SE*	RM	76115	62056	71067	76061
1750	†	**CX**	A	*SC*	BI	76080	62021	70699	76039
1751	†	**CX**	A	*SC*	BI	76125	62066	71051	76071
1752	§	**CX**	A	*SC*	BI	76119	62060	70717	76065

1753	†	CX	A	*SC*	BI	76102	62043	70721	76048
Spare		N	A		PY		62053	71068	76058

Class 421/4. Phase 2 units.

1801	†	CX	P	*SC*	BI	76848	71095	62415	76777
1802	†	CX	P	*SC*	BI	76754	62392	71072	76825
1803	†	CX	A	*SC*	BI	76780	62418	71098	76851
1804	†	CX	A	*SC*	BI	76778	62416	71096	76849
1805	†	CX	A	*SC*	BI	76782	62420	71100	76853
1806		N	H	*SE*	RM	76783	62421	71101	76854
1807		N	H	*SE*	RM	76784	62422	71102	76855
1808		N	H	*SE*	RM	76785	62423	71103	76856
1809		N	H	*SE*	RM	76786	62424	71104	76857
1810		N	H	*SE*	RM	76787	62425	71105	76858
1811		N	H	*SE*	RM	76781	62419	71099	76852
1812	d	N	H		ZG	76757	62395	71075	76828
1813		N	H	*SE*	RM	76859	62430	71106	76860
1831	†	CX	A	*SC*	BI	76598	62304	70984	76628
1832	†	CX	A	*SC*	BI	76719	62357	71037	76790
1833	†	CX	A	*SC*	BI	76582	62288	70968	76612
1834	†	CX	A	*SC*	BI	76566	62284	70988	76576
1835	†	CX	A	*SC*	BI	76601	62307	70987	76631
1837	†	CX	A	*SC*	BI	76722	62360	71040	76793
1839		N	H	*SE*	RM	76607	62313	70993	76637
1840		N	H	*SE*	RM	76724	62362	71042	76795
1841		N	H	*SE*	RM	76603	62309	70989	76633
1842		N	H	*SE*	RM	76725	62363	71043	76796
1843		N	H	*SE*	RM	76731	62369	71049	76802
1845	†	CX	A	*SC*	BI	76599	62305	70985	76718
1846	†	CX	A	*SC*	BI	76737	62375	71055	76808
1847	†	CX	A	*SC*	BI	76600	62306	70986	76630
1848	†	CX	A	*SC*	BI	76605	62311	70991	76635
1850	†	CX	A	*SC*	BI	76629	62356	71036	76789
1851	†	U	A	*SC*	BI	76721	62359	71039	76792
1853	†	U	A	*SC*	BI	76606	62312	70992	76636
1854	†	GA	A	*SC*	BI	76738	62376	71056	76809
1855	†	GA	A	*SC*	BI	76720	62358	71038	76791
1856	†	GA	A	*SC*	BI	76739	62377	71057	76810
1857	†	GA	A	*SC*	BI	76610	62316	70996	76640
1858	§	GA	A	*SC*	BI	76604	62310	70990	76634
1859	§	GA	A	*SC*	BI	76727	62365	71045	76798
1860	§	GA	A	*SC*	BI	76752	62390	71070	76823
1861	§	GA	A	*SC*	BI	76735	62373	71053	76806
1862	†	GA	A	*SC*	BI	76736	62374	71054	76807
1863	†	CX	A	*SC*	BI	76742	62380	71060	76813
1864	†	CX	A	*SC*	BI	76741	62379	71059	76812
1865	†	GA	A	*SC*	BI	76745	62383	71063	76639
1866	†	CX	A	*SC*	BI	76743	62381	71061	76814
1867	†	CX	A	*SC*	BI	76744	62382	71062	76815
1868	†	CX	A	*SC*	BI	76751	62389	71069	76822
1869	†	CX	A	*SC*	BI	76753	62391	71071	76804

1870		CX	H	*SE*	RM	76108	62409	71089	76842
1871		N	H	*SE*	RM	76756	62394	71074	76827
1872		N	H	*SE*	RM	76771	62396	71076	76829
1873		N	H	*SE*	RM	76759	62397	71077	76830
1874	†	CX	A	*SC*	BI	76755	62393	71073	76826
1876		N	H	*SE*	RM	76761	62399	71079	76832
1877		N	H	*SE*	RM	76763	62401	71081	76834
1878		N	H	*SE*	RM	76768	62406	71086	76839
1879		N	H	*SE*	RM	76760	62398	71078	76831
1880		ST	H	*SW*	FR	76770	62408	71088	76841
1881		ST	H	*SW*	FR	76762	62400	71080	76833
1882		ST	H	*SW*	FR	76765	62403	71083	76836
1883		ST	H	*SW*	FR	76764	62402	71082	76835
1884		ST	H	*SW*	FR	76767	62405	71085	76838
1885		ST	H	*SW*	FR	76769	62407	71087	76840
1886		ST	H	*SW*	FR	76772	62410	71090	76843
1887		ST	H	*SW*	FR	76766	62404	71084	76837
1888		ST	H	*SW*	FR	76773	62411	71091	76844
1889		ST	H	*SW*	FR	76774	62412	71092	76845
1890		ST	H	*SW*	FR	76775	62413	71093	76846
1891		ST	H	*SW*	FR	76776	62414	71094	76847

Former numbers of converted buffet cars used in Phase 1 sets:

| 71766 (69303) | 71767 (69314) | 71768 (69317) | 71769 (69305) |
| 71770 (69308) | | | |

Note: No new lot numbers were issued for the above conversions

Class 421/9. Phase 1 units fitted with ex-Class 432 Mark 6 motor bogies.

1901	†	CX	P	*SC*	BI	76082	62023	70701	76028
1902	†	CX	P	*SC*	BI	76100	62041	71768	76046
1903	†	CX	A	*SC*	BI	76081	62022	70700	76027
1904	†	CX	A	*SC*	BI	76107	62048	70726	76053
1905	§	CX	A	*SC*	BI	76099	62040	70718	76045
1906	†	CX	A	*SC*	BI	76105	62046	70724	76113
1907	†	CX	A	*SC*	BI	76104	62045	70723	76050
1908	†	GA	A	*SC*	BI	76096	62037	70715	76042

CLASS 423   BR

Outer suburban units. Facelifted with fluorescent lighting.

SR designation: 4 Vep.
Formation: DTCso(A)–MBSO–TSO–DTCso(B).
Construction: Steel.   **Doors:** Slam.
Gangways: Throughout.   **Electrical Equipment:** 1966-type.
Traction Motors: Four EE507 of 185 kW.   **Couplers:** Buckeye.
Bogies: Two Mk. 4 motor bogies (MBSO). B5 (SR) bogies (trailer cars).
Maximum Speed: 90 m.p.h.   **Dimensions:** 20.18 x 2.82 m
Seating Layout: 1: Compartments, 2: 3+2 facing or compartments.
Braking: Tread brakes.

Multiple Working: Within class and with Classes 411, 412, 423, 438 and locos of Classes 33/1 and 73.
62121–62140. MBSO. Dia. ED266. Lot No. 30760 Derby 1967. –/76. 49 t.
62182–62216. MBSO. Dia. ED266. Lot No. 30773 York 1967–1968. –/76. 49 t.
62217–62266. MBSO. Dia. ED266. Lot No. 30794 York 1968–1969. –/76. 49 t.
62267–62276. MBSO. Dia. ED266. Lot No. 30800 York 1970. –/76. 49 t.
62317–62354. MBSO. Dia. ED266. Lot No. 30813 York 1970–1973. –/76. 49 t.
62435–62475. MBSO. Dia. ED266. Lot No. 30851 York 1973–1974. –/76. 49 t.
70781–70800. TSO. Dia. EH291. Lot No. 30759 Derby 1967. –/98. 31.5 t.
70872–70906. TSO. Dia. EH291. Lot No. 30772 York 1967–1968. –/98. 31.5 t.
70907–70956. TSO. Dia. EH291. Lot No. 30793 York 1968–1969. –/98. 31.5 t.
70957–70966. TSO. Dia. EH291. Lot No. 30801 York 1970. –/98. 31.5 t.
70997–71034. TSO. Dia. EH291. Lot No. 30812 York 1970–1973. –/98. 31.5 t.
71115–71155. TSO. Dia. EH291. Lot No. 30852 York 1973–1974. –/98. 31.5 t.
76230–76269. DTCso. Dia. EE373. Lot No. 30758 York 1967. 18/46 1T. 35 t.
76275. DTSO (Class 438). Dia. EE266. Lot No. 30764 York 1966. –/64 32 t.
(Converted from hauled TSO 3929). Now in unit 3582.
76333–76402. DTCso. Dia. EE373. Lot No. 30771 York 1967–1968. 18/46 1T. 35 t.
76441–76540. DTCso. Dia. EE373. Lot No. 30792 York 1968–1969. 18/46 1T. 35 t.
76541–76560. DTCso. Dia. EE373. Lot No. 30799 York 1970. 18/46 1T. 35 t.
76641–76716. DTCso. Dia. EE373. Lot No. 30811 York 1970–1973. 18/46 1T. 35 t.
76861–76942. DTCso. Dia. EE373. Lot No. 30853 York 1973–1974. 18/46 1T. 35 t.

Class 423/1. Standard units.

3401	**ST**	H	*SW*	WD	76871	62276	70781	76872
3402	**ST**	H	*SW*	WD	76233	62123	70782	76232
3403	**CX**	H	*SC*	BI	76234	62254	70783	76235
3404	**ST**	H	*SW*	WD	76378	62261	70894	76236
3405	**ST**	H	*SW*	WD	76239	62271	70785	76238
3406	**ST**	H	*SW*	WD	76241	62130	70786	76240
3407	**ST**	H	*SW*	WD	76243	62348	70787	76242
3408	**ST**	H	*SW*	WD	76244	62435	70788	76245
3409	**ST**	H	*SW*	WD	76246	62239	70789	76247
3410	**ST**	H	*SW*	WD	76369	62442	70790	76249
3411	**ST**	H	*SW*	WD	76250	62342	70791	76251
3412	**CX**	A	*SE*	RM	76252	62340	70792	76253
3413	**ST**	H	*SW*	WD	76255	62441	70793	76254
3414	**ST**	H	*SW*	WD	76257	62446	70794	76248
3415	**N**	H	*SW*	WD	76258	62462	70795	76259
3416	**CX**	A	*SE*	RM	76261	62451	70796	76260
3417	**ST**	H	*SW*	WD	76262	62236	70797	76263
3418	**ST**	H	*SW*	WD	76265	62133	70875	76264
3419	**ST**	H	*SW*	WD	76267	62354	70799	76266
3420	**ST**	H	*SW*	WD	76269	62349	70800	76268
3421	**CX**	A	*SE*	RM	76889	62449	71129	76890
3422	**CX**	A	*SE*	RM	76372	62201	70891	76371
3423	**CX**	A	*SE*	RM	76452	62222	70912	76451
3424	**CX**	A	*SE*	RM	76354	62185	70882	76353
3425	**ST**	H	*SW*	WD	76338	62192	70874	76358
3426	**ST**	H	*SW*	WD	76386	62208	70898	76385
3427	**ST**	H	*SW*	WD	76374	62184	70892	76373

3428	**ST**	H	*SW*	WD	76360	62223	70913	76453
3429	**ST**	H	*SW*	WD	76334	62202	70872	76333
3430	**ST**	H	*SW*	WD	76348	62189	70879	76347
3431	**ST**	H	*SW*	WD	76458	62182	70915	76457
3432	**ST**	H	*SW*	WD	76400	62225	70905	76399
3433	**ST**	H	*SW*	WD	76444	62215	70908	76443
3434	**ST**	H	*SW*	WD	76462	62218	70917	76461
3435	**CX**	P	*SC*	BI	76342	62228	70876	76341
3436	**CX**	P	*SC*	BI	76350	62190	70880	76349
3437	**CX**	P	*SC*	BI	76346	62186	70878	76345
3445	**CX**	A	*SE*	RM	76450	62242	70911	76449
3446	**CX**	A	*SE*	RM	76532	62243	70952	76531
3447	**CX**	A	*SE*	RM	76380	62199	70895	76379
3448	**CX**	A	*SE*	RM	76376	62221	70886	76375
3449	**CX**	A	*SE*	RM	76336	62205	70873	76335
3450	**CX**	A	*SE*	RM	76460	62203	70916	76459
3451	**CX**	A	*SE*	RM	76488	62240	70930	76487
3452	**CX**	A	*SE*	RM	76340	62183	71021	76690
3453	**CX**	A	*SE*	RM	76382	62226	70896	76381
3454	**CX**	A	*SE*	RM	76390	62200	70798	76389
3455	**ST**	H	*SW*	WD	76388	62206	70899	76387
3456	**ST**	H	*SW*	WD	76455	62210	70914	76230
3457	**ST**	H	*SW*	WD	76392	62197	70901	76391
3458	**ST**	H	*SW*	WD	76394	62209	70902	76393
3459	**ST**	H	*SW*	WD	76396	62224	70903	76395
3466	**ST**	H	*SW*	WD	76464	62214	70918	76463
3467	**ST**	H	*SW*	WD	76446	62217	70909	76445
3468	**ST**	H	*SW*	WD	76448	62267	70910	76447
3469	**ST**	H	*SW*	WD	76546	62219	70959	76545
3470	**ST**	H	*SW*	WD	76496	62220	70934	76495
3471	**CX**	A	*SE*	RM	76498	62269	70935	76497
3472	**CX**	A	*SE*	RM	76500	62244	70936	76499
3473	**CX**	A	*SE*	RM	76502	62245	70937	76339
3474	**CX**	A	*SE*	RM	76504	62246	70938	76503
3475	**CX**	A	*SE*	RM	76552	62270	70962	76551
3479	**CX**	H	*SC*	BI	76655	62272	71004	76656
3480	**ST**	H	*SW*	WD	76474	62233	70923	76473
3481	**ST**	H	*SW*	WD	76647	62324	70900	76648
3482	**CX**	H	*SC*	BI	76657	62320	71005	76658
3483	**CX**	H	*SC*	BI	76661	62233	71007	76662
3484	**CX**	H	*SC*	BI	76476	62325	70924	76475
3485	**CX**	H	*SC*	BI	76508	62327	70940	76507
3486	**CX**	H	*SC*	BI	76478	62234	70925	76477
3487	**CX**	A	*SC*	BI	76645	62250	70941	76509
3488	**CX**	H	*SC*	BI	76663	62235	71008	76664
3489	**CX**	H	*SC*	BI	76665	62251	71009	76666
3490	**CX**	H	*SC*	BI	76695	62328	71024	76696
3491	**CX**	A	*SE*	RM	76337	62436	70927	76481
3492	**CX**	A	*SE*	RM	76667	62344	71010	76662
3493	**CX**	A	*SE*	RM	76669	62237	71011	76670
3494	**CX**	A	*SE*	RM	76675	62330	71014	76676

3495	CX	A	*SE*	RM	76699	62331	71026	76700
3496	CX	A	*SE*	RM	76673	62334	71013	76674
3497	CX	A	*SE*	RM	76671	62346	71012	76672
3498	CX	A	*SE*	RM	76701	62333	71027	76702
3499	CX	A	*SE*	RM	76901	62347	71135	76902
3500	CX	A	*SE*	RM	76470	62455	70921	76469
3501	CX	P	*SC*	BI	76512	62332	70942	76511
3503	CX	P	*SC*	BI	76681	62231	71017	76682
3504	CX	P	*SC*	BI	76711	62351	71032	76712
3505	CX	P	*SC*	BI	76472	62352	70922	76471
3508	ST	H	*SW*	WD	76643	62273	70998	76644
3509	ST	H	*SW*	WD	76560	62275	70966	76559
3510	ST	H	*SW*	WD	76641	62318	70997	76642
3511	CX	A	*SE*	RM	76893	62135	70999	76646
3512	CX	P	*SC*	BI	76679	62337	71016	76680
3514	GA	P	*SC*	BI	76683	62136	71018	76684
3515	CX	P	*SC*	BI	76544	62319	70958	76543
3516	ST	H	*SW*	WD	76693	62268	71023	76694
3517	CX	P	*SC*	BI	76685	62338	71019	76686
3518	CX	P	*SC*	BI	76689	62343	70887	76363
3519	ST	H	*SW*	WD	76556	62274	70964	76555
3520	ST	H	*SW*	WD	76697	62131	71025	76359
3521	CX	A	*SE*	RM	76484	62345	70928	76483
3523	CX	H	*SC*	BI	76651	62139	71002	76652
3524	CX	H	*SC*	BI	76466	62322	70919	76370
3529	CX	H	*SC*	BI	76659	62257	71006	76660
3530	CX	H	*SC*	BI	76468	62256	70920	76467
3531	CX	H	*SC*	BI	76649	62230	71001	76650
3535	CX	P	*SC*	BI	76677	62335	71015	76678
3536	ST	H	*SW*	WD	76384	62207	70897	76383
3539	ST	H	*SW*	WD	76861	62122	71115	76862
3540	ST	H	*SW*	WD	76863	62128	71116	76864
3542	ST	H	*SW*	WD	76480	62127	70926	76479
3543	N	A	*SC*	BI	76899	62137	71134	76900
3544	CX	A	*SE*	RM	76892	62454	71131	76894
3545	CX	A	*SE*	RM	76875	62121	71122	76876
3546	CX	P	*SC*	BI	76687	62339	71020	76688
3547	CX	A	*SE*	RM	76895	62126	71132	76896
3548	CX	A	*SE*	RM	76903	62452	71136	76904
3549	CX	P	*SC*	BI	76707	62132	71030	76708
3551	CX	P	*SC*	BI	76465	62456	71033	76714
3552	ST	H	*SW*	WD	76715	62353	71034	76716
3553	CX	A	*SE*	RM	76913	62241	71141	76914
3554	CX	A	*SE*	RM	76905	62461	71137	76906
3555	ST	H	*SW*	WD	76865	62140	71117	76866
3556	CX	A	*SE*	RM	76885	62457	71127	76886
3557	ST	H	*SW*	WD	76869	62437	71119	76870
3558	ST	H	*SW*	WD	76352	62447	70881	76351
3559	ST	H	*SW*	WD	76486	62439	70929	76485
3560	CX	A	*SE*	RM	76897	62191	71133	76898
3561	ST	H	*SW*	WD	76867	62453	71118	76868

3562	**CX**	A	*SE*	RM	76907	62129	71138	76908
3563	**ST**	H	*SW*	WD	76873	62438	71121	76874
3564	**CX**	A	*SE*	RM	76883	62458	71126	76884
3565	**CX**	A	*SE*	RM	76877	62134	71123	76878
3566	**CX**	A	*SE*	RM	76915	62443	71142	76916
3568	**CX**	A	*SE*	RM	76887	62440	71128	76888
3569	**ST**	H	*SW*	WD	76344	62448	70877	76343
3570	**CX**	A	*SE*	RM	76909	62187	71139	76910
3571	**CX**	A	*SE*	RM	76927	62463	71148	76928
3572	**CX**	A	*SE*	RM	76879	62468	71124	76880
3573	**CX**	A	*SE*	RM	76919	62444	71144	76920
3574	**CX**	A	*SE*	RM	76929	62464	71149	76930
3575	**CX**	A	*SE*	RM	76931	62469	71150	76932
3576	**ST**	H	*SW*	WD	76362	62196	70890	76361
3577	**CX**	A	*SE*	RM	76933	62459	71151	76934
3578	**ST**	H	*SW*	WD	76356	62193	70883	76355
3579	**CX**	A	*SE*	RM	76935	62471	71152	76936
3581	**ST**	H	*SW*	WD	76366	62198	70888	76365
3582	**CX**	A	*SE*	RM	76891	62472	71130	76275
3583	**CX**	A	*SE*	RM	76937	62450	71153	76938
3584	**CX**	A	*SE*	RM	76881	62473	71125	76882
3585	**CX**	A	*SE*	RM	76939	62445	71154	76940
3586	**CX**	A	*SE*	RM	76921	62474	71145	76922
3587	**CX**	A	*SE*	RM	76925	62465	71147	76926
3588	**CX**	A	*SE*	RM	76923	62467	71146	76924
3589	**CX**	A	*SE*	RM	76911	62466	71140	76912
3590	**CX**	A	*SE*	RM	76941	62460	71155	76942
3591	**CX**	A	*SE*	RM	76917	62475	71143	76918
3801	**CX**	P	*SE*	RM	76522	62229	70947	76521
3802	**CX**	P	*SE*	RM	76534	62188	70953	76533
3803	**CX**	P	*SE*	RM	76494	62263	70933	76493
3804	**CX**	P	*SE*	RM	76368	62204	70889	76367
3805	**CX**	P	*SE*	RM	76540	62211	70956	76539
3806	**CX**	P	*SE*	RM	76538	62212	70955	76537
3807	**CX**	P	*SE*	RM	76542	62264	70957	76541
3808	**CX**	P	*SE*	RM	76550	62248	70961	76549
3809	**N**	P	*SW*	WD	76516	62253	70944	76515
3810	**N**	P	*SW*	WD	76709	62252	71031	76710
3811	**N**	P	*SW*	WD	76514	62249	70943	76513
3812	**ST**	P	*SW*	WD	76703	62238	71028	76704
Spare	**ST**	H		ZG	76698	62195	70885	
Spare	**ST**	H		ZA		62138		
Spare	**ST**	H		ZG	76456		71120	76231
Spare	**N**	H		ZG	76454			
Spare	**N**	H		WD		62470		

Class 423/2. Units converted for "South London Metro" service.

SR designation: 4 Vop.
Formation: DTSso(A)–MBSO–TSO–DTSso(B).
DTSso seats –/70 1T.
Note: Vehicle 70954 in unit 3903 carries number 70904 in error.

3901	**CX**	P	*SC*	Bl	76402	62227	70906	76401
3902	**CX**	P	*SC*	Bl	76364	62260	70949	76525
3903	**CX**	P	*SC*	Bl	76536	62213	70954	76535
3904	**CX**	P	*SC*	Bl	76691	62336	71022	76692
3905	**CX**	P	*SC*	Bl	76398	62266	70904	76397
3906	**CX**	P	*SC*	Bl	76490	62350	70931	76489
3907	**CX**	P	*SC*	Bl	76506	62259	70939	76505
3908	**CX**	P	*SC*	Bl	76442	62265	70907	76441
3909	**CX**	P	*SC*	Bl	76705	62341	71029	76706
3910	**CX**	P	*SC*	Bl	76530	62262	70951	76529
3911	**CX**	P	*SC*	Bl	76548	62247	70960	76547
3912	**CX**	P	*SC*	Bl	76492	62216	70932	76491
3913	**CX**	P	*SC*	Bl	76653	62125	71003	76654
3914	**CX**	P	*SC*	Bl	76520	62326	70946	76519
3915	**CX**	P	*SC*	Bl	76524	62255	70948	76523
3916	**CX**	P	*SC*	Bl	76518	62258	70945	76517
3917	**CX**	P	*SC*	Bl	76558	62232	70965	76557
3918	**CX**	P	*SC*	Bl	76528	62321	70950	76527
3919	**CX**	P	*SC*	Bl	76554	62317	70963	76553

CLASS 438   BR

Unpowered units converted from loco-hauled stock.

SR designation: 4 TC.
Formation: DTSO–TBSK–TFK–DTSO.
Construction: Steel.   **Doors:** Slam.
Gangways: Throughout.   **Electrical Equipment:** 1966-type.
Bogies: B5 (SR).   **Couplers:** Buckeye.
Maximum Speed: 90 m.p.h.   **Dimensions:** 20.18 x 2.82 m
Saloon Seating Layout: 1: Compartments, 2: 2+2 facing.
Braking: Tread brakes.
Multiple Working: Within class and with Classes 411, 412, 421, 423 and locos of Classes 33/1 and 73.

DTSO. Dia. EE266. Lot No. 30764 York 1966–1967. –/64. 32 t.
TFK. Dia. EH160. Lot No. 30766 York 1966–1967. 42/– 2T. 33.5 t.
TBSK. Dia. EJ260. Lot No. 30765 York 1966–1967. –/32 1T. 35.5 t.

417	**B**	CM	KT	76301	70826	70860	76302
Spare	**B**	CM	KT		70812		

Former numbers of converted hauled stock:

70812 (34987)	70826 (34980)	70860 (13019)	76301 (4375)
70302 (4382)			

CLASS 442   WESSEX EXPRESS   BREL DERBY

Stock built for Waterloo–Bournemouth–Weymouth service. Now also used on certain Portsmouth Harbour services. Can be hauled and heated by any ETH fitted locomotive.

SR designation: 5 Wes.
Formation: DTFso–TSO(A)–MBRSM–TSO(B)–DTSO.
Construction: Steel.   **Doors:** Sliding plug.
Gangways: Throughout.   **Electrical Equipment:** 1986-type.
Traction Motors: Four EE546 of 300 kW recovered from class 432.
Bogies: Two BREL P7 motor bogies (MBSO). T4 bogies (trailer cars).
Maximum Speed: 100 m.p.h.   **Couplers:** Buckeye.
Seating Layout: 1: 2+2 facing/compartments, 2: 2+2 facing/unidirectional.
Dimensions: 23.15/23.00 x 2.74 m.   **Braking:** Tread brakes.
Heating & Ventilation: Air conditioning.
Multiple Working: Within class and with Classes 411, 412, 423, 438 and locos of
Classes 33/1 and 73 in emergency.

DTFso. Dia. EE160. Lot No. 31030 Derby 1988–1989. 50/– 1T. (36 in six
compartments and 14 in one saloon). Public Telephone. 38.2 t.
TSO (A). Dia. EH288. Lot No. 31032 Derby 1988–1989. –/82 2T. 35.3 t.
MBRSM. Dia. ED268. Lot No. 31034 Derby 1988–1989. Modified Adtranz Crewe
1998. –/52 1W. 54.9 t.
TSO (B). Dia. EH289. Lot No. 31033 Derby 1988–1989. –/78 2T 1W. 35.4 t.
DTSO. Dia. EE273. Lot No. 31031 Derby 1988–1989. –/78 1T. 35.7 t.

2401	**SW**	A	*SW*	BM	77382	71818	62937	71842	77406
2402	**SW**	A	*SW*	BM	77383	71819	62938	71843	77407
2403	**SW**	A	*SW*	BM	77384	71820	62941	71844	77408
2404	**SW**	A	*SW*	BM	77385	71821	62939	71845	77409
2405	**SW**	A	*SW*	BM	77386	71822	62944	71846	77410
2406	**SW**	A	*SW*	BM	77389	71823	62942	71847	77411
2407	**SW**	A	*SW*	BM	77388	71824	62943	71848	77412
2408	**SW**	A	*SW*	BM	77387	71825	62945	71849	77413
2409	**SW**	A	*SW*	BM	77390	71826	62946	71850	77414
2410	**SW**	A	*SW*	BM	77391	71827	62948	71851	77415
2411	**SW**	A	*SW*	BM	77392	71828	62940	71858	77422
2412	**SW**	A	*SW*	BM	77393	71829	62947	71853	77417
2413	**SW**	A	*SW*	BM	77394	71830	62949	71854	77418
2414	**SW**	A	*SW*	BM	77395	71831	62950	71855	77419
2415	**SW**	A	*SW*	BM	77396	71832	62951	71856	77420
2416	**SW**	A	*SW*	BM	77397	71833	62952	71857	77421
2417	**SW**	A	*SW*	BM	77398	71834	62953	71852	77416
2418	**SW**	A	*SW*	BM	77399	71835	62954	71859	77423
2419	**SW**	A	*SW*	BM	77400	71836	62955	71860	77424
2420	**SW**	A	*SW*	BM	77401	71837	62956	71861	77425
2421	**SW**	A	*SW*	BM	77402	71838	62957	71862	77426
2422	**SW**	A	*SW*	BM	77403	71839	62958	71863	77427
2423	**SW**	A	*SW*	BM	77404	71840	62959	71864	77428
2424	**SW**	A	*SW*	BM	77405	71841	62960	71865	77429

Names (carried on MBRSM):

2401	BEAULIEU
2402	COUNTY OF HAMPSHIRE
2403	THE NEW FOREST
2404	BOROUGH OF WOKING

2405	CITY OF PORTSMOUTH
2406	VICTORY
2407	THOMAS HARDY
2408	COUNTY OF DORSET
2409	BOURNEMOUTH ORCHESTRAS
2410	MERIDIAN TONIGHT
2412	SPECIAL OLYMPICS
2415	MARY ROSE
2416	MUM IN A MILLION 1997, DOREEN SCANLON
2417	WOKING HOMES
2418	WESSEX CANCER TRUST
2419	BBC SOUTH TODAY
2420	CITY OF SOUTHAMPTON
2422	OPERATION OVERLORD
2423	COUNTY OF SURREY
2424	FATHER OF THE YEAR GERRY NEWSON

CLASS 444   DESIRO UK   SIEMENS

New 5-car express units for South West Trains.
Formation: DMCO–TSRMB–TSO–TSO–DMSO.
Construction: Aluminium. **Doors:** Single-leaf sliding plug.
Traction Motors: 4 Siemens 1TB2016-0GB02 asynchronous of 250 kW.
Gangways: Throughout. **Bogies:** SGP SF5000.
Couplers: Dellner 12. **Maximum Speed:** 100 m.p.h.
Seating Layout: 1: 2+1, 2: 2+2 mainly unidirectional.
Dimensions: 23.57 x 2.74 m.
Heating & Ventilation: Air conditioning.
Braking: Disc and rheostatic.
Multiple Working: Within class and with Class 450.

DMSO. Dia. EA2 . Siemens Wien 2002–2004. –/76. . t.
TSO. Dia. EH2 . Siemens Wien 2002–2004. –/76 1T. . t.
TSO. Dia. EH2 . Siemens Wien 2002–2004. –/76 1T. . t.
TSORMB. Dia. EH2 . Siemens Wien 2002–2004. –/47 2W 1T 1TD. . t.
DMCO. Dia. EA3 . Siemens Wien 2002–2004. 35/24. . t.

444 001	SW	A	63801	67101	67151	67201	63851
444 002	SW	A	63802	67102	67152	67202	63852
444 003	SW	A	63803	67103	67153	67203	63853
444 004	SW	A	63804	67104	67154	67204	63854
444 005	SW	A	63805	67105	67155	67205	63855
444 006	SW	A	63806	67106	67156	67206	63856
444 007	SW	A	63807	67107	67157	67207	63857
444 008	SW	A	63808	67108	67158	67208	63858
444 009	SW	A	63809	67109	67159	67209	63859
444 010	SW	A	63810	67110	67160	67210	63860
444 011	SW	A	63811	67111	67161	67211	63861
444 012	SW	A	63812	67112	67162	67212	63862
444 013	SW	A	63813	67113	67163	67213	63863
444 014	SW	A	63814	67114	67164	67214	63864
444 015	SW	A	63815	67115	67165	67215	63865

444 016	SW	A	63816	67116	67166	67216	63866
444 017	SW	A	63817	67117	67167	67217	63867
444 018	SW	A	63818	67118	67168	67218	63868
444 019	SW	A	63819	67119	67169	67219	63869
444 020	SW	A	63820	67120	67170	67220	63870
444 021	SW	A	63821	67121	67171	67221	63871
444 022	SW	A	63822	67122	67172	67222	63872
444 023	SW	A	63823	67123	67173	67223	63873
444 024	SW	A	63824	67124	67174	67224	63874
444 025	SW	A	63825	67125	67175	67225	63875
444 026	SW	A	63826	67126	67176	67226	63876
444 027	SW	A	63827	67127	67177	67227	63877
444 028	SW	A	63828	67128	67178	67228	63878
444 029	SW	A	63829	67129	67179	67229	63879
444 030	SW	A	63830	67130	67180	67230	63880
444 031	SW	A	63831	67131	67181	67231	63881
444 032	SW	A	63832	67132	67182	67232	63882
444 033	SW	A	63833	67133	67183	67233	63883
444 034	SW	A	63834	67134	67184	67234	63884
444 035	SW	A	63835	67135	67185	67235	63885
444 036	SW	A	63836	67136	67186	67236	63886
444 037	SW	A	63837	67137	67187	67237	63887
444 038	SW	A	63838	67138	67188	67238	63888
444 039	SW	A	63839	67139	67189	67239	63889
444 040	SW	A	63840	67140	67190	67240	63890
444 041	SW	A	63841	67141	67191	67241	63891
444 042	SW	A	63842	67142	67192	67242	63892
444 043	SW	A	63843	67143	67193	67243	63893
444 044	SW	A	63844	67144	67194	67244	63894
444 045	SW	A	63845	67145	67195	67245	63895

CLASS 450   DESIRO UK   SIEMENS

New 4-car and 5-car suburban units now being delivered for South West Trains.
Formations: Various.
Construction: Aluminium.   **Doors:** Sliding plug.
Traction Motors: 4 Siemens 1TB2016-0GB02 asynchronous of 250 kW.
Gangways: Throughout.   **Bogies:** SGP SF5000.
Couplers: Dellner 12.   **Maximum Speed:** 100 m.p.h.
Seating Layout: 1: 2+2, 2: 3+2 facing/unidirectional.
Dimensions: 20.40 x 2.79 m.
Heating & Ventilation: Air conditioning.
Braking: Disc and rheostatic.
Multiple Working: Within class and with Class 444.

Class 450/1   4-car units. DMSO–TCO–TSO–DMSO.

DMSO(A). Dia. EA291. Siemens Uerdingen/Wien 2002–2004. –/69. 46.0 t.
TCO. Dia. EH365. Siemens Uerdingen/Wien 2002–2004. 24/36 1T. 35.0 t.
TSO. Dia. EH200. Siemens Uerdingen/Wien 2002–2004. –/60 2W 1TD. 35.0 t.
DMSO(B). Dia. EA291. Siemens Uerdingen/Wien 2002–2004. –/69. 46.0 t.

450 001	**SD**	A		63201	64201	68101	63601
450 002	**SD**	A		63202	64202	68102	63602
450 003	**SD**	A		63203	64203	68103	63603
450 004	**SD**	A		63204	64204	68104	63604
450 005	**SD**	A		63205	64205	68105	63605
450 006	**SD**	A		63206	64206	68106	63606
450 007	**SD**	A		63207	64207	68107	63607
450 008	**SD**	A		63208	64208	68108	63608
450 009	**SD**	A		63209	64209	68109	63609
450 010	**SD**	A		63210	64210	68110	63610
450 011	**SD**	A		63211	64211	68111	63611
450 012	**SD**	A		63212	64212	68112	63612
450 013	**SD**	A		63213	64213	68113	63613
450 014	**SD**	A		63214	64214	68114	63614
450 015	**SD**	A		63215	64215	68115	63615
450 016	**SD**	A		63216	64216	68116	63616
450 017	**SD**	A		63217	64217	68117	63617
450 018	**SD**	A		63218	64218	68118	63618
450 019	**SD**	A		63219	64219	68119	63619
450 020	**SD**	A		63220	64220	68120	63620
450 021	**SD**	A		63221	64221	68121	63621
450 022	**SD**	A		63222	64222	68122	63622
450 023	**SD**	A		63223	64223	68123	63623
450 024	**SD**	A		63224	64224	68124	63624
450 025	**SD**	A		63225	64225	68125	63625
450 026	**SD**	A		63226	64226	68126	63626
450 027	**SD**	A		63227	64227	68127	63627
450 028	**SD**	A		63228	64228	68128	63628
450 029	**SD**	A		63229	64229	68129	63629
450 030	**SD**	A		63230	64230	68130	63630
450 031	**SD**	A		63231	64231	68131	63631
450 032	**SD**	A		63232	64232	68132	63632
450 033	**SD**	A		63233	64233	68133	63633
450 034	**SD**	A		63234	64234	68134	63634
450 035	**SD**	A		63235	64235	68135	63635
450 036	**SD**	A		63236	64236	68136	63636
450 037	**SD**	A		63237	64237	68137	63637
450 038	**SD**	A		63238	64238	68138	63638
450 039	**SD**	A		63239	64239	68139	63639
450 040	**SD**	A		63240	64240	68140	63640
450 041	**SD**	A		63241	64241	68141	63641
450 042	**SD**	A		63242	64242	68142	63642
450 043	**SD**	A		63243	64243	68143	63643
450 044	**SD**	A		63244	64244	68144	63644
450 045	**SD**	A		63245	64245	68145	63645
450 046	**SD**	A		63246	64246	68146	63646
450 047	**SD**	A		63247	64247	68147	63647
450 048	**SD**	A		63248	64248	68148	63648
450 049	**SD**	A		63249	64249	68149	63649
450 050	**SD**	A		63250	64250	68150	63650
450 051	**SD**	A		63251	64251	68151	63651

450 052	SD	A	63252	64252	68152	63652
450 053	SD	A	63253	64253	68153	63653
450 054	SD	A	63254	64254	68154	63654
450 055	SD	A	63255	64255	68155	63655
450 056	SD	A	63256	64256	68156	63656
450 057	SD	A	63257	64257	68157	63657
450 058	SD	A	63258	64258	68158	63658
450 059	SD	A	63259	64259	68159	63659
450 060	SD	A	63260	64260	68160	63660
450 061	SD	A	63261	64261	68161	63661
450 062	SD	A	63262	64262	68162	63662
450 063	SD	A	63263	64263	68163	63663
450 064	SD	A	63264	64264	68164	63664
450 065	SD	A	63265	64265	68165	63665
450 066	SD	A	63266	64266	68166	63666
450 067	SD	A	63267	64267	68167	63667
450 068	SD	A	63268	64268	68168	63668
450 069	SD	A	63269	64269	68169	63669
450 070	SD	A	63270	64270	68170	63670
450 071	SD	A	63271	64271	68171	63671
450 072	SD	A	63272	64272	68172	63672
450 073	SD	A	63273	64273	68173	63673
450 074	SD	A	63274	64274	68174	63674
450 075	SD	A	63275	64275	68175	63675
450 076	SD	A	63276	64276	68176	63676
450 077	SD	A	63277	64277	68177	63677
450 078	SD	A	63278	64278	68178	63678
450 079	SD	A	63279	64279	68179	63679
450 080	SD	A	63280	64280	68180	63680
450 081	SD	A	63281	64281	68181	63681
450 082	SD	A	63282	64282	68182	63682
450 083	SD	A	63283	64283	68183	63683
450 084	SD	A	63284	64284	68184	63684
450 085	SD	A	63285	64285	68185	63685
450 086	SD	A	63286	64286	68186	63686
450 087	SD	A	63287	64287	68187	63687
450 088	SD	A	63288	64288	68188	63688
450 089	SD	A	63289	64289	68189	63689
450 090	SD	A	63290	64290	68190	63690
450 091	SD	A	63291	64291	68191	63691
450 092	SD	A	63292	64292	68192	63692
450 093	SD	A	63293	64293	68193	63693
450 094	SD	A	63294	64294	68194	63694
450 095	SD	A	63295	64295	68195	63695
450 096	SD	A	63296	64296	68196	63696
450 097	SD	A	63297	64297	68197	63697
450 098	SD	A	63298	64298	68198	63698
450 099	SD	A	63299	64299	68199	63699
450 100	SD	A	63300	64300	68200	63700

Class 450/2 5-car units. DMSO–TSO–TSO–TSO–DMSO.

DMSO(A). Dia. EA2 . Siemens Uerdingen/Wien 2003–2004. –/69. . t.
TSO(A). Dia. EH2 . Siemens Uerdingen/Wien 2003–2004. –/82. . t.
TSO(B). Dia. EH2 . Siemens Uerdingen/Wien 2003–2004. –/78 1T. . t.
TSO(C). Dia. EH2 . Siemens Uerdingen/Wien 2003–2004. –/68 2W 1TD. . t.
DMSO(B). Dia. EA2 . Siemens Uerdingen/Wien 2003–2004. –/69. . t.

450 201	**SD**	A	63701	66801	66851	66901	63751
450 202	**SD**	A	63702	66802	66852	66902	63752
450 203	**SD**	A	63703	66803	66853	66903	63753
450 204	**SD**	A	63704	66804	66854	66904	63754
450 205	**SD**	A	63705	66805	66855	66905	63755
450 206	**SD**	A	63706	66806	66856	66906	63756
450 207	**SD**	A	63707	66807	66857	66907	63757
450 208	**SD**	A	63708	66808	66858	66908	63758
450 209	**SD**	A	63709	66809	66859	66909	63759
450 210	**SD**	A	63710	66810	66860	66910	63760
450 211	**SD**	A	63711	66811	66861	66911	63761
450 212	**SD**	A	63712	66812	66862	66912	63762
450 213	**SD**	A	63713	66813	66863	66913	63763
450 214	**SD**	A	63714	66814	66864	66914	63764
450 215	**SD**	A	63715	66815	66865	66915	63765
450 216	**SD**	A	63716	66816	66866	66916	63766
450 217	**SD**	A	63717	66817	66867	66917	63767
450 218	**SD**	A	63718	66818	66868	66918	63768
450 219	**SD**	A	63719	66819	66869	66919	63769
450 220	**SD**	A	63720	66820	66870	66920	63770
450 221	**SD**	A	63721	66821	66871	66921	63771
450 222	**SD**	A	63722	66822	66872	66922	63772
450 223	**SD**	A	63723	66823	66873	66923	63773
450 224	**SD**	A	63724	66824	66874	66924	63774
450 225	**SD**	A	63725	66825	66875	66925	63775
450 226	**SD**	A	63726	66826	66876	66926	63776
450 227	**SD**	A	63727	66827	66877	66927	63777
450 228	**SD**	A	63728	66828	66878	66928	63778
450 229	**SD**	A	63729	66829	66879	66929	63779
450 230	**SD**	A	63730	66830	66880	66930	63780
450 231	**SD**	A	63731	66831	66881	66931	63781
450 232	**SD**	A	63732	66832	66882	66932	63782

CLASS 455   BR YORK

South West Trains/South Central inner suburban units.

Formation: DTSO–MSO–TSO–DTSO.
Construction: Steel. Class 455/7 TSOs have a steel underframe with an aluminium alloy body & roof.
Doors: Sliding.
Gangways: Throughout.   **Electrical Equipment:** 1966-type.
Traction Motors: Four GEC507-20J of 185 kW.
Couplers: Tightlock.

Bogies: P7 (motor) and T3 (455/8 & 455/9) BX1 (455/7) trailer.
Maximum Speed: 75 m.p.h.   **Seating Layout:** 3+2 facing.
Dimensions: 20.18 x 2.82 m.   **Braking:** Disc brakes.
Heating & Ventilation: Various
Multiple Working: Within class and with Class 456.

Class 455/7. Second series with TSOs originally in Class 508. Pressure heating and ventilation.

DTSO. Dia. EE218. Lot No. 30976 1984–1985. –/74. 29.5 t.
MSO. Dia. EC203. Lot No. 30975 1984–1985. –/84. 45 t.
TSO. Dia. EH219. Lot No. 30944 1977–1980. –/86. 25.48 t.

5701	ST	P	SW	WD	77727	62783	71545	77728
5702	N	P	SW	WD	77729	62784	71547	77730
5703	ST	P	SW	WD	77731	62785	71540	77732
5704	ST	P	SW	WD	77733	62786	71548	77734
5705	N	P	SW	WD	77735	62787	71565	77736
5706	N	P	SW	WD	77737	62788	71534	77738
5707	N	P	SW	WD	77739	62789	71536	77740
5708	N	P	SW	WD	77741	62790	71560	77742
5709	N	P	SW	WD	77743	62791	71532	77744
5710	N	P	SW	WD	77745	62792	71566	77746
5711	N	P	SW	WD	77747	62793	71542	77748
5712	N	P	SW	WD	77749	62794	71546	77750
5713	ST	P	SW	WD	77751	62795	71567	77752
5714	ST	P	SW	WD	77753	62796	71539	77754
5715	ST	P	SW	WD	77755	62797	71535	77756
5716	ST	P	SW	WD	77757	62798	71564	77758
5717	N	P	SW	WD	77759	62799	71528	77760
5718	N	P	SW	WD	77761	62800	71557	77762
5719	ST	P	SW	WD	77763	62801	71558	77764
5720	ST	P	SW	WD	77765	62802	71568	77766
5721	ST	P	SW	WD	77767	62803	71553	77768
5722	ST	P	SW	WD	77769	62804	71533	77770
5723	ST	P	SW	WD	77771	62805	71526	77772
5724	ST	P	SW	WD	77773	62806	71561	77774
5725	ST	P	SW	WD	77775	62807	71541	77776
5726	ST	P	SW	WD	77777	62808	71556	77778
5727	ST	P	SW	WD	77779	62809	71562	77780
5728	ST	P	SW	WD	77781	62810	71527	77782
5729	ST	P	SW	WD	77783	62811	71550	77784
5730	ST	P	SW	WD	77785	62812	71551	77786
5731	ST	P	SW	WD	77787	62813	71555	77788
5732	ST	P	SW	WD	77789	62814	71552	77790
5733	ST	P	SW	WD	77791	62815	71549	77792
5734	ST	P	SW	WD	77793	62816	71531	77794
5735	ST	P	SW	WD	77795	62817	71563	77796
5736	ST	P	SW	WD	77797	62818	71554	77798
5737	ST	P	SW	WD	77799	62819	71544	77800
5738	ST	P	SW	WD	77801	62820	71529	77802
5739	ST	P	SW	WD	77803	62821	71537	77804

5740	**ST**	P	*SW*	WD	77805	62822	71530	77806
5741	**ST**	P	*SW*	WD	77807	62823	71559	77808
5742	**ST**	P	*SW*	WD	77809	62824	71543	77810
5750	**ST**	P	*SW*	WD	77811	62825	71538	77812

Names (carried on TSO):

5711	SPIRIT OF RUGBY
5731	VARIETY CLUB
5735	The Royal Borough of Kingston
5750	Wimbledon Train Care

Class 455/8. First series. Pressure heating and ventilation.

DTSO. Dia. EE218. Lot No. 30972 York 1982–1984. –/74. 29.5 t.
MSO. Dia. EC203. Lot No. 30973 York 1982–1984. –/84. 45.6 t.
TSO. Dia. EH221. Lot No. 30974 York 1982–1984. –/84. 27.1 t.

Advertising liveries:

5853 Cotes du Rhone wine (All over deep red with various images).
5856 Legoland Windsor (Yellow, blue and red with various images).
5860, 5870 South West Trains days out – "You really should get out more" (Blue and red with various images).
5864 Old Royal British Legion poppy appeal (grey with poppy images).
5868 Golden Jubilee/Hampton Court Palace (Gold with various images).
5869 New Royal British Legion poppy appeal (white with poppy images).

5801	**N**	H	*SC*	SU	77579	62709	71637	77580
5802	**CX**	H	*SC*	SU	77581	62710	71664	77582
5803	**CX**	H	*SC*	SU	77583	62711	71639	77584
5804	**CX**	H	*SC*	SU	77585	62712	71640	77586
5805	**CX**	H	*SC*	SU	77587	62713	71641	77588
5806	**CX**	H	*SC*	SU	77589	62714	71642	77590
5807	**CX**	H	*SC*	SU	77591	62715	71643	77592
455 808	**SN**	H	*SC*	SU	77593	62716	71644	77594
455 809	**SN**	H	*SC*	SU	77595	62717	71645	77596
5810	**CX**	H	*SC*	SU	77597	62718	71646	77598
5811	**CX**	H	*SC*	SU	77599	62719	71647	77600
455 812	**SN**	H	*SC*	SU	77601	62720	71648	77602
5813	**N**	H	*SC*	SU	77603	62721	71649	77604
5814	**CX**	H	*SC*	SU	77605	62722	71650	77606
5815	**CX**	H	*SC*	SU	77607	62723	71651	77608
5816	**N**	H	*SC*	SU	77609	62724	71652	77633
5817	**N**	H	*SC*	SU	77611	62725	71653	77612
5818	**CX**	H	*SC*	SU	77613	62726	71654	77614
455 819	**SN**	H	*SC*	SU	77615	62727	71655	77616
5820	**CX**	H	*SC*	SU	77617	62728	71656	77618
5821	**CX**	H	*SC*	SU	77619	62729	71657	77620
5822	**CX**	H	*SC*	SU	77621	62730	71658	77622
5823	**N**	H	*SC*	SU	77623	62731	71659	77624
455 824	**SN**	H	*SC*	SU	77637	62732	71660	77626
455 825	**SN**	H	*SC*	SU	77627	62733	71661	77628
5826	**N**	H	*SC*	SU	77629	62734	71662	77630

5827	CX	H	*SC*	SU	77610	62735	71663	77632
5828	N	H	*SC*	SU	77631	62736	71638	77634
5829	N	H	*SC*	SU	77635	62737	71665	77636
5830	N	H	*SC*	SU	77625	62743	71666	77638
5831	N	H	*SC*	SU	77639	62739	71667	77640
5832	U	H	*SC*	SU	77641	62740	71668	77642
455 833	SN	H	*SC*	SU	77643	62741	71669	77644
5834	N	H	*SC*	SU	77645	62742	71670	77646
455 835	SN	H	*SC*	SU	77647	62738	71671	77648
5836	N	H	*SC*	SU	77649	62744	71672	77650
5837	N	H	*SC*	SU	77651	62745	71673	77652
455 838	SN	H	*SC*	SU	77653	62746	71674	77654
5839	N	H	*SC*	SU	77655	62747	71675	77656
5840	N	H	*SC*	SU	77657	62748	71676	77658
455 841	SN	H	*SC*	SU	77659	62749	71677	77660
5842	N	H	*SC*	SU	77661	62750	71678	77662
5843	N	H	*SC*	SU	77663	62751	71679	77664
5844	N	H	*SC*	SU	77665	62752	71680	77666
5845	N	H	*SC*	SU	77667	62753	71681	77668
5846	N	H	*SC*	SU	77669	62754	71682	77670
5847	ST	P	*SW*	WD	77671	62755	71683	77672
5848	ST	P	*SW*	WD	77673	62756	71684	77674
5849	ST	P	*SW*	WD	77675	62757	71685	77676
5850	ST	P	*SW*	WD	77677	62758	71686	77678
5851	ST	P	*SW*	WD	77679	62759	71687	77680
5852	ST	P	*SW*	WD	77681	62760	71688	77682
5853	AL	P	*SW*	WD	77683	62761	71689	77684
5854	ST	P	*SW*	WD	77685	62762	71690	77686
5855	ST	P	*SW*	WD	77687	62763	71691	77688
5856	AL	P	*SW*	WD	77689	62764	71692	77690
5857	ST	P	*SW*	WD	77691	62765	71693	77692
5858	ST	P	*SW*	WD	77693	62766	71694	77694
5859	ST	P	*SW*	WD	77695	62767	71695	77696
5860	AL	P	*SW*	WD	77697	62768	71696	77698
5861	ST	P	*SW*	WD	77699	62769	71697	77700
5862	ST	P	*SW*	WD	77701	62770	71698	77702
5863	N	P	*SW*	WD	77703	62771	71699	77704
5864	AL	P	*SW*	WD	77705	62772	71700	77706
5865	ST	P	*SW*	WD	77707	62773	71701	77708
5866	N	P	*SW*	WD	77709	62774	71702	77710
5867	ST	P	*SW*	WD	77711	62775	71703	77712
5868	AL	P	*SW*	WD	77713	62776	71704	77714
5869	AL	P	*SW*	WD	77715	62777	71705	77716
5870	AL	P	*SW*	WD	77717	62778	71706	77718
5871	N	P	*SW*	WD	77719	62779	71707	77720
5872	ST	P	*SW*	WD	77721	62780	71708	77722
5873	N	P	*SW*	WD	77723	62781	71709	77724
5874	ST	P	*SW*	WD	77725	62782	71710	77726

Class 455/9. Third series. Convection heating.

DTSO. Dia. EE226. Lot No. 30991 York 1985. –/74. 29.5 t.
MSO. Dia. EC206. Lot No. 30992 York 1985. –/84. 45.6 t.
TSO. Dia. EH224. Lot No. 30993 York 1985. –/84. 27.1 t.
TSO †. Dia. EH236. Lot No. 30932 Derby 1981. –/84. 27.1 t.

Note: † Prototype vehicle (67400) converted from a Class 210 DEMU.

Advertising livery:

5904 South West Trains days out – "You really should get out more"
(Blue and red with various images).

5901		**ST**	P	*SW*	WD	77813	62826	71714	77814
5902		**ST**	P	*SW*	WD	77815	62827	71715	77816
5903		**ST**	P	*SW*	WD	77817	62828	71716	77818
5904		**AL**	P	*SW*	WD	77819	62829	71717	77820
5905		**ST**	P	*SW*	WD	77821	62830	71725	77822
5906		**ST**	P	*SW*	WD	77823	62831	71719	77824
5907		**ST**	P	*SW*	WD	77825	62832	71720	77826
5908		**ST**	P	*SW*	WD	77827	62833	71721	77828
5909		**ST**	P	*SW*	WD	77829	62834	71722	77830
5910		**ST**	P	*SW*	WD	77831	62835	71723	77832
5911		**ST**	P	*SW*	WD	77833	62836	71724	77834
5912	†	**ST**	P	*SW*	WD	77835	62837	67400	77836
5913		**ST**	P	*SW*	WD	77837	62838	71726	77838
5914		**ST**	P	*SW*	WD	77839	62839	71727	77840
5915		**ST**	P	*SW*	WD	77841	62840	71728	77842
5916		**ST**	P	*SW*	WD	77843	62841	71729	77844
5917		**ST**	P	*SW*	WD	77845	62842	71730	77846
5918		**ST**	P	*SW*	WD	77847	62843	71732	77848
5919		**ST**	P	*SW*	WD	77849	62844	71718	77850
5920		**N**	P	*SW*	WD	77851	62845	71733	77852
Spare		**ST**	P		ZG			71731	

CLASS 456   BREL YORK

South Central inner suburban units.

Formation: DMSO–DTSO.
Construction: Steel underframe, aluminium alloy body & roof.
Doors: Sliding.
Gangways: Within unit.   **Electrical Equipment:** 1966-type.
Traction Motors: Two GEC507-20J of 185 kW.
Bogies: P7 (motor) and T3 (trailer).   **Couplers:** Tightlock.
Maximum Speed: 75 m.p.h.   **Seating Layout:** 3+2 facing.
Dimensions: 20.18 x 2.82 m.   **Braking:** Disc brakes.
Heating & Ventilation: Convection.
Multiple Working: Within class and with Class 455.

DMSO. Dia. EA267. Lot No. 31073 1990–1991. –/79. 41.1 t.
DTSO. Dia. EE276. Lot No. 31074 1990–1991. –/73 1T. 31.4 t.

456 001	N	P	SC	SU	64735	78250
456 002	N	P	SC	SU	64736	78251
456 003	N	P	SC	SU	64737	78252
456 004	N	P	SC	SU	64738	78253
456 005	N	P	SC	SU	64739	78254
456 006	N	P	SC	SU	64740	78255
456 007	N	P	SC	SU	64741	78256
456 008	N	P	SC	SU	64742	78257
456 009	N	P	SC	SU	64743	78258
456 010	N	P	SC	SU	64744	78259
456 011	N	P	SC	SU	64745	78260
456 012	N	P	SC	SU	64746	78261
456 013	N	P	SC	SU	64747	78262
456 014	N	P	SC	SU	64748	78263
456 015	N	P	SC	SU	64749	78264
456 016	N	P	SC	SU	64750	78265
456 017	N	P	SC	SU	64751	78266
456 018	N	P	SC	SU	64752	78267
456 019	N	P	SC	SU	64753	78268
456 020	N	P	SC	SU	64754	78269
456 021	N	P	SC	SU	64755	78270
456 022	N	P	SC	SU	64756	78271
456 023	N	P	SC	SU	64757	78272
456 024	CX	P	SC	SU	64758	78273

Name (carried on DTSO): 456 024 Sir Cosmo Bonsor.

CLASS 458   JUNIPER   ALSTOM BIRMINGHAM

Formation: DMCO(A)–PTSO–MSO–DMCO(B).
SR designation: 4 Jop.
Construction: Steel.
Gangways: Throughout.
Seating Layout: 1: 2+2 facing, 2: 3+2 facing/unidirectional.
Traction Motors: Two Alstom ONIX 800 of 270 kW.
Couplers: Scharfenberg.
Maximum Speed: 100 m.p.h.
Dimensions: 21.01 x 2.82 m.
Heating & Ventilation: Air conditioning.

Doors: Sliding plug.
Electrical Equipment: IGBT control.

Bogies: ACR.
Braking: Disc and regenerative brakes.
Multiple Working: Within class.

DMCO(A). Dia. EA302. 1998–2000. 12/63. 45.2 t.
PTSO. Dia. EH250. 1998–2000. –/49 1TD 2W. 33.3 t.
MSO. Dia. EC226. 1998–2000. –/75 1T. 40.6 t.
DMCO(B). Dia. EA303. 1998–2000. 12/63. 45.2 t.

8001	SW	P			67601	74001	74101	67701
8002	SW	P	SW	WD	67602	74002	74102	67702
8003	SW	P			67603	74003	74103	67703
8004	SW	P	SW	WD	67604	74004	74104	67704
8005	SW	P	SW	WD	67605	74005	74105	67705
8006	SW	P	SW	WD	67606	74006	74106	67706
8007	SW	P	SW	WD	67607	74007	74107	67707

8008	**SW**	P	*SW*	WD	67608	74008	74108	67708
8009	**SW**	P	*SW*	WD	67609	74009	74109	67709
8010	**SW**	P	*SW*	WD	67610	74010	74110	67710
8011	**SW**	P	*SW*	WD	67611	74011	74111	67711
8012	**SW**	P	*SW*	WD	67612	74012	74112	67712
8013	**SW**	P	*SW*	WD	67613	74013	74113	67713
8014	**SW**	P	*SW*	WD	67614	74014	74114	67714
8015	**SW**	P	*SW*	WD	67615	74015	74115	67715
8016	**SW**	P	*SW*	WD	67616	74016	74116	67716
8017	**SW**	P	*SW*	WD	67617	74017	74117	67717
8018	**SW**	P	*SW*	WD	67618	74018	74118	67718
8019	**SW**	P	*SW*	WD	67619	74019	74119	67719
8020	**SW**	P	*SW*	WD	67620	74020	74120	67720
8021	**SW**	P	*SW*	WD	67621	74021	74121	67721
8022	**SW**	P	*SW*	WD	67622	74022	74122	67722
8023	**SW**	P	*SW*	WD	67623	74023	74123	67723
8024	**SW**	P	*SW*	WD	67624	74024	74124	67724
8025	**SW**	P	*SW*	WD	67625	74025	74125	67725
8026	**SW**	P	*SW*	WD	67626	74026	74126	67726
8027	**SW**	P	*SW*	WD	67627	74027	74127	67727
8028	**SW**	P	*SW*	WD	67628	74028	74128	67728
8029	**SW**	P	*SW*	WD	67629	74029	74129	67729
8030	**SW**	P			67630	74030	74130	67730

CLASS 460   GEC-ALSTHOM JUNIPER

Gatwick Express units.

Formation: DMLFO–TFO–TCO–2MSO–TSO–MSO–DMSO.
SR designation: 8 Gat.
Construction: Steel.
Gangways: Within unit.
Traction Motors: Two Alstom ONIX 800 of 270 kW.
Couplers: Scharfenberg.
Maximum Speed: 100 m.p.h.
Doors: Sliding plug.
Electrical Equipment: IGBT control.
Bogies: ACR.
Seating Layout: 1: 2+1 facing, 2: 2+2 facing/unidirectional.
Dimensions: 21.0 m/19.9 m x 2.82 m. **Braking:** Disc and regenerative brakes.
Heating & Ventilation: Air conditioning. **Multiple Working:** Within class.

DMLFO. Dia. EA101. 2000–2001. 10/– 42.6 t.
TFO. Dia. EH161 2000–2001. 28/– 1TD 1W. 33.5 t.
TCO. Dia. EH364 2000–2001. 9/42 1T. 34.9 t.
MSO(A). Dia. EC227 2000–2001. –/60. 42.5 t.
MSO(B). Dia. EC228 2000–2001. –/60. 42.5 t.
TSO. Dia. EH251 2000–2001. –/38 1TD 1W. 35.2 t.
MSO(C). Dia. EC229 2000–2001. –/60. 40.5 t.
DMSO. Dia. EA274 2000–2001. –/56. 45.3 t.

460 001	**GV**	P	*GX*	SL	67901	74401	74411	74421
					74431	74441	74451	67911
460 002	**GV**	P	*GX*	SL	67902	74402	74412	74422
					74432	74442	74452	67912

460 003	**GV**	P	*GX*	SL	67903	74403	74413	74423
					74433	74443	74453	67913
460 004	**GV**	P	*GX*	SL	67904	74404	74414	74424
					74434	74444	74454	67914
460 005	**GV**	P	*GX*	SL	67905	74405	74415	74425
					74435	74445	74455	67915
460 006	**GV**	P	*GX*	SL	67906	74406	74416	74426
					74436	74446	74456	67916
460 007	**GV**	P	*GX*	SL	67907	74407	74417	74427
					74437	74447	74457	67917
460 008	**GV**	P	*GX*	SL	67908	74408	74418	74428
					74438	74448	74458	67918

CLASS 465   NETWORKER

Formation: DMSO–TSO–TSO–DMSO.
Construction: Welded aluminium alloy.
Doors: Sliding plug.   **Couplers:** Tightlock.
Gangways: Within unit.   **Electrical Equipment:** GTO inverters.
Traction Motors: Four Brush TIM970 (Classes 465/0 and 465/1) or GEC-Alsthom
G352AY (Class 465/2) three-phase induction motors of 280 kW.
Bogies: BREL P3/T3 (Classes 465/0 and 465/1) SRP BP62/BT52 (Class 465/2).
Maximum Speed: 75 m.p.h.   **Dimensions:** 20.89/20.16 x 2.82 m.
Seating Layout: 3+2 (* 2+2) facing/unidirectional.
Braking: Disc, rheostatic and regenerative.
Multiple Working: Within class and with Classes 365 and 466.

64759–64808. DMSO(A). Dia. EA268. Lot No. 31100 BREL York 1991–1993.
–/86 (* –/74). 38.9 t.
64809–64858. DMSO(B). Dia. EA268. Lot No. 31100 BREL York 1991–1993.
–/86 (* –/74). 39 t.
65700–65749. DMSO(A). Dia. EA269. Lot No. 31103 Metro-Cammell 1991–1993.
–/86. 38.8 t.
65750–65799. DMSO(B). Dia. EA269. Lot No. 31103 Metro-Cammell 1991–1993.
–/86. 38.9 t.
65800–65846. DMSO(A). Dia. EA268. Lot No. 31130 ABB York 1993–1994.
–/86. 38.9 t.
65847–65893. DMSO(B). Dia. EA268. Lot No. 31130 ABB York 1993–1994.
–/86. 39 t.
72028–72126 (even Nos.). TSO. Dia. EH293. Lot No. 31102 BREL York 1991–
1993. –/90 (* –/80). 29.5 t.
72029–72127 (odd Nos.). TSO. Dia. EH292. Lot No. 31101 BREL York 1991–
1993. –/86 1T (* –/76 1T). 28.6 t.
72719–72817 (odd Nos.). TSO. Dia. EH294. Lot No. 31104 Metro-Cammell
1991–1992. –/86 1T. 30.2 t.
72720–72818 (even Nos.). TSO. Dia. EH295. Lot No. 31105 Metro-Cammell
1991–1992. –/90. 29.1 t.
72900–72992 (even Nos.). TSO. Dia. EH293. Lot No. 31102 ABB York 1993–1994.
–/90. 29.5 t.
72901–72993 (odd Nos.). TSO. Dia. EH294. Lot No. 31101 ABB York 1993–
1994. –/86 1T. 28.6 t.

▲ First Great Eastern expects to withdraw most of its Class 312s when all the new "Desiros" are delivered. On 15/07/02 312 722 passes through the Essex countryside near Jacques Hall with the 10.46 Manningtree–Harwich Town.　　**Alan Sargeant**

▼ 313 115 is seen in the attractive Silverlink livery at West Hampstead on the North London line with the 14.44 Richmond–North Woolwich on 25/09/02.
Robert Pritchard

▲ WAGN are currently painting their 313, 315 and 317 fleets into their new purple livery. On 02/02/02 315 861 pauses at Bethnal Green with a Liverpool Street–Chingford service. **David Cable**

▼ On 08/11/02 dedicated Stansted Express Class 317 No. 317 719 passes through Bethnal Green with the 12.15 Liverpool Street–Stansted Airport. **Alan Yearsley**

▲ Strathclyde PTE liveried 318 261 waits at Milngavie on 26/08/02 with the 13.52 to Lanark. **Murdoch Currie**

▼ Thameslink liveried 319 455 and 319 439 pass Copyhold Junction, Haywards Heath with a Bedford–Brighton service on 01/06/02. **Hector Denman**

▲ 320 318 stands at Dalmuir on 04/09/01 with a service to Bellgrove via Airdrie.
Hugh Ballantyne

▼ First Great Eastern liveried 321 341 passes Shenfield on 28/07/02 with the 11.20 Ipswich–London Liverpool Street.
Iain Scotchman

▲ Newly painted into First Group corporate livery, 323 235 approaches Stockport with the 14.55 Manchester Piccadilly–Hazel Grove on 23/08/02.   **Alan Sherratt**

▼ Half of Arriva's Class 333s were strengthened to 4-car units in 2002 with the remainder to be completed in 2003. Here 333 005 pauses at Keighley with the 14.48 Bradford Forster Square–Skipton on 04/08/02.   **Robert Pritchard**

On 10/09/02 332 001 and 332 012 pass Southall with the 09.55 Heathrow Terminal 4–London Paddington. The front driving car of the front unit carries an advertising livery for the Royal Bank of Scotland.

Alex Dasi-Sutton

▲ A pair of Class 334 units led by 334 017 pause at Irvine on 21/07/02 with the 16.30 Glasgow Central–Ayr. **Tom Heavyside**

▼ All Class 357s are now in service with c2c and are in the new livery. On 25/09/02 357 210 pauses at Tilbury Town with the 12.50 London Fenchurch Street–Southend Central. **Robert Pritchard**

Govia South Central liveried 375 325 and 375 333 (to be renumbered in the Class 377 number range) are seen near Coldwaltham with a Lovers Walk (Brighton)–Dorking test run on 16/08/02.

Chris Wilson

▲ Virgin West Coast's new Class 390 "Pendolino" fleet are expected to enter service on all West Coast routes during 2003. Here 390 001 "Virgin Pioneer" passes Penrith with a test train. **Bob Sweet**

▼ Class 411/5 (4 Cep) unit 1612 in Stagecoach livery leaves Basingstoke with a Waterloo service on 23/06/01. **Jonathan Allen**

▲ Class 421/3 (4 Cig) unit 1321 leaves Egham on 21/06/01 with a Reading–Ascot service. **Jason Rogers**

▼ Class 423 (4 Vep) unit 3420 is seen at Guildford with the 14.22 to Waterloo on 13/09/02. **Colin Scott-Morton**

▲ South West Trains liveried Class 442s Nos. 2405 and 2401 pass Raynes Park with the 07.20 Wareham–Waterloo on 04/09/02. **Alex Dasi-Sutton**

▼ New South West Trains "Desiro" Class 450 450 001 at its launch at the Wildenrath test centre, Germany on 24/04/02. **Peter Fox**

▲ Class 455/9 No. 5904 in South West Trains advertising livery arrives at Clapham Junction with the 12.27 Windsor & Eton Riverside–Waterloo on 04/04/02.
Andy Flowers

▼ Class 458 "Juniper" No. 8017 passes Worting Junction with a Basingstoke–Eastleigh test train on 23/04/02.
Anthony Kay

Connex South Eastern liveried 466 002 leads an NSE liveried Class 465 past Swanley
with the 09.13 Blackfriars–Sevenoaks on 14/08/02.   **Alex Dasi-Sutton**

▲ Class 460 No. 460 002 is seen near Coulsdon with the 15.30 Victoria–Gatwick Airport Gatwick Express working on 16/04/02. **Anthony Kay**

▼ Ex-London Underground stock is still in use on Island line. Here 483 004 in "Dinosaur" livery leaves Ryde Esplanade with a Shanklin–Ryde Pier Head service on 15/07/02. **Martyn Hilbert**

▲ New Merseyrail liveried 507 003 calls at Ainsdale on 23/09/02 with a Hunts Cross–Southport service. **Martyn Hilbert**

▼ Railtrack liveried Sandite/De-icing unit No. 930 203 passes Chelsfield on 12/10/01. **Rodney Lissenden**

Regional Eurostar set 3314/3313 passes Otford Jn. on a test run from North Pole depot to Dolland's Moor on 13/09/02.
Chris Wilson

Class 465/0. Built by BREL/ABB.

465 001	**CB**	H	*SE*	SG	64759	72028	72029	64809
465 002	**CB**	H	*SE*	SG	64760	72030	72031	64810
465 003	**CB**	H	*SE*	SG	64761	72032	72033	64811
465 004	**NT**	H	*SE*	SG	64762	72034	72035	64812
465 005	**NT**	H	*SE*	SG	64763	72036	72037	64813
465 006	**CB**	H	*SE*	SG	64764	72038	72039	64814
465 007	**CB**	H	*SE*	SG	64765	72040	72041	64815
465 008	**CB**	H	*SE*	SG	64766	72042	72043	64816
465 009	**CB**	H	*SE*	SG	64767	72044	72045	64817
465 010	**CB**	H	*SE*	SG	64768	72046	72047	64818
465 011	**CB**	H	*SE*	SG	64769	72048	72049	64819
465 012	**CB**	H	*SE*	SG	64770	72050	72051	64820
465 013	**CB**	H	*SE*	SG	64771	72052	72053	64821
465 014	* **CB**	H	*SE*	SG	64772	72054	72055	64822
465 015	**CB**	H	*SE*	SG	64773	72056	72057	64823
465 016	**CB**	H	*SE*	SG	64774	72058	72059	64824
465 017	**CB**	H	*SE*	SG	64775	72060	72061	64825
465 018	**CB**	H	*SE*	SG	64776	72062	72063	64826
465 019	**CB**	H	*SE*	SG	64777	72064	72065	64827
465 020	**CB**	H	*SE*	SG	64778	72066	72067	64828
465 021	**NT**	H	*SE*	SG	64779	72068	72069	64829
465 022	**NT**	H	*SE*	SG	64780	72070	72071	64830
465 023	**NT**	H	*SE*	SG	64781	72072	72073	64831
465 024	**NT**	H	*SE*	SG	64782	72074	72075	64832
465 025	**NT**	H	*SE*	SG	64783	72076	72077	64833
465 026	**NT**	H	*SE*	SG	64784	72078	72079	64834
465 027	**NT**	H	*SE*	SG	64785	72080	72081	64835
465 028	**NT**	H	*SE*	SG	64786	72082	72083	64836
465 029	**NT**	H	*SE*	SG	64787	72084	72085	64837
465 030	**NT**	H	*SE*	SG	64788	72086	72087	64838
465 031	**NT**	H	*SE*	SG	64789	72088	72089	64839
465 032	**NT**	H	*SE*	SG	64790	72090	72091	64840
465 033	**NT**	H	*SE*	SG	64791	72092	72093	64841
465 034	**NT**	H	*SE*	SG	64792	72094	72095	64842
465 035	**NT**	H	*SE*	SG	64793	72096	72097	64843
465 036	**NT**	H	*SE*	SG	64794	72098	72099	64844
465 037	**NT**	H	*SE*	SG	64795	72100	72101	64845
465 038	**NT**	H	*SE*	SG	64796	72102	72103	64846
465 039	**NT**	H	*SE*	SG	64797	72104	72105	64847
465 040	**NT**	H	*SE*	SG	64798	72106	72107	64848
465 041	**NT**	H	*SE*	SG	64799	72108	72109	64849
465 042	**NT**	H	*SE*	SG	64800	72110	72111	64850
465 043	**NT**	H	*SE*	SG	64801	72112	72113	64851
465 044	**NT**	H	*SE*	SG	64802	72114	72115	64852
465 045	**NT**	H	*SE*	SG	64803	72116	72117	64853
465 046	**NT**	H	*SE*	SG	64804	72118	72119	64854
465 047	**NT**	H	*SE*	SG	64805	72120	72121	64855
465 048	**NT**	H	*SE*	SG	64806	72122	72123	64856
465 049	**NT**	H	*SE*	SG	64807	72124	72125	64857
465 050	**NT**	H	*SE*	SG	64808	72126	72127	64858

Class 465/1. Built by BREL/ABB. Similar to Class 465/0 but with detail differences.

465 151	**NT**	H	*SE*	SG	65800	72900	72901	65847
465 152	**NT**	H	*SE*	SG	65801	72902	72903	65848
465 153	**NT**	H	*SE*	SG	65802	72904	72905	65849
465 154	**NT**	H	*SE*	SG	65803	72906	72907	65850
465 155	**NT**	H	*SE*	SG	65804	72908	72909	65851
465 156	**NT**	H	*SE*	SG	65805	72910	72911	65852
465 157	**NT**	H	*SE*	SG	65806	72912	72913	65853
465 158	**NT**	H	*SE*	SG	65807	72914	72915	65854
465 159	**NT**	H	*SE*	SG	65808	72916	72917	65855
465 160	**NT**	H	*SE*	SG	65809	72918	72919	65856
465 161	**NT**	H	*SE*	SG	65810	72920	72921	65857
465 162	**NT**	H	*SE*	SG	65811	72922	72923	65858
465 163	**NT**	H	*SE*	SG	65812	72924	72925	65859
465 164	**NT**	H	*SE*	SG	65813	72926	72927	65860
465 165	**NT**	H	*SE*	SG	65814	72928	72929	65861
465 166	**NT**	H	*SE*	SG	65815	72930	72931	65862
465 167	**NT**	H	*SE*	SG	65816	72932	72933	65863
465 168	**NT**	H	*SE*	SG	65817	72934	72935	65864
465 169	**NT**	H	*SE*	SG	65818	72936	72937	65865
465 170	**NT**	H	*SE*	SG	65819	72938	72939	65866
465 171	**NT**	H	*SE*	SG	65820	72940	72941	65867
465 172	**NT**	H	*SE*	SG	65821	72942	72943	65868
465 173	**NT**	H	*SE*	SG	65822	72944	72945	65869
465 174	**NT**	H	*SE*	SG	65823	72946	72947	65870
465 175	**NT**	H	*SE*	SG	65824	72948	72949	65871
465 176	**NT**	H	*SE*	SG	65825	72950	72951	65872
465 177	**NT**	H	*SE*	SG	65826	72952	72953	65873
465 178	**NT**	H	*SE*	SG	65827	72954	72955	65874
465 179	**NT**	H	*SE*	SG	65828	72956	72957	65875
465 180	**NT**	H	*SE*	SG	65829	72958	72959	65876
465 181	**NT**	H	*SE*	SG	65830	72960	72961	65877
465 182	**NT**	H	*SE*	SG	65831	72962	72963	65878
465 183	**NT**	H	*SE*	SG	65832	72964	72965	65879
465 184	**NT**	H	*SE*	SG	65833	72966	72967	65880
465 185	**NT**	H	*SE*	SG	65834	72968	72969	65881
465 186	**NT**	H	*SE*	SG	65835	72970	72971	65882
465 187	**NT**	H	*SE*	SG	65836	72972	72973	65883
465 188	**NT**	H	*SE*	SG	65837	72974	72975	65884
465 189	**NT**	H	*SE*	SG	65838	72976	72977	65885
465 190	**NT**	H	*SE*	SG	65839	72978	72979	65886
465 191	**NT**	H	*SE*	SG	65840	72980	72981	65887
465 192	**NT**	H	*SE*	SG	65841	72982	72983	65888
465 193	**NT**	H	*SE*	SG	65842	72984	72985	65889
465 194	**NT**	H	*SE*	SG	65843	72986	72987	65890
465 195	**NT**	H	*SE*	SG	65844	72988	72989	65891
465 196	**NT**	H	*SE*	SG	65845	72990	72991	65892
465 197	**NT**	H	*SE*	SG	65846	72992	72993	65893

Class 465/2. Built by Metro-Cammell.

465 201	**NT**	A	*SE*	SG	65700	72719	72720	65750
465 202	**NT**	A	*SE*	SG	65701	72721	72722	65751
465 203	**NT**	A	*SE*	SG	65702	72723	72724	65752
465 204	**NT**	A	*SE*	SG	65703	72725	72726	65753
465 205	**NT**	A	*SE*	SG	65704	72727	72728	65754
465 206	**CN**	A	*SE*	SG	65705	72729	72730	65755
465 207	**CN**	A	*SE*	SG	65706	72731	72732	65756
465 208	**NT**	A	*SE*	SG	65707	72733	72734	65757
465 209	**NT**	A	*SE*	SG	65708	72735	72736	65758
465 210	**NT**	A	*SE*	SG	65709	72737	72738	65759
465 211	**NT**	A	*SE*	SG	65710	72739	72740	65760
465 212	**NT**	A	*SE*	SG	65711	72741	72742	65761
465 213	**CN**	A	*SE*	SG	65712	72743	72744	65762
465 214	**NT**	A	*SE*	SG	65713	72745	72746	65763
465 215	**NT**	A	*SE*	SG	65714	72747	72748	65764
465 216	**CN**	A	*SE*	SG	65715	72749	72750	65765
465 217	**NT**	A	*SE*	SG	65716	72751	72752	65766
465 218	**NT**	A	*SE*	SG	65717	72753	72754	65767
465 219	**NT**	A	*SE*	SG	65718	72755	72756	65768
465 220	**NT**	A	*SE*	SG	65719	72757	72758	65769
465 221	**NT**	A	*SE*	SG	65720	72759	72760	65770
465 222	**NT**	A	*SE*	SG	65721	72761	72762	65771
465 223	**NT**	A	*SE*	SG	65722	72763	72764	65772
465 224	**CN**	A	*SE*	SG	65723	72765	72766	65773
465 225	**NT**	A	*SE*	SG	65724	72767	72768	65774
465 226	**NT**	A	*SE*	SG	65725	72769	72770	65775
465 227	**NT**	A	*SE*	SG	65726	72771	72772	65776
465 228	**NT**	A	*SE*	SG	65727	72773	72774	65777
465 229	**NT**	A	*SE*	SG	65728	72775	72776	65778
465 230	**NT**	A	*SE*	SG	65729	72777	72778	65779
465 231	**NT**	A	*SE*	SG	65730	72779	72780	65780
465 232	**NT**	A	*SE*	SG	65731	72781	72782	65781
465 233	**NT**	A	*SE*	SG	65732	72783	72784	65782
465 234	**NT**	A	*SE*	SG	65733	72785	72786	65783
465 235	**CN**	A	*SE*	SG	65734	72787	72788	65784
465 236	**NT**	A	*SE*	SG	65735	72789	72790	65785
465 237	**CN**	A	*SE*	SG	65736	72791	72792	65786
465 238	**NT**	A	*SE*	SG	65737	72793	72794	65787
465 239	**NT**	A	*SE*	SG	65738	72795	72796	65788
465 240	**CN**	A	*SE*	SG	65739	72797	72798	65789
465 241	**CN**	A	*SE*	SG	65740	72799	72800	65790
465 242	**NT**	A	*SE*	SG	65741	72801	72802	65791
465 243	**CN**	A	*SE*	SG	65742	72803	72804	65792
465 244	**NT**	A	*SE*	SG	65743	72805	72806	65793
465 245	**NT**	A	*SE*	SG	65744	72807	72808	65794
465 246	**NT**	A	*SE*	SG	65745	72809	72810	65795
465 247	**NT**	A	*SE*	SG	65746	72811	72812	65796
465 248	**NT**	A	*SE*	SG	65747	72813	72814	65797
465 249	**NT**	A	*SE*	SG	65748	72815	72816	65798
465 250	**NT**	A	*SE*	SG	65749	72817	72818	65799

CLASS 466   NETWORKER   GEC-ALSTHOM

Formation: DMSO–DTSO.
Construction: Welded aluminium alloy.
Doors: Sliding plug.
Gangways: Within unit.   **Electrical Equipment:** GTO inverters.
Traction Motors: Four GEC-Alsthom G352AY three-phase induction motors of 280 kW.
Couplers: Tightlock.   **Bogies:** SRP BP62/BT52.
Maximum Speed: 75 m.p.h.   **Dimensions:** 20.89 x 2.82 m.
Seating Layout: 3+2 (* 2+2) facing/unidirectional.
Braking: Disc, rheostatic and regenerative.
Multiple Working: Within class and with Classes 365 and 465.

DMSO. Dia. EA271. Lot No. 31128 Birmingham 1993–1994. –/86 (* –72). 38.8 t.
DTSO. Dia. EE279. Lot No. 31129 Birmingham 1993–1994. –/82 1T (* –/68 1T). 33.2 t.

466 001	NT	A	SE	SG	64860	78312
466 002	CN	A	SE	SG	64861	78313
466 003	CN	A	SE	SG	64862	78314
466 004	CN	A	SE	SG	64863	78315
466 005	CN	A	SE	SG	64864	78316
466 006	CN	A	SE	SG	64865	78317
466 007	CN	A	SE	SG	64866	78318
466 008	NT	A	SE	SG	64867	78319
466 009	NT	A	SE	SG	64868	78320
466 010	NT	A	SE	SG	64869	78321
466 011	NT	A	SE	SG	64870	78322
466 012	NT	A	SE	SG	64871	78323
466 013	NT	A	SE	SG	64872	78324
466 014	NT	A	SE	SG	64873	78325
466 015	NT	A	SE	SG	64874	78326
466 016	NT	A	SE	SG	64875	78327
466 017 *	NT	A	SE	SG	64876	78328
466 018	CN	A	SE	SG	64877	78329
466 019	NT	A	SE	SG	64878	78330
466 020	CN	A	SE	SG	64879	78331
466 021	CN	A	SE	SG	64880	78332
466 022	CN	A	SE	SG	64881	78333
466 023	CN	A	SE	SG	64882	78334
466 024	NT	A	SE	SG	64883	78335
466 025	CN	A	SE	SG	64884	78336
466 026	NT	A	SE	SG	64885	78337
466 027	NT	A	SE	SG	64886	78338
466 028	NT	A	SE	SG	64887	78339
466 029	NT	A	SE	SG	64888	78340
466 030	NT	A	SE	SG	64889	78341
466 031	NT	A	SE	SG	64890	78342
466 032	NT	A	SE	SG	64891	78343
466 033	CN	A	SE	SG	64892	78344
466 034	CN	A	SE	SG	64893	78345

466 035	**CN**	A	*SE*	SG	64894	78346
466 036	**NT**	A	*SE*	SG	64895	78347
466 037	**CN**	A	*SE*	SG	64896	78348
466 038	**NT**	A	*SE*	SG	64897	78349
466 039	**NT**	A	*SE*	SG	64898	78350
466 040	**NT**	A	*SE*	SG	64899	78351
466 041	**NT**	A	*SE*	SG	64900	78352
466 042	**NT**	A	*SE*	SG	64901	78353
466 043	**NT**	A	*SE*	SG	64902	78354

CLASS 483   METRO-CAMMELL

Built 1938 onwards for LTE. Converted 1989–1990 for Isle of Wight Line.

Formation: DMSO(A)–DMSO(B).
System: 660 V DC third rail.
Construction: Steel.
Gangways: None. End doors.
Doors: Sliding.
Electrical Equipment: IGBT control.
Traction Motors: Two Crompton Parkinson/GEC/BTH LT100 of 125 kW.
Couplers: Wedglock.
Bogies: LT design.
Maximum Speed: 45 m.p.h.
Seating Layout: Longitudinal.
Dimensions: 16.00 x 2.69 m.
Braking: Tread brakes.
Multiple Working: Within class.
Notes: The last three numbers of the unit number only are carried.
Former London Underground numbers are shown in parentheses.

DMSO (A). Lot No. 31071. Dia. EA265. –/42. 27.5 t.
DMSO (B). Lot No. 31072. Dia. EA266. –/42. 27.5 t.

Non-standard livery: 483 007 is original London Transport Maroon and cream.

483 002	**IL**	H	*IL*	RY	122	(10221)	225	(11142)
483 003	**N**	H		RY	123	(10116)	221	(11184)
483 004	**IL**	H	*IL*	RY	124	(10205)	224	(11205)
483 006	**IL**	H	*IL*	RY	126	(10297)	226	(11297)
483 007	**O**	H	*IL*	RY	127	(10291)	227	(11291)
483 008	**IL**	H	*IL*	RY	128	(10255)	228	(11255)
483 009	**IL**	H	*IL*	RY	129	(10289)	229	(11229)

CLASS 488   BR DERBY

Converted 1983–1984 from Mk. 2F FOs and TSOs for Victoria–Gatwick services.
The seating layout was modified with and the removal of one toilet to provide
additional luggage space. The position with these vehicles is in a state of flux
with many stored out of use. Two sets were still in use as this book closed for
press, covering for non-available Class 460s.

Formation: TFOH–TSO (Class 488/3 only)–TSOH.
Construction: Steel.
Gangways: Throughout.
Bogies: B4.
Doors: Slam.
Couplers: Buckeye.
Maximum Speed: 90 m.p.h.
Seating Layout: 1: 2+1 facing, 2: 2+2 facing.

Dimensions: 20.18 x 2.82 m. **Braking:** Tread brakes.
Heating & Ventilation: Air conditioning.
Multiple Working: SR.

72500–72509. TFOH. Dia. EP101. Lot No. 30859 Derby 1973–1974. 41/– 1T. 35 t.
72602–72614/72616–72618/72620–72644/72646/72647. TSOH. Dia. EP202. Lot No. 30860 Derby 1973–1974. –/48 1T. 35 t.
72615/72619/72645. TSOH. Dia. EP202. Lot No. 30846 Derby 1973. –/48 1T. 35 t.
72701–72718. TSO. Dia. EH285. Lot No. 30860 Derby 1973–1974. –/48 1T. 35 t.

Note: Vehicles 72630 and 72631 from set 8316 are regularly used in the Network Rail Ultrasonic Test Train.

Advertising livery: As **GX** but with a deep blue instead of a white lower bodyside, advertising Continental Airlines.

CLASS 488/2. TFOH–TSOH. Note: TFOH fitted with public telephone.

8201	**GX**	GB		PY	72500 (3413)	72638 (6068)	
8202	**GX**	P	*GX*	SL	72501 (3382)	72617 (6086)	
8203	**AL**	NR		ZA	72502 (3321)	72640 (6097)	
8204	**RK**	NR	*SO*	ZA	72503 (3407)	72641 (6079)	
8205	**GX**	P		ZG	72504 (3406)	72628 (6058)	
8206	**GX**	P	*GX*	SL	72505 (3415)	72629 (6048)	
8207	**AL**	P		PY	72506 (3335)	72642 (6076)	
8208	**AL**	GB		PY	72507 (3412)	72643 (6040)	
8209	**GX**	P	*GX*	SL	72508 (3409)	72644 (6039)	
8210	**AL**	P		PY	72509 (3398)	72635 (6128)	

CLASS 488/3. TSOH–TSO–TSOH.

8302	**GX**	P	*GX*	SL	72602 (6130)	72701 (6088)	72604 (6087)
8303	**GX**	NR		ZA	72603 (6093)	72702 (6099)	72608 (6077)
8304	**AL**	P		PY	72606 (6084)	72703 (6075)	72611 (6083)
8306	**GX**	P		PY	72607 (6020)	72705 (6032)	72610 (6074)
8307	**RK**	NR	*SO*	ZA	72612 (6156)	72706 (6143)	72613 (6126)
8308	**RK**	NR	*SO*	ZA	72614 (6090)	72707 (6127)	72615 (5938)
8309	**RK**	NR	*SO*	ZA	72616 (6007)	72708 (6095)	72639 (6070)
8310	**AL**	P		PY	72618 (6044)	72709 (5982)	72619 (5909)
8311	**GX**	P	*GX*	SL	72620 (6140)	72710 (6003)	72621 (6108)
8312	**GX**	GB		PY	72622 (6004)	72711 (6109)	72623 (6118)
8313	**GX**	P	*GX*	SL	72624 (5972)	72712 (6091)	72625 (6085)
8315	**GX**	GB		PY	72636 (6071)	72714 (6092)	72645 (5942)
8316	**RK**	NR	*SO*	ZA	72630 (6094)	72715 (6019)	72631 (6096)
8317	**GX**	P		PY	72632 (6072)	72716 (6114)	72633 (6129)
Spare	**AL**	CD		MM		72704 (6132)	
Spare	**AL**	CD		MM		72713 (6023)	
Spare	**GX**	CD		MM		72717 (6069)	
Spare	**AL**	CD		MM		72718 (5979)	

CLASS 489 BR EASTLEIGH

Converted 1983–1984 from Class 414/3 (2 Hap) DMBSOs to work with Class 488.

Formation: DMLV.
Construction: Steel.
Gangways: Gangwayed at inner end only.
Traction Motors: Two EE507 of 185 kW.
Bogies: Mark 4.
Dimensions: 20.45 x 2.82 m.
Multiple Working: SR.

Doors: Slam.
Electrical Equipment: 1966-type.
Couplers: Buckeye.
Maximum Speed: 90 m.p.h.
Braking: Tread brakes.

DMLV. Dia. EB501. Lot No. 30452 1959. 40.5 t.

9101	GX	P		PY	68500	(61269)
9102	GX	NR		ZA	68501	(61281)
9103	GX	P		ZG	68502	(61274)
9104	GX	P	GX	SL	68503	(61277)
9105	GX	GB		PY	68504	(61286)
9106	GX	GB		PY	68505	(61299)
9107	GX	P		PY	68506	(61292)
9108	GX	P	GX	SL	68507	(61267)
9109	GX	NR		ZA	68508	(61272)
9110	GX	P	GX	SL	68509	(61280)

CLASS 507 BREL YORK

Formation: BDMSO–TSO–DMSO.
System: 750 V DC third rail.
Traction Motors: Four GEC G310AZ of 82.125 kW.
Construction: Steel underframe, aluminium alloy body and roof.
Doors: Sliding.
Gangways: Within unit + end doors.
Couplers: Tightlock
Seating Layout: 3+2 facing.
Braking: Disc and rheostatic.
Multiple Working: Within class and with Class 508.

Bogies: BX1.
Maximum Speed: 75 m.p.h.
Dimensions: 20.18 x 2.82 m.

BDMSO. Dia. EI202. Lot No. 30906 1978–1980. –/68. 37.06 t.
TSO. Dia. EH205. Lot No. 30907 1978–1980. –/86. 25.60 t.
DMSO. Dia. EA201. Lot No. 30908 1978–1980. –/68. 35.62 t.

507 001	MT	A	ME	BD	64367	71342	64405
507 002	MT	A	ME	BD	64368	71343	64406
507 003	MY	A	ME	BD	64369	71344	64407
507 004	MY	A	ME	BD	64388	71345	64408
507 005	MY	A	ME	BD	64371	71346	64409
507 006	MY	A	ME	BD	64372	71347	64410
507 007	MT	A	ME	BD	64373	71348	64411
507 008	MY	A	ME	BD	64374	71349	64412
507 009	MY	A	ME	BD	64375	71350	64413
507 010	MT	A	ME	BD	64376	71351	64414

507 011	MT	A	ME	BD	64377	71352	64415
507 012	MY	A	ME	BD	64378	71353	64416
507 013	MY	A	ME	BD	64379	71354	64417
507 014	MT	A	ME	BD	64380	71355	64418
507 015	MT	A	ME	BD	64381	71356	64419
507 016	MT	A	ME	BD	64382	71357	64420
507 017	MT	A	ME	BD	64383	71358	64421
507 018	MT	A	ME	BD	64384	71359	64422
507 019	MT	A	ME	BD	64385	71360	64423
507 020	MT	A	ME	BD	64386	71361	64424
507 021	MY	A	ME	BD	64387	71362	64425
507 023	MT	A	ME	BD	64389	71364	64427
507 024	MY	A	ME	BD	64390	71365	64428
507 025	MY	A	ME	BD	64391	71366	64429
507 026	MY	A	ME	BD	64392	71367	64430
507 027	MT	A	ME	BD	64393	71368	64431
507 028	MT	A	ME	BD	64394	71369	64432
507 029	MT	A	ME	BD	64395	71370	64433
507 030	MT	A	ME	BD	64396	71371	64434
507 031	MT	A	ME	BD	64397	71372	64435
507 032	MY	A	ME	BD	64398	71373	64436
507 033	MT	A	ME	BD	64399	71374	64437

CLASS 508   BREL YORK

Formation: DMSO–TSO–BDMSO.
System: 750 V DC third rail.
Traction Motors: Four GEC G310AZ of 82.125 kW.
Construction: Steel underframe, aluminium alloy body and roof.
Doors: Sliding.
Gangways: Within unit + end doors.   **Bogies:** BX1.
Couplers: Tightlock.   **Maximum Speed:** 75 m.p.h.
Seating Layout: 3+2 facing.   **Dimensions:** 20.18 x 2.82 m.
Braking: Disc and rheostatic.
Multiple Working: Within class and with Class 507.

DMSO. Dia. EA208. Lot No. 30979 1979–1980. –/68. 36.2 t.
TSO. Dia. EH218. Lot No. 30980 1979–1980. –/86. 26.7 t.
BDMSO. Dia. EI203. Lot No. 30981 1979–1980. –/68. 36.6 t.

Class 508/1. Standard design.

Note: Units currently shown as stored out of use at Alstom, Eastleigh (ZG) are
being refurbished for Arriva Trains Merseyside.

508 103	MT	A	ME	BD	64651	71485	64694
508 104	MT	A	ME	BD	64652	71486	64695
508 108	MT	A		ZG	64656	71490	64699
508 110	MT	A		ZG	64658	71492	64701
508 111	MY	A	ME	BD	64659	71493	64702
508 112	MT	A	ME	BD	64660	71494	64703
508 114	MT	A	ME	BD	64662	71496	64705

508 115	**MY**	A	*ME*	BD	64663	71497	64706
508 117	**MY**	A	*ME*	BD	64665	71499	64708
508 120	**MT**	A		ZG	64668	71502	64711
508 122	**MT**	A		ZG	64670	71504	64713
508 124	**MT**	A	*ME*	BD	64672	71506	64715
508 125	**MT**	A	*ME*	BD	64673	71507	64716
508 126	**MT**	A	*ME*	BD	64674	71508	64717
508 127	**MY**	A	*ME*	BD	64675	71509	64718
508 128	**MY**	A	*ME*	BD	64676	71510	64719
508 130	**MT**	A	*ME*	BD	64678	71512	64721
508 131	**MT**	A		ZG	64679	71513	64722
508 134	**MT**	A	*ME*	BD	64682	71516	64725
508 136	**MT**	A	*ME*	BD	64684	71518	64727
508 137	**MT**	A	*ME*	BD	64685	71519	64728
508 138	**MY**	A	*ME*	BD	64686	71520	64729
508 139	**MT**	A	*ME*	BD	64687	71521	64730
508 140	**MT**	A	*ME*	BD	64688	71522	64731
508 141	**MT**	A	*ME*	BD	64689	71523	64732
508 143	**MT**	A	*ME*	BD	64691	71525	64734
Spare	**MY**	A		ZA	64671		
Spare	**MT**	A		KT		71505	64714

Class 508/2. Facelifted Connex South Eastern units. Refurbished 1998–1999 by Wessex Traincare/Alstom, Eastleigh.

DMSO. Dia. EA211. Lot No. 30979 1979–1980. –/66. 36.2 t.
TSO. Dia. EH246. Lot No. 30980 1979–1980. –/79. 26.7 t.
BDMSO. Dia. EI204. Lot No. 30981 1979–1980. –/74. 36.6 t.

508 201	(508 101)	**CX**	A	*SE*	GI	64649	71483	64692
508 202	(508 105)	**CX**	A	*SE*	GI	64653	71487	64696
508 203	(508 106)	**CX**	A	SE	GI	64654	71488	64697
508 204	(508 107)	**CX**	A	*SE*	GI	64655	71489	64698
508 205	(508 109)	**CX**	A	*SE*	GI	64657	71491	64700
508 206	(508 113)	**CX**	A	*SE*	GI	64661	71495	64704
508 207	(508 116)	**CX**	A	*SE*	GI	64664	71498	64707
508 208	(508 119)	**CX**	A	*SE*	GI	64667	71501	64710
508 209	(508 121)	**CX**	A	*SE*	GI	64669	71503	64712
508 210	(508 129)	**CX**	A	*SE*	GI	64677	71511	64720
508 211	(508 132)	**CX**	A	*SE*	GI	64680	71514	64723
508 212	(508 133)	**CX**	A	*SE*	GI	64681	71515	64724

Class 508/3. Facelifted units for Silverlink for use on Euston–Watford Junction services. Refurbished 2002–2003 by Alstom, Eastleigh. Details as Class 508/1.

508 301	(508 102)	**SL**	A	*SL*	WN	64650	71484	64693
508 302	(508 135)	**SL**	A	*SL*	WN	64683	71517	64726
508 303	(508 142)	**SL**	A	*SL*	WN	64690	71524	64733

4.3. EUROSTAR UNITS (CLASS 373)

Eurostar units were built for and are normally used on services between Britain and Continental Europe via the Channel Tunnel. Apart from such workings units may be used as follows:
• SNCF-owned units 3203/3204/3225/3226/3227/3228 have been removed from the Eurostar pool, and are in a pool which normally only operate SNCF-internal services between Paris and Lille.
• Certain 8-car sets are used on a daily basis by GNER for its "White Rose" services.

Each train consists of two Eurostar units coupled, with a motor car at each driving end. Services starting from/terminating at London Waterloo International are formed of two 10-car units coupled, whilst those to/from other British destinations (yet to commence) will be formed of two 8-car units coupled. All units are articulated with an extra motor bogie on the coach adjacent to the motor car.

DM–MSO–4TSO–RB–2TFO–TBFO or DM–MSO–3TSO–RB–TFO–TBFO.
Gangwayed within pair of units. Air conditioned.
Construction: Steel.
Supply Systems: 25 kV AC 50 Hz overhead or 3000 V DC overhead or 750 V DC third rail (* also equipped for 1500 V DC overhead operation).
Wheel Arrangement: Bo–Bo + Bo–2–2–2–2–2–2–2–2–2.
Length: 22.15 m (DM), 21.85 m (MS & TBF), 18.70 m (other cars).
Maximum Speed: 300 km/h.
Built: 1992-1993 by GEC-Alsthom/Brush/ANF/De Dietrich/BN Construction/ACEC.
Note: DM vehicles carry the set numbers indicated below.

10-Car Sets. Built for services starting from/terminating at London Waterloo. Individual vehicles in each set are allocated numbers 373xxx0 + 373xxx1 + 373xxx2 + 373xxx3 + 373xxx4 + 373xxx5 + 373xxx6 + 373xxx8 + 373xxx9, where 3xxx denotes the set number.

Non-standard Livery: 0 – grey with silver ends, TGV symbol and green or blue doors.
AL – Sets 373011 and 373012 have adverts for "Cafe Noir" on the buffet car vehicles.

373xxx0 series. DM. Dia. LA501. Lot No. 31118 1992–1995. 68.5 t.
373xxx1 series. MS. Dia. LB202. Lot No. 31119 1992–1995. –/48 2T. 44.6 t.
373xxx2 series. TS. Dia. LC202. Lot No. 31120 1992–1995. –/58 1T. 28.1 t.
373xxx3 series. TS. Dia. LD202. Lot No. 31121 1992–1995. –/58 2T. 29.7 t.
373xxx4 series. TS. Dia. LE202. Lot No. 31122 1992–1995. –/58 1T. 28.3 t.
373xxx5 series. TS. Dia. LF202. Lot No. 31123 1992–1995. –/58 2T. 29.2 t.
373xxx6 series. RB. Dia. LG502. Lot No.31124 1992–1995. 31.1 t.
373xxx7 series. TF. Dia. LH102. Lot No. 31125 1992–1995. 39/– 1T. 29.6 t.
373xxx8 series. TF. Dia. LJ102. Lot No. 31126 1992–1995. 39/– 1T. 32.2 t.
373xxx9 series.TBF. Dia. LK102. Lot No. 31127 1992–1995. 25/– 1TD. 39.4 t.

3001	**EU**	EU	*EU*	NP		3006	**EU**	EU	*EU*	NP
3002	**EU**	EU	*EU*	NP		3007	**EU**	EU	*EU*	NP
3003	**EU**	EU	*EU*	NP		3008	**EU**	EU	*EU*	NP
3004	**EU**	EU	*EU*	NP		3009	**EU**	EU	*EU*	NP
3005	**EU**	EU	*EU*	NP		3010	**EU**	EU	*EU*	NP

3011	**AL**	EU	*EU*	NP	3207*	**EU**	SF	*EU*	LY
3012	**AL**	EU	*EU*	NP	3208*	**EU**	SF	*EU*	LY
3013	**EU**	EU	*EU*	NP	3209*	**EU**	SF	*EU*	LY
3014	**EU**	EU	*EU*	NP	3210*	**EU**	SF	*EU*	LY
3015	**EU**	EU	*EU*	NP	3211	**EU**	SF	*EU*	LY
3016	**EU**	EU	*EU*	NP	3212	**EU**	SF	*EU*	LY
3017	**EU**	EU	*EU*	NP	3213	**EU**	SF	*EU*	LY
3018	**EU**	EU	*EU*	NP	3214	**EU**	SF	*EU*	LY
3019	**EU**	EU	*EU*	NP	3215*	**EU**	SF	*EU*	LY
3020	**EU**	EU	*EU*	NP	3216*	**EU**	SF	*EU*	LY
3021	**EU**	EU	*EU*	NP	3217	**EU**	SF	*EU*	LY
3022	**EU**	EU	*EU*	NP	3218	**EU**	SF	*EU*	LY
3101	**EU**	SB	*EU*	FF	3219	**EU**	SF	*EU*	LY
3102	**EU**	SB	*EU*	FF	3220	**EU**	SF	*EU*	LY
3103	**EU**	SB	*EU*	FF	3221	**EU**	SF	*EU*	LY
3104	**EU**	SB	*EU*	FF	3222	**EU**	SF	*EU*	LY
3105	**EU**	SB	*EU*	FF	3223*	**EU**	SF	*EU*	LY
3106	**EU**	SB	*EU*	FF	3224*	**EU**	SF	*EU*	LY
3107	**EU**	SB	*EU*	FF	3225*	**0**	SF	*EU*	LY
3108	**EU**	SB	*EU*	FF	3226*	**0**	SF	*EU*	LY
3201 *	**EU**	SF	*EU*	LY	3227*	**0**	SF	*EU*	LY
3202 *	**EU**	SF	*EU*	LY	3228*	**0**	SF	*EU*	LY
3203 *	**0**	SF	*EU*	LY	3229*	**EU**	SF	*EU*	LY
3204 *	**0**	SF	*EU*	LY	3230*	**EU**	SF	*EU*	LY
3205	**EU**	SF	*EU*	LY	3231	**EU**	SF	*EU*	LY
3206	**EU**	SF	*EU*	LY	3232	**EU**	SF	*EU*	LY

8-Car Sets. Built for Regional Eurostar services. Individual vehicles in each set are allocated numbers 373xxx0 + 373xxx1 + 373xxx3 + 373xxx2 + 373xxx5 + 373xxx6 + 373xxx7 + 373xxx9, where 3xxx denotes the set number.

3733xx0 series. DM. Dia. LA502. 68.5 t.
3733xx1 series. MS. Dia. LB203. –/48 1T. 44.6 t.
3733xx3 series. TS. Dia. LD203. –/58 2T. 29.7 t.
3733xx2 series. TS. Dia. LC203. –/58 1T. 28.1 t.
3733xx5 series. TS. Dia. LF203. –/58 1T. 29.2 t.
3733xx6 series. RB. Dia. LG503. 31.1 t.
3733xx7 series. TF. Dia. LH103. 39/– 1T. 29.6 t.
3733xx9 series. TBF. Dia. LK103. 18/– 1TD. 39.4 t.

3301	**GN**	EU	*GN*	NP		3308	**EU**	EU		NP
3302	**GN**	EU	*GN*	NP		3309	**EU**	EU	*GN*	NP
3303	**GN**	EU	*GN*	NP The White Rose		3310	**EU**	EU	*GN*	NP
3304	**GN**	EU	*GN*	NP The White Rose		3311	**EU**	EU	*GN*	NP
3305	**GN**	EU	*GN*	NP		3312	**EU**	EU	*GN*	NP
3306	**GN**	EU	*GN*	NP Golden Jubilee		3313	**EU**	EU		NP
3307	**EU**	EU		NP		3314	**EU**	EU		NP

Spare DM:

3999	**EU**	EU		NP

4.4. SERVICE UNITS

CLASS 930/0   SANDITE/DE-ICING UNIT

Converted from Class 405.

Formation: DMB–DMB.
Supply System: 750 V DC third rail.
Traction Motors: Two English Electric 507 of 185 kW.
Construction: Steel.   **Doors:** Slam.
Gangways: Within unit.   **Bogies:** Central 43 inch.
Couplers: Buckeye.   **Maximum Speed:** 75 m.p.h.
Braking: Tread brakes.   **Dimensions:** 19.05 x 2.74 m.
Multiple Working: SR type.

977586/587/604/605. DMB. Dia. EZ512. Lot No. 3231 Southern Railway
   Eastleigh 1947. 39.0 t.
975588/589/592/595/597–600/602/603. DMB. Dia. EZ512 Lot No. 1060.
   Southern Railway Eastleigh 1941. 39.0 t.
975590/591/596/601. DMB. Dia. EZ512. Lot No. 3384 Eastleigh 1948. 39.0 t.
975593/594. DMB. Dia. EZ512. Lot No. 3618 Eastleigh 1950. 39.0 t.
975896/897. DMB. Dia. EZ512. Lot No. 3506 Eastleigh 1950. 39.0 t.

930 002	**RK**	NR	*SE*	RM	975896	(11387)	975897	(11388)
930 003	**RO**	NR	*SC*	SU	975594	(12658)	975595	(10994)
930 004	**RO**	NR	*SW*	WD	975586	(10907)	975587	(10908)
930 005	**RK**	NR	*SW*	WD	975588	(10981)	975589	(10982)
930 006	**RO**	NR	*SW*	WD	975590	(10833)	975591	(10834)
930 007	**RO**	NR	*SE*	GI	975592	(10993)	975593	(12659)
930 008	**RK**	NR	*SE*	GI	975596	(10844)	975597	(10987)
930 009	**RK**	NR		DY	975604	(10939)	975599	(10990)
930 010	**RK**	NR		DY	975600	(10988)	975601	(10843)
930 011	**RK**	NR	*SC*	SU	975602	(10991)	975603	(10992)
Spare	**RO**	NR		AF(S)	975598	(10989)	975605	(10940)

CLASS 930/0   ROUTE LEARNING UNIT

Converted from Class 411/4.

Formation: DM–TB–DM.
Supply System: 750 V DC third rail.
Traction Motors: Two English Electric 507 of 185 kW.
Construction: Steel.   **Doors:** Slam.
Gangways: Within unit.   **Bogies:** Mk. 4/Commonwealth.
Couplers: Buckeye.   **Maximum Speed:** 90 m.p.h.
Braking: Tread brakes.   **Dimensions:** 20.34 x 2.82 m.
Multiple Working: SR type.

977861. DM. Dia. EZ536. Lot No. 30111 Eastleigh 1956. 44.2 t.
977862. TB. Dia. EZ542. Lot No. 30110 Eastleigh 1956. 36.2 t.
977863. DM. Dia. EZ536. Lot No. 30108 Eastleigh 1956. 43.5 t.

930 082	**CX**	SC	*SC*	SU	977861	(61044)	977862	(70039)
					977863	(61038)		

CLASS 930/1   TRACTOR UNIT

Converted from Class 416/2.

Formation: DMB–DMB.
Supply System: 750 V DC third rail.
Traction Motors: Two English Electric 507 of 185 kW.
Construction: Steel.   **Doors:** Slam.
Gangways: Within unit.   **Bogies:** Mk. 4 and Mk. 3B/Commonwealth.
Couplers: Buckeye.   **Maximum Speed:** 90 m.p.h.
Braking: Tread brakes.   **Dimensions:** 20.42 x 2.82 m.
Multiple Working: SR type.

977207. DMB. Dia. EZ522. Lot No. 30388 Eastleigh 1958. 40.5 t.
977609. DMB. Dia. EZ522. Lot No. 30617 Eastleigh 1961. 40.5 t.

930 101	**N**	NR		AF	977207	(65414)	977609	(61658)

CLASS 930/1   SANDITE UNIT

Converted from Class 416.

Formation: DMB–DMB.
Supply System: 750 V DC third rail.
Traction Motors: Two English Electric 507 of 185 kW.
Construction: Steel.   **Doors:** Slam.
Gangways: Within unit.   **Bogies:** Central 40 inch.
Couplers: Buckeye.   **Maximum Speed:** 75 m.p.h.
Braking: Tread brakes.   **Dimensions:** 19.23 x 2.74 m.
Multiple Working: SR type.

977533. DMB. Dia. EZ512. Lot No. 4016 Eastleigh 1954–55. 40.5 t.
977534. DMB. Dia. EZ512. Lot No. 4099 Eastleigh 1955–56. 40.5 t.

930 102	**RK**	NR	*SW*	FR	977533	(14273)	977534	(14384)

CLASS 930/2   SANDITE/DE-ICING UNIT

Converted from Class 416/2.

Formation: DMB–DMB.
Supply System: 750 V DC third rail.
Traction Motors: Two English Electric 507 of 185 kW.
Construction: Steel.   **Doors:** Slam.
Gangways: Within unit.   **Bogies:** Mk. 3B.
Couplers: Buckeye.   **Maximum Speed:** 75 m.p.h.
Braking: Tread brakes.   **Dimensions:** 20.44 x 2.82 m.
Multiple Working: SR type.

977566/567. DMB. Dia. EZ525. Lot No. 30116 Eastleigh 1954–55. 40.5 t.
977804/864. DMB. Dia. EZ522. Lot No. 30119 Eastleigh 1954. 40.5 t.
977805/865/871. DMB. Dia. EZ522. Lot No. 30167 Eastleigh 1955. 40.5 t.

977872/924/925. DMB. Dia. EZ522. Lot. No. 30314. Eastleigh 1956–58. 40.5 t.
977874/875. DMB. Dia. EZ522. Lot No. 30114 Eastleigh 1954. 40.5 t.

930 201	**RK**	NR	*SW*	FR	977566	(65312)	977567	(65314)
930 202	**RK**	NR	*SW*	FR	977804	(65336)	977805	(65357)
930 203	**RK**	NR	*SE*	RM	977864	(65341)	977865	(65355)
930 204	**RK**	NR	*SE*	RM	977874	(65302)	977875	(65304)
930 205	**RO**	NR	*SE*	RM	977871	(65353)	977872	(65367)
930 206	**RO**	NR	*SW*	WD	977924	(65382)	977925	(65379)

CLASS 931   ROUTE LEARNING UNIT

DT–DMB or DMB–DT. Gangwayed within unit. Converted from Class 416/2.

Construction: Steel.
Supply System: 750 V DC third rail.
Traction Motors: Two English Electric 507 of 185 kW each.
Dimensions: 20.44 x 2.82 x 3.86 m. **Doors:** Manually operated slam.
Maximum Speed: 75 m.p.h. **Bogies:** Mk. 3B.
Couplings: Buckeye. **Multiple Working:** SR type.

977856. DT. Dia. EZ541. Lot No. 30168 Eastleigh 1955. 30.5 t.
977857. DMB. Dia. EZ522. Lot No. 30167 Eastleigh 1955. 40.5 t.
977917. DMB. Dia. EZ541. Lot No. 30119 Eastleigh 1954. 40.5 t.
977918. DT. Dia. EZ541. Lot No. 30120 Eastleigh 1954. 30.5 t.

931 001	**N**	SE	*SE*	RM	977857	(65346)	977856	(77531)
931 002	**N**	SE	*SE*	RM	977917	(65331)	977918	(77516)

CLASS 931   CARRIAGE CLEANING FLUID UNIT

Converted from Class 416/2. For details see 931 001/2., except:
Formation: DMB–DMB.

DMB. Dia. EZ525. Lot No. 30116 Eastleigh 1954-55. 40.5 t.

931 062	**N**	SE	*SE*	RM	977559	(65313)	977560	(65320)

CLASS 931   TRACTOR UNIT

DM. Non gangwayed. Previously Class 419.

Formation: DM.
Supply System: 750 V DC third rail or battery power.
Traction Motors: Two English Electric 507 of 185 kW.
Construction: Steel. **Doors:** Slam.
Gangways: Throughout. **Bogies:** Mk. 3B.
Couplers: Buckeye. **Maximum Speed:** 90 m.p.h.
Braking: Tread brakes. **Dimensions:** 19.64 x 2.82 m.
Multiple Working: SR type.

68002. DM. Dia. EX560. Lot No. 30458 Eastleigh 1959. 45.5 t.

931 092	**N**	P	*SW*	BM	68002

CLASS 932 TEST UNIT

Converted from Class 411. Test unit for manufacturers' traction packages.

Formation: DM–TB–T–DM.
Supply System: 750 V DC third rail or 25 kV AC 50 Hz overhead.
Traction Motors: Two English Electric 507 of 185 kW.
Construction: Steel. **Doors:** Slam.
Gangways: Throughout. **Bogies:** Mk. 4 /Commonwealth.
Couplers: Buckeye. **Maximum Speed:** 90 m.p.h.
Braking: Tread brakes. **Dimensions:** 20.34 x 2.82 m.
Multiple Working: SR type.

Non-standard Livery: One side of each car painted in GEC-Alsthom white and orange livery and the other side of each car painted in livery **P**. Vehicle 70653 is in livery **CX**

61948. DM. Dia. EA264. Lot No. 30708 Eastleigh 1963. 41.0 t.
70653. TB. Dia. EJ361. Lot No. 30709 Eastleigh 1963. 31.5 t.
70660. TB. Dia. EH282. Lot No. 30709 Eastleigh 1963. 31.5 t.
61949. DM. Dia. EA264. Lot No. 30708 Eastleigh 1963. 44.9 t.

932 620	**0**	P		ZG	61948 70653 70660 61949		

CLASS 960/1 CAB SIGNALLING TEST UNIT

Converted from Class 309/2 units by Alstom Eastleigh 2001.

Supply System: 25 kV AC 50 Hz overhead.
BDTC–MBS–DTS. Gangwayed throughout.
Construction: Steel.
Traction Motors: Four GEC WT401 of 210 kW each.
Dimensions: 20.18 x 2.82 x 3.90 m.
Maximum Speed: 100 m.p.h. **Doors:** Slam.
Couplings: Buckeye. **Bogies:** Commonwealth.
Multiple Working: Within class.

Non-standard Livery: Light blue & white.

977962. BDTC. Dia. EF305. Lot No. 30679 York 1962. 40.0 t.
977965. BDTC. Dia. EF305. Lot No. 30675 York 1962. 40.0 t.
977963. MBS. Dia. ED218. Lot No. 30680 York 1962. 57.7 t.
977966. MBS. Dia. ED218. Lot No. 30676 York 1962. 57.7 t.
977964. DTS. Dia. EE229. Lot No. 30682 York 1962. 36.6 t.
977967. DTS. Dia. EE229. Lot No. 30678 York 1962. 36.6 t.

960 101	**0**	NR	*AM*	Old	977962	(75642)	977963	(61937)
				Dalby	977964	(75981)		
960 102	**0**	NR	*AM*	Old	977965	(75965)	977966	(61928)
				Dalby	977967	(75972)		

Names:

960 101 West Coast Flyer
960 102 New Dalby

4.5. EMUS AWAITING DISPOSAL

The list below comprises vehicles awaiting disposal which are stored on Network Rail, together
with those stored at other locations which, although awaiting disposal, remain NR registered.

25 kV AC 50 Hz Overhead Units:

305 506	**GM**	A	PY	75429	61415	75448	
305 511	**GM**	A	PY	75434	61420	75453	
305 516	**GM**	A	PY	75439	61425	75458	
308 134	**WY**	A	PY	75879	61912	75888	
308 136	**WY**	A	PY	75881	61886	75890	
308 137	**WY**	A	PY	75882	61887	75891	
308 141	**WY**	A	PY	75886	61881	75895	
308 147	**WY**	A	PY	75901	61897	75934	
308 152	**WY**	A	PY	75913	61902	75939	
308 154	**WY**	A	PY	75908	61904	75941	
308 155	**WY**	A	PY	75909	61905	75942	
308 159	**WY**	A	PY	75906	61909	75946	
308 161	**WY**	A	PY	75911	61911	75948	
308 162	**WY**	A	PY	75916	61884	75949	
308 163	**WY**	A	PY	75917	61913	75950	
308 164	**WY**	A	PY	75918	61915	75951	
308 165	**WY**	A	PY	75919	61915	75952	
309 613	**RN**	A	PY	75639	61934	71756	75978
309 617	**RN**	A	ZG	75643	61938		75982
309 623	**RN**	A	PY	75641	61927	71758	75980
309 627	**RN**	A	PY	75644	61931	70259	75975
310 046	**N**	H	PY	76130	62071	70731	76180
310 047	**N**	H	PY	76131	62072	70732	76181
310 049	**N**	H	KT	76133	62074	70734	76183
310 050	**N**	H	KT	76134	62075	70735	76184
310 051	**N**	H	KT	76135	62076	70736	76185
310 052	**N**	H	PY	76136	62077	70737	76186
310 057	**N**	H	PY	76141	62082	70742	76191
310 058	**N**	H	PY	76142	62083	70743	76192
310 059	**N**	H	KT	76143	62084	70744	76205
310 060	**N**	H	PY	76144	62085	70745	76194
310 064	**N**	H	PY	76148	62089	70749	76198
310 066	**N**	H	PY	76228	62091	70751	76200
310 067	**N**	H	PY	76151	62092	70752	76201
310 068	**N**	H	PY	76152	62093	70753	76202
310 069	**N**	H	PY	76153	62094	70754	76203
310 070	**N**	H	PY	76154	62099	70755	76204
310 074	**N**	H	PY	76145	62099	70759	76208
310 075	**N**	H	PY	76159	62100	70760	76209
310 077	**N**	MD	MoD Caerwent	76161			76211
310 079	**N**	H	PY	76163	62104	70764	76222
310 080	**N**	H	KT	76164	62105	70765	76214
310 081	**N**	H	KT	76165	62106	70766	76215
310 082	**N**	H	KT	76166	62107	70767	76216

Unit							
310 083	**N**	H	KT	76167	62108	70768	76217
310 084	**N**	H	PY	76168	62109	70769	76206
310 085	**N**	H	PY	76169	62110	70770	76219
310 086	**N**	H	PY	76170	62111	70771	76220
310 087	**N**	H	PY	76171	62112	70772	76221
310 088	**N**	H	PY	76172	62113	70773	76213
310 089	**N**	H	PY	76173	62114	70774	76223
310 091	**N**	H	PY	76175	62116	70776	76225
310 092	**N**	H	KT	76176	62117	70777	76226
310 093	**N**	H	PY	76177	62118	70778	76190
310 094	**N**	H	PY	76998	62119	70780	76193
310 095	**N**	H	PY	76179	62120	70779	76229
310 101	**RR**	H	PY	76157	62098		76207
310 102	**RR**	H	PY	76139	62080		76189
310 103	**RR**	H	PY	76160	62101		76210
310 104	**RR**	H	PY	76162	62103		76212
310 105	**RR**	H	PY	76174	62115		76224
310 107	**RR**	H	PY	76146	62087		76196
310 108	**RR**	H	PY	76132	62073		76182
310 109	**RR**	H	ZA	76137	62078		76187
310 110	**RR**	H	PY	76138	62079		76188
310 111	**RR**	H	PY	76147	62088		76197
310 112	**RR**	H	PY	76140	62086		76227
310 113	**RR**	H	ZA	76158	62090		76195

Spare Cars:

Cl. 302	**N**	H	PY	61060	61063	61072	61075	61077	61080
				61084	61085	61091	61193		
				75088	75097	75100	75191	75194	75197
				75198	75199	75201	75205		
Cl. 303	**S**	A	PY	75773	75824				
Cl. 303	**S**	A	GW	75624					
Cl. 307	**BG**	E	KT	75023					
Cl. 308	**N**	A	PY	70612	70621	70622	70631	70640	
Cl. 309	**RN**	A	ZG	70256	71759				
Cl. 309	**RN**	A	PY	71760					
Cl. 310	**RR**	H	PY	62102	76156				
Cl. 310	**RR**	H	LT	76218					

750 V DC Third Rail Units:

4308	**N**	NR	PY	61275	75395		
5001	**G**	H	KT	14001	15101	15207	14002
6213	**BG**	NR	PY	65327	77512		
6308	**N**	NR	PY	14564	16108		
6309	**N**	NR	PY	14562	16106		
6402	**N**	NR	PY	65362	77547		

Spare Cars:

Cl. 416	**B**	NR ZG	977296 (65319)	Cl. 438	**B**	AM ZG	76288
Cl. 421	**BG**	AM ZG	70995	Cl. 438	**B**	NR ZG	977764
Cl. 423	**N**	P ZG	76510				(70866)

5. NON-PASSENGER-CARRYING COACHING STOCK

The notes shown for locomotive-hauled passenger stock generally apply also to non-passenger-carrying coaching stock (often abbreviated to NPCCS).

TOPS TYPE CODES

TOPS type codes for NPCCS are made up as follows:

(1) Two letters denoting the type of the vehicle:

AX	Nightstar generator van
AY	Eurostar barrier vehicle
NA	Propelling control vehicle.
NB	High security brake van (100 m.p.h.).
NC	Gangwayed brake van modified for newspaper conveyance (100 m.p.h.).
ND	Gangwayed brake van (90 m.p.h.).
NE	Gangwayed brake van (100 m.p.h.).
NF	Gangwayed brake van with guard's safety equipment removed.
NG	Motorail loading wagon.
NH	Gangwayed brake van (110 m.p.h.).
NI	High security brake van (110 m.p.h.).
NJ	General utility van (90 m.p.h.).
NK	High security general utility van (100 m.p.h.).
NL	Newspaper van.
NN	Courier vehicle.
NO	General utility van (100 m.p.h. e.t.h. wired).
NP	General utility van for post office use or Motorail van (110 m.p.h.).
NQ	High security brake van (110 m.p.h.).
NR	BAA container van (100 m.p.h.).
NS	Post office sorting van.
NT	Post office stowage van.
NU	Brake post office stowage van.
NV	Motorail van (side loading).
NX	Motorail van (100 m.p.h.).
NY	Exhibition van.
NZ	Driving brake van (also known as driving van trailer).
YR	Ferry van (special Southern Region version of NJ with two pairs of side doors instead of three).

(2) A third letter denoting the brake type:

A	Air braked
V	Vacuum braked
X	Dual braked

OPERATING CODES

The normal operating codes are given in parentheses after the TOPS type codes. These are as follows:

BG	Gangwayed brake van.
BPOT	Brake post office stowage van.
DLV	Driving brake van (also known as driving van trailer – DVT).
GUV	General utility van.
PCV	Propelling control van.
POS	Post office sorting van.
POT	Post office stowage van.

5.1. CAPITAL STOCK

AK51 (RK)   KITCHEN CAR

Dia. AK503. Mark 1. Converted 1989 from RBR. Fluorescent lighting. Commonwealth bogies. ETH 2X.

Lot No. 30628 Pressed Steel 1960–61. 39 t.

Note: Kitchen cars have traditionally been numbered in the NPCCS series, but have passenger coach diagram numbers!

| 80041 | (1690) | | x | **M** | RS | *SS* | BN |

NN   COURIER VEHICLE

Dia. NN504. Mark 1. Converted 1986–7 from BSKs. One compartment retained for courier use. Roller shutter doors. ETH 2.

80204/11/13/17. Lot No. 30699 Wolverton 1962. Commonwealth bogies. 37 t.
80207. Lot No. 30721 Wolverton 1963. Commonwealth bogies. 37 t.
80220. Lot No. 30573 Gloucester 1960. B4 bogies. 33 t.

Non-Standard Livery: 80211 is purple.

80204	(35297)	x	**M**	WC	*LS*	CS
80207	(35466)	x	**PC**	VS	*SS*	SL
80211	(35296)		**0**	NR		DY
80213	(35316)	x	**CH**	RV	*SS*	CP
80217	(35299)	x	**M**	14	*LS*	NY
80220	(35276)	x	**G**	NE		NY

Name: 80207 is branded 'BAGGAGE CAR No.11'.

NP   POST OFFICE GUV

Dia. NP502. Mark 1. Converted 1991–93 from newspaper vans. Short frames (57'). Originally converted from GUV. Fluorescent lighting, toilet and gangways fitted. Load 14 t. B5 bogies. ETH 3X.

Lot No. 30922 Wolverton or Doncaster 1977–78. 31 t.

80255	(86098, 94019)	x	**RM**	E	OC
80256	(86408, 94013)	x	**RM**	E	OC
80258	(86651, 94002)		**RM**	E	OC
80259	(86845, 94005)	x	**RM**	E	OC

NS (POS)   POST OFFICE SORTING VAN

Used in travelling post office (TPO) trains. Mark 1. Various diagrams. Pressure ventilated. Fluorescent lighting. B5 bogies. ETH 4X (5X*).

80319–80327. Dia. NS504. Lot No. 30778 York 1968–69. 35 t.
80331–80337. Dia. NS505. Lot No. 30779 York 1968–69. 35 t.
80339–80355. Dia. NS506. Lot No. 30780 York 1968–69. 35 t.
80356–80380. Dia. NS501. Lot No. 30839 York 1972–73. 37 t.

80319	**RM**	E	*E*	EN	80353	**RM**	E	*E*	EN
80320	**RM**	E	*E*	EN	80354	**RM**	E	*E*	EN
80321	**RM**	E	*E*	BK	80355	**RM**	E	*E*	BK
80322	**RM**	E	*E*	EN	80356	**RM**	E	*E*	EN
80323	**RM**	E	*E*	EN	80357	**RM**	E	*E*	BK
80324	**RM**	E	*E*	EN	80358	**RM**	E	*E*	EN
80325	**RM**	E	*E*	EN	80359	**RM**	E	*E*	BK
80326	**RM**	E	*E*	EN	80360	**RM**	E	*E*	EN
80327	**RM**	E	*E*	BK	80361	**RM**	E	*E*	EN
80331	**RM**	E	*E*	EN	80362	**RM**	E	*E*	EN
80332	**RM**	E	*E*	EN	80363	**RM**	E	*E*	BK
80333	**RM**	E	*E*	EN	80364	**RM**	E	*E*	BK
80334	**RM**	E	*E*	BK	80365	**RM**	E	*E*	EN
80337	**RM**	E	*E*	EN	80366	**RM**	E	*E*	EN
80339	**RM**	E	*E*	BK	80367	**RM**	E	*E*	EN
80340	**RM**	E	*E*	BK	80368	**RM**	E	*E*	BK
80341	**RM**	E	*E*	BK	80369	**RM**	E	*E*	EN
80342	**RM**	E	*E*	BK	80370	**RM**	E	*E*	BK
80343	**RM**	E	*E*	BK	80371 *	**RM**	E	*E*	BK
80344	**RM**	E	*E*	BK	80372	**RM**	E	*E*	EN
80345	**RM**	E	*E*	EN	80373	**RM**	E	*E*	EN
80346	**RM**	E	*E*	EN	80374	**RM**	E	*E*	EN
80347	**RM**	E	*E*	EN	80375	**RM**	E	*E*	BK
80348	**RM**	E	*E*	BK	80376	**RM**	E	*E*	BK
80349	**RM**	E	*E*	BK	80377	**RM**	E	*E*	EN
80350	**RM**	E	*E*	BK	80378	**RM**	E	*E*	EN
80351	**RM**	E	*E*	EN	80379	**RM**	E	*E*	EN
80352	**RM**	E	*E*	BK	80380	**RM**	E	*E*	BK

Names:

80320	The Borders Mail	80360	Derek Carter
80327	George James	80367	M.G. Berry
80339	Brian Quinn	80368	George Economou
80345	Richard Yeo		

80381–80395. Lot No. 30900 Wolverton 1977. Dia NS531. Converted from SK. 38 t.

80381	(25112)	**RM**	E	*E*	EN	80385	(25083)	**RM**	E	*E*	EN
80382	(25109)	**RM**	E	*E*	EN	80386	(25099)	**RM**	E	*E*	EN
80383	(25033)	**RM**	E	*E*	EN	80387	(25045)	**RM**	E	*E*	EN
80384	(25078)	**RM**	E	*E*	EN	80390	(25047)	**RM**	E	*E*	EN

80392	(25082)	**RM** E	*E*	EN	80394	(25156)	**RM** E	*E*	EN
80393	(25118)	**RM** E	*E*	EN	80395	(25056)	**RM** E	*E*	EN

Names:

80384	C W Pennell MBE	80390	Ernie Gosling
80385	Paul Rushton		

NT (POT)   POST OFFICE STOWAGE VAN

Mark 1. Open vans used for stowage of mail bags in conjunction with POS.

Lot No. 30488 Wolverton 1959. Dia. NT502. Originally built with nets for collecting mail bags in motion. Equipment now removed. B5 bogies. ETH 3. 35 t.

80400	**RM** E	*E*	BK	80402	**RM** E	*E*	BK
80401	**RM** E	*E*	EN				

The following eight vehicles were converted at York from BSK to lot 30143 (80403) and 30229 (80404–80414). No new lot number was issued. Dia. NT503. B5 bogies. 35 t. (* Dia. NT501 BR2 bogies 38 t.). ETH 3 (3X*).

80403	(34361)	**RM** E *E*	BK	80411	(35003)	*	**RM** E *E*	EN
80404	(35014)	**RM** E *E*	BK	80412	(35002)	*	**RM** E *E*	EN
80405	(35009)	**RM** E *E*	BK	80413	(35004)	*	**RM** E *E*	EN
80406	(35022)	**RM** E *E*	EN	80414	(35005)	*	**RM** E *E*	EN

Lot No. 30781 York 1968. Dia. NT505. Pressure ventilated. B5 bogies. ETH 4. 34 t.

80415	**RM** E	*E*	EN	80421	**RM** E	*E*	EN
80416	**RM** E	*E*	EN	80422	**RM** E	*E*	EN
80417	**RM** E	*E*	EN	80423	**RM** E	*E*	EN
80419	**RM** E	*E*	EN	80424	**RM** E	*E*	EN
80420	**RM** E	*E*	BK				

Lot No. 30840 York 1973. Dia. NT504. Pressure ventilated. fluorescent lighting. B5 bogies. ETH 4X. 35 t.

80425	**RM** E	*E*	BK	80428	**RM** E	*E*	EN
80426	**RM** E	*E*	EN	80429	**RM** E	*E*	BK
80427	**RM** E	*E*	EN	80430	**RM** E	*E*	EN

Lot No. 30901 Wolverton 1977. converted from SK. Dia. NT521. Pressure ventilated. Fluorescent lighting. B5 bogies. ETH 4X. 35 t.

80431	(25104)	**RM** E *E*	EN	80436	(25077)	**RM** E *E*	EN
80432	(25071)	**RM** E *E*	EN	80437	(25068)	**RM** E *E*	EN
80433	(25150)	**RM** E *E*	BK	80438	(25139)	**RM** E *E*	BK
80434	(25519)	**RM** E *E*	EN	80439	(25127)	**RM** E *E*	BK
80435	(25117)	**RM** E *E*	EN				

NU (BPOT) BRAKE POST OFFICE STOWAGE VAN

Dia. NU502. Mark 1. As NT but with brake compartment. Pressure ventilated. B5 bogies. ETH4.

Lot No. 30782 York 1968. 36 t.

| 80456 | RM E | *E* | EN | | 80458 | RM E | *E* | EN |
| 80457 | RM E | *E* | EN | | | | | |

ND (BG) GANGWAYED BRAKE VAN (90 m.p.h.)

Dia. ND501. Mark 1. Short frames (57'). Load 10t. All vehicles were built with BR Mark 1 bogies. ETH 1. Vehicles numbered 81xxx had 3000 added to the original numbers to avoid confusion with Class 81 locomotives. The full lot number list is listed here for reference purposes with renumbered vehicles. No unmodified vehicles remain in service.

80525. Lot No. 30009 Derby 1952–53. 31 t.
80621. Lot No. 30046 York 1954. 31.5 t.
80777. Lot No. 30140 BRCW 1955–56. 31.5 t.
80826. Lot No. 30144 Cravens 1955. 31.5 t.
80855–80959. Lot No. 30162 Pressed Steel 1956–57. 32 t.
80971–81014. Lot No. 30173 York 1956. 31.5 t.
81025–81049. Lot No. 30224 Cravens 1956. 31.5 t.
81061–81175. Lot No. 30228 Metro-Cammell 1957–58. 31.5 t.
81182–81186. Lot No. 30234 Cravens 1956–57. 31.5 t.
81205–81265. Lot No. 30163 Pressed Steel 1957. 31.5 t.
81266–81309. Lot No. 30323 Pressed Steel 1957. 32 t.
81325–81497. Lot No. 30400 Pressed Steel 1957–58. 32 t.
81498–81568. Lot No. 30484 Pressed Steel 1958. 32 t.
81606. Lot No. 30716 Gloucester 1962. 31 t.

Non-standard Livery: 81025 is British racing green with gold lining.

The following vehicle is an ND rebogied with Commonwealth bogies and adapted for use as exhibition van 1998 at Lancastrian Carriage & Wagon Co. Ltd. 33 t.

81025   (81025, 84025)   **0**   RA *SS*   CP

Name: 81025 VALIANT

NZ (DLV)   DRIVING BRAKE VAN (110 m.p.h.)

Dia. NZ501. Mark 3B. Air conditioned. T4 bogies. dg. ETH 5X (6X*).

Lot No. 31042 Derby 1988. 45.18 t.

82101	**V**	P	*VW*	OY		82113	**V**	P	*VW*	OY
82102	**V**	P	*VW*	MA		82114	**V**	P	*VW*	MA
82103	**V**	P	*VW*	OY		82115	**V**	P	*VW*	MA
82104	**V**	P	*VW*	MA		82116	**V**	P	*VW*	MA
82105	**V**	P	*VW*	MA		82117	**V**	P	*VW*	MA
82106	**V**	P	*VW*	OY		82118	**V**	P	*VW*	OY
82107	**V**	P	*VW*	MA		82119	**V**	P	*VW*	MA
82108	**V**	P	*VW*	MA		82120	**V**	P	*VW*	MA
82109	**V**	P	*VW*	MA		82121	**V**	P	*VW*	MA
82110	**V**	P	*VW*	MA		82122	**V**	P	*VW*	OY
82111	**V**	P	*VW*	MA		82123	**V**	P	*VW*	MA
82112	**V**	P	*VW*	MA		82124	**V**	P	*VW*	MA

82125	V	P	VW	MA	82139	V	P	VW	MA
82126	V	P	VW	OY	82140	V	P	VW	MA
82127	V	P	VW	OY	82141	V	P	VW	MA
82128	V	P	VW	OY	82142	V	P	VW	MA
82129	V	P	VW	OY	82143	V	P	VW	OY
82130	V	P	VW	MA	82144	V	P	VW	OY
82131	V	P	VW	OY	82145	V	P	VW	MA
82132	V	P	VW	OY	82146	V	P	VW	MA
82133	V	P	VW	MA	82147	V	P	VW	MA
82134	V	P	VW	OY	82148	V	P	VW	MA
82135	V	P	VW	MA	82149	V	P	VW	OY
82136	V	P	VW	MA	82150	V	P	VW	MA
82137	V	P	VW	MA	82151	V	P	VW	OY
82138	V	P	VW	MA	82152	V	P	VW	MA

Names:

82101	101 Squadron
82115	Liverpool John Moores University
82120	Liverpool Chamber of Commerce
82121	Carlisle Cathedral
82124	The Girls' Brigade
82126	G8 Summit Birmingham 1998
82132	INDUSTRY 96 West Midlands
82134	Sir Henry Doulton 1820–1897
82135	Spirit of Cumbria
82147	The Red Devils
82148	International Spring Fair

NZ (DLV)   DRIVING BRAKE VAN (140 m.p.h.)

Dia. NZ502. Mark 4. Air conditioned. Swiss-built (SIG) bogies. dg. ETH 6X.

Lot No. 31043 Metro-Cammell 1988. 45.18 t.

82200	GN	H	GN	BN	82216	GN	H	GN	BN
82201	GN	H	GN	BN	82217	GN	H	GN	BN
82202	GN	H	GN	BN	82218	GN	H	GN	BN
82203	GN	H	GN	BN	82219	GN	H	GN	BN
82204	GN	H	GN	BN	82220	GN	H	GN	BN
82205	GN	H	GN	BN	82222	GN	H	GN	BN
82206	GN	H	GN	BN	82223	GN	H	GN	BN
82207	GN	H	GN	BN	82224	GN	H	GN	BN
82208	GN	H	GN	BN	82225	GN	H	GN	BN
82209	GN	H	GN	BN	82226	GN	H	GN	BN
82210	GN	H	GN	BN	82227	GN	H	GN	BN
82211	GN	H	GN	BN	82228	GN	H	GN	BN
82212	GN	H	GN	BN	82229	GN	H	GN	BN
82213	GN	H	GN	BN	82230	GN	H	GN	BN
82214	GN	H	GN	BN	82231	GN	H	GN	BN
82215	GN	H	GN	BN					

NB   HIGH SECURITY BRAKE VAN

Dia. NB501. Converted at Wembley Heavy Repair Depot from ND in 1985.
Gangways removed. B4 bogies. 100 m.p.h.

Lot No. 30400 Pressed Steel 1957–58. 32 t.

84387	(81387, 80461)	x	**B**	E	CW
84477	(81477, 80463)	x	**B**	E	CW

NJ (GUV)   GENERAL UTILITY VAN

Dia. NJ501. Mark 1. Short frames. Load 14 t. Screw couplings. These vehicles
had 7000 added to the original numbers to avoid confusion with Class 86
locomotives. The full lot number list is listed here for reference purposes with
renumbered vehicles. No unmodified vehicles remain in service. All vehicles
were built with BR Mark 2 bogies. ETH 0 or 0X*.

86081–86499. Lot No. 30417 Pressed Steel 1958–59. 30 t.
86508–86518. Lot No. 30343 York 1957. 30 t.
86521–86651. Lot No. 30403 York/Glasgow 1958–60. 30 t.
86656–86834. Lot No. 30565 Pressed Steel 1959. 30 t.
86845–86973. Lot No. 30616 Pressed Steel 1959–60. 30 t.

NE/NH (BG)   GANGWAYED BRAKE VAN (100/110 m.p.h.)

Dia. NE501 or NH501. NE are ND but rebogied with B4 bogies suitable for 100
m.p.h. NH are identical but are allowed to run at 110 m.p.h. with special
maintenance of the bogies. For lot numbers refer to original number series.
Deduct 1.5t from weights. All NHA are *pg. ETH 1 (1X*).

† Emergency equipment removed. Dia. NF509.
b In use as Pendolino barrier vehicle.
92175 is leased to Riviersa Trains.

Non-standard Livery: 92116 is purple.

92100	(81391)	to		RV		CP
92111	(81432)	NHAb		LW	*FL*	CP
92114	(81443)	NHA		NR		DY
92116	(81450)	to	**0**	NR		DY
92125	(81470)	to		DR		KM
92146	(81498)	NHA		NR		DY
92159	(81534)	NHA		H		CP
92174	(81567)	NHA		H		PY
92175	(81568)	pg		H	*SS*	CP
92194	(81606)	to		H		PY
92234	(81336, 84336)	*	**RX**	E		DY
92238	(81563, 84563)	†	**RY**	E		DY
92261	(80988)	x*	**RY**	E		BK

NE (BG) GANGWAYED BRAKE VAN (100 m.p.h.)

As ND but rebogied with Commonwealth bogies suitable for 100 m.p.h. ETH 1 (1X*). For lot numbers refer to original number series. Add 1.5 t to weights to allow for the increased weight of the Commonwealth bogies. ETH 1 (1X*§).

†§ Emergency equipment removed. Dia. NF509†, NF510§.

92303	(81427, 84427)			RX	E	DY
92311	(81453, 84453)	x		RY	E	CW
92314	(80777)	x*		RY	E	CW
92321	(81566, 84566)			RY	E	FP
92347	(81326, 84326)			RX	E	DY
92350	(81049, 84049)	*		RY	E	DY
92355	(81517, 84517)	x		RX	E	DY
92356	(81535, 84535)	x			E	OC
92363	(81294, 84294)	x		RY	E	CW
92377	(80928)	*		RX	E	DY
92382	(81561, 84561)			RX	E	DY
92384	(80893)			RY	E	CW
92400	(81211, 84211)	†			E	CW
92410	(81469, 84469)	†			E	CW
92412	(81354, 84354)	§		RY	E	CW
92413	(81472, 84472)	§		RY	E	CW

NB   HIGH SECURITY BRAKE VAN (100 m.p.h.)

Dia. NB501. Mark 1. Converted from ND at Wembley Heavy Repair Depot in 1985. Gangways removed. Now used for movement of materials between EWS maintenance depots. B4 bogies.

92530	(81461, 84461)	x	RX	E	*E*	EN

NF (BG) GANGWAYED BRAKE VAN (100 m.p.h.)

Dia. NF509 (NF510*). As NE but with emergency equipment removed. For details and lot numbers refer to original number series. Commonwealth bogies. ETH 1 (1X*).

92831	(81365, 92331)	x	RX	E	OC
92842	(81397, 92342)	x	RY	E	OC
92852	(81182, 92352)	*	RX	E	DY
92859	(81275, 92359)	*	RX	E	DY
92872	(81362, 92372)	x	RY	E	CW

NE/NH (BG)   GANGWAYED BRAKE VAN (100/110 m.p.h.)

Dia. NE501 or NH501. Renumbered from 920xx series by adding 900 to number to avoid conflict with Class 92 locos. Class continued from 92261.

b In use as Pendolino barrier vehicle.
92936 is leased to Riviera Trains.

92901	(80855, 92001)	NHA		H		PY
92904	(80867, 92004)	*pg	**G**	VS		SL
92908	(80895, 92008)	NHA	**M**	WC	*VL*	CF
92912	(80910, 92012)	*pg		H		KT
92923	(80971, 92023)	*pg		NR		DY
92927	(81061, 92027)	NHA		NR		DY
92928	(81064, 92028)	NHA		NR		DY
92929	(81077, 92029)	NHA		LW	*FL*	CP
92931	(81102, 92031)	NHA		H		PY
92934	(81142, 92034)	NHA		NR		DY
92935	(81150, 92035)	*pg		H		PY
92936	(81158, 92036)	NHA		H	*SS*	OC
92937	(81165, 92037)	NHA		NR		DY
92938	(81173, 92038)	NHA		H		PY
92939	(81175, 92039)	NHA		NR		DY
92940	(81186, 92040)	pg		H		IS
92946	(81214, 92046)	NHA		H		PY
92961	(81231, 92061)			NR		DY
92986	(81282, 92086)	to		H		CP
92988	(81284, 92088)	to		NR		DY
92991	(81308, 92091)	to		NR		DY
92998	(81381, 92098)	NHA		NR		DY

NL   NEWSPAPER VAN

Dia. NL501. Mark 1. Short frames (57'). Converted from NJ (GUV). Fluorescent lighting, toilets and gangways fitted. Load 14 t. All except 94003/6, now used for materials storage, are out of use. B5 Bogies. ETH 3X.

Lot No. 30922 Wolverton or Doncaster 1977–78. 31 t.

94003	(86281, 93999)	x	**RX**	FG	*GW*	OO
94006	(86202, 85506)		**RX**	FG	*GW*	OO
94016	(86317, 85516)	x	**B**	E		OC
94020	(86220, 85520)	x	**RY**	E		OC
94027	(86732, 85527)		**R**	E		FP

NKA   HIGH SECURITY GENERAL UTILITY VAN

Dia. NK501. Mark 1. These vehicles are GUVs further modified with new floors, three roller shutter doors per side and the end doors removed. For lot Nos. see original number series. Commonwealth bogies. Add 2 t to weight. ETH0X.

94100	(86668, 95100)	**RX**	E	*E*	BK
94101	(86142, 95101)	**RX**	E	*E*	BK
94102	(86762, 95102)	**RX**	E	*E*	BK
94103	(86956, 95103)	**RX**	E	*E*	BK
94104	(86942, 95104)	**RX**	E	*E*	EN
94106	(86353, 95106)	**RX**	E	*E*	BK
94107	(86576, 95107)	**RX**	E	*E*	EN
94108	(86600, 95108)	**RX**	E	*E*	BK
94110	(86393, 95110)	**RX**	E	*E*	BK

94111	(86578, 95111)	**RX**	E	*E*	EN
94112	(86673, 95112)	**RX**	E	*E*	EN
94113	(86235, 95113)	**RX**	E	*E*	BK
94114	(86081, 95114)	**RX**	E	*E*	BK
94116	(86426, 95116)	**RX**	E	*E*	BK
94117	(86534, 95117)	**RX**	E	*E*	BK
94118	(86675, 95118)	**RX**	E	*E*	EN
94119	(86167, 95119)	**RX**	E	*E*	EN
94121	(86518, 95121)	**RX**	E	*E*	BK
94123	(86376, 95123)	**RX**	E	*E*	BK
94126	(86692, 95126)	**RX**	E	*E*	BK
94132	(86607, 95132)	**RX**	E	*E*	EN
94133	(86604, 95133)	**RX**	E	*E*	BK
94137	(86610, 95137)	**RX**	E	*E*	EN
94138	(86212, 95138)	**RX**	E	*E*	EN
94140	(86571, 95140)	**RX**	E	*E*	BK
94146	(86648, 95146)	**RX**	E	*E*	BK
94147	(86091, 95147)	**RX**	E	*E*	BK
94148	(86416, 95148)	**RX**	E	*E*	EN
94150	(86560, 95150)	**RX**	E	*E*	BK
94153	(86798, 95153)	**RX**	E	*E*	EN
94155	(86820, 95155)	**RX**	E	*E*	EN
94157	(86523, 95157)	**RX**	E	*E*	EN
94160	(86581, 95160)	**RX**	E	*E*	BK
94164	(86104, 95164)	**RX**	E	*E*	EN
94166	(86112, 95166)	**RX**	E	*E*	BK
94168	(86914, 95168)	**RX**	E	*E*	BK
94170	(86395, 95170)	**RX**	E	*E*	BK
94172	(86429, 95172)	**RX**	E	*E*	EN
94174	(86852, 95174)	**RX**	E	*E*	EN
94175	(86521, 95175)	**RX**	E	*E*	BK
94176	(86210, 95176)	**RX**	E	*E*	EN
94177	(86411, 95177)	**RX**	E	*E*	BK
94180	(86362, 95141)	**RX**	E	*E*	EN
94182	(86710, 95182)	**RX**	E	*E*	BK
94190	(86624, 95350)	**RX**	E	*E*	EN
94191	(86596, 95351)	**RX**	E	*E*	BK
94192	(86727, 95352)	**RX**	E	*E*	EN
94193	(86514, 95353)	**RX**	E	*E*	EN
94195	(86375, 95355)	**RX**	E	*E*	BK
94196	(86478, 95356)	**RX**	E	*E*	BK
94197	(86508, 95357)	**RX**	E	*E*	BK
94198	(86195, 95358)	**RX**	E	*E*	BK
94199	(86854, 95359)	**RX**	E	*E*	BK
94200	(86207, 95360)	**RX**	E	*E*	EN
94202	(86563, 95362)	**RX**	E	*E*	BK
94203	(86345, 95363)	**RX**	E	*E*	BK
94204	(86715, 95364)	**RX**	E	*E*	BK
94205	(86857, 95365)	**RX**	E	*E*	BK
94207	(86529, 95367)	**RX**	E	*E*	BK
94208	(86656, 95368)	**RX**	E	*E*	EN

94209	(86390, 95369)	**RX**	E	*E*	BK
94211	(86713, 95371)	**RX**	E	*E*	EN
94212	(86728, 95372)	**RX**	E	*E*	EN
94213	(86258, 95373)	**RX**	E	*E*	EN
94214	(86367, 95374)	**RX**	E	*E*	BK
94215	(86862, 94077)	**RX**	E	*E*	BK
94216	(86711, 93711)	**RX**	E	*E*	EN
94217	(86131, 93131)	**RX**	E	*E*	BK
94218	(86541, 93541)	**RX**	E	*E*	BK
94221	(86905, 93905)	**RX**	E	*E*	BK
94222	(86474, 93474)	**RX**	E	*E*	EN
94223	(86660, 93660)	**RX**	E	*E*	BK
94224	(86273, 93273)	**RX**	E	*E*	BK
94225	(86849, 93849)	**RX**	E	*E*	BK
94226	(86525, 93525)	**RX**	E	*E*	BK
94227	(86585, 93585)	**RX**	E	*E*	BK
94228	(86511, 93511)	**RX**	E	*E*	BK
94229	(86720, 93720)	**RX**	E	*E*	BK

NAA   PROPELLING CONTROL VEHICLE

Dia. NA508. Mark 1. Class 307 driving trailers converted for use in propelling mail trains out of termini. Fitted with roller shutter doors. Equipment fitted for communication between cab of PCV and locomotive. B5 bogies. ETH 2X.

Lot No. 30206 Eastleigh 1954–56. Converted at Hunslet-Barclay, Kilmarnock 1994–6.

94302	(75124)	**RX**	E	*E*	BK		94323	(75110)	**RX**	E	*E*	EN
94303	(75131)	**RX**	E	*E*	EN		94324	(75103)	**RX**	E	*E*	EN
94304	(75107)	**RX**	E	*E*	EN		94325	(75113)	**RX**	E	*E*	EN
94305	(75104)	**RX**	E	*E*	EN		94326	(75123)	**RX**	E	*E*	BK
94306	(75112)	**RX**	E	*E*	BK		94327	(75116)	**RX**	E	*E*	EN
94307	(75127)	**RX**	E	*E*	EN		94331	(75022)	**RX**	E	*E*	BK
94308	(75125)	**RX**	E	*E*	EN		94332	(75011)	**RX**	E	*E*	EN
94309	(75130)	**RX**	E	*E*	EN		94333	(75016)	**RX**	E	*E*	EN
94310	(75119)	**RX**	E	*E*	EN		94334	(75017)	**RX**	E	*E*	EN
94311	(75105)	**RX**	E	*E*	EN		94335	(75032)	**RX**	E	*E*	BK
94312	(75126)	**RX**	E	*E*	BK		94336	(75031)	**RX**	E	*E*	EN
94313	(75129)	**RX**	E	*E*	BK		94337	(75029)	**RX**	E	*E*	EN
94314	(75109)	**RX**	E	*E*	BK		94338	(75008)	**RX**	E	*E*	EN
94315	(75132)	**RX**	E	*E*	EN		94339	(75024)	**RX**	E	*E*	BK
94316	(75108)	**RX**	E	*E*	EN		94340	(75012)	**RX**	E	*E*	BK
94317	(75117)	**RX**	E	*E*	EN		94341	(75007)	**RX**	E	*E*	BK
94318	(75115)	**RX**	E	*E*	EN		94342	(75005)	**RX**	E	*E*	BK
94319	(75128)	**RX**	E	*E*	EN		94343	(75027)	**RX**	E	*E*	EN
94320	(75120)	**RX**	E	*E*	EN		94344	(75014)	**RX**	E	*E*	BK
94321	(75122)	**RX**	E	*E*	EN		94345	(75004)	**RX**	E	*E*	EN
94322	(75111)	**RX**	E	*E*	BK							

NBA HIGH SECURITY BRAKE VAN (100 m.p.h.)

Dia. NB501. Mark 1. These vehicles are NEs further modified with sealed gangways, new floors, built-in tail lights and roller shutter doors. For lot Nos. see original number series. B4 bogies. 31.4 t. ETH 1X.

94400	(81224, 92954)	**RX**	E	*E*	BK
94401	(81277, 92224)	**RX**	E	*E*	EN
94403	(81479, 92629)	**RX**	E	*E*	BK
94404	(81486, 92135)	**RX**	E	*E*	BK
94405	(80890, 92233)	**RX**	E	*E*	EN
94406	(81226, 92956)	**RX**	E	*E*	BK
94407	(81223, 92553)	**RX**	E	*E*	BK
94408	(81264, 92981)	**RX**	E	*E*	BK
94410	(81205, 92941)	**RX**	E	*E*	EN
94411	(81378, 92997)	**RX**	E	*E*	EN
94412	(81210, 92945)	**RX**	E	*E*	EN
94413	(80909, 92236)	**RX**	E	*E*	EN
94414	(81377, 92996)	**RX**	E	*E*	BK
94415	(81309, 92992)	**RX**	E	*E*	EN
94416	(80929, 92746)	**RX**	E	*E*	BK
94418	(81248, 92244)	**RX**	E	*E*	BK
94420	(81325, 92263)	**RX**	E	*E*	BK
94422	(81516, 92651)	**RX**	E	*E*	BK
94423	(80923, 92914)	**RX**	E	*E*	BK
94424	(81400, 92103)	**RX**	E	*E*	EN
94427	(80894, 92754)	**RX**	E	*E*	BK
94428	(81550, 92166)	**RX**	E	*E*	BK
94429	(80870, 92232)	**RX**	E	*E*	EN
94431	(81401, 92604)	**RX**	E	*E*	BK
94432	(81383, 92999)	**RX**	E	*E*	EN
94433	(81495, 92643)	**RX**	E	*E*	EN
94434	(81268, 92584)	**RX**	E	*E*	EN
94435	(81485, 92134)	**RX**	E	*E*	EN
94436	(81237, 92565)	**RX**	E	*E*	BK
94437	(81403, 92208)	**RX**	E	*E*	EN
94438	(81425, 92251)	**RX**	E	*E*	BK
94439	(81480, 92130)	**RX**	E	*E*	BK
94440	(81497, 92645)	**RX**	E	*E*	BK
94441	(81492, 92140)	**RX**	E	*E*	BK
94442	(80932, 92723)	**RX**	E	*E*	BK
94443	(81473, 92127)	**RX**	E	*E*	BK
94444	(81484, 92133)	**RX**	E	*E*	BK
94445	(81444, 92615)	**RX**	E	*E*	EN
94446	(80857, 92242)	**RX**	E	*E*	EN
94447	(81515, 92266)	**RX**	E	*E*	EN
94448	(81541, 92664)	**RX**	E	*E*	BK
94449	(81536, 92747)	**RX**	E	*E*	BK
94450	(80927, 92915)	**RX**	E	*E*	BK
94451	(80955, 92257)	**RX**	E	*E*	EN
94452	(81394, 92602)	**RX**	E	*E*	BK

94453	(81170, 92239)	**RX**	E	*E*	EN
94454	(81465, 92124)	**RX**	E	*E*	EN
94455	(81239, 92264)	**RX**	E	*E*	BK
94458	(81255, 92974)	**RX**	E	*E*	BK
94459	(81490, 92138)	**RX**	E	*E*	BK
94460	(81266, 92983)	**RX**	E	*E*	EN
94461	(81487, 92136)	**RX**	E	*E*	EN
94462	(81289, 92270)	**RX**	E	*E*	EN
94463	(81375, 92995)	**RX**	E	*E*	EN
94464	(81240, 92262)	**RX**	E	*E*	EN
94465	(81481, 92131)	**RX**	E	*E*	BK
94466	(81236, 92964)	**RX**	E	*E*	EN
94467	(81245, 92969)	**RX**	E	*E*	BK
94468	(81259, 92978)	**RX**	E	*E*	BK
94469	(81260, 92979)	**RX**	E	*E*	BK
94470	(81442, 92113)	**RX**	E	*E*	EN
94471	(81518, 92152)	**RX**	E	*E*	BK
94472	(81256, 92975)	**RX**	E	*E*	BK
94473	(81262, 92272)	**RX**	E	*E*	EN
94474	(81452, 92618)	**RX**	E	*E*	EN
94475	(81208, 92943)	**RX**	E	*E*	EN
94476	(81209, 92944)	**RX**	E	*E*	BK
94477	(81494, 92642)	**RX**	E	*E*	BK
94478	(81488, 92637)	**RX**	E	*E*	EN
94479	(81482, 92132)	**RX**	E	*E*	BK
94480	(81411, 92608)	**RX**	E	*E*	EN
94481	(81493, 92641)	**RX**	E	*E*	BK
94482	(81491, 92639)	**RX**	E	*E*	EN
94483	(81500, 92647)	**RX**	E	*E*	EN
94484	(81426, 92110)	**RX**	E	*E*	BK
94485	(81496, 92644)	**RX**	E	*E*	EN
94486	(81254, 92973)	**RX**	E	*E*	BK
94487	(81413, 92609)	**RX**	E	*E*	BK
94488	(81405, 92105)	**RX**	E	*E*	BK
94490	(81409, 92606)	**RX**	E	*E*	EN
94492	(80888, 92721)	**RX**	E	*E*	BK
94493	(80944, 92919)	**RX**	E	*E*	BK
94494	(81451, 92617)	**RX**	E	*E*	BK
94495	(80871, 92755)	**RX**	E	*E*	BK
94496	(81514, 92650)	**RX**	E	*E*	BK
94497	(80877, 92717)	**RX**	E	*E*	BK
94498	(81225, 92555)	**RX**	E	*E*	BK
94499	(81258, 92577)	**RX**	E	*E*	BK

NBA/NIA/NQA
HIGH SECURITY BRAKE VAN (100/110 m.p.h.)

Dia. NB501, NI501 or NQ501. Mark 1. These vehicles are NEs further modified with sealed gangways, new floors, built-in tail lights and roller shutter doors. For lot Nos. see original number series. B4 bogies. 31.4 t. ETH 1X.

These vehicles are identical to the 94400–94499 series. Certain vehicles are being given a special maintenance regime whereby tyres are reprofiled more frequently than normal and are then allowed to run at 110 m.p.h. Vehicles from the 94400 series upgraded to 110 m.p.h. are being renumbered in this series. Vehicles are NBA (100 m.p.h.) unless marked NIA or NQA (110 m.p.h.). NQA are vehicles which were modified for haulage by Class 90/2 locomotives which were fitted with composition brake blocks.

94500	(81457, 92121)	NIA	**RX**	E	*E*	ML
94501	(80891, 92725)		**RX**	E	*E*	BK
94502	(80924, 92720)	NQA	**RX**	E	*E*	ML
94503	(80873, 92709)	NIA	**RX**	E	*E*	ML
94504	(80935, 92748)	NQA	**RX**	E	*E*	BK
94505	(81235, 92750)	NIA	**RX**	E	*E*	ML
94506	(80958, 92922)	NIA	**RX**	E	*E*	ML
94507	(80876, 92505)	NIA	**RX**	E	*E*	ML
94508	(80887, 92722)	NQA	**RX**	E	*E*	ML
94509	(80897, 92509)	NQA	**RX**	E	*E*	ML
94510	(80945, 92265)		**RX**	E	*E*	BK
94511	(81504, 92714)	NIA	**RX**	E	*E*	ML
94512	(81265, 92582)		**RX**	E	*E*	BK
94513	(81257, 92576)		**RX**	E	*E*	BK
94514	(81459, 92122)	NIA	**RX**	E	*E*	ML
94515	(80916, 92513)	NQA	**RX**	E	*E*	ML
94516	(81267, 92211)	NQA	**RX**	E	*E*	ML
94517	(81489, 92243)	NIA	**RX**	E	*E*	BK
94518	(81346, 92258)		**RX**	E	*E*	BK
94519	(80930, 92916)	NQA	**RX**	E	*E*	ML
94520	(80940, 92917)	NQA	**RX**	E	*E*	ML
94521	(80900, 92510)	NIA	**RX**	E	*E*	ML
94522	(80880, 92907)	NIA	**RX**	E	*E*	ML
94523	(81509, 92649)	NIA	**RX**	E	*E*	BK
94524	(81454, 94457)	NQA	**RX**	E	*E*	ML
94525	(80902, 92229)	NIA	**RX**	E	*E*	ML
94526	(80941, 92518)	NIA	**RX**	E	*E*	ML
94527	(80921, 92728)	NQA	**RX**	E	*E*	ML
94528	(81404, 92267)		**RX**	E	*E*	BK
94529	(80959, 92252)	NQA	**RX**	E	*E*	ML
94530	(81511, 94409)	NIA	**RX**	E	*E*	ML
94531	(80879, 94456)	NQA	**RX**	E	*E*	BK
94532	(81423, 94489)	NQA	**RX**	E	*E*	BK
94534	(80908, 94430)	NIA	**RX**	E	*E*	BK
94535	(80858, 94419)	NIA	**RX**	E	*E*	BK
94536	(80936, 94491)	NIA	**RX**	E	*E*	BK
94537	(81230, 94421)	NIA	**RX**	E	*E*	BK
94538	(81283, 94426)	NQA	**RX**	E	*E*	ML

NBA HIGH SECURITY BRAKE VAN (100 m.p.h.)

Dia. NB501. Mark 1. Details as for 94400–99 but fitted with Commonwealth bogies. 34.4 t. ETH 1X.

94539	(81501, 92302)	**RX**	E	*E*	BK
94540	(81431, 92860)	**RX**	E	*E*	BK
94541	(80980, 92316)	**RX**	E	*E*	BK
94542	(80995, 92330)	**RX**	E	*E*	BK
94543	(81026, 92389)	**RX**	E	*E*	BK
94544	(81083, 92345)	**RX**	E	*E*	BK
94545	(81001, 92327)	**RX**	E	*E*	BK
94546	(81339, 92804)	**RX**	E	*E*	BK
94547	(80861, 92392)	**RX**	E	*E*	BK
94548	(81154, 92344)	**RX**	E	*E*	BK

NO (GUV)   GENERAL UTILITY VAN (100 m.p.h.)

Dia. NO513. Mark 1. For lot Nos. see original number series. Commonwealth bogies. Add 2 t to weight. ETH 0X.

| 95128 | (86764, 93764) | x | **RY** | E | | CW |
| 95129 | (86347, 93347) | x | **RY** | E | | CW |

NCX   NEWSPAPER VAN (100 m.p.h.)

Dia. NC501. Mark 1. BGs modified to carry newspapers. As EWS does not now carry newspaper traffic these are now all out of use. For lot Nos. refer to original number series. Commonwealth bogies. Add 2 t to weight. ETH3.

| 95228 | (81014, 95332) | x | **RX** | E | | NC |
| 95230 | (80525, 95321) | x | **RX** | E | | DY |

NAA   PROPELLING CONTROL VEHICLE

Dia. NA508. Mark 1. Class 307 driving trailers converted for use in propelling mail trains out of termini. Fitted with roller shutter doors. Equipment was fitted for communication between cab of PCV and locomotive but this is now isolated. ETH 2X.

Lot No. 30206 Eastleigh 1954–56. Converted at RTC, Derby 1993.

| 95300 | (75114, 94300) | **E** | E | *E* | ML |
| 95301 | (75102, 94301) | **E** | E | *E* | ML |

NRX   BAA CONTAINER VAN (100 m.p.h.)

Dia. NR503. Mark 1. Modified for carriage of British Airports Authority containers with roller shutter doors and roller floors and gangways removed. Now used for general parcels traffic. For lot Nos. see original number series. Commonwealth bogies. Add 2 t to weight. ETH3.

| 95400 | (80621, 95203) | **E** | E | *E* | ML |
| 95410 | (80826, 95213) | **E** | E | *E* | ML |

NOA   HIGH SECURITY GENERAL UTILITY VAN

Dia. NO516. Mark 1. These vehicles are GUVs further modified with new floors, two roller shutter doors per side, middle doors sealed and end doors removed.

For lot Nos. see original number series. Commonwealth bogies. Add 2 t to weight.
ETH 0X.

95715	(86174, 95115)	**R**	E	*E*	EN
95727	(86323, 95127)	**R**	E	*E*	EN
95734	(86462, 95134)	**RX**	E	*E*	EN
95739	(86172, 95139)	**R**	E	*E*	EN
95743	(86485, 95143)	**RX**	E	*E*	EN
95749	(86265, 95149)	**R**	E	*E*	EN
95754	(86897, 95154)	**R**	E	*E*	EN
95758	(86499, 95158)	**RX**	E	*E*	EN
95759	(86084, 95159)	**RX**	E	*E*	EN
95761	(86205, 95161)	**RX**	E	*E*	EN
95762	(86122, 95162)	**RX**	E	*E*	EN
95763	(86407, 95163)	**R**	E	*E*	EN

NP/NX/NV (GUV)   MOTORAIL VAN (100 m.p.h.)

Dia. NX501. Mark 1. For details and lot numbers see original number series.
ETH 0 (0X*).

Notes: 96100 was authorised for 110 m.p.h. and is classified NP504.
96101 has a new prototype body built 1998 by Marcroft Engineering with side
loading and one end sealed (Dia. NV502).

b In use as Pendolino barrier vehicle.

96100	(86734, 93734)	*B5		H			KT
96101	(86741, 93741)	*B5	**HB**	H			PY
96110	(86738, 93738)	*C		H			PY
96130	(86736, 93736)	*C		H			KT
96131	(86737, 93737)	*C		H			KT
96132	(86754, 93754)	*C		H			LT
96135	(86755, 93755)	C		H			CP
96139	(86751, 93751)	C		H		*VW*	MA
96163	(86646, 93646)	*C		H			KT
96164	(86880, 93880)	*C		H			LT
96165	(86784, 93784)	*C		H			KT
96166	(86834, 93834)	*C		H			KT
96167	(86756, 93756)	*C		H			KT
96170	(86159, 93159)	x*C		H			KT
96172	(86363, 93363)	x*C		H			KT
96173	(86440, 93440)	x*C		H			KT
96175	(86628, 93628)	x*C		H			KT
96176	(86641, 93641)	x*C		H			KT
96178	(86782, 93782)	*C		H			KT
96179	(86910, 93910)	*C		H			LT
96181	(86875, 93875)	*C		H			ZH
96182	(86944, 93944)	*Cb	**K**	LW	*FL*		CP
96187	(86168, 93168)	x*C		H			LT
96188	(86320, 93320)	x*C		H			KT
96190	(86448, 93448)	x*C		H			LT
96191	(86665, 93665)	x*C		H			KT

| 96192 | (86669, 93669) | x*C | H | KT |
| 96194 | (86949, 93949) | x*C | H | LT |

NP (GUV)   MOTORAIL VAN (110 m.p.h.)

Dia. NP503. Mark 1. Vehicles modified with concertina end doors. For details and lot numbers see original number series. B5 Bogies. ETH 0X.

96210	(86355, 96159)		NR		ZA
96212	(86443, 96161)		NR		ZA
96218	(86286, 96151)		NR		ZA

AX5G   NIGHTSTAR GENERATOR VAN

Dia. AX502. Mark 3A. Generator vans converted from sleeping cars for use on 'Nightstar' services. Designed to operate between two Class 37/6 locomotives. Gangways removed. Two Cummins diesel generator groups providing a 1500 V train supply. Hydraulic parking brake. 61-way ENS interface jumpers. BT10 bogies.

Lot No. 30960 Derby 1981–83. 46.01 t.

96371	(10545, 6371)	**EP**	EU	*EU*	NP
96372	(10564, 6372)	**EP**	EU	*EU*	NP
96373	(10568, 6373)	**EP**	EU	*EU*	NP
96374	(10585, 6374)	**EP**	EU	*EU*	NP
96375	(10587, 6375)	**EP**	EU	*EU*	NP

AY5 (BV)   EUROSTAR BARRIER VEHICLE

Dia. AY501. Mark 1. Converted from GUVs. Bodies removed. B4 bogies.

96380–96382/9. Lot No. 30417 Pressed Steel 1958–59. 40 t.
96383. Lot No. 30565 Pressed Steel 1959. 40 t.
96384/6/7. Lot No. 30616 Pressed Steel 1959–60. 40 t.
96385. Lot No. 30343 York 1957. 40 t.
96388. Lot No. 30403 Glasgow 1958–60. 40 t.

96380	(86386, 6380)	**B**	EU	*EU*	NP
96381	(86187, 6381)	**B**	EU	*EU*	NP
96382	(86295, 6382)	**B**	EU	*EU*	NP
96383	(86664, 6383)	**B**	EU	*EU*	NP
96384	(86955, 6384)	**B**	EU	*EU*	NP
96385	(86515, 6385)	**B**	EU	*EU*	NP
96386	(86859, 6386)	**B**	SM		CP
96387	(86973, 6387)	**B**	SM		CP
96388	(86562, 6388)	**B**	EU	*EU*	NP
96389	(86135, 6389)	**B**	EU	*EU*	NP

NG   MOTORAIL LOADING WAGON

Dia. NG503. These vehicles have been converted and renumbered from weltrol wagons and were used for loading purposes.
Built Swindon 1960. Wagon Lot No. 3102 (3192*).

96452	(B900917)		H	MB
96453	(B900926)	*	H	MB

NVA   MOTORAIL VAN (100 m.p.h.)

Dia. NV502. Mark 1. Built 1998–9 by Marcroft Engineering using underframe and running gear from Motorail GUVs. Side loading with one end sealed. The vehicles run in pairs and access is available to the adjacent vehicle. For details and lot numbers see original number series. B5 bogies. ETH 0X.

96602	(86097, 96150)	**FP**	H	*GW*	PZ
96603	(86334, 96155)	**FP**	H	*GW*	PZ
96604	(86337, 96156)	**FP**	H	*GW*	PZ
96605	(86344, 96157)	**FP**	H	*GW*	PZ
96606	(86324, 96213)	**FP**	H	*GW*	PZ
96607	(86351, 96215)	**FP**	H	*GW*	PZ
96608	(86385, 96216)	**FP**	H	*GW*	PZ
96609	(86327, 96217)	**FP**	H	*GW*	PZ

NY   EXHIBITION VAN

Dia. NY530. Converted Railway Age, Crewe 1996 from SO. Originally FO. B4 bogies. Electric heating from shore supply. B4 bogies.

Non-Standard Livery: Varies according to job being undertaken.

Lot No. 30821 Derby 1971

99664	(3189, 6231)	**0**	NR		ZN

NY   ULTRASONIC TEST COACH

Dia. NY532. Converted Railway Age, Crewe 1996 from FO to Exhibition Van. Further converted at Alstom, Wolverton Works 2002 to Ultrasonic Test Coach. B4 bogies.

Non-Standard Livery: All over Railtrack blue.

Lot No. 30843 Derby 1972–73.

99666	(3250)	**0**	NR	*SO*	ZA

YR   FERRY VAN

Dia. YR025. This vehicle was built to a wagon lot although the design closely resembles that of NJ except it only has two sets of doors per side. Short Frames (57'). Load 14 t. Commonwealth bogies.

Built Eastleigh 1958. Wagon Lot. No. 2849. 30 t.

Non-Standard Livery: 889202 is Pullman Car umber with gold lining and lettering.

889202	**0**	VS	*SS*	CP

Name: 889202 is branded 'BAGGAGE CAR No.8'.

5.2. SERVICE STOCK

Vehicles in this section are numbered in the former BR departmental number series. They are used for internal purposes within the railway industry, i.e. they do not generate revenue from outside the industry.

EMU TRANSLATOR VEHICLES

These vehicles are used to move EMU vehicles around the national system in the same way as other vehicles included in this book. Similar vehicles numbered in the BR capital stock series are included elsewhere in this book. Various diagrams. Converted from Mark 1 TSO, RSOs, RUOs, BSKs and GUVs (NP/NL).

975864. Lot No. 30054 Eastleigh 1951–54. Commonwealth bogies.
975867. Lot No. 30014 York 1950–51. Commonwealth bogies.
975875. Lot No. 30143 Charles Roberts 1954–55. Commonwealth bogies.
975971–975978. Lot No. 30647 Wolverton 1959–61. Commonwealth bogies.
977087. Lot No. 30229 Metro–Cammell 1955–57. Commonwealth bogies.
977942/948. Lot No. 30417 Pressed Steel 1958–59. B5 bogies.
977943/949. Lot No. 30565 Pressed Steel 1959. B5 bogies.

Non-standard livery: 975974 and 975978 are in plain grey.

975864	(3849)	**HB**	H	*SR*	GW
975867	(1006)	**HB**	H	*SR*	GW
975875	(34643)	**HB**	H	*WN*	HE
975971	(1054)	**P**	P	*E*	CJ
975972	(1039)	**P**	P	*E*	CJ
975973	(1021)	**P**	P	*E*	CJ
975974	(1030)	**0**	A	*ME*	BD
975975	(1042)	**P**	P	*E*	CJ
975976	(1033)		A		KT
975977	(1023)		A		KT
975978	(1025)	**0**	A	*ME*	BD
977087	(34971)	**HB**	H	*WN*	HE
977942	(86467, 80251)	**E**	E	*E*	CF
977943	(86718, 80252)	**E**	E	*E*	CF
977948	(86733, 94028)	**E**	E	*E*	CF
977949	(86377, 94025)	**E**	E	*E*	CF

CLASS 390 PENDOLINO BARRIER VEHICLES

These vehicles are used to move Class 390 EMUs around the national system in the same way as other vehicles included in this book. Various diagrams. Converted from Mark 1 GUVs (NL).

977944–977946. Lot No. 30417 Pressed Steel 1958–59. B5 bogies.
977947. Lot No. 30565 Pressed Steel 1959. B5 bogies.

977944	(86151, 94010)	**E** E	TO
977945	(86437, 94011)	**E** E	TO
977946	(86106, 94024)	**E** E	TO
977947	(86730, 94032)	**E** E	TO

LABORATORY, TESTING & INSTRUCTION COACHES

These coaches are used for research, development, instruction, testing and inspection on the Network Rail system. Many are fitted with sophisticated technical equipment.

Non-Standard Livery: 975000/46/76 are in BR research white and red with a grey stripe.

Laboratory Coach. Converted from BR Mark 1 RSO. Lot No. 30014 York 1950–51. B4 bogies.

975000	(1003)	**O**	AE		ZA

Structure Gauging Driving Trailer Coach. Converted from BR Mark 1 BSK. Lot No. 30699 Wolverton 1961–63. B4 bogies.

975081	(35313)	**SO**	NR	*SO*	ZA

Overhead Line Equipment Test Coach. Can either be locomotive hauled or included between DMU vehicles 977391/2. Converted from BR Mark 1 BSK Lot No. 30142 Gloucester 1954–5. B4 bogies.

975091	(34615)	**Y**	NR	*SO*	ZA

Structure Gauging Train Dormitory and Generator Coach. Converted from BR Mark 1 BCK Lot No. 30732 Derby 1962–4. B4 bogies.

975280	(21263)	**RK**	NR		ZA

Test Coach. Converted from BR Mark 2 FK Lot No. 30734 Derby 1962–64. B4 bogies.

975290	(13396)	**SO**	SO	*SO*	ZA

Test Coach. Converted from BR Mark 1 BSK Lot No. 30699 Wolverton 1961–63. Commonwealth bogies.

975397	(35386)	**SO**	SO	*SO*	ZA

Cinema Coach. Converted from BR Mark 1 TSO Lot No. 30243 York 1955–57. BR Mark 1 bogies.

975403	(4598)	**FG**	FG	*GW*	PM

Test Coach. Converted from BR Mark 1 BSK Lot No. 30223 Charles Roberts 1955–56. B5 bogies.

975422	(34875)	**SO**	SO	*SO*	ZA

High Speed Track Recording Train Coach. Converted from prototype HST TF Lot No. 30848 Derby 1972. BT10 bogies.

975814	(11000,41000)	**RK**	NR		Hunslet-Barclay, Kilmarnock

Test Coach. Converted from Mark 3 TRUB Lot No. 30849 Derby 1972–3. BT10 bogies.

975984 (10000, 40000)   **SO**   SO   *SO*   ZA

High Speed Track Recording Train Generator Coach. Converted from Class 438 driving trailer. Lot No. 30764 York 1965–67, which in turn had been converted from BR Mark 1 TSO Lot No. 30149 Swindon 1956–57. B5 (SR) bogies.

977335 (4005, 76277)   **SO**   NR   *SO*   ZA

High Speed Track Recording Train Dormitory Coach. Converted from BR Mark 2 BSO. Lot No 30757 Derby 1965–66. B4 bogies.

977337 (9395)   **SO**   NR   *SO*   ZA

High Speed Track Recording Train Brake & Stores Coach. Converted from Mark 2 BSO. Lot No. 30757 Derby 1965–66. B4 bogies.

977338 (9387)   **SO**   NR   *SO*   ZA

Test Train Staff and Dormitory Coach. Converted from BR Mark 3 SLEP. Lot No. 30960 Derby 1979–83. BT10 bogies.

977855 (10576)   **SO**   NR   *SO*   ZA

Instruction Coach. Converted from BR Mark 2E TSO. Lot No. 30844 Derby 1972–73. B4 bogies.

977867 (5841)   **AR**   AR   *AR*   NC

Radio Equipment Survey Coaches. Converted from BR Mark 2E TSO. Lot No. 30844 Derby 1972–73. B4 bogies.

977868 (5846)   **RK**   NR   *SO*   ZA
977869 (5858)   **RK**   NR   *SO*   ZA

Laboratory Coach. Converted from BR Mark 2E TSO. Lot No. 30844 Derby 1972–73. B4 bogies.

977974 (5854)   **AE**   AE   *AE*   ZA

Inspection Coach. Converted from BR Inspection Saloon. BR Wagon Lot No. 3095. Swindon 1957. B4 bogies.

999506   **M**   NR   *SO*   ZA

Track Recording Coach. Converted from BR Inspection Saloon. BR Wagon Lot No. 3379. Swindon 1960. B4 bogies.

999508   **SO**   NR   *SO*   ZA

High Speed Track Recording Coach. Can either be locomotive hauled (accompanied by 977335/7/8) or included between DMU vehicles 977391/2. Purpose built Mark 2. B4 bogies.

999550   **RK**   NR   *SO*   ZA

TEST TRAIN BRAKE FORCE RUNNERS

These vehicles are included in test trains to provide brake force and are not used for any other purposes. Other vehicles included in this book may also be similarly used on a temporary basis if required. Converted from BR Mark 1 BSK, RKB, RB, RU, SK, TSO, FK, FOs and BR Mark 2 TSO, SO, FK, BFKs.

975051. Lot No. 30025 Wolverton 1950–52. B4 bogies.
977084. Lot No. 30514 Cravens 1958–61. B5 bogies.
977085. Lot No. 30633 Swindon 1959–62. Commonwealth bogies.
977193. Lot No. 30632 Swindon 1959–61. Commonwealth bogies.
977331. Lot No. 30721 Swindon 1961–63. Commonwealth bogies.
977390. Lot No. 30810 Derby 1969–70. B4 bogies.
977449/450. Lot No. 30472 BRCW 1957–59. B4 bogies.
977468/470/801/2. Lot No. 30751 Derby 1964–7. B4 bogies.
977595. Lot No. 30825 Derby 1969–72. B4 bogies.
977788/94. Lot No. 30823 Derby 1969–72. B4 bogies.
977789. Lot No. 30837 Derby 1971–72. B4 bogies.
977790/1/2/6. Lot No. 30844 Derby 1972–73. B4 bogies.
977793. Lot No. 30795 Derby 1969–70. B4 bogies.
977905. Lot No. 30573 GRCW 1959–60. B4 bogies.
977970. Lot No. 30717 Swindon 1959–60. Commonwealth bogies.
977971. Lot No. 30690 Wolverton 1961–62. Commonwealth bogies.
977972/973. Lot No. 30667 Swindon 1962. Commonwealth bogies.
977982. Lot No. 30685 Derby 1960–62. Commonwealth bogies.

Non-Standard Livery: 977788–94 are Adtranz White with yellow stripe.

975051	(34133)	**B**	E		CW
977084	(1505)	**B**	E		CW
977085	(336, 1637)	**B**	E		CW
977193	(1989)	**B**	E		CW
977331	(35444)	**BG**	H		MB
977390	(3164, 6410)	**B**	E		CW
977449	(3086)	**B**	E		CW
977450	(3087)	**B**	E		CW
977468	(5169)	**SO**	SO	*SO*	ZA
977470	(5134)	**SO**	SO	*SO*	ZA
977595	(13573)	**BG**	E		CW
977788	(14157, 17157)	**O**	BT	*E*	ZF
977789	(5765)	**O**	BT	*E*	ZF
977790	(5830)	**O**	BT	*E*	ZF
977791	(5855)	**O**	BT	*E*	ZF
977792	(5856)	**O**	BT	*E*	ZF
977793	(5596)	**O**	BT	*E*	ZF
977794	(14139, 17139)	**O**	BT	*E*	ZF
977796	(5898)	**BG**	H		ZH
977801	(5153)	**SO**	NR	*SO*	ZA
977802	(5176)	**SO**	NR	*SO*	ZA
977905	(35292, 80215)	**SO**	SO	*SO*	ZA
977970	(3136)		WC		CS

977971	(4939)		SO	*SO*	ZA
977972	(13318)		SO	*SO*	ZA
977973	(13341)	**WR**	SO	*SO*	ZA
977982	(25729, 18729)	**CH**	SO	*SO*	ZA

BREAKDOWN TRAIN COACHES

These coaches are formed in trains used for the recovery of derailed railway vehicles and were converted from BR Mark 1 BCK, BG, BSK and SK. The current use of each vehicle is given. 975611–613 were previously converted to trailer luggage vans in 1968. BR Mark 1 bogies.

975080. Lot No. 30155 Wolverton 1955–56.
975087. Lot No. 30032 Wolverton 1951–52.
975463/573. Lot No. 30156 Wolverton 1954–55.
975465/477/494. Lot No. 30233 GRCW 1955–57.
975471. Lot No. 30095 Wolverton 1953–55.
975481/482/484/574. Lot No. 30141 GRCW 1954–55.
975498. Lot No. 30074 Wolverton 1953–54.
975611–613. Lot No. 30162 Pressed Steel 1954–57.
975639, 977088/235. Lot No. 30229 Metro-Cammell 1955–57.
977095/107. Lot No. 30425 Metro-Cammell 1956–58.

975080	(25079)	r	**Y**	NR	*E*	TO	Tool Van
975087	(34289)	r	**Y**	NR		DY	Generator Van
975463	(34721)	r	**Y**	NR	*E*	TE	Staff Coach
975465	(35109)	r	**Y**	NR	*E*	TO	Staff Coach
975471	(34543)	r	**Y**	NR		DY	Staff & Tool Coach
975477	(35108)	r	**Y**	NR		DY	Staff Coach
975481	(34606)	r	**Y**	NR	*E*	TO	Generator Van
975482	(34602)	r	**Y**	NR	*E*	TE	Generator Van
975484	(34591)		**Y**	DR		CS	Generator Van
975494	(35082)	r	**Y**	NR	*E*	CF	Generator Van
975498	(34367)	r	**Y**	NR	*E*	TE	Tool Van
975573	(34729)	r	**Y**	NR	*E*	CF	Staff Coach
975574	(34599)	r	**Y**	NR	*E*	OC	Staff Coach
975611	(80915, 68201)	r	**Y**	NR	*E*	OC	Generator Van
975612	(80922, 68203)	r	**Y**	NR	*E*	CF	Tool Van
975613	(80918, 68202)	r	**Y**	NR	*E*	OC	Tool Van
975639	(35016)		**Y**	DR		CS	Tool Van
977088	(34990)		**Y**	NR	*E*	CD	Generator Van
977095	(21210)		**Y**	DR		CS	Staff Coach
977107	(21202)		**Y**	NR	*E*	CD	Staff Coach
977235	(34989)		**Y**	NR	*E*	CD	Tool Van

INFRASTRUCTURE MAINTENANCE COACHES

Overhead Line Maintenance Coaches

These coaches are formed in trains used for the maintenance, repair and renewal of overhead lines and were converted from BR Mark 1 BSK, CK and SK. The current use of each vehicle is given. BR Mark 1 bogies.

Non-standard livery: All vehicles are light grey.

975697/698, 975700. Lot No. 30025 Wolverton 1950–52.
975699. Lot No. 30233 GRCW 1955–57.
975713/744. Lot No. 30350 Wolverton 1956–57.
975714. Lot No. 30374. York 1958.
975723/743. Lot No. 30349 Wolverton 1956–57.
975724. Lot No. 30471 Metro-Cammell 1957–59.
975733. Lot No. 30351 Wolverton 1956–57.
975734. Lot No. 30426 Wolverton 1956–58.

975697	(34147)	r	0	CA	CA	RU	Pantograph coach
975698	(34148)	r	0	CA	CA	RU	Pantograph coach
975699	(35105)	r	0	CA	CA	Preston	Pantograph coach
975700	(34138)	r	0	CA	CA	RU	Pantograph coach
975713	(25420)	r	0	CA	CA	RU	Stores van
975714	(25466)	r	0	CA	CA	Preston	Stores van
975723	(25388)	r	0	CA	CA	RU	Stores & generator van
975724	(16079)	r	0	CA	CA	Preston	Stores & generator van
975733	(16001)	r	0	CA	CA	RU	Stores & roof access coach
975734	(25695)	r	0	CA	CA	Preston	Stores & roof access coach
975743	(25358)	r	0	CA	CA	RU	Staff & office coach
975744	(25440)	r	0	CA	CA	Preston	Staff & office coach

Snowblower Train Coaches

These coaches work with Snowblower ADB 968501. They were converted from BR Mark 1 BSK. The current use of each vehicle is given. BR Mark 1 bogies.

975464. Lot No. 30386 Charles Roberts 1956–58.
975486. Lot No. 30025 Wolverton 1950–52.

975464	(35171)	N	NR	E	Hunslet-Barclay, Kilmarnock	Staff & dormitory coach
975486	(34100)	N	NR	E	Hunslet-Barclay, Kilmarnock	Tool van

Severn Tunnel Emergency Train Coaches

These coaches are formed in a train used in the event of incidents in the Severn Tunnel. They were converted from BR Mark 1 BSK & BG. The current use of each vehicle is given. 975615 was previously converted to a trailer luggage van in 1968.

975497. Lot No. 30427 Wolverton 1956–59. BR Mark 1 bogies.
975615. Lot No. 30162 Pressed Steel 1954–57. BR Mark 1 bogies.
977526. Lot No. 30229 Metro-Cammell 1955–57. Commonwealth bogies.

975497	(35218)	Y	NR	E	Sudbrook	Tool & generator van

| 975615 | (80951, 68206) | Y | NR | *E* | Sudbrook | Tool van |
| 977526 | (35010) | **BG** | NR | *E* | Sudbrook | Emergency casualty coach |

Miscellaneous Infrastructure Coaches

These coaches are used for various infrastructure projects on Network Rail.

99016. Lot No. 30732 Derby 1964. Commonwealth bogies.
99018. Lot No. 30219 Swindon 1955–57. Commonwealth bogies.
99019. Lot No. 30702 Wolverton 1961–62. Commonwealth bogies.
99025/26. Lot No. 30565 Pressed Steel 1959. B5 bogies.
99027. Lot No. 30417 Pressed Steel 1958–59. B5 bogies.
977163/165/166. Lot No. 30721 Wolverton 1961–63. Commonwealth bogies.
977167. Lot No. 30699 Wolverton 1961–63. Commonwealth bogies.
977168. Lot No. 30573 GRCW 1959–60. B4 bogies.
977169. Lot No. 30232 GRCW 1955–56. B4 bogies.
977591. Lot No. 30756 Derby 1965–66. B4 bogies.
977787. Lot No. 30820 Derby 1969–71. B4 bogies.
977912/913. Lot No. 30796 Derby 1969–70. B4 bogies.
977922/923. Wagon Lot No. 3472 Ashford 1963. 4-wheeled.

Non-standard liveries:

99016/18, 977163/165–168 are all over white.
977591 is red and yellow.
977922/923 are light blue.

99016	(21275)	**0**	BB		AP	Staff & dormitory coach
99018	(4393)	**0**	BB		AP	Generator & stores coach
99019	(1870)	**RK**	NR	*SO*	DY	Spray coach
99025	(86744, 96103)	**RK**	NR	*E*	DY	Spray coach
99026	(86745, 96211)	**RK**	NR	*E*	DY	Spray coach
99027	(86331, 96214)	**RK**	NR	*E*	DY	Spray coach
977163	(35487)	**0**	BB	*BB*	AP	Staff & generator coach
977165	(35408)	**0**	BB	*BB*	AP	Staff & generator coach
977166	(35419)	**0**	BB	*BB*	AP	Staff & generator coach
977167	(35400)	**0**	BB	*BB*	AP	Staff & generator coach
977168	(35289)	**0**	BB	*BB*	AP	Staff & generator coach
977169	(35027)	**E**	E		OC	Staff & tool coach
977591	(14033, 17033)	**0**	E	*E*	Newport	Staff & tool coach
977787	(9453)	**CE**	NR		DY	Staff, tool & generator coach
977912	(14115, 17115)	**N**	NR		CS	Staff, tool & generator coach
977913	(14120, 17120)	**N**	NR		CS	Staff & tool coach
977922	(787245)	**0**	J		Doncaster Roberts Road	Staff & dormitory van
977923	(787253)	**0**	J		Doncaster Roberts Road	Staff & dormitory van

5.3. NPCCS AWAITING DISPOSAL

This list contains the last known locations of NPCCS vehicles awaiting disposal. The definition of which vehicles are "awaiting disposal" is somewhat vague, but generally speaking these are vehicles of types not now in normal service or vehicles which have been damaged by fire, vandalism or collision.

230	Horsham Yard	321047	Temple Mills Yard
80330	Bristol Pylle Hill	395896	Wavertree Yard, Liverpool
80336	Bristol East Yard	975066	Ripple Lane WRD
80338	Bristol East Yard	975071	Heaton ECD
80389	ZG	975379	York Leeman Road
80865	Hornsey Sand Terminal	975454	TO
82221	ZF	975456	Horsham Yard
84197	Worksop	975462	Three Bridges WRD
84364	Doncaster West Yard	975491	TO
84519	Crewe South Yard	975550	Doncaster Hexthorpe Sidings
92193	Preston Carriage Sidings	975551	Doncaster Hexthorpe Sidings
92198	ZB	975552	Doncaster Hexthorpe Sidings
92306	Oxford Hinksey Yard*	975554	Doncaster West Yard
92325	Oxford Hinksey Yard*	975555	Doncaster West Yard
92328	ZG	975557	Carstairs
92333	Oxford Hinksey Yard*	975558	Carstairs
92341	Oxford Hinksey Yard*	975559	Carstairs
92353	Oxford Hinksey Yard*	975638	Horsham Yard
92357	Oxford Hinksey Yard*	975680	Carstairs
92370	ZG	975681	Portobello
92401	Oxford Hinksey Yard*	975682	Portobello
92402	Oxford Hinksey Yard*	975683	Carstairs
92404	CL	975684	Carstairs
92562	OC	975685	Portobello
92873	Oxford Hinksey Yard*	975686	Portobello
92897	ZG	975687	Portobello
93180	Derby South Dock Siding	975688	Portobello
93234	Hayes & Harlington	975691	Doncaster Hexthorpe Sidings
93358	Mossend Yard	975701	Preston Dock Street Sidings
93446	Crewe South Yard	975702	Preston Dock Street Sidings
93482	Bedford Civil Engineers Sdgs	975703	Rugby OTPD
93542	Hayes & Harlington	975704	Rugby OTPD
93579	DY	975706	Oxford Hinksey Yard*
93723	Bletchley T&RSMD	975707	Bletchley Middle Road Siding
93930	Crewe South Yard	975708	Bletchley Middle Road Siding
95227	Oxford Hinksey Yard*	975710	Doncaster Hexthorpe Sidings
95366	Bristol East Yard	975715	Preston Dock Street Sidings
96177	CP	975717	Oxford Hinksey Yard*
99645	FP	975718	Bletchley Middle Road Siding
99646	FP	975720	Doncaster Hexthorpe Sidings
99648	Eastleigh East Yard	975721	Doncaster West Yard
150144	Bristol East Yard	975725	Preston Dock Street Sidings
320645	York Leeman Road	975727	Oxford Hinksey Yard*

975728	Bletchley Middle Road Sdg	977063	Three Bridges WRD
975730	Doncaster Hexthorpe Sdgs	977077	Ripple Lane WRD
975735	Preston Dock Street Sdgs	977111	Ripple Lane WRD
975737	Oxford Hinksey Yard*	977112	Ripple Lane WRD
975738	Bletchley Middle Road Sdg	977116	Three Bridges WRD
975740	Doncaster Hexthorpe Sdgs	977144	PY
975745	Preston Dock Street Sdgs	977182	Eastleigh Down CS
975747	Oxford Hinksey Yard*	977183	Eastleigh Down CS
975748	Bletchley Middle Road Sdg	977359	ZN
975750	Doncaster Hexthorpe Sdgs	977399	NL
975757	Doncaster Hexthorpe Sdgs	977510	FP
975761	Doncaster Hexthorpe Sdgs	977618	Bletchley T&RSMD
975769	Doncaster Hexthorpe Sdgs	977695	Eastleigh Down CS
975797	Heaton ECD	977726	Wavertree Yard, Liverpool
975966	Three Bridges WRD	977795	ZN
975991	Crewe South Yard	977908	NC
975995	Wolverhampton Low Level Stn		

* In use as environmental sound protection barrier.

6. CODES

6.1. LIVERY CODES

Livery codes are used to denote the various liveries carried. It is impossible in a publication of this size to list every livery variation which currently exists. In particular items ignored for the purposes of this publication include:

• Minor colour variations.
• Omission of logos.
• All numbering, lettering and branding.

Descriptions quoted are thus a general guide only. Logos as appropriate for each livery are normally deemed to be carried.

Note: Loco-hauled coaching stock vehicles are in Intercity (light grey/red stripe/ white stripe/dark grey) livery unless otherwise indicated. For traditional two-colour carriage liveries the colour of the lower half of the bodyside is stated first.

Code Description

AE	AEA Technology (dark blue with a white stripe).
AL	Advertising livery (see class heading for details).
AN	Anglia Railways Class 170s (white & turquoise with blue vignette).
AR	Anglia Railways (turquoise blue with a white stripe).
AV	Arriva Trains Northern (turquoise blue with white doors).
B	BR blue.
BG	BR blue & grey lined out in white.
BI	"Visit Bristol" promotional livery (deep blue with various images).
BL	BR blue with yellow cabs, grey roof & large numbers.
BR	BR blue with a red solebar stripe.
C2	c2c Rail (blue with metallic grey doors & pink c2c branding).
CB	Old Connex South Eastern (NSE blue with a yellow lower bodyside).
CD	Cotswold Rail (silver with blue & red logo).
CE	BR Engineers (yellow & grey with black cab doors & window surrounds).
CH	BR Western Region/GWR (chocolate & cream).
CO	Centro (grey/green with light blue, white & yellow stripes).
CN	New Connex South Eastern (white with yellow doors, black window surrounds & grey lower band).
CR	Chiltern Railways (blue & white with a thin red stripe).
CS	ScotRail Caledonian Sleepers (two-tone purple with silver stripe).
CT	Central Trains (two-tone green with yellow doors. Blue flash and red stripe at vehicle ends).
CX	Connex (white with yellow lower body & blue solebar).
DC	Scenic lines of Devon & Cornwall promotional livery (black with gold cantrail stripe).
DG	BR Departmental (plain dark grey with black cab doors & window surrounds).
DR	Direct Rail Services (dark blue with light blue or dark grey roof).
E	English Welsh & Scottish Railway (maroon bodyside & roof with a gold band).
EB	Eurotunnel (two-tone grey with a broad blue stripe).

EN	Enron Teesside Operations (trafalgar blue with red solebar stripe).
EP	European Passenger Services (two-tone grey with dark blue roof).
ES	Eurailscout GB (deep yellow with a blue and purple logo).
ET	Eurotunnel (two-tone grey & white with green & blue bands).
EU	Eurostar (white with dark blue & yellow stripes).
F	BR Trainload Freight (two-tone grey with black cab doors & window surrounds. Various logos).
FB	Revised Fragonset Railways (Black with large bodyside FRAGONSET lettering).
FE	Railfreight Distribution International (two tone-grey with black cab doors & dark blue roof).
FF	Freightliner (two-tone grey with black cab doors & window surrounds. Freightliner logo).
FG	First Group corporate Inter-City livery (indigo blue with a white roof & gold, pink & white stripes).
FL	Freightliner (dark green with yellow cabs).
FO	BR Railfreight (grey bodyside, yellow cabs & large BR double arrow).
FP	First Great Western (green & ivory with thin green & broad gold stripes).
FR	Fragonset Railways (black with silver roof & a red bodyside band lined out in white).
FS	First Group corporate regional/suburban livery (indigo blue with pink & white stripes).
FX	Felixstowe Dock Company.
FY	Foster Yeoman (blue/silver. Cast numberplates).
G	BR Green (plain green, with white stripe on main line locomotives).
G	BR Southern Region/SR or BR DMU (green with straw stripe on coaching stock).
GA	GoVia South Central "Heritage" EMUs (white & dark green with light green semi-circular patchs at cab ends. Light green stripe along length of unit).
GB	GB Railfreight (blue with orange cantrail & solebar stripes, orange cabs).
GC	British racing green and cream.
GE	First Great Eastern (grey, green, blue & white).
GG	BR Green (two-tone green).
GIF	GIF (Spain) light blue with dark blue band.
GL	First Great Western Locos (green with gold stripe).
GM	Greater Manchester PTE (light grey/dark grey with red & white stripes).
GN	Great North Eastern Railway (dark blue with a red stripe).
GP	Ginsters Cornish Pasties promotional livery (Black and red with various images and cartoons etc.).
GS	Royal Scotsman/Great Scottish & Western Railway (maroon).
GV	Gatwick Express EMU (red, white & indigo blue with mauve & blue doors).
GW	Great Western Railway (green, lined out in black & orange. Cast numberplates).
GX	Gatwick Express IC (dark grey/white/burgundy/white).
GY	Eurotunnel (grey & yellow).
HA	Hanson Quarry Products (dark blue & silver).
HB	HSBC Rail (Oxford blue & white)
HE	Heathrow Express (silver grey & indigo blue with black window surrounds).
HN	Harry Needle Railroad Company (grey/orange, lined out in black).
HW	Heart of Wales Line promotional livery (orange with yellow doors).
I	BR InterCity (dark grey/white/red/white).
IL	Island Line (light blue, with illustrations featuring dinosaurs etc).

IM	BR Mainline (dark grey/white/red/light grey & yellow lower cabsides except shunters).
IR	Ian Riley Engineering (grey with light green band).
K	Black.
LH	BR Loadhaul (black with orange cabsides).
LN	LNER Tourist (green & cream).
LW	LNWR black with grey red lining.
M	BR maroon (Maroon lined out in straw & black).
MA	Maintrain (Light blue).
ME	New Merseyrail Electrics (details to follow).
ML	BR Mainline Freight (Aircraft blue with silver stripe).
MM	Midland Mainline (Teal green with cream lower body sides & three orange stripes).
MN	New Midland Mainline Meridian (details to follow).
MR	Mendip Rail (Green, red & silver).
MT	Old Merseytravel (yellow/white with grey & black stripes).
MY	New Merseytravel (yellow/white with grey stripe).
N	BR Network SouthEast (white & blue with red lower bodyside stripe, grey solebar & cab ends).
NB	Provincial services (As RR but with the red stripe repainted blue).
NS	Northern Spirit/Arriva Trains Northern (turquoise blue with lime green 'N').
NT	BR Network SouthEast (white & blue with red lower bodyside & cantrail stripes).
NW	North West Trains/First North Western (blue with a gold cant rail stripe & star).
O	Non standard livery (see class heading for details).
P	Porterbrook Leasing Company (purple & grey or white).
PC	Pullman Car Company (umber & cream with gold lettering).
PS	Provincial (dark blue/grey with light blue & white stripes).
R	Plain red.
RE	Provincial/Regional Railways Express (light grey/buff/dark grey with white, dark blue & light blue stripes).
RG	BR Parcels (dark grey & red).
RK	New Railtrack (blue & green).
RL	RMS Locotech (blue & red).
RM	Royal Mail (red with yellow stripes above solebar).
RN	North West Regional Railways (dark blue/grey with green & white stripes).
RO	Old Railtrack (orange with white & grey stripes).
RP	Royal Train (claret, lined out in red & black).
RR	Regional Railways (dark blue/grey with light blue & white stripes, three narrow dark blue stripes at cab ends).
RT	RT Rail (Michael Owen) (black, lined out in red).
RV	Riviera Trains (Oxford blue & cream [Oxford blue for locos], lined out in gold).
RX	Rail Express Systems (dark grey & red with or without blue markings).
RY	BR Parcels sector (red with yellow stripes above solebar).
S	Old Strathclyde PTE (orange & black lined out in white).
SC	New Strathclyde PTE (carmine & cream lined out in black & gold).
SD	South West Trains suburban livery (deep blue with red doors & orange & red cab sides).
SL	Silverlink (indigo blue with white stripe, green lower body & yellow doors).

SN   GoVia South Central (white & dark green with light green semi-circles at both ends of each vehicle. Light grey band at solebar level).

SO   Serco Railtest (red/grey).

SP   New Strathcltde PTE Class 170/334 livery (Carmine and cream with a turqouise stripe.)

SR   ScotRail (white, terracotta, purple & aquamarine).

ST   Stagecoach/South West Trains (white & blue with orange & red stripes).

SW   South West Trains (long-distance stock) (white & dark blue with black window surounds, red doors & red panel with orange stripe at unit ends.)

SX   Stansted Express (two-tone metallic blue with grey doors).

TR   Thameslink Rail (dark blue with a broad orange stripe & two narrower white bodyside stripes plus white cantrail stripe).

TT   Thames Trains (blue with lime green doors).

TW   Tyne & Wear PTE (white & yellow with blue stripe).

TX   Arriva Trans-Pennine Express (plum with gold 'N').

U   Plain white or grey undercoat.

V   Virgin Trains (red with black doors extending into bodysides, three white lower bodysides stripes).

VL   Valley Lines (dark green & red with white & light green stripes. Light green doors).

VN   Venice Simplon Orient Express 'Northern Belle' (crimson lake & cream).

VP   Virgin Trains shunters (black with a large black & white chequered flag on the bodyside).

VT   New Virgin Trains (silver, with black window surrounds & red roof. Red swept down at unit/loco ends. Black and white strpied doors on units.)

VW   "Visit Wales" promotional livery (green & red with various images).

WA   Wabtec Rail (black).

WB   Wales & Borders Alphaline (metallic silver with blue doors).

WN   Old West Anglia Great Northern (white with blue, grey & orange stripes).

WP   New West Anglia Great Northern (deep purple with grey doors).

WR   Waterman Railways (maroon with cream stripes).

WV   Waterman Railways VIP (West Coast Joint Stock-style lined purple lake).

WX   Heart of Wessex Line promotional livery (red with yellow doors).

WT   Wessex Trains Alphaline (metallic silver with maroon doors).

WY   Old West Yorkshire PTE (red/cream with thin yellow stripe).

WZ   Wessex Trains promotional livery (claret with various images).

Y   Plain yellow.

YN   West Yorkshire PTE (red with light grey 'N').

YP   New West Yorkshire PTE (red with grey semi-circles).

YO   Foster Yeoman (blue/silver/blue. Cast numberplates).

6.2. OWNER CODES

Locomotives and rolling stock are owned by various companies and private owners and are allotted codes as follows:

Code   Owner

14	75014 Locomotive Operators Group.
24	6024 Preservation Society.
50	The Fifty Fund.
62	The Princess Royal Class Locomotive Trust.
71	71A locomotives Ltd.
90	Deltic 9000 Locomotives.
A	Angel Trains.
AE	AEA Technology.
AM	Alstom UK.
AR	Anglia Railways.
B1	Thompson B1 Locomotive Society.
BB	Balfour Beatty Rail Plant.
BC	Bridgend County Borough Council.
BK	The Scottish Railway Preservation Society.
BT	Bombardier Transportation.
CA	Carillion Rail Plant.
CD	Cotswold Rail.
CM	Cambrian Trains.
CN	The Carriage and Traction Company Ltd.
DP	The Deltic Preservation Society.
DR	Direct Rail Services.
DT	The Diesel Traction Group.
E	English Welsh & Scottish Railway.
EF	EWS Finance.
EN	Enron Teesside Operations.
ER	Eastleigh Railway Preservation Society.
ES	Eurailscout GB.
ET	Eurotunnel.
EU	Eurostar (UK).
FG	First Great Western.
FL	Freightliner.
FR	Fragonset Railways.
FS	Flying Scotsman Railways.
FX	The Felixstowe Dock & Railway Company.
FY	Foster Yeoman.
GB	GB Rail.
GS	The Great Scottish & Western Railway Company.
GW	The Great Western Society.
H	HSBC Rail (UKI).
HA	The Hanson Group.
HD	Hastings Diesels.
HE	British Airports Authority.
HJ	Howard Johnston Engineering.
HN	Harry Needle Railroad Company.

HS	Harry Schneider.
HX	Halifax Asset Finance.
IE	Ian Storey Engineering
IR	Ian Riley Engineering.
J	Jarvis Rail.
JK	Dr. John Kennedy.
LW	London & North Western Railway Company.
MA	Maintrain.
MD	Ministry of Defence.
ME	Arriva Trains Merseyside.
MH	Mid-Hants Railway.
MN	Merchant Navy Locomotive Preservation Society.
NE	North Eastern Locomotive Preservation Group.
NR	Network Rail.
NY	North Yorkshire Moors Railway
P	Porterbrook Leasing Company.
PD	Project Defiance.
PO	Other/Privately owned.
RA	Railfilms.
RD	Rhondda Cynon Taff District Council
RI	Rail Assets Investments.
RL	RMS Locotech.
RM	Royal Mail.
RS	Rail Charter Services
RT	RT Rail Tours.
RV	Riviera Trains.
SA	Sea Containers Rail Services
SB	SNCB/NMBS (Société Nationale des Chemins de fer Belges/Nationale Maatschappij der belgische Spoorwegen).
SC	GoVia South Central.
SE	Connex South Eastern.
SF	SNCF (Société Nationale des Chemins de fer Français).
SH	Scottish Highland Railway Company.
SM	Siemens.
SO	Serco Railtest.
SV	Severn Valley Railway.
SW	South West Trains.
VS	Venice Simplon Orient Express.
VT	Vintage Trains
VW	West Coast Trains.
W	Wiltshire Leasing Company.
WA	Wabtec Rail.
WB	Wales & Borders Trains.
WC	West Coast Railway Company.
WF	Western Falcon Rail (Alan and Tracy Lear).
WN	West Anglia Great Northern Railway.
WT	Wessex Trains.
X	Sold for scrap/further use or owner unknown.

6.3. LOCOMOTIVE POOL CODES

Locomotives are split into operational groups ('pools') for diagramming and maintenance purposes. The official codes used to denote these pools are shown in this publication.

Code	Pool
ATLO	Virgin West Coast/Cross-Country locomotives (Alstom controlled).
CDJD	Serco Railtest. Class 08.
CREL	Cotswold Rail Engineering. Serviceable locomotives.
CROL	Cotswold Rail Engineering. Stored locomotives.
DFFT	Freightliner. Class 47 with "Dock Mode" for the Felixstowe branch.
DFGC	Freightliner. Class 86/5.
DFGM	Freightliner. Class 66/5, intermodal traffic.
DFHH	Freightliner Heavy Haul. Classes 66/5 and 66/6.
DFLC	Freightliner. Class 90.
DFLH	Freightliner Heavy Haul. Class 47.
DFLM	Freightliner. Class 47 with multiple working equipment.
DFLS	Freightliner. Class 08.
DFNC	Freightliner. Class 86/6.
DFRT	Freightliner. Class 66/5. Railtrack contracts and general traffic.
DFTZ	Freightliner. Class 57.
DHLT	Freightliner. Locomotives awaiting maintenance/repair/disposal.
DNLL	Deltic 9000 Locomotives Limited locomotives.
GBCM	GB Railfreight Class 66. Railfreight contracts.
GBRT	GB Railfreight Class 66. Railtrack contracts.
GBZZ	GB Rail. Stored/General pool.
GPSN	Eurostar (UK). Class 73.
GPSS	Eurostar (UK). Class 08.
GPSV	Eurostar (UK). Class 37.
HBSH	Wabtec. Hire Locomotives.
HGSS	Maintrain. Class 08 (Tyseley)
HISE	Maintrain. Class 08 (Derby).
HISL	Maintrain. Class 08 (Neville Hill).
HJSE	First Great Western. Class 08 (Landore).
HJSL	First Great Western. Class 08 (Laira).
HJXX	First Great Western. Class 08 (Old Oak HST & St. Phillips Marsh).
HLSV	Wales & Borders. Class 08. Hire locomotive.
HNRL	Harry Needle Railroad Company. Hire locomotives.
HNRS	Harry Needle Railroad Company. Stored locomotives.
HQXX	West Anglia Great Northern Railway. Class 03.
HWSU	South Central. Class 09.
HYSB	South West Trains. Standby locomotives.
IANA	Anglia Railways. Classes 47 & 86.
ICCM	Virgin Cross-Country Class 43.
ICCP	Virgin Cross-Country/Virgin West Coast Class 43.
IECA	Great North Eastern Railway. Class 91.
IECB	Great North Eastern Railway. Class 89.
IECP	Great North Eastern Railway. Class 43.
IMLP	Midland Mainline. Class 43.

IVGA	Gatwick Express. Class 73.
IWCA	Virgin West Coast. Classes 87 & 90.
IWLA	First Great Western. Classes 47 & 57.
IWPA	Virgin West Coast. Class 86.
IWRP	First Great Western. Class 43.
KCSI	Bombardier. Class 08 (Ilford).
KDSD	Bombardier. Class 08 (Doncaster).
KESE	Alstom. Class 08 (Eastleigh).
KGSS	Bombardier. Class 08 (Glasgow).
KWSW	Bombardier. Class 08 (Wolverton).
MBDL	Non TOC owned diesel locomotives.
MOLO	RT Rail Tours (Michael Owen).
QADD	Network Rail. Class 31.
QAED	Network Rail. Class 73.
RFSH	Wabtec. Hire fleet.
RTLO	Riviera Trains. Operational Fleet.
SAXL	HSBC Rail (UK). Off lease.
SBXL	Porterbrook Leasing. Off lease.
SDFR	Fragonset Railways. Operational locomotives.
SDMS	Fragonset Railways. Museum locomotives.
SDXL	Fragonset Railways. Stored locomotives.
WAAK	EWS. Class 67.
WBAH	EWS. Class 66 Anglia & Southern.
WBAI	EWS. Class 66 North Eastern (South).
WBAK	EWS. Class 66 Great Western.
WBAM	EWS. Class 66 Scotland, non-RETB fitted.
WBAN	EWS. Class 66 Midland.
WBAT	EWS. Class 66 North Eastern (North).
WBBM	EWS. Class 66 Scotland RETB fitted.
WCAI	EWS. Class 60 North Eastern (South).
WCAK	EWS. Class 60 Great Western.
WCAN	EWS. Class 60 Midland.
WCAT	EWS. Class 60 North Eastern (North).
WDAG	EWS. Class 59/2.
WEFE	EWS. Class 90.
WFGA	EWS. Class 58 for hire contract to the Netherlands.
WGAI	EWS. Class 56 North Eastern (South).
WGAT	EWS. Class 56 North Eastern (North).
WHCD	EWS. Class 47/7 Dual braked.
WHDD	EWS. Class 47 Dual braked.
WHRD	EWS. Class 47 Special Trains.
WHTN	EWS. Class 47 Hired to Serco Railtest.
WKAC	EWS. Class 37 Anglia & Southern.
WKAD	EWS. Class 37 Midlands & North West.
WKAM	EWS. Class 37 Motherwell. Non-RETB.
WKBM	EWS. Class 37 RETB equipped.
WKCK	EWS. Class 37 Hired to Wales & Borders.
WKGR	EWS. Class 37. On hire to Italy.
WKGS	EWS. Class 37. On hire to Spain.
WMOC	EWS. Heritage locomotives.
WNSS	EWS. Main line locomotives – stored serviceable.

WNTR	EWS. Main line locomotives – tactical reserve.
WNWX	EWS. Main line locomotives – for major repairs.
WNXX	EWS. Main line locomotives – stored unserviceable.
WNYX	EWS. Main line locomotives – authorised for component recovery.
WNZX	EWS. Main line locomotives/Shunting locomotives – awaiting disposal.
WPAG	EWS. Class 73.
WSAS	EWS. Shunting locomotives (Anglia & Southern Zone).
WSAW	EWS. Shunting locomotives (on hire to Allied Steel & Wire).
WSGW	EWS. Shunting locomotives (Great Western Zone).
WSMD	EWS. Shunting locomotives (Midlands Zone).
WSNE	EWS. Shunting locomotives (North East England).
WSNW	EWS. Shunting locomotives (North West England).
WSSC	EWS. Shunting locomotives (Scotland).
WSWX	EWS. Shunting locomotives – Locos for repair.
WSXX	EWS. Shunting locomotives – Stored.
WSYX	EWS. Shunting locomotives – component recovery only.
WTAE	EWS. Class 92 Dollands Moor–Wembley–Mossend–Doncaster & Crewe–Trafford Park Routes.
WTWE	EWS. Class 92 Eurotunnel only.
XHSD	Direct Rail Services. Operational locomotives.
XHSS	Direct Rail Services. Stored locomotives.
XYPA	Mendip Rail. Class 59/0.
XYPO	Mendip Rail. Class 59/1.

PLATFORM 5 MAIL ORDER

BRITISH MULTIPLE UNITS VOLUME 1: DMUs & DEMUs

Coorlea Publishing

A complete listing of all DMU and DEMU vehicles built for Britain's railways. For each vehicle details of build date, withdrawal date, disposal date and disposal location are given. Also includes details of use conversions, renumberings and vehicles in preservation. Spiral bound. 72 pages. **£7.95**.

BRITISH MULTIPLE UNITS VOLUME 2: EPBs, Haps, Saps and Caps

Coorlea Publishing

A second volume of multiple unit data covering electric multiple units of classes EPB, Hap, Sap and Cap. Includes detailed information for every vehicle as listed in volume 1. 48 pages. **£6.95**.

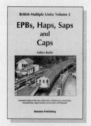

BRITISH MULTIPLE UNITS VOLUME 3: Classes 302-390

Coorlea Publishing

Complete listing of all AC Electric Multiple Units of classes 302-390. Shows introduction to service dates for every vehicle, unit formations, subsequent reformations, renumberings, withdrawal dates and disposal information. Includes a listing in set number order, plus a full index in vehicle number order. Also covers departmental vehicles. 84 pages. **£9.95**.

Please add postage: 10% UK, 20% Europe, 30% Rest of World.

Telephone, fax or send your order to the Platform 5 Mail Order Department. See page 384 of this book for details.

6.4. OPERATOR CODES

Operator codes are used to denote the normal usage of the vehicles listed – i.e. the services of which company any vehicle will normally be used upon. Where no operation code is shown, vehicles are currently not in use.

Code	Operation
A	Angel Trains.
AE	AEA Technology Rail.
AM	Alstom.
AR	Anglia Railways.
AV	Arriva Trains Northern.
BB	Balfour Beatty Rail.
C2	c2c Rail.
CA	Carillion Rail.
CR	Chiltern Railways.
CT	Central Trains.
DR	Direct Rail services.
E	English Welsh & Scottish Railway.
EU	Eurostar (UK).
FL	Freightliner.
GB	GB Railfreight.
GE	First Great Eastern.
GN	Great North Eastern Railway.
GW	First Great Western.
GX	Gatwick Express.
H	HSBC Rail (UK)
HE	Heathrow Express.
IL	Island Line.
J	Jarvis Rail.
LS	Locomotive support coach.
ME	Arriva Trains Merseyside.
MM	Midland Mainline.
NW	First North Western.
P	Porterbrook Leasing Company.
RP	Royal Train.
SC	GoVia South Central.
SE	Connex South Eastern.
SL	Silverlink.
SO	Serco Railtest.
SR	ScotRail.
SS	Normally used on special or charter services.
SW	South West Trains.
TR	Thameslink Rail.
TT	Thames Trains
VL	Wales & Borders Trains (Valley Lines Business Unit)
VW	Virgin West Coast.
VX	Virgin Cross-Country
WB	Wales & Borders Trains.
WN	West Anglia Great Northern
WX	Wessex Trains

6.5. ALLOCATION & LOCATION CODES

Allocation codes are used in this publication to denote the normal maintenance base of each operational locomotive. However, maintenance may be carried out at other locations and may also be carried out by mobile maintenance teams.

Location codes are used to denote common storage locations whilst the full place name is used for other locations. The designation (S) denotes stored. However, when a loco pool code denotes that a loco is stored then the (S) is not shown.

Code	Depot	Operator
AF	Ashford Chart Leacon T&RSMD (Kent)	Bombardier Transportation
AL	Aylesbury TMD	Chiltern Railways
AP*	Ashford Rail Plant Depot (Kent)	Balfour Beatty Rail
AN	Allerton T&RSMD (Liverpool)	EWS
AY	Ayr SD	EWS
BA	Basford Hall Yard (Crewe)	*Storage location only*
BD	Birkenhead North T&RSMD	Arriva Trains Merseyside
BG*	Billingham T&RSMD	Enron Teesside Operations
BF*	Beechbrook Farm (Ashford)	
BH	Barrow Hill T&RSMD (Chesterfield)	Barrow Hill Engine Shed Society
BI	Brighton T&RSMD	South Central
BK	Barton Hill T&RSMD (Bristol)	EWS
BM	Bournemouth T&RSMD	South West Trains
BN	Bounds Green T&RSMD (London)	Great North Eastern Railway
BP	Blackpool North CS	*Storage location only*
BQ	Bury T&RSMD	East Lancashire Railway
BS	Bescot TMD (Walsall)	EWS
BT	Bo'ness (West Lothian)	Bo'ness & Kinneil Railway
BY	Bletchley T&RSMD	Silverlink
CA*	Carlisle Kingmoor Yard	EWS
CD	Crewe Diesel TMD	EWS
CE	Crewe International Electric T&RSMD	EWS
CF	Cardiff Canton TMD	EWS
CH	Chester TMD	First North Western
CJ	Clapham Yard CSD (London)	South West Trains
CK	Corkerhill TMD (Glasgow)	ScotRail
CL	Carlisle Upperby (closed)	*Storage location only*
CO	Coquelles T&RSMD (France)	Eurotunnel
CP	Crewe Carriage T&RSMD	London & North Western Railway
CQ	Crewe (The Railway Age) T&RSMD	Carriage & Traction Company
CS	Carnforth T&RSMD	West Coast Railway Company
CU	Carlisle Currock WRD	*Storage location only*
CW*	Crewe South Yard	*Storage location only*
CZ	Central Rivers T&RSMD (Burton)	Bombardier Transportation
DD*	Doncaster Wood Yard	*Storage location only*
DE	Dewsbury T&RSMD	RMS Locotech
DF	Derby RTC	Fragonset Railways
DI	Didcot Railway Centre	Great Western Society
DP*	Devonport Dockyard (Plymouth)	Devonport Maintenance Ltd.
DR	Doncaster TMD	EWS

DY	Derby Etches Park T&RSMD	Maintrain
EC	Edinburgh Craigentinny T&RSMD	Great North Eastern Railway
EH	Eastleigh T&RSMD	EWS
EM	East Ham T&RSMD	c2c
EN	Euston Downside CARMD (London)	EWS
ES*	On hire to Spain	GIF
FB	Ferrybridge T&RSMD	EWS
FD	Freightliner diesels (general code)	Freightliner
FE	Freightliner electrics (general code)	Freightliner
FF	Forest T&RSMD (Brussels)	SNCB/NMBS
FP	Ferme Park CSD (London)	GNER
FR	Fratton T&RSMD	South West Trains
FX*	Felixstowe TMD	Felixstowe Dock & Railway Company
GI	Gillingham T&RSMD (Kent)	Connex South Eastern
GW	Shields Road T&RSMD (Glasgow)	ScotRail/Alstom
HA	Haymarket TMD (Edinburgh)	ScotRail
HE	Hornsey T&RSMD (London)	West Anglia Great Northern
HG	Hither Green TMD (London)	EWS
HM	Healey Mills SD (Wakefield)	EWS
HT	Heaton T&RSMD (Newcastle)	Arriva Trains Northern
IL	Ilford T&RSD (London)	First Great Eastern
IM	Immingham T&RSMD	EWS
IP	Ipswich SD	EWS
IR	Immingham Railfreight Terminal	*Storage location only*
IS	Inverness T&RSMD	ScotRail
IT*	Italy	On hire
KM	Carlisle Kingmoor T&RSMD	Direct Rail Services
KR	Kidderminster T&RSMD	Severn Valley Railway
KT	MoD Kineton DM	MoD Defence Rail Group
KY	Knottingley T&RSMD	EWS
LA	Laira T&RSMD (Plymouth)	First Great Western
LB	Loughborough	Brush Traction
LC	Lancastrian C&W Co. Heysham	Lancastrian C&W Company
LE	Landore T&RSMD (Swansea)	First Great Western
LG	Longsight Electric T&RSMD (Manchester)	First North Western
LL	Edge Hill (Liverpool)	
LO	Longsight Diesel (Manchester) TMD	First North Western
LR	Leicester SD	EWS
LT	MoD Longtown DM	MoD Defence Rail Group
LY	Le Landy T&RSMD (Paris)	SNCF
MA	Manchester Longsight CARMD	West Coast Traincare
MB	MoD DSDA (Bicester)	MoD Defence Rail Group
MD	Merehead T&RSMD	Mendip Rail
MG	Margam SD (Port Talbot)	EWS
MH	Millerhill SD (Edinburgh)	EWS
ML	Motherwell T&RSMD (Glasgow)	EWS
MM	Fire Service College Moreton-in-Marsh	Cotswold Rail
NC	Norwich Crown Point T&RSMD	Anglia Railways
NH	Newton Heath TMD (Manchester)	First North Western
NL	Neville Hill T&RSMD (Leeds)	Maintrain/Arriva Trains Northern
NP	North Pole International (London)	Eurostar (UK)

NY	Grosmont (North Yorkshire)	North Yorkshire Moors Railway
OC	Old Oak Common TMD (London)	EWS
OH	Old Oak Common EMUD (London)	Heathrow Express
OM	Old Oak Common CARMD (London)	First Great Western
OO	Old Oak Common HST T&RSMD (London)	First Great Western
OY	Oxley T&RSMD (Wolverhampton)	West Coast Traincare
PB	Peterborough Yard	EWS
PC	Polmadie T&RSMD (Glasgow)	West Coast Traincare
PM	St. Philips Marsh T&RSMD (Bristol)	First Great Western
PR	Peak Rail (Darley Dale)	Peak Rail
PY	MoD DERA Pigs Bay (Shoeburyness)	MoD Defence Rail Group
PZ	Penzance CARMD	First Great Western
RG	Reading TMD	Thames Trains
RL	Ropley T&RSMD	Mid Hants Railway
RM	Ramsgate T&RSMD	Connex South Eastern
RU*	Rugby Rail Plant Depot	Carillion Rail
RY	Ryde T&RSMD (Isle of Wight)	Island Line
SA	Salisbury TMD	South West Trains
SD	Sellafield SD (Cumbria)	Direct Rail Services
SE	St. Leonards TMD (Hastings)	St. Leonards Railway Engineering
SG	Slade Green T&RSMD (London)	Connex South Eastern
SI	Soho T&RSMD (Birmingham)	Maintrain
SK	Swanwick Jn. (Derbyshire)	Midland Railway Centre
SL	Stewarts Lane T&RSMD (London)	Gatwick Express
SP	Springs Branch CRDC (Wigan)	EWS
SU	Selhurst T&RSMD (Croydon)	South Central
SY	Saltley SD (Birmingham)	EWS
SZ	Southampton Maritime T&RSMD	Freightliner
TE	Thornaby T&RSMD (Middlesbrough)	EWS
TM	Tyseley Museum T&RSMD (Birmingham)	Fragonset Railways
TO	Toton TMD (Nottinghamshire)	EWS
TS	Tyseley T&RSMD (Birmingham)	Maintrain
TT	Toton Training School Compound (Notts)	*Storage location only*
TY	Tyne Yard SD (Newcastle)	EWS
WA	Warrington Arpley SD	EWS
WD	Wimbledon T&RSMD	South West Trains
WN	Willesden TMD (London)	West Coast Train Care
YK	National Railway Museum (York)	National Railway Museum
ZA	Railway Technical Centre (Derby)	Serco Railtest/AEA Technology
ZB	Doncaster Works	Wabtec
ZC	Crewe Works	Bombardier Transportation
ZD	Derby Litchurch Lane Works	Bombardier Transportation
ZF	Doncaster Works	Bombardier Transportation
ZG	Eastleigh Works	Alstom
ZH	Springburn Works (Glasgow)	Alstom
ZI	Ilford	Bombardier Transportation
ZN	Wolverton Works	Alstom
ZP	Horbury (Wakefield)	Bombardier Transportation

*Unofficial code

6.6. ABBREVIATIONS

The following general abbreviations are used in this book:

AC	Alternating Current (i.e. Overhead supply).
BR	British Railways.
BSI	Bergische Stahl Industrie.
DC	Direct Current (i.e. Third Rail).
DEMU	Diesel Electric Multiple Unit.
Dia.	Diagram number.
DMU	Diesel Multiple Unit (general term).
EMU	Electric Multiple Unit.
GNER	Great North Eastern Railway
GWR	Great Western Railway
H-B	Hunslet-Barclay.
h.p.	horse power.
HNRC	Harry Needle Railroad Co.
Hz	Hertz.
kN	kilonewtons.
km/h	kilometres per hour.
kW	kilowatts.
lbf	pounds force.
LT	London Transport.
LUL	London Underground Limited.
m.	metres.
mm.	millimetres.
m.p.h.	miles per hour.
RCH	Railway Clearing House.
r.p.m.	revolutions per minute.
RR	Rolls Royce.
RSL	Rolling Stock Library.
SR	BR Southern Region.
t.	tonnes.
T	Toilets.
TD	Toilets suitable for disabled passengers.
TDM	Time Division Multiplex.
V	volts.
w	wheelchair spaces.

Depot/location type abbreviations

CARMD	Carriage Maintenance Depot
CSD	Carriage Servicing Depot
DERA	Defence Evaluation & Research Agency
DM	Defence Munitions
DSDA	Defence Distribution and Agency
MoD	Ministry of Defence
TMD	Traction Maintenance Depot
T&RSMD	Traction and Rolling Stock Maintenance Depot

6.7 BUILDERS

These are shown in class headings. The workshops of British Railways and the pre-nationalisation and pre-grouping companies were first transferred to a wholly-owned subsidiary called 'British Rail Engineering Ltd.', abbreviated to BREL. These workshops were later privatised, BREL then becoming 'BREL Ltd.'. Some of the works were then taken over by ABB, which was later merged with Daimler-Benz Transportation to become 'Adtranz'. This company has now been taken over by Bombardier Transportation, which had taken over Procor at Horbury previously. Bombardier also builds vehicles for the British market in Brugge, Belgium.

Other workshops were the subject of separate sales, Springburn, Glasgow and Wolverton becoming 'Railcare' and Eastleigh becoming 'Wessex Traincare'. These are now owned by Alstom (previously GEC-Alsthom), as is the former Metro-Cammell Works in Birmingham.

Note: Part of Doncaster works was sold to RFS Engineering, which became insolvent and was bought out and renamed RFS Industries. This has now been taken over by Wabtec.

The builder details in the class headings show the owner at the time of vehicle construction followed by the works as follows:

Ashford	Ashford Works (Note that this is not the same as the current Bombardier Ashford depot which is at Chart Leacon)
Birmingham	The former Metro-Cammel works at Saltley, Birmingham.
Cowlairs	Cowlairs Works, Glasgow
Derby	Derby Carriage Works (also known as Litchurch Lane)
Doncaster	Doncaster Works.
Eastleigh	Eastleigh Works.
Swindon	Swindon Works.
Wolverton	Wolverton Works.
York	York Carriage Works.

Other builders are:

Alexander	Walter Alexander, Falkirk.
Barclay	Andrew Barclay, Caledonia Works, Kilmarnock (now Hunslet-Barclay).
BRCW	Birmingham Railway Carriage & Wagon, Smethwick.
CAF	Construcciones y Auxiliar de Ferrocarriles, Zaragosa, Spain.
Cravens	Cravens, Sheffield.
Gloucester	Gloucester Railway Carriage & Wagon, Gloucester.
Hunslet-Barclay	Hunslet-Barclay, Caledonia Works, Kilmarnock.
Hunslet TPL	Hunslet Transportation Projects, Leeds.
Lancing	SR, Lancing Works.
Leyland Bus	Leyland Bus, Workington.
Metro-Cammell	Metropolitan-Cammell, Saltley, Birmingham
Pressed Steel	Pressed Steel, Linwood.
Charles Roberts	Charles Roberts, Horbury Junction, Wakefield.
SGP	Simmering-Graz-Pauker, Austria (now owned by Siemens).
Siemens	Siemens Transportaion Systems (various works in Germany and Austria).
SRP	Specialist Rail Products Ltd (A subsidiary of RFS).